MW00476133

ESSENTIAL DOCUMENTS OF
AMERICAN
HISTORY

VOLUME
I

From Colonial Times to the Civil War

EDITED BY BOB BLAISDELL

DOVER PUBLICATIONS
Garden City, New York

Bibliographical Note

Essentials Documents of American History, Volume I: From Colonial Times to the Civil War, first published by Dover Publications in 2016, is a new compilation of historic American documents. The source of each one has been abbreviated in brackets at the end of the respective document and the Source and Author Guide can be found in the last section of this collection.

International Standard Book Number
ISBN-13: 978-0-486-79730-4
ISBN-10: 0-486-79730-9

Manufactured in the United States of America
79730905   2021
www.doverpublications.com

Note

IT'S ENLIVENING AND enlightening to read about events as they happen through these 154 documents*—dating from 1606 to 2008—that make us eyewitnesses to history. For example, during the Constitutional Convention in the summer of 1787, we can imagine some of the Founding Fathers shaking their heads ruefully during the debate over the continuance of slavery.

George Mason of Virginia lamented, "Every master of slaves is born a petty tyrant. They bring the judgment of heaven on a country. As nations cannot be rewarded or punished in the next world they must be in this." Was Mason prescient about the Civil War of 1861–1865 or simply possessed of an unusually acute moral sense?

In 1789, we learn through his first Inaugural Address that George Washington was apprehensive as he warily accepted the duties of president of the newly established nation: "Among the vicissitudes incident to life no event could have filled me with greater anxieties than that of which the notification was transmitted by your order ... On the one hand, I was summoned by my country, whose voice I can never hear but with veneration and love, from a retreat which I had chosen with the fondest predilection, and, in my flattering hopes, with an immutable decision, as the asylum of my declining years ..." Less than three years after serving his second term of office, the great man died at the longed for "asylum" of his Mount Vernon home.

Thomas Jefferson, the primary author in 1776 of the Declaration of Independence, was, as the third president, excited as he imagined the world that his chosen proxy, Captain Meriwether Lewis, would encounter in the wilderness in and beyond the recently purchased

*Volume I contains 83 documents, spanning 1606 to 1865. Volume II (ISBN-13: 978-0-486-80908-3) contains 71 documents, spanning 1866 to 2008.

Louisiana Territory and made his way to the Pacific Ocean. More than any other U.S. president of the eighteenth century, Jefferson demonstrated respect for the native peoples by instructing Lewis:

> In all your intercourse with the natives treat them in the most friendly & conciliatory manner which their own conduct will admit; allay all jealousies as to the object of your journey, satisfy them of it's innocence, make them acquainted with the position, extent, character, peaceable & commercial dispositions of the U. S. of our wish to be neighborly, friendly & useful to them, & of our dispositions to a commercial intercourse with them; confer with them on the points most convenient as mutual emporiums, & the articles of most desirable interchange for them & us. if a few of their influential chiefs, within practicable distance, wish to visit us, arrange such a visit with them, and furnish them with authority to call on our officers, on their entering the U. S. to have them conveyed to this place at public expense. if any of them should wish to have some of their young people brought up with us, & taught such arts as may be useful to them, we will receive, instruct & take care of them, such a mission, whether of influential chiefs, or of young people, would give some security to your own party, carry with you some matter of the kine-pox, inform those of them with whom you may be of it' efficacy as a preservative from the small-pox; and instruct & encourage them in the use of it. This may be especially done wherever you winter.[1]

(We have preserved Jefferson's clipped and special spellings.)

Native American oratory is justly admired, and as recorded by witnesses, we can read the speakers' cogent arguments and discourses about this great land they love and the naive concessions they made to the multitudes of immigrants from across the Atlantic. In 1811, Tecumseh, the chief of the Shawnees, tried to unify various tribes in an alliance against the encroaching, treaty-breaking European settlers. When we learn that his persuasive, carefully reasoned arguments fell on deaf ears, we can only wonder what else he might have said to convince them.

---

[1] *Original Journals of the Lewis and Clark Expedition: 1804–1806*. Vol. 7. Edited by Reuben Gold Thwaites. New York: Dodd, Mead and Company. 1904. 250.

Too often as students of history we are like readers of tragedies, hoping that what we know is about to happen won't. Would Senator John C. Calhoun, a firebrand from South Carolina, really have stoked the flames of secession by defending and lauding the region's "peculiar institution" of slavery had he known the consequences of the Civil War, in which more than 600,000 soldiers died? Could this country of immigrants really have set out on genocidal policies against the Native peoples? As proud as we are to be Americans, our history will often shock us. Along with the glory of unprecedented achievement, there is also the shame and regret of injustice and wrongdoing.

But it's not over until it's over; improvements beckon. Lord knows we haven't achieved gender or racial equality yet, much less agreement about health care, economic and international policy, or guns and drugs. Our history shows that we've made tremendous moral progress, that in spite of each age's prejudices and limitations, we are driven toward making adjustments and corrections.

Political stand-offs can be infuriatingly frustrating, no doubt about it, and if we weren't much more than political animals, it would be hard to feel hopeful. But Americans are *social* beings, and at our best we're curious and reflective, and we can clearly see the veering of our nation's course in retrospect while wondering where we're veering now. The leaders of the American Revolution seemed to have no intention of declaring independence until they did so; the history they encountered and created surprised them, and someday the history we're making now will surprise us too. In fact, a few of the more recent documents can evoke memories of unexpected events of our own time. For instance, the 9/11 Commission Report recounting the minute-by-minute confusion and terror of the attack on the World Trade Center towers may stir haunting memories from that day for many readers.

Does our sense of history lay too much blame or credit at the feet of politicians, who, in their twists and turns, bombast and eloquence, we see speaking to the wishes and furies of the people? Probably! But these documents are not just written or spoken by the privileged; they include the bewildered and outraged viewpoints of the comparatively powerless. In his 1852 address, "What to the Slave Is the Fourth of July?" the ex-slave Frederick Douglass, one of the most extraordinary Americans in our history, forcefully expresses the contradictory feelings in the air: "I am not included within the pale of this glorious anniversary! Your high independence only reveals the immeasurable distance between us. The blessings in which you, this day, rejoice, are not enjoyed in common. The rich inheritance of justice, liberty, prosperity and independence, bequeathed by your fathers, is shared by you, not by me. The sunlight that brought light and healing to you, has brought stripes and death to me. This Fourth of July is yours, not mine. You may rejoice, I must mourn. To drag a man in fetters into the grand illuminated temple of liberty, and call upon him to join you in joyous anthems, were inhuman mockery and sacrilegious irony."

I have tried to include all the most famous documents as long as they can now be read with engagement, while avoiding blowhard self-congratulatory speeches and pronouncements, which unfortunately in political matters are always a looming part of the weather. There are documents I haven't included only because they would take a cleverer and more knowledgeable writer and reader than I to introduce them in a succinct way. For example, concerning our own time, I didn't know how to make use of the flood of documents that have been released concerning our government's squirrelly approbation of the use of torture after the 9/11 catastrophe. Given another decade or two, I might figure out which of these outrageous documents to include.

While it's impossible to sympathize with any argument for the post–Civil War's Jim Crow laws or segregation, I have chosen to let the Georgia governor George C. Wallace try to make the argument himself in 1963. His voice was loud; he spoke for himself and others. If we're ashamed by much of our history, there's plenty of shame left to think of our own personal failures and sins. The most thoughtless "truths" we once accepted as a country or individuals can now, in reflection, fill us with horror and disgust.

Just personally, on the (big open) other hand, Abraham Lincoln's words almost always make me proud to be an American. You might argue, sensibly, that not only I but nobody alive today had anything to do with anything he said or did, and so why should I feel proud for what he said or ashamed for what his opposite number, the Confederate president Jefferson Davis, said and did? Because that's the way despair of and pride in one's nation works. We agonize with not only the weaknesses of those who came before us but identify with their accomplishments. Senator Margaret Chase Smith's speech in 1950, in which she calls out a horde of her fellow senators during the Red Scare for trying to "ride to political victory on the Four

Horsemen of Calumny—Fear, Ignorance, Bigotry, and Smear," gives me hope that it's possible to be brave in the face of cynically induced hysteria; Martin Luther King, Jr.'s "I Have a Dream" speech never stops being inspiring and alluring; through the astronauts' accounts of their Apollo 11 moon landing in 1969, it seems now even more wonderful to me than when it happened in my boyhood.

Finally, the word "Documents" in our anthology title shouldn't suggest we have the facts or that we are establishing *a* truth or *the* truths about American history. We could, by substituting the word *Artifacts* for *Documents* remind ourselves that these pieces are, famous or not, maybe no more significant than *millions* of other pieces that could help us form an idea of America's history, but that, as *artifacts,* they represent only a fraction of each event yet can, nonetheless, tell us so much about the culture in which they were produced.

There are many anthologies and histories I have relied on for pointing me to some of the definitely great and famous documents of our history, and I have also relied on many previous compilers and editors for their astute introductory notes to the selections. I particularly thank Dover's senior editor, John Grafton, for his guidance over the course of this project and for several of the most informative introductory notes.

—*Bob Blaisdell*
New York City, April 2015

Contents

THE FIGHT FOR INDEPENDENCE

THE EARLY REPUBLIC AND THE CONSTITUTION

THE NEW NATION

Colonial America

King James I,
First Charter of Virginia

April 10, 1606

This charter, granted by King James I. on April 10, 1606, to the oldest of the English colonies in America, is a typical example of the documents issued by the British government, authorizing "Adventurers" to establish plantations in the New World. The name "Virginia" was at that time applied to all that part of North America claimed by Great Britain.

— Note by Charles W. Eliot.

I JAMES, BY the Grace of God, King of *England, Scotland, France* and *Ireland,* Defender of the Faith, &c. WHEREAS our loving and well-disposed Subjects, Sir *Thomas Gates,* and Sir *George Somers,* Knights, *Richard Hackluit,* Prebendary of *Westminster,* and *Edward-Maria Wingfield, Thomas Hanham,* and *Ralegh Gilbert,* Esqrs. *William Parker,* and *George Popham,* Gentlemen, and divers others of our loving Subjects, have been humble Suitors unto us, that We would vouchsafe unto them our License, to make Habitation, Plantation, and to deduce a Colony of sundry of our People into that Part of *America,* commonly called VIRGINIA, and other Parts and Territories in *America,* either appertaining unto us, or which are not now actually possessed by any *Christian* Prince or People, situate, lying, and being all along the Sea Coasts, between four and thirty Degrees of *Northerly* Latitude from the Equinoctial Line, and five and forty Degrees of the same Latitude, and in the main Land between the same four and thirty and five and forty Degrees, and the Islands thereunto adjacent, or within one hundred Miles of the Coasts thereof;

II. And to that End, and for the more speedy Accomplishment of their said intended Plantation and Habitation there, are desirous to divide themselves into two several Colonies and Companies; The one consisting of certain Knights, Gentlemen, Merchants, and other Adventurers, of our City of *London* and elsewhere, which are, and from time to time shall be, joined unto them, which do desire to begin their Plantation and Habitation in some fit and convenient Place, between four and thirty and one and forty Degrees of the said Latitude, along the Coasts of *Virginia* and Coasts of *America* aforesaid; And the other consisting of sundry Knights, Gentlemen, Merchants, and other Adventurers, of our Cities of *Bristol* and *Exeter,* and of our Town of *Plimouth,* and of other Places, which do join themselves unto that Colony, which do desire to begin their Plantation and Habitation in some fit and convenient Place, between eight and thirty Degrees and five and forty Degrees of the said Latitude, all amongst the said Coast of *Virginia* and *America,* as that Coast lyeth:

III. We, greatly commending, and graciously accepting of, their Desires for the Furtherance of so noble a Work, which may, by the Providence of Almighty God, hereafter tend to the Glory of his Divine Majesty, in propagating of *Christian* Religion to such People, as yet live in Darkness and miserable Ignorance of the true Knowledge and Worship of God, and may in time bring the Infidels and Savages, living in those Parts, to human Civility, and to a settled and quiet Government; DO, by these our Letters Patents, graciously accept of, and agree to, their humble and well-intended Desires;

IV. And do therefore, for Us, our Heirs, and Successors, GRANT and agree, that the said Sir *Thomas Gates,* Sir *George Somers, Richard Hackluit,* and *Edward-Maria Wingfield,* Adventurers of and for our City of *London,* and all such others, as are, or shall be, joined unto them of that Colony, shall be called the *first Colony;* And they shall and may begin their said first Plantation and Habitation, at any Place upon the said Coast of *Virginia* or *America,* where they shall think fit and convenient, between the said four and thirty and one and forty Degrees of the said Latitude; And that they shall have all the Lands, Woods, Soil, Grounds, Havens, Ports, Rivers, Mines, Minerals, Marshes, Waters, Fishings, Commodities, and Hereditaments, whatsoever, from the said first Seat of their Plantation and Habitation by the Space of fifty Miles of *English* Statute Measure, all along the said Coast of *Virginia* and *America,* towards the *West* and *Southwest,* as the Coast lyeth, with all the Islands within one

hundred Miles directly over against the same Sea Coast; And also all
the Lands, Soil, Grounds, Havens, Ports, Rivers, Mines, Minerals,
Woods, Waters, Marshes, Fishings, Commodities, and Hereditaments,
ments, whatsoever, from the said Place of their first Plantation and
Habitation for the space of fifty like *English* Miles all amongst the
said Coast of *Virginia* and *America,* towards the *East and Northeast,* or
towards the *North,* as the Coast lyeth, together with all the Islands
within one hundred Miles, directly over against the said Sea Coast;
And also all the Lands, Woods, Soil, Grounds, Havens, Ports, Rivers, Mines, Minerals, Marshes, Waters, Fishings, Commodities, and
Hereditaments, whatsoever, from the same fifty Miles every way on
the Sea Coast, directly into the main Land by the Space of one
hundred like *English* Miles; And shall and may inhabit and remain
there; and shall and may also build and fortify within any the same,
for their better Safeguard and Defense, according to their best Discretion, and the Discretion of the Council of that Colony; And that
no other of our Subjects shall be permitted, or suffered, to plant or
inhabit behind, or on the Backside of them, towards the main Land,
without the Express License or Consent of the Council of that
Colony, thereunto in Writing first had and obtained.

V. And we do likewise, for Us, our Heirs, and Successors, by
these Presents, GRANT and agree, that the said *Thomas Hanham,* and
Ralegh Gilbert, William Parker, and *George Popham,* and all others of
the Town of *Plimouth* in the County of *Devon,* or elsewhere, which
are, or shall be, joined unto them of that Colony, shall be called the
second Colony; And that they shall and may begin their said Plantation and Seat of their first Abode and Habitation, at any Place upon
the said Coast of *Virginia* and *America,* where they shall think fit and
convenient, between eight and thirty Degrees of the said Latitude,
and five and forty Degrees of the same Latitude; And that they shall
have all the Lands, Soils, Grounds, Havens, Ports, Rivers, Mines,
Minerals, Woods, Marshes, Waters, Fishings, Commodities, and
Hereditaments, whatsoever from the first Seat of their Plantation
and Habitation by the Space of fifty like *English* Miles as is aforesaid,
all amongst the said Coast of *Virginia* and *America,* towards the *West*
and *Southwest,* or towards the *South,* as the Coast lyeth, and all the
Islands within one hundred Miles, directly over against the said Sea
Coast; And also all the Lands, Soils, Grounds, Havens, Ports,
Rivers, Mines, Minerals, Woods, Marshes, Waters, Fishings, Commodities, and Hereditaments, whatsoever, from the said Place of
their first Plantation and Habitation for the Space of fifty like Miles,

all alongst the said Coast of *Virginia* and *America,* towards the *East* and *Northeast,* or towards the *North,* as the Coast lyeth, and all the Islands also within one hundred Miles directly over against the same Sea Coast; And also all the Lands, Soils, Grounds, Havens, Ports, Rivers, Woods, Mines, Minerals, Marshes, Waters, Fishings, Commodities, and Hereditaments, whatsoever, from the Same fifty Miles every way on the Sea Coast, directly into the main Land, by the Space of one hundred like *English* Miles; And shall and may inhabit and remain there; and shall and may also build and fortify within any the same for their better Safeguard, according to their best Discretion, and the Discretion of the Council of that Colony; And that none of our Subjects shall be permitted, or suffered, to plant or inhabit behind, or on the back of them, towards the main Land, without the express License of the Council of that Colony, in Writing thereunto first had and obtained.

VI. Provided always, and our Will and Pleasure herein is, that the Plantation and Habitation of such of the said Colonies, as shall last plant themselves, as aforesaid, shall not be made within one hundred like *English* Miles of the other of them, that first began to make their Plantation, as aforesaid.

VII. And we do also ordain, establish, and agree, for Us, our Heirs, and Successors, that each of the said Colonies shall have a Council, which shall govern and order all Matters and Causes, which shall arise, grow, or happen, to or within the same several Colonies, according to such Laws, Ordinances, and Instructions, as shall be, in that behalf, given and signed with Our Hand or Sign Manual, and pass under the Privy Seal of our Realm of *England;* Each of which Councils shall consist of thirteen Persons, to be ordained, made, and removed, from time to time, according as shall be directed, and comprised in the same instructions; And shall have a several Seal, for all Matters that shall pass or concern the same several Councils; [...]

VIII. And that also there shall be a Council established here in *England,* which shall, in like Manner, consist of thirteen Persons, to be, for that Purpose, appointed by Us, our Heirs and Successors, which shall be called our *Council of Virginia;* And shall, from time to time, have the superior Managing and Direction, only of and for all Matters, that shall or may concern the Government, as well of the said several Colonies, as of and for any other Part or Place, within the aforesaid Precincts of four and thirty and five and forty

Degrees, abovementioned; Which Council shall, in like manner, have a Seal. [...]

IX. And moreover, we do GRANT and agree, for Us, our Heirs and Successors, that the said several Councils, of and for the said several Colonies, shall and lawfully may, by Virtue hereof, from time to time, without any Interruption of Us, our Heirs, or Successors, give and take Order, to dig, mine, and search for all Manner of Mines of Gold, Silver, and Copper, as well within any part of their said several Colonies, as for the said main Lands on the Backside of the same Colonies; And to HAVE and enjoy the Gold, Silver, and Copper, to be gotten thereof, to the Use and Behoof of the same Colonies, and the Plantations thereof; YIELDING therefore, to Us, our Heirs and Successors, the fifth Part only of all the same Gold and Silver, and the fifteenth Part of all the same Copper, so to be gotten or had, as is aforesaid, without any other Manner or Profit or Account, to be given or yielded to Us, our Heirs, or Successors, for or in Respect of the same:

X. And that they shall, or lawfully may, establish and cause to be made a Coin, to pass current there between the People of those several Colonies, for the more Ease of Traffick and Bargaining between and amongst them and the Natives there, of such Metal, and in such Manner and Form, as the said several Councils there shall limit and appoint.

XI. And we do likewise, for Us, our Heirs, and Successors, by these Presents, give full Power and Authority to the said Sir *Thomas Gates,* Sir *George Somers, Richard Hackluit, Edward-Maria Wingfield, Thomas Hanham, Ralegh Gilbert, William Parker,* and *George Popham,* and to every of them, and to the said several Companies, Plantations, and Colonies, that they, and every of them, shall and may, at all and every time and times hereafter, have, take, and lead in the said Voyage, and for and towards the said several Plantations and Colonies, and to travel thitherward, and to abide and inhabit there, in every the said Colonies and Plantations, such and so many of our Subjects, as shall willingly accompany them, or any of them, in the said Voyages and Plantations; With sufficient Shipping and Furniture of Armor, Weapons, Ordinance, Powder, Victual, and all other things, necessary for the said Plantations, and for their Use and Defense there: PROVIDED always, that none of the said Persons be such, as shall hereafter be specially restrained by Us, our Heirs, or Successors.

XII. Moreover, we do, by these Presents, for Us, our Heirs, and Successors, GIVE AND GRANT Licence unto the said Sir *Thomas Gates,* Sir *George Somers, Richard Hackluit, Edward-Maria Wingfield, Thomas Hanham, Ralegh Gilbert, William Parker,* and *George Popham,* and to every of the said Colonies, that they, and every of them, shall and may, from time to time, and at all times for ever hereafter, for their several Defences, encounter, expulse, repel, and resist, as well by Sea as by Land, by all Ways and Means whatsoever, all and every such Person and Persons, as without the especial Licence of the said several Colonies and Plantations, shall attempt to inhabit within the said several Precincts and Limits of the said several Colonies and Plantations, or any of them, or that shall enterprise or attempt, at any time hereafter, the Hurt, Detriment, or Annoyance, of the said several Colonies or Plantations.

XIII. Giving and granting, by these Presents, unto the said Sir *Thomas Gates,* Sir *George Somers, Richard Hackluit, Edward-Maria Wingfield,* and their Associates of the said first Colony, and unto the said *Thomas Hanham, Ralegh Gilbert, William Parker,* and *George Popham,* and their Associates of the said second Colony, and to every of them, from time to time, and at all times for ever hereafter, Power and Authority to take and surprise, by all Ways and Means whatsoever, all and every Person and Persons, with their Ships, Vessels, Goods and other Furniture, which shall be found trafficking, into any Harbour or Harbours, Creek or Creeks, or Place, within the Limits or Precincts of the said several Colonies and Plantations, not being of the same Colony, until such time, as they, being of any Realms or Dominions under our Obedience, shall pay, or agree to pay, to the Hands of the Treasurer of that Colony, within whose Limits and Precincts they shall so traffick, two and a half upon every Hundred, of any thing, so by them trafficked, bought, or sold; And being Strangers, and not Subjects under our Obeysance, until they shall pay five upon every Hundred, of such Wares and Merchandise, as they shall traffick, buy, or sell, within the Precincts of the said several Colonies, wherein they shall so traffick, buy, or sell, as aforesaid, WHICH Sums of Money, or Benefit, as aforesaid, for and during the Space of one and twenty Years, next ensuing the Date hereof, shall be wholly emploied to the Use, Benefit, and Behoof of the said several Plantations, where such Traffick shall be made; And after the said one and twenty Years ended, the same shall be taken to the Use of Us, our Heirs, and

Successors, by such Officers and Ministers, as by Us, our Heirs, and Successors, shall be thereunto assigned or appointed.

XIV. And we do further, by these Presents, for Us, our Heirs, and Successors, GIVE AND GRANT unto the said Sir *Thomas Gates,* Sir *George Somers, Richard Hackluit,* and *Edward-Maria Wingfield,* and to their Associates of the said first Colony and Plantation, and to the said *Thomas Hanham, Ralegh Gilbert, William Parker,* and *George Popham,* and their Associates of the said second Colony and Plantation, that they, and every of them, by their Deputies, Ministers and Factors, may transport the Goods, Chattels, Armour, Munition, and Furniture, needful to be used by them, for their said Apparel, Food, Defence, or otherwise in Respect of the said Plantations, out of our Realms of *England* and *Ireland,* and all other our Dominions, from time to time, for and during the Time of seven Years, next ensuing the Date hereof, for the better Relief of the said several Colonies and Plantations, without any Custom, Subsidy, or other Duty, unto Us, our Heirs, or *Successors,* to be yielded or paid for the same.

XV. Also we do, for Us, our Heirs, and Successors, DECLARE, by these Presents, that all and every the Persons, being our Subjects, which shall dwell and inhabit within every or any of the said several Colonies and Plantations, and every of their children, which shall happen to be born within any of the Limits and Precincts of the said several Colonies and Plantations, shall HAVE and enjoy all Liberties, Franchises, and Immunities, within any of our other Dominions, to all Intents and Purposes, as if they had been abiding and born, within this our Realm of *England,* or any other of our said Dominions.[…]

[AHD]

Powhatan, Wahunsonacock, Speech to Captain John Smith at Jamestown

c. 1609

Powhatan (c. 1547–1618) was the head of a confederacy that spanned hundreds of miles and thirty-two tribes. (He is well known today because of his favorite daughter, Pocahontas, who rescued the English captain John Smith from execution in 1608.) In 1607 Powhatan's confederacy allowed the English to establish their first colony at Jamestown. In 1609, when the same Captain Smith, dissatisfied with trade negotiations, resorted to bluster and threats, Powhatan made the following reply.

I AM NOW grown old, and must soon die; and the succession must descend, in order, to my brothers, Opitchapan, Opekankanough, and Catataugh, and then to my two sisters, and their two daughters. I wish their experience was equal to mine; and that your love to us might not be less than ours to you. Why should you take by force that from us which you can have by love? Why should you destroy us, who have provided you with food? What can you get by war? We can hide our provisions, and fly into the woods; and then you must consequently famish by wronging your friends. What is the cause of your jealousy? You see us unarmed, and willing to supply your wants, if you will come in a friendly manner, and not with swords and guns, as to invade an enemy. I am not so simple, as not to know it is better to eat good meat, lie well, and sleep quietly with my women and children; to laugh and be merry with the English; and, being their friend, to have copper, hatchets, and whatever else I want, than to fly from all, to lie cold in the woods, feed upon acorns, roots, and such trash, and to be so hunted, that I cannot rest, eat, or sleep. In such circumstances, my men must watch, and if a twig should but break, all would cry out, *"Here comes Capt. Smith;"* and so, in this miserable manner, to end my miserable life; and, Capt. Smith, this *might* be soon your fate too, through your rashness and unadvisedness. I, therefore, exhort you to peaceable councils; and, above all, I insist that the guns and swords, the cause of all our jealousy and uneasiness, be removed and sent away.

[GSNA]

The Pilgrims of Cape Cod, Mayflower Compact

November 11, 1620

The need of this compact is thus set forth by one of the Pilgrims: "Some of the strangers among them had let fall from them in the ship that when they came ashore they would use their own liberty, for none had power to command them, the patent they had being for Virginia and not for New England, which belonged to another government, with which the Virginia Company had nothing to do. [The historian George] Bancroft lauds it in the highest terms: "Here was the birth of popular constitutional liberty. The middle ages had been familiar with charters and constitutions; but they had been merely compacts for immunities, partial enfranchisements, patents of nobility, concessions of municipal privileges, or limitations of the sovereign power in favor of feudal institutions. In the cabin of the Mayflower humanity recovered its rights, and instituted government on the basis of 'equal laws,' enacted by all the people for the 'general good.' " Somewhat similar compacts were drawn up by the settlers of Portsmouth, R. I., 1638, and Newport, 1639, and Exeter, N. H., 1639.

Plymouth obtained a patent for their lands from the New England Company, and though never successful in their numerous applications for a royal charter maintained an independent existence until its incorporation with Massachusetts in 1691.

— Note by Howard W. Preston

IN THE NAME of God, Amen; We, whose names are underwritten, the loyall subjects of our dread soveraigne King James, by the grace of God, of Great Britaine, France, and Ireland King, defender of the faith, etc., haveing undertaken, for the glorie of God, and advancemente of the Christian faith and honor of our king and countrie, a voyage to plant the first colonie in the Northerne parts of Virginia, doe, by these presents, solemnly and mutually, in the presence of God, and one of another, covenant and combine our-selves together into a civill body politick, for our better ordering and preservation and furtherance of the ends aforesaid: and, by vertue heareof, to enacte, constitute, and frame, such just and equal laws, ordenances, acts, constitutions and offices, from time to time, as shall be thought most meete and convenient for the general good of the Colonie. Unto which we promise all due submission and obedience. In witnes whereof we have hereunder subscribed our names, at Cap Codd, the 11th of November, in the year of the raigne of our sovereigne lord, King James, of England, France, and Ireland the eighteenth, and of Scotland the fifty-fourth, Anno Domini, 1620.

[DIH]

Captain John Underhill, Narrative of the Pequot War

1637

In his Newes from America, *published in 1638, Captain John Underhill of Massachusetts narrated his experiences leading the English troops against the Pequot tribe in northern Connecticut. The Pequot War was instigated by the Puritans in revenge against the Pequots of Block Island. In this passage, Underhill justifies the massacre of 400 native men, women and children at Mystic Fort on May 26, 1637. The war, in which the English were aided by the Pequots' enemies the native Narragansett and Mohegan tribes, ended a few months later.*

— *Note by Albert Bushnell Hart*

. . . THE PEQUEATS HAVING slaine one Captain *Norton,* and Captain *Stone,* with seven more of their company, order was given us to visit them, sailing along the *Nahanticot* shore with five vessels, the Indians spying of us came running in multitudes along the water side, crying, what cheere Englishmen, what cheere, what doe you come for? They not thinking we intended warre went on cheerefully untill they come to Pequeat riuer. We thinking it the best way did forbeare to answer them; first, that we might the better bee able to runne through the worke. Secondly, that by delaying of them, we might drive them in securitie, to the end wee might have the more advantage of them: but they seeing wee would make no answer, kept on their course, and cryed, what Englishman, what cheere, what cheere, are you hoggerie, will you cram us? That is, are you angry, will you kill us, and doe you come to fight. That night the *Nahanticot* Indians, and the *Pequeats,* made fire on both sides of the River, fearing we would land in the night. They made most dolefull, and wofull cryes all the night, (so that wee could scarce rest) hollowing one to another, and giving the word from place to place, to gather their forces together, fearing the English were come to warre against them.

The next morning they sent early aboard an Ambassadour, a grave Senior, a man of good understanding, portly, cariage grave, and majesticall in his expressions; he demanded of us what the end of our comming was, to which we answered, that the Governours of the *Bay* sent us to demand the heads of those persons that had slaine Captain *Norton,* and Captain *Stone,* and the rest of their company, and that it was not the custome of the English to suffer murtherers to live, and therefore if they desired their owne peace and welfare, they will peaceably answer our expectation, and give us the heads of the murderers.

They being a witty and ingenious Nation, their Ambassadour labored to excuse the matter, and answered, we know not that any of ours have slaine any English: true it is, saith he, we have slaine such a number of men, but consider the ground of it; . . . we distinguish not betweene the *Dutch* and *English,* but tooke them to be one Nation, and therefore we doe not conceive that we wronged you, for they slew our king; and thinking these Captaines to be of the same Nation and people, as those that slew him, made us set upon this course of revenge.

Our answer was, they were able to distinguish between *Dutch* and *English,* having had sufficient experience of both Nations, and therefore seeing you have slaine the king of *Englands* subjects, we come to demand an account of their blood, for we our selves are lyable to account for them. . . .

But wee seeing their drift was to get our Arms, we rather chose to beat up the Drum and bid them battell, marching into a champion field we displayed our colours, but none would come neere us, but standing remotely off did laugh at us for our patience, wee suddenly set upon our march, and gave fire to as many as we could come neere, firing their Wigwams, spoyling their corne, and many other necessaries that they had buried in the ground we raked up, which the soldiers had for bootie. Thus we spent the day burning and spoyling the Countrey, towards night imbarqued our selves the next morning, landing on the *Nahanticot* shore, where we were served in like nature, no *Indians* would come neere us, but runne from us, as the Deere from the dogges; but having burnt and spoyled what we could light on, wee imbarqued our men, and set sayle for the *Bay*, having ended this exploit came off, having one man wounded in the legge; but certaine numbers of theirs slaine, and many wounded; this was the substance of the first yeares service: now followeth the service performed in the second yeare.

This insolent Nation, seeing wee had used so much Lenitie towards them, and themselves not able to make good use of our patience, set upon a course of greater insolencie then before, and slew all they found in their way: they came neere *Seabrooke* fort, and made many proud challenges, and dared them out to fight. . . .

The *Conetticot* Plantation understanding the insolencie of the enemie to bee so great, sent downe a certaine number of soldiers under the conduct of Captaine *John Mason* for to strengthen the Fort. The enemy lying hovering about the Fort, continually tooke notice of the supplies that were come, and forbore drawing neere it as before: and Letters were immediately sent to the *Bay*, to that Right worshipfull Gentleman, Master *Henry Vane*, for a speedy supply to strengthen the Fort. For assuredly without supply suddenly came in reason all would be lost, and fall into the hands of the enemy; This was the trouble and perplexity that lay upon the spirits of the poore garrisons. Upon serious consideration the Governour and Councell sent forth my selfe with 20. armed souldiers to supply the necessitie of those distressed persons, and to take the government of that place for the space of three moneths: reliefe being come, Captaine *John Mason* with the rest of his company returned to the Plantation againe: we sometimes fell out with a matter of twentie souldiers to see whether we could discover the enemy or no; they seeing us (lying in ambush) gave us leave to passe by them, considering we were too hot for them to meddle with us; our men being compleatly armed, with Corslets, Muskets, bandileeres, rests, and swords (as they themselves related afterward), did much daunt them; thus we spent a matter of six weeks before we could have any thing to doe with them, perswading our selves that all things had beene well. But they seeing there was no advantage more to be had against the Fort, they enterprized a new action, and fell upon *Water towne*, now called *Wethersfield* with two hundred *Indians*; before they came to attempt the place, they put into a certaine River, an obscure small river running into the maine, where they incamped, and refreshed themselves, and fitted themselves for their service, and by breake of day attempted their enterprise, and slew nine men, women and children, having finished their action, they suddenly returned againe, bringing with them two maids captives, having put poles in their Conoos, as we put Masts in our boats, and upon them hung our English mens and womens shirts and smocks, in stead of sayles, and in way of bravado came along in sight of us as we stood upon *Seybrooke* Fort, and seeing them passe along in such a triumphant manner, wee much fearing they had enterprised some desperate action upon the *English,* wee gave fire with a peece of Ordnance, and shotte among their Conoos. And though they were a mile from us, yet the bullet grazed not above twentie yards over the Conooe, where the poore maids were; it was a speciall providence of God it did not hit them, for then should we have beene deprived of the sweet observation of Gods providence in their deliverance: we were not able to make out after them, being destitute of meanes, Boats, and the like. . . .

I told you before, that when the *Pequeats* heard and saw *Seabrooke* Fort was supplied, they forbore to visit us: But the old Serpent according to his first malice stirred them up against the Church of Christ, and in such a furious manner, as our people were so farre disturbed, and affrighted with their boldnesse that they scarce durst rest in their beds: threatning persons and cattell to take them, as indeed they did: so insolent were these wicked imps growne, that like the divell their commander, they runne up and downe as roaring Lyons, compassing all corners of the Countrey for a prey, seeking whom they might devoure: It being death to them for to rest without some wicked imployment or other, they still plotted how they might wickedly attempt some bloody enterprise upon our poore native Countrey-men. . . .

Having imbarqued our soldiers, wee weighed ankor at *Seabrooke* Fort, and set sayle for the *Narraganset Bay,* deluding the *Pequeats* thereby, for they expected us to fall into *Pequeat* River; but crossing their expectation, bred in them a securitie: wee landed our men in the *Narraganset Bay,* and marched over land above two dayes journey before wee came to *Pequeat;* quartering the last nights march within two miles of the place, wee set forth about one of the clocke in the morning, having sufficient intelligence that they knew nothing of our comming: Drawing neere to the Fort yeelded up our selves to God, and intreated his assistance in so waightie an enterprize. We set on our march to surround the Fort, Captaine *John Mason,* approching to the West end, where it had an entrance to passe into

it, my selfe marching to the Southside, surrounding the Fort, placing the *Indians,* for wee had about three hundred of them without,
side of our souldiers in a ring battalia, giving a volley of shotte upon
the Fort, so remarkable it appeared to us, as wee could not but
admire at the providence of God in it, that souldiers so unexpert in
the use of their armes, should give so compleat a volley, as though
the finger of God had touched both match and flint: which volley
being given at breake of day, and themselves fast asleepe for the
most part, bred in them such a terrour, that they brake forth into a
most dolefull cry, so as if God had not fitted the hearts of men for
the service, it would have bred in them a commiseration towards
them: but every man being bereaved of pitty fell upon the worke
without compassion, considering the bloud they had shed of our
native Countrey-men, and how barbarously they had dealt with
them, and slaine first and last about thirty persons. Having given
fire, wee approached neere to the entrance which they had stopped
full, with armes of trees, or brakes: my selfe approching to the entrance found the worke too heavie for mee, to draw out all those
which were strongly forced in. We gave order to one Master *Hedge,*
and some other souldiers to pull out those brakes, having this done,
and laid them betweene me and the entrance, and without order
themselves, proceeded first on the South end of the Fort: but remarkable it was to many of us; men that runne before they are sent,
most commonly have an ill reward. Worthy Reader, let mee intreate
you to have a more charitable opinion of me (though unworthy to
be better thought of) then is reported in the other Booke: you may
remember there is a passage unjustly laid upon mee, that when wee
should come to the entrance, I should put forth this question: shall
we enter? others should answer againe; What came we hither for
else? It is well knowne to many, it was never my practise in time
of my command, when we are in garrison, much to consult with a
private souldier, or to aske his advise in point of Warre, much less
in a matter of so great a moment as that was, which experience had
often taught mee, was not a time to put forth such a question, and
therefore pardon him that hath given the wrong information: having our swords in our right hand, our Carbins or Muskets in our
left hand, we approched the Fort. Master *Hedge* being shot thorow
both armes, and more wounded; though it bee not commendable
for a man to make mention of any thing that might tend to his
owne honour; yet because I would have the providence of God

observed, and his Name magnified, as well for my selfe as others, I dare not omit, but let the world know, that deliverance was given to us that command, as well as to private souldiers. Captaine *Mason* and my selfe entring into the Wigwams, hee was shot, and received many Arrowes against his head-peece, God preserved him from any wounds; my selfe received a shotte in the left hippe, through a sufficient Buffe coate, that if I had not been supplyed with such a garment, the Arrow would have pierced through me; another I received betweene necke and shoulders, hanging in the linnen of my Head-peece, others of our souldiers were shot some through the shoulders, some in the face, some in the head, some in the legs: Captaine *Mason* and my selfe losing each of us a man, and had neere twentie wounded: most couragiously these *Pequeats* behaved themselves: but seeing the Fort was to hotte for us, wee devised a way how wee might save our selves and prejudice them, Captaine *Mason* entring into a Wigwam, brought out a fire-brand, after hee had wounded many in the house, then hee set fire on the West-side where he entered, my selfe set fire on the South end with a traine of Powder, the fires of both meeting in the center of the Fort blazed most terribly, and burnt all in the space of halfe an houre; many couragious fellowes were unwilling to come out, and fought most desperately through the Palisadoes, so as they were scorched and burnt with the very flame, and were deprived of their armes, in regard the fire burnt their very bowstrings, and so perished valiantly: mercy they did deserve for their valour, could we have had opportunitie to have bestowed it; many were burnt in the Fort, both men, women, and children, others forced out, and came in troopes to the *Indians,* twentie, and thirtie at a time, which our souldiers received and entertained with the point of the sword; downe fell men, women, and children, those that scaped us, fell into the hands of the *Indians,* that were in the reere of us; it is reported by themselves, that there were about foure hundred soules in this Fort, and not above five of them escaped out of our hands. Great and dolefull was the bloudy sight to the view of young souldiers that never had beene in Warre, to see so many soules lie gasping on the ground so thicke in some places, that you could hardly passe along. It may bee demanded, Why should you be so furious (as some have said) should not Christians have more mercy and compassion? But I would referre you to *Davids* warre, when a people is growne to such a height of bloud, and sinne against God and man, and all confederates in the action, there hee hath no respect to persons, but harrowes them, and sawes them, and puts them to the sword, and the most terriblest death that may bee: sometimes the Scripture declareth women and children must perish with their parents; some time the case alters: but we will not dispute it now. We had sufficient light from the word of God for our proceedings. . . .

SOURCE: Captaine John Underhill, *Newes from America* (London, 1638), 9–40 *passim*.

[AHC]

Nathaniel Ward, the Liberties of the Massachusetts Collonie in New England

December 1641

The Massachusetts "Body of Liberties," the first code of laws established in New England, was compiled by Nathaniel Ward (c. 1578–1652) a leading English Puritan minister, who had been trained as a lawyer. He came to the colony in 1634, and was for a time pastor at Ipswich. The "Liberties" were established by the Massachusetts General Court in December, 1641.
— Note by Charles W. Eliot

THE FREE FRUITION of such liberties, Immunities, and priveledges as humanitie, Civilitie, and Christianitie call for as due to every man in his place and proportion, without impeachment, and infringement, hath ever bene and ever will be the tranquillitie and Stabilitie of Churches and Commonwealths. And the deniall or deprivall thereof, the disturbance if not the ruine of both.

We hould it therefore our dutie and safetie whilst we are about the further establishing of this Government to collect and expresse all such freedomes as for present we foresee may concerne us, and our posteritie after us, And to ratify them with our sollemne consent.

Wee doe therefore this day religiously and unanimously decree and confirme these following Rites, liberties, and priveledges concerneing our Churches, and Civill State to be respectively, impartiallie, and inviolably enjoyed and observed throughout our Jurisdiction for ever.

1. No mans life shall be taken away, no mans honour or good name shall be stayned, no mans person shall be arested, restrayned, banished, dismembred, nor any wayes punished, no man shall be deprived of his wife or children, no mans goods or estaite shall be taken away from him, nor any way indammaged under colour of law or Countenance of Authoritie, unless it be by vertue or equitie of some expresse law of the Country waranting the same, established by a generall Court and sufficiently published, or in case of the defect of a law in any partecular case by the word of God. And in Capitall cases, or in cases concerning dismembring or banishment according to that word to be judged by the Generall Court.

2. Every person within this Jurisdiction, whether Inhabitant or forreiner, shall enjoy the same justice and law, that is generall for the plantation, which we constitute and execute one towards another without partialitie or delay.

3. No man shall be urged to take any oath or subscribe any articles, covenants or remonstrance, of a publique and Civill nature, but such as the Generall Court hath considered, allowed, and required.

4. No man shall be punished for not appearing at or before any Civill Assembly, Court, Councell, Magistrate, or Officer, nor for the omission of any office or service, if he shall be necessarily hindred by any apparent Act or providence of God, which he could neither foresee nor avoid. Provided that this law shall not prejudice any person of his just cost or damage, in any civill action.

5. No man shall be compelled to any publique worke or service unlesse the presse be grounded upon some act of the generall Court, and have reasonable allowance therefore.

6. No man shall be pressed in person to any office, worke, warres, or other publique service, that is necessarily and suffitiently exempted by any naturall or personall impediment, as by want of yeares, greatnes of age, defect of minde, fayling of sences, or impotencie of Lymbes.

7. No man shall be compelled to goe out of the limits of this plantation upon any offensive warres which this Commonwealth or any of our friends or confederats shall volentarily undertake. But onely upon such vindictive and defensive warres in our owne behalfe or the behalfe of our freinds and confederats as shall be enterprized by the Counsell and consent of a Court generall, or by authority derived from the same.

8. No mans Cattel or goods of what kinde soever shall be pressed or taken for any publique use or service, unlesse it be by warrant grounded upon some act of the generall Court, nor without such reasonable prices and hire as the ordinarie rates of the Countrie do afford. And if his Cattel or goods shall perish or suffer damage in such service, the owner shall be suffitiently recompenced.

9. No monopolies shall be granted or allowed amongst us, but of such new Inventions that are profitable to the Countrie, and that for a short time.

10. All our lands and heritages shall be free from all fines and licenses upon Alienations, and from all hariotts, wardships, Liveries, Primer-seisins, yeare day and wast, Escheates, and forfeitures, upon the deaths of parents or Ancestors, be they naturall, casuall or Juditiall.

11. All persons which are of the age of 21 yeares, and of right understanding and meamories, whether excommunicate or condemned shall have full power and libertie to make there wills and testaments, and other lawfull alienations of theire lands and estates.

12. Every man whether Inhabitant or fforreiner, free or not free shall have libertie to come to any publique Court, Councel, or Towne meeting, and either by speech or writeing to move any lawfull, seasonable, and materiall question, or to present any necessary motion, complaint, petition, Bill or information, whereof that meeting hath proper cognizance, so it be done in convenient time, due order, and respective manner.

13. No man shall be rated here for any estaite or revenue he hath in England, or in any forreine partes till it be transported hither.

14. Any Conveyance or Alienation of land or other estaite what so ever, made by any woman that is married, any childe under age, Ideott or distracted person, shall be good if it be passed and ratified by the consent of a generall Court.

15. All Covenous or fraudulent Alienations or Conveyances of lands, tenements, or any hereditaments, shall be of no validitie to defeat any man from due debts or legacies, or from any just title, clame or possession, of that which is so fraudulently conveyed.

16. Every Inhabitant that is an howse holder shall have free fishing and fowling in any great ponds and Bayes, Coves and Rivers, so farre as the sea ebbes and flowes within the presincts of the towne where they dwell, unlesse the free men of the same Towne or the Generall Court have otherwise appropriated them, provided

that this shall not be extended to give leave to any man to come upon others proprietie without there leave.

17. Every man of or within this Jurisdiction shall have free libertie, notwithstanding any Civill power to remove both himselfe, and his familie at their pleasure out of the same, provided there be no legall impediment to the contrarie.

RITES, RULES, AND LIBERTIES CONCERNING JUDITIALL PROCEEDINGS

18. No mans person shall be restrained or imprisoned by any authority whatsoever, before the law hath sentenced him thereto, if he can put in sufficient securitie, bayle or mainprise, for his appearance, and good behaviour in the meane time, unlesse it be in Crimes Capitall, and Contempts in open Court, and in such cases where some expresse act of Court doth allow it.

19. If in a general Court any miscariage shall be amongst the Assistants when they are by themselves that may deserve an Admonition or fine under 20 sh. it shall be examined and sentenced amongst themselves, If amongst the Deputies when they are by themselves, it shall be examined and sentenced amongst themselves, If it be when the whole Court is togeather, it shall be judged by the whole Court, and not severallie as before.

20. If any which are to sit as Judges in any other Court shall demeane themselves offensively in the Court, The rest of the Judges present shall have power to censure him for it, if the cause be of a high nature it shall be presented to and censured at the next superior Court.

21. In all cases where the first summons are not served six dayes before the Court, and the cause breifly specified in the warrant, where appearance is to be made by the partie summoned, it shall be at his libertie whether he will appeare or no, except all cases that are to be handled in Courts suddainly called, upon extraordinary occasions, In all cases where there appeares present and urgent cause any assistant or officer apointed shal have power to make our attaichments for the first summons.

22. No man in any suit or action against an other shall falsely pretend great debts or damages to vex his adversary, if it shall

appeare any doth so, The Court shall have power to set a reasonable fine on his head. […]

26. Every man that findeth himselfe unfit to plead his owne cause in any Court shall have Libertie to imploy any man against whom the Court doth not except, to helpe him, Provided he give him noe fee or reward for his paines. This shall not exempt the partie him selfe from Answering such Questions in person as the Court shall thinke meete to demand of him. […]

34. If any man shall be proved and Judged a common Barrator vexing others with unjust frequent and endlesse suites, It shall be in the power of Courts both to denie him the benefit of the law, and to punish him for his Barratry. […]

42. No man shall be twise sentenced by Civill Justice for one and the same Crime, offence, or Trespasse.

43. No man shall be beaten with above 40 stripes, nor shall any true gentleman, nor any man equall to a gentleman be punished with whipping, unles his crime be very shamefull, and his course of life vitious and profligate.

44. No man condemned to dye shall be put to death within fower dayes next after his condemnation, unles the Court see spetiall cause to the contrary, or in case of martiall law, nor shall the body of any man so put to death be unburied 12 howers unlesse it be in case of Anatomie.

45. No man shall be forced by Torture to confesse any Crime against himselfe nor any other unlesse it be in some Capitall case, where he is first fullie convicted by cleare and suffitient evidence to be guilty, After which if the cause be of that nature, That it is very apparent there be other conspiratours, or confederates with him, Then he may be tortured, yet not with such Tortures as be Barbarous and inhumane.

46. For bodilie punishments we allow amongst us none that are inhumane Barbarous or cruel.

47. No man shall be put to death without the testimony of two or three witnesses or that which is equivalent thereunto. […]

57. Whensoever any person shall come to any very suddaine untimely and unnaturall death, Some assistant, or the Constables of that Towne shall forthwith sumon a Jury of twelve free men to inquire of the cause and manner of their death, and shall present a true verdict thereof to some neere Assistant, or the next Court to be helde for that Towne upon their oath.

LIBERTIES MORE PECULIARLIE CONCERNING THE FREE MEN

58. Civill Authoritie hath power and libertie to see the peace, ordinances and Rules of Christ observed in every church according to his word, so it be done in a Civill and not in an Ecclesiastical way.

59. Civill Authoritie hath power and libertie to deale with any Church member in a way of Civill Justice, notwithstanding any Church relation, office or interest. [...]

65. No custome or prescription shall ever pervaile amongst us in any morall cause, our meaneing is maintaine anythinge that can be proved to be morrallie sinfull by the word of god. [...]

75. It is and shall be the libertie of any member or members of any Court Councell or Civill Assembly in cases of makeing or executing any order or law, that properlie concerne religion, or any cause capitall, or warres, or Subscription to any publique Articles or Remonstrance, in case they cannot in Judgement and conscience consent to that way the Major vote or suffrage goes, to make their contra Remonstrance or protestation in speech or writeing, and upon request to have their dissent recorded in the Rolles of that Court. So it be done Christianlie and respectively for the manner. And their dissent onely be entered without the reasons thereof, for the avoiding of tediousnes.

76. Whensoever any Jurie of trialls or Jurours are not cleare in their Judgments or consciences conserneing any cause wherein they are to give their verdict, They shall have libertie in open Court to advise with any man they thinke fitt to resolve or direct them, before they give in their verdict.

77. In all cases wherein any freeman is to give his vote, be it in point of Election, makeing constitutions and orders or passing sentence in any case of Judicature or the like, if he cannot see reason to give it positively one way or an other, he shall have libertie to be silent, and not pressed to a determined vote. [...]

LIBERTIES OF WOMEN

79. If any man at his death shall not leave his wife a competent portion of his estaite, upon just complaint made to the Generall Court she shall be relieved.

80. Everie marryed woeman shall be free from bodilie correction or stripes by her husband, unless it is in his owne defence upon her assalt. If there be any just cause of correction complaint shall be made to Authoritie assembled in some Court, from which onely she shall receive it.

LIBERTIES OF CHILDREN

81. When parents die intestate, the Elder sonne shall have a doble portion of his whole estate reall and personall, unlesse the Generall Court upon just cause alleadged shall judge otherwise.

82. When parents dye intestate haveing noe heires males of their bodies their Daughters shall inherit as Copartners, unles the Generall Court upon just reason shall judge otherwise.

83. If any parents shall wilfullie and unreasonably deny any childe timely or convenient marriage, or shall exercise any unnaturall severitie towards them, such children shall have free libertie to complaine to Authoritie for redresse.

84. No Orphan dureing their minoritie which was not committed to tuition or service by the parents in their life time, shall afterwards be absolutely disposed of by any kindred, friend, Executor, Towneship, or Church, nor by themselves without the consent of some Court, wherein two Assistants at least shall be present.

LIBERTIES OF SERVANTS

85. If any servants shall flee from the Tiranny and crueltie of their masters to the howse of any freeman of the same Towne, they shall be there protected and susteyned till due order be taken for their relife. Provided due notice thereof be speedily given to their maisters from whom they fled. And the next Assistant or Constable where the partie flying is harboured.

86. No servant shall be put of for above a yeare to any other neither in the life time of their maister nor after their death by their Executors or Administrators unlesse it be by consent of Authoritie assembled in some Court or two Assistants.

87. If any man smite out the eye or tooth of his manservant, or maid servant, or otherwise mayme or much disfigure him, unlesse it be by meere casualtie, he shall let them goe free from his

service. And shall have such further recompense as the Court shall allow him.

88. Servants that have served deligentlie and faithfully to the benefitt of their maisters seaven yearse, shall not be sent away emptie. And if any have bene unfaithfull, negligent or unprofitable in their service, notwithstanding the good usage of their maisters, they shall not be dismissed till they have made satisfaction according to the Judgement of Authoritie.

LIBERTIES OF FOREIGNERS AND STRANGERS

89. If any people of other Nations professing the true Christian Religion shall flee to us from the Tiranny or oppression of their persecutors, or from famyne, warres, or the like necessary and compulsarie cause, They shall be entertayned and succoured amongst us, according to that power and prudence, god shall give us.

90. If any ships or other vessels, be it freind or enemy, shall suffer shipwrack upon our Coast, there shall be no violence or wrong offered to their persons or goods. But their persons shall be harboured, and relieved, and their goods preserved in safety till Authoritie may be certified thereof, and shall take further order therein.

91. There shall never be any bond slaverie, villinage or Captivitie amongst us unless it be lawfull Captives taken in just warres, and such strangers as willingly selle themselves or are sold to us. And these shall have all the liberties and Christian usages which the law of god established in Israell concerning such persons doeth morally require. This exempts none from servitude who shall be Judged thereto by Authoritie.

OFF THE BRUITE CREATURE

92. No man shall exercise any Tirranny or Crueltie towards any bruite Creature which are usuallie kept for man's use.

93. If any man shall have occasion to leade or drive Cattel from place to place that is far of, so that they be weary, or hungry, or fall sick, or lambe, It shall be lawful to rest or refresh them, for competant time, in any open place that is not Corne, meadow, or inclosed for some peculiar use.

94. CAPITAL LAWS

1.

If any man after legall conviction shall have or worship any other god, but the lord god, he shall be put to death.[1]

2.

If any man or woeman be a witch, (that is hath or consulteth with a familiar spirit,) they shall be put to death.[2]

3.

If any person shall Blaspheme the name of god, the father, Sonne or Holie Ghost, with direct, expresse, presumptuous or high handed blasphemie, or shall curse god in the like manner, he shall be put to death.[3]

4.

If any person committ any wilfull murther, which is manslaughter, committed upon premeditated malice, hatred, or Crueltie, not in a mans necessarie and just defence, nor by meere casualtie against his will, he shall be put to death.[4]

5.

If any person slayeth another suddenly in his anger or Crueltie of passion, he shall be put to death.[5]

6.

If any person shall slay an other through guile, either by poysoning or other such divelish practice, he shall be put to death.[6]

---

[1] Deut. xiii. 6, 10. Deut. xvii. 2, 6. Ex. xxii. 20.
[2] Ex. xxii. 18. Lev. xx. 27. Deut. xviii. 10.
[3] Lev. xxiv. 15, 16.
[4] Ex. xxi. 22. Numb. xxxv. 13, 14, 30, 31.
[5] Numb. xxv. 20, 21. Lev. xxiv. 17.
[6] Ex. xxi. 14.

7.

If any man or woeman shall lye with any beaste or bruite creature by Carnall Copulation, They shall surely be put to death. And
the beast shall be slaine, and buried and not eaten.[7]

8.

If any man lyeth with mankinde as he lyeth with a woeman, both
of them have committed abhomination, they both shall surely be
put to death.[8]

9.

If any person committeth Adultery with a maried or espoused
wife, the Adulterer and Adulteresse shall surely be put to death.[9]

10.

If any man stealeth a man or mankinde, he shall surely be put to
death.[10]

11.

If any man rise up by false witnes, wittingly and of purpose to
take away any mans life, he shall be put to death.[11]

12.

If any man shall conspire and attempt any invasion, insurrection,
or publique rebellion against our commonwealth, or shall endeavor
to surprize any Towne or Townes, fort or forts therein, or shall
treacherously and perfediouslie attempt the alteration and subversion of our frame of politie or Government fundamentallie, he shall
be put to death.

---

[7] Lev. xx. 15, 16.
[8] Lev. xx. 13.
[9] Lev. xx. 19, and 18, 20. Deut. xxii. 23, 24.
[10] Ex. xxi. 16.
[11] Deut. xix. 16, 18, 19.

95. A DECLARATION OF THE LIBERTIES THE LORD JESUS HATH GIVEN TO THE CHURCHES

1.

All the people of god within this Jurisdiction who are not in a church way, and be orthodox in Judgement, and not scandalous in life, shall have full libertie to gather themselves into a Church Estaite. Provided they doe it in a Christian way, with due observation of the rules of Christ revealed in his word. [...]

[AHD]

Massachusetts School Laws

April 14, 1642 and November 11, 1647

Note: The earliest colonial law about education is credited to the Massachusetts Colony in 1642. A clarification or justification of that law, concerning now "the old deluder Satan," followed in 1647.

(1642)

THIS CO^RT, TAKING into consideration the great neglect of many parents & masters in training up their children in learning, & labo^r, & other implyments which may be proffitable to the common wealth, do hereupon order and decree, that in euery towne ye chosen men appointed for managing the prudentiall affajres of the same shall henceforth stand charged with the care of the redresse of this evill, so as they shalbee sufficiently punished by fines for the neglect thereof, upon presentment of the grand iury, or other information or complaint in any Court within this iurisdiction; and for this end they, or the greater numbe^r of them, shall have power to take account from time to time of all parents and masters, and of their children, concerning their calling and implyment of their children, especially of their ability to read & understand the principles of religion & the capitall lawes of this country, and to impose fines upon such as shall refuse to render such accounts to them when they shall be required; and they shall have power, with consent of any Court or the magistrate, to put forth apprentices the children of such as they shall (find) not to be able & fitt to employ and bring them up. They shall take . . . that boyes and girles be not suffered to converse together, so as may occasion any wanton, dishonest, or immodest behavio^r; & for their better performance of this trust committed to them, they may divide the towne amongst them, appointing to every of the said townesmen a certaine number of families to have special oversight of. They are also to provide that a sufficient quantity of materialls, as hemp, flaxe, ec^{ra}, may be raised in their severall townes, & tooles & implements provided for working out the same; & for their assistance in this so needfull and beneficiall imploym^t, if they meete wth any difficulty or opposition wch they cannot well master by their own power, they may have reco^{r}se to some of the ma^{trats}, who shall take such course for their help & incuragm^t as the occasion shall require according to iustice; & the said townesmen, at the next Co^{r}t in those limits, after the end of their year, shall give a briefe account in writing of their proceedings herein, provided that they have been so required by some Co^{r}t or magistrate a month at least before; & this order to continue for two years, & till the Co^{r}t shall take further order.

(1647)

It being one chiefe proiect of ye ould deluder, Satan, to keepe men from the knowledge of ye Scriptures, as in form^r times by keeping y^m in an unknowne tongue, so in these latt^r times by perswading from ye use of tongues, y^t so at least ye true sence & meaning of ye originall might be clouded by false glosses of saint seeming deceivers, y^t learning may not be buried in y^o grave of o^r fath^{rs} in ye church and cornmonwealth, the Lord assisting o^r endeavo^{r}s,—

It is therefore ord^{r}ed, y^t ev^{r}y towneship in this iurisdiction, aft^r ye Lord hath increased y^m number to 50 househol^{rs}, shall then forthwth appoint one wth in their towne to teach all such children as shall resort to him to write & reade, whose wages shall be paid eith^r by ye parents or mast^{rs} of such children, or by ye inhabitants in gen^{r}all, by way of supply, as ye maior part of those y^t ord^r ye prudentials ye twone shall appoint; provided, those y^t send their children be not oppressed by paying much more y^m they can have y^m taught for in oth^r townes; & it is furth^r ordered, y^t where any towne shall increase to ye numb^r of 100 families or household^{rs}, they shall set up a grammer schoole, ye m^r thereof being able to instruct youth so farr as they shall be fitted for ye university, provided, y^t if any towne neglect ye performance hereof above one yeare, y^t every such towne shall pay 5 pounds to ye next schoole till they shall perform this order.

[RHE]

The Germantown Mennonite Protest Against Slavery

February 18, 1688

Drawn up at Thomas Kunder's house February, 1688, and sent to the quarterly and yearly meetings of the Quakers, only to be of too great importance "to meddle with," this protest is, so far as is known, the first public protest against the holding of slaves in America.

— Note by Peter George Mode

"This is to ye Monthly Meeting held at Rigert Worrells. These are the reasons why we are against the traffick of mens-body as followeth: Is there any that would be done or handled at this manner? viz. to be sold or made a slave for all the time of his life? How fearfull and fainthearted are many on sea when they see a strange vessel being afraid it should be a Turck, and they should be tacken and sold for Slaves in Turckey. Now what is this better done as Turcks doe? yea rather is it worse for them, wch say they are Christians for we hear, that ye most part of such Negers are brought heither against their will & consent, and that many of them are stollen. Now tho' they are black, we cannot conceive there is more liberty to have them slaves, as it is to have other white ones. There is a saying, that we shall doe to all men, licke as we will be done our selves: macking no difference of what generation, descent, or Colour they are. And those who steal or robb men, and those who buy or purchase them, are they not all alicke? Here is liberty of Conscience, wch is right & reasonable, here ought to be lickewise liberty of ye body, except of evildoers, wch is another case. But to bring men hither, or to robb and sell them against their will, we

stand against. In Europe there are many oppressed for Conscience
Sacke; and here there are those oppressed wch are of a black Colour.
And we, who know that men must not commit adultery, some do
commit adultery in others, separating wifes from their housbands,
and giving them to others and some sell the children of those poor
Creatures to other men. Oh, doe consider well this things, you who
doe it, if you would be done at this manner? And if it is done according Christianity? you surpass Holland and Germany in this
thing. This mackes an ill report in all those Countries of Europe,
where they hear off, that ye Quackers doe here handel men, Licke
they handel there ye Cattle, and for that reason some have no mind
or inclination to come hither. And who shall maintaine this your
cause or plaid for it! Truely we can not do so except you shall inform us better hereof, viz. that christians have liberty to practise this
things. Pray! What thing in the world can be done worse towarts us
then if men should robb or steal us away & sell us for slaves to
strange Countries, separating housband from their wife & children.
Being now this is not done at that manner we will be done at,
therefore we contradict & are against this traffick of men body. And
we who profess that it is not lawfull to steal, must lickewise avoid
to purchase such things as are stolen, but rather help to stop this
robbing and stealing if possibel and such men ought to be delivred
out of ye hands of ye Robbers and set free as well as in Europe.
Then is Pensilvania to have a good report, in stead it hath now a
bad one for this sacke in other Countries. Especially whereas ye
Europeans are desirous to know in what manner ye Quackers doe
rule in their Province & most of them doe loock upon us with an
envious eye. But if this is done well, what shall we say, is don evil?

If once these slaves (wch they say are so wicked and stubbern
men) should joint themselves, fight for their freedom and handel
their masters & mastrisses, as they did handel them before; will these
masters & mistrisses tacke the sword at hand & warr against these
poor slaves, licke we are able to believe, some will not refuse to doe?
Or have these negers not as much right to fight for their freedom,
as you have to keep them slaves?

Now consider well this thing, if it is good or bad? and in case
you find it to be good to handel these blacks at that manner, we
desire & require you hereby lovingly that you may informe us
herein, which at this time never was done, viz. that Christians have
Liberty to do so, to the end we shall be satisfied in this point, &

satisfie lickewise our good friends & acquaintances in our natif Country, to whose it is a terrour or fairfull thing that men should be handeld so in Pensilvania.

"This is from our meeting at Germantown hold ye 18 of the 2 month 1688 to be delivered to the monthly meeting at Richard Warrels.

GERRET HENDRICKS
DERICK OP DE GRAEFF
FRANCIS DANIELL PASTORIUS
ABRAHAM OP DEN GRAEF."

[ACH]

Reverend Deodat Lawson, Statement on the Salem Witches and Witches' Testimony

1692

Lawson was minister at Salem Village (now Danvers), where the witchcraft excitement first broke out. His account is paralleled by those of Calef and Increase Mather.

— Note by Albert Bushnell Hart

IT PLEASED GOD in the Year of our Lord 1692. to visit the People at a place called *Salem Village* in NEW-ENGLAND, with a very Sore and Grievous Affliction, in which they had reason to believe, that the Sovereign and Holy GOD was pleased to permit **Satan** and his Instruments, to Affright and Afflict, those poor Mortals in such an Astonishing and Unusual manner.

Now, I having for some time before, attended the work of the Ministry in that Village, the Report of those *Great Afflictions,* came quickly to my notice; and the more readily, because the first Person Afflicted, was in the Minister's Family, who succeeded me, after I was removed from them; in pitty therefore to my Christian Friends, and former Acquaintance there, I was much concerned about them, frequently consulted with them, and fervently (by Divine Assistance) prayed for them; but especially my Concern was augmented, when it was Reported, at an Examination of a Person suspected for Witchcraft, that my Wife and Daughter, who Dyed Three Years before, were sent out of the World under the Malicious Operations of the Infernal Powers; as is more fully

represented in the following Remarks. I did then *Desire,* and was
also *Desired,* by some concerned in the Court, to be there present,
that I might hear what was alleged in that respect; observing therefore, when I was amongst them, that the Case of the Afflicted was
very amazing, and deplorable; and the Charges brought against the
Accused, such as were Ground of Suspicions yet very intricate, and
difficult to draw up right Conclusions about them. ...

1. One or two of the first that were Afflicted, Complaining of
unusual Illness, their Relations used *Physick* for their *Cure,* but it
was altogether in vain.

2. They were oftentimes, very *stupid* in their Fits, and could
neither hear nor understand, in the apprehension of the Standers
by, so that when *Prayer* hath been made, with some of them, in
such a manner as might be audible in a great Congregation; yet
when their Fit was off, they declared they did not hear so much as
one Word thereof.

3. It was several times Observed, that when they were discoursed
with, about GOD or CHRIST, or the Things of *Salvation,* they
were presently afflicted at a dreadful Rate, and hence were oftentimes *Outragious,* if they were permitted to be in the Congregation,
in the Time of the Public Worship. . . .

5. They affirm'd, That they saw the *Ghosts* of several departed
Persons, who at their appearing, did instigate them, to discover
such as (they said) were Instruments to hasten their Deaths; threatening sorely to afflict them, if they did not make it known to the
Magistrates; they did affirm at the Examination, and again at the
Tryal of an accused Person, that they saw the Ghosts of his two
Wives (to whom he had carryed very ill in their Lives, as was
proved by several Testimonies) and also that they saw the Ghosts of
My Wife and *Daughter,* (who dyed above three Years before) and
they did affirm, that when the very Ghosts looked on the Prisoner
at the Bar, they looked red, as if the Blood would fly out of their
Faces, with Indignation at him: The Manner of it was thus; Several
Afflicted being before the Prisoner at the Bar, on a sudden they
fixed all their Eyes together, on a certain Place of the Floor before
the Prisoner; neither moving their Eyes nor Bodies, for some few
Minutes, nor answering to any Question which was asked them; so
soon as that Trance was over, some being removed out of Sight and
Hearing, they were all one after another asked what they saw, and
they did all agree, that they saw those *Ghosts* above mentioned; I

was present, and heard and saw the whole of what passed upon that Account, during the Tryal of that Person who was accused to be the Instrument of 𝕾𝖆𝖙𝖆𝖓's Malice therein.

6. In this (*worse than Gallick*) Persecution by the *Dragoons* of Hell, the Persons afflicted were harassed at such a dreadful rate, to write their Names in a Devil-Book, presented by a Spectre unto them; and One in my hearing said, *I will not, I will not Write, it is none of God's Book, it is none of God's Book; it is the Devil's Book for ought I know:* And when they stedfastly refused to sign, they were told if they would but touch or take hold of the Book it should do: And *Lastly,* The Diabolical Propositions were so low and easy, that if they would but let their Clothes, or any thing about them, touch the Book, they should be at ease from their Torments, it being their Consent that is aimed at by the Devil in those Representations and Operations.

7. One who had been long afflicted at a stupendous rate, by two or three Spectres, when they were (to speak after the manner of Men) *tyred out* with tormenting of her, to *Force* or *Fright* her to sign a Covenant with the Prince of Darkness, they said to her, as in a Diabolical and Accursed Passion, *Go your ways and the Devil go with you, for we will be no more pestred and plagued about you.* And ever after that she was well, and no more afflicted that ever I heard of.

8. Sundry Pins have been taken out of the Wrists and Arms of the Afflicted; and one in time of Examination of a suspected Person, had a Pin ran through both her *Vpper* and her *Lower* Lip, when she was called to speak; yet no apparent festering followed thereupon, after it was taken out.

9. Some of the Afflicted, as they were striving in their Fits, in open Court, have (by invisible means) had their Wrists bound fast together with a real Cord, so as it could hardly be taken off without cutting. Some Afflicted have been found with their Arms tyed, and hanged upon an Hook, from whence others have been forced to take them down that they might not expire in that Posture.

10. Some Afflicted have been drawn under Tables and Beds, by undiscerned Force, so as they could hardly be pull[ed] out: And one was drawn half way over the Side of a Well, and was with much difficulty recovered back again.

11. When they were most grievously afflicted, if they were brought to the Accused, and the suspected Persons Hand but laid upon them, they were immediately relieved out of their Tortures; but if the Accused did but look on them, they were instantly struck down again. Wherefore, they use to cover the Face of the Accused,

while they laid their Hands on the Afflicted, and then it obtained the desired Issue; for it hath been experienced (both in Examinations and Tryals) that so soon as the Afflicted, came in sight of the Accused, they were immediately cast into their Fits; yea, though the Accused were among the Crowd of People unknow to the Sufferers, yet on the first view were they struck down; which was observed in a Child of four or five Years of Age, when it was apprehended, that so many as she could look upon, either directly or by turning her Head, were immediately struck into their Fits.

12. An iron Spindle of a woolen Wheel, being taken very strangely out of an House at *Salem* Village, was used by a Spectre, as an Instrument of Torture to a Sufferer, not being discernable to the Standers by; until it was by the said Sufferer snatched out of the Spectres Hand, and then it did immediately appear to the Persons present to be really the same iron Spindle.

13. Sometimes in their Fits, they have had their Tongues drawn out of their Mouths to a fearful length, their Heads turned very much over their Shoulders; and while they have been so strained in their Fits, and had their Arms and Legs, *&c.* wrested, as if they were quite dislocated, the Blood hath gushed plentifully out of their Mouths, for a considerable time together; which some, that they might be satisfied that it was real Blood, took upon their Finger and rubbed on their other Hand. I saw several together thus violently strained and bleeding in their Fits, to my very great astonishment, that my fellow-Mortals should be so grievously distressed by the invisible Powers of Darkness. For certainly, all considerate Persons, who beheld these things, must needs be convinced, that their Motions in their Fits were Præternatural and Involuntary, both as to the *Manner* which was so strange, as a well Person could not (at least without great Pain) screw their Bodies into; and as to the *violence* also, they were Præternatural Motions, being much beyond the ordinary Force of the same Persons when they were in their right Minds. So that being such grievous Sufferers, it would seem very hard and unjust to censure them of consenting *To,* or holding any voluntary Converse or Familiarity *with* the 𝔇𝔢𝔳𝔦𝔩.

14. Their Eyes were for the most part fast closed in their Trance-Fits, and when they were asked a Question, they could give no Answer; and I do verily believe, they did not hear at that time, yet did they discourse with the Spectres as with real Persons; asserting Things, and receiving Answers, affirmative or negative, as the Matter was. For Instance, One in my hearing thus argued *with,* and

railed *at* a Spectre, *Goodn——* be gone! be gone! be gone! Are you not ashamed, a Woman of your Profession, to afflict a poor Creature so? What hurt did I ever do you in my Life? You have but two Years to live, and then the 𝔇𝔢𝔳𝔦𝔩 will torment your Soul for this: Your Name is blotted out of God's Book, and it shall never be put into God's Book again. Be gone for shame, are you not afraid of what is coming upon you? I know, I know, what will make you afraid, the Wrath of an angry God: I am sure that will make you afraid. Be gone, do not torment me; I know what you would have, *(we judged she meant her Soul:)* but it is out of your reach, it is clothed with the white Robes of Christ's Righteousness. This Sufferer I was well acquainted with, and knew her to be a very sober and pious Woman, so far as I could judge; and it appears that she had not in that Fit, voluntary Converse with the 𝔇𝔢𝔳𝔦𝔩; for then she might have been helped to a better Guess about that Woman above-said, as to her living but two Years, for she lived not many Months after that time. . . .

16. Some of them were asked how it came to pass that they were not affrighted when they saw the *Black-man,* they said they were at first, but not so much afterwards.

17. Some of them affirmed, they saw the *Black-man* sit on the Gallows, and that he whispered in the Ears of some of the *Condemned Persons* when they were just ready to be turn'd off; even while they were making their last Speech. . . .

19. Some of them, have sundry times seen a *White-man* appearing amongst the Spectres, and as soon as he appeared, the *Black-Witches* vanished. They said: This *White-man* had often foretold them, what respite they should have from their Fits; as sometimes a day or two, or more, which fell out accordingly. One of the Afflicted said she saw him in her Fit, and was with him in a *Glorious Place,* which had no *Candle* nor *Sun,* yet was full of Light and Brightness; where there was a multitude in *white Glittering Robes,* and they sang the Song in *Rev.* 5. 9. *Psal.* 110. *Psal.* 149. she was loth to leave that Place, and said *how long shall I stay here, let me be along with you?* She was grieved, she could stay no longer in that Place and Company.

20. A young Woman that was afflicted at a fearful rate, had a Spectre appeared to her, with a white Sheet wrapped about it, not visible to the Standers by, until this Sufferer *(violently striving in her Fit)* snatched at, took hold, and tore off a Corner of that Sheet; her Father being by her, endeavored to lay hold upon it with her, that

she might retain what she had gotten; but at the passing away of the Spectre, he had such a violent Twitch of his Hand, as if it would have been torn off; immediately thereupon appeared in the Sufferers hand, the Corner of a Sheet, *a real cloth, visible* to the Spectators, which *(as it is said)* remains still to be seen.

SOURCE: Deodat Lawson, *Christ's Fidelity the only Shield against Satan's Malignity* (Boston, 1704), Appendix, 93–109 *passim*.

WITCHES' TESTIMONY

The original minutes of the witch trials at Salem [taken by the clerk Ezekiel Cheever], still well preserved, afford the most striking proof of the inadequacy of the evidence and of the terror of the prosecutors.

— Note by Albert Bushnell Hart

SALEM FFEB[y] THE 29th 169½

WHEREAS M[rs] Joseph Hutcheson, Thomas Putnam, Edward Putnam, and Thomas Preston, Yeomen of Salem Village in ye County of Essex, personally appeared before vs and made Complaint on Behalf of their Majes[ts] against Sarah Good the wife of William Good of Salem Village aboves[d] for suspition of Witchcraft by her Committed, and thereby much Injury done by Eliz. Paris, Abigail Williams, Anne Putnam and Elizabeth Hubert all of Salem Village afores[d] Sundry times within this two moneths and Lately also don, at Salem Village Contrary to y[e] peace of our Souer[n] L[d] and Lady W[m] & Mary, King & Queen of Engld &c — You are therefore in theire Majesties names hereby required to apprehe[d] & bring before vs, the said Sarah Good to morrow aboute ten of y[e] clock in y[e] forenoon at y[e] house of Lt Nathaniele Ingersalls in Salem Village or as soon as may be then and there to be Examined Relating to y[e] aboves[d] premises and hereof you are not to faile at your perile.

Dated. Salem, feb[r] 29th 1692.

JOHN HATHORNE } Assis[ta].
JONATHAN CORWIN }

To Constable George Locker.

I brought the person of Saragh Good the wife of William Good according to the tenor of the within warrant, as is Attest by me
1 March 1692   GEORGE LOCKER — Constable

Anno: Regis et Reginee Willm et Mariae
nunc Anglice &c. Quarto

Essex ss.

The Juro^{rs} for our Sovereigne Lord and Lady the King and Queen, pr^{e}sent, That Sarah Good the wife of William Good of Salem Village in the County of Essex, Husbandman, the Second Day of May in the forth year of the Reigne of our Sovereigne Lord and Lady William and Mary by the Grace of God of England, Scotland ffrance & Ireland King and Queen Defenders of the ffaith &c and Divers other Days and times as well before as after, certaine Detestable arts called Witchcrafts and Sorceries, Wickedly and ffeloniously hath vsed, Practiced and Exorcised, at and within the Township of Salem in the County of Essex aforesaid, in, upon and against one Sarah Vibber wife of John Vibber of Salem aforesaid, Husbandman, by which said wicked Arts, she the said Sarah Vibber the said Second Day of May in the fourth year abovsaid and divers other Days and times as well before as after was and is Tortuered Afflicted, Pined, Consumed, wasted and Tormented, and also for Sundry other Acts of witchcraft by said Sarah Good committed and done before and since that time ag^t the Peace of our Sovereigne Lord & Lady the King & Queen theire Crowne and Dignity and ag^t the forme of the Statute in that case made and Provided.

Witnesses
Sarah Vibber Jurat
Abigail Williams Jurat
Elizabeth Hubbard "
Ann Putnam Jurat
Jno Vibber   Sworne . . .

The examination of Sarah Good before the worshipfull Assts John Harthorn Jonathan Curran
(H.) Sarah Good what evil Spirit have you familiarity with
(S. G.) None.

(H.) Have you made no contracte with the devil
    Good answered no.
(H.) Why doe you hurt these children
(g) I doe not hurt them. I scorn it.
(H) Who doe you imploy then to doe it.
(g) I imploy no body
(H) What creature do you imploy then.
(g) no creature but I am falsely accused.
(H) why did you go away muttering from Mr Parris his house.
(g) I did not mutter but I thanked him for what he gave my child.
(H) have you made no contract with the devil.
(g) no.
(H) desired the children all of them to look upon her and see if this were the person that had hurt them and so they all did looke upon her, and said this was one of the persons that did torment them — presently they were all tormented.

(H) Sarah Good do you not see now what you have done, why doe you not tell us the truth, why doe you thus torment these poor children.
(g) I doe not torment them.
(H) who do you imploy then.
(g) I imploy nobody I scorn it.
(H) how came they thus tormented
(g) what doe I know you bring others here and now you charge me with it.
(H) why who was it.
(g) I doe not know but it was some you brought into the meeting house with you.
(H) wee brought you into the meeting house.
(g) but you brought in two more.
(H) who was it then that tormented the children.
(g) it was osburn.
(H) what is it you say when you go muttering away from persons houses
(g) if I must tell I will tell.
(H) doe tell us then
(g) if I must tell, I will tell, it is the commandments. I may say my commandments I hope.
(H.) what commandment is it.
(g) if I must tell, I will tell, it is a psalm.

(H) what psalm.

(g) after a long time shee muttered over some part of a psalm.

(H) who doe you serve

(g) I serve God

(H) what God doe you serve.

(g) the God that made heaven and earth. though shee was not willing to mention the word God. her answers were in a very wicked spitfull manner, reflecting and retorting against the authority with base and abussive words and many lies shee was taken in it was here said that her husband had said that he was afraid that she either was a witch or would be one very quickly. the worsh. Mr. Harthon asked him his reason why he said so of her, whether he had ever seen any thing by her, he answered no, not in this nature, but it was her bad carriage to him, and indeed said he I may say with tears that shee is an enemy to all good.

Salem Village March the 1st 169½

Written by Ezekiell Chevers

Salem Village March th 1st 169½ . . .

Salem Village March the 1st 169½

Sarah Osburne the wife of Alexander Osburne of Salem Village brought before vs by Joseph Herrick constable in Salem, to answer Joseph Hutcheson and Thomas putnam &c yeomen in s^d Salem Village Complainants on behalfe of theire Majes^{ts} against s^d Sarah Osburne for Suspition of Witchcraft by her Committed and thereby much Injury don to the bodys of Elizabeth Parris, Abigail Williams Anna Putnam and Elizabeth Hubert, all of Salem Village aforesaid, according to theire Complaint, according to a Warrant, Dated Salem ffebu^y 29th 169½

Sarah Osburne vpon Examination denyed ye matter of fact (viz) y^t she ever vnderstood or vsed any Witchcraft, or hurt any of ye aboue s^d children.

The children aboue named being all personally present accused her face to face which being don, thay ware all hurt, afflicted and tortured very much; which being ouer and thay out of theire fitts thay sayd y^t said Sarah Osburne, did then come to them and hurt them, Sarah Osburn being then keept at a distance personally from them. S. Osburne was asked why she then hurt them, she denyed it, it being asked of her how she could soe pinch and hurt them and yet she be at that distance personally from y^m, she Answered she did not then hurt them, nor never did, she was asked who then did it, or who she Imploy to doe it, she Answered she did not know y^t ye Divell goes aboute in her likeness to doe any hurt. Sarah Osburn being told y^t Sarah Good one of her Companions had vpon Examination accused her, she nottwithstanding denyed ye same, according to her Examination, wch is mor at Large giuen in as therein will appeare.

p. vs. JOHN HATHORNE } Assits.
JONATHAN CORWIN

(H) what evil spirit have you familiarity with.

(O) none.

(H) have you made no contract with the devill.

(O) no I never saw the devill in my life.

(H) why doe you hurt these children.

(O) I doe not hurt them.

(H) who do you imploy then to hurt them.

(O) I imploy no body.

(H) what familiarity have you with Sarah Good.

(O) none. I have not seen her these 2 years.

(H) where did you see her then.

(O) one day a going to town.

(H) what communications had you with her.

(O) I had none, only, how doe you doe or so, I did not know her by name.

(H) what did you call her then.

Osburn made a stand at that, at last said, shee called her Sarah.

(H) Sarah Good saith that it was you that hurt the children.

(O) I doe not know that the devil goes about in my likeness to doe any hurt.

Mr Hathorn desired all the children to stand up and look upon her and see if they did know her, which they all did and every one of them said that this was one of the women that did afflict them, and that they had constantly seen her in the very habit, that shee was now in, theire evidence do stand that shee said this morning that shee was more like to be bewitched, than that shee was a witch. Mr Hathorn asked her what made her say so, shee answered that shee was frighted one time in her sleep and either saw or dreamed that shee saw a thing like an indian all black which did prick her in her neck and pulled her by the back part of her head to the dore of the house

(H) did you never see anything else.

(O) no.

it was said by some in the meeting house that shee had said that shee would never be tied to that lying spirit any more.

(H) what lying spirit is this, hath the devil ever deceived you and been false to you.

(O) I doe not know the devil I never did see him.

(H) what lying spirit was it then.

(O) it was a voice that I thought I heard.

(H) what did it propound to you.

(O) that I should goe no more to meeting, but I said I would and did goe the next Sabbath day.

(H) were you never tempted furder.

(O) no.

(H) why did you yield thus far to the devil as never to goe to meeting since

(O) Alas. I have been sike and not able to goe. her husband and others said that she had not been at meeting this yeare and two months. . . .

Salem Village March 1st 1692

Titiba an Indian woman brought before vs by Const Joseph Herrick of Salem vpon Suspition of witchcraft by her committed according to ye complaint of Jos. Hutcheson and Thomas Putnam &c of Salem Village as appears p warrant granted Salem 29 ffeby 169½ Titiba vpon examination and after some deny all acknowledged ye matter of fact according to her examination giuen in more fully will appeare, and who also charged Sarah Good and Sarah Osborne with ye same . . .

(H) Titibe whan evil spirit have you familiarity with.

(T) none.

(H) why do you hurt these children.

(T) I do not hurt them,

(H) who is it then.

(T) the devil for ought I know.

(H) Did you never see the devil.

(T) The devil came to me and bid me serve him.

(H) Who have you seen.

(T) Four women sometimes hurt the children.

(H) Who were they.

(T) Goode Osburn and Sarah Good and I doe not know who the other were. Sarah Good and Osburne would have me hurt the children but I would not she further saith there was a tale man of Boston that she did see.

(H) when did you see them.

(T) Last night at Boston.

(H) what did they say to you.
     they said hurt the children

(H) and did you hurt them

(T) no there is 4 women and one man they hurt the children and they lay all upon me and they tell me if I will not hurt the children they will hurt me.

(H) but did you not hurt them

(T) yes, but I will hurt them no more.

(H) are you not sorry you did hurt them.

(T) yes.

(H) and why then doe you hurt them.

(T) they say hurt children or wee will doe worse to you.

(H) what have you seen.
     an man come to me and say serve me.

(H) what service.

(T) hurt the children and last night there was an appearance that said kill the children and if I would no go on hurting the children they would do worse to me.

(H) what is this appearance you see.

(T) Sometimes it is like a hog and sometimes like a great dog, this appearance shee saith shee did see 4 times.

(H) what did it say to you

(T) it s the black dog said serve me but I said I am afraid he said if I did not he would doe worse to me.

(H) what did you say to it.

(T) I will serve you no longer, then he said he would hurt me and then he looked like a man and threatens to hurt me, shee said that this man had a yellow bird that kept with him and he told me he had more pretty things that he would give me if I would serve him.

(H) what were these pretty things.

(T) he did not show me them.

(H) what also have you seen

(T) two rats, a red rat and a black rat.

(H) what did they say to you.

(T) they said serve me.

(H) when did you see them.

(T) last night and they said serve me, but I said I would not

(H) what service.

(T) shee said hurt the children.

(H) did you not pinch Elizabeth Hubbard this morning

(T) the man brought her to me and made me pinch her

(H) why did you go to Thomas Putnams last night and hurt his child.

(T) they pull and hall me and make me goe

(H) and what would have you doe.

    Kill her with a knif.

Left. Fuller and others said at this time when the child saw these persons and was tormented by them that she did complayn of a knife, that they would have her cut her head off with a knife.

(H) how did you go

(T) we ride upon stickes and are there presently.

(H) doe you goe through the trees or over them.

(T) we see nothing but are there presently.

[H] why did you not tell your master.

[T] I was afraid they said they would cut of my head if I told.

[H] would you not have hurt others if you cold.

[T] They said they would hurt others but they could not

[H] what attendants hath Sarah Good.

[T] a yellow bird and shee would have given me one

[H] what meate did she give it

[T] it did suck her between her fingers.

[H] did not you hurt Mr Currins child

[T] goode good and goode Osburn told that they did hurt Mr Currens child and would have had me hurt him two, but I did not.

[H] what hath Sarah Osburn.

[T] yellow dog, shee had a thing with a head like a woman with 2 legges, and wings. Abigail Williams that lives with her Uncle Parris said that she did see the same creature, and it turned into the shape of Goode Osburn.

[H] what else have you seen with Osburn.

[T] another thing, hairy it goes upright like a man it hath only 2 leggs.

[H] did you not see Sarah Good upon Elizabeth Hubbard, last Saterday.

[T] I did see her set a wolfe upon her to afflict her, the persons with this maid did say that she did complain of a wolfe.

T. shee further saith that shee saw a cat with good at another time.

[H] What cloathes doth the man go in

[T] he goes in black clouthes a tal man with white hair I thinke

[H] How doth the woman go

[T] in a white whood and a black whood with a top knot

[H] doe you see who it is that torments these children now.

[T] yes it is Goode Good, shee hurts them in her own shape

[H] and who is it that hurts them now.

[T] I am blind now. I cannot see.

Salem Village   Written by Ezekiell Cheevers.
March the 1st 169½   Salem Village March 1st 169½

[AHC]

Benjamin Franklin, Plan of Union

1754

Viewing with apprehension the encroachments of France in America, the Lords of Trade in 1753 directed the governors to recommend their respective assemblies to appoint delegates to a congress to meet at time and place to be fixed by the Governor of New York. The congress was to treat with the Six Nations [an alliance of native American tribes] of New York, and secure their alliance in a possible war with France. It was suggested that the colonies form a league for mutual defence. Commissioners from seven colonies met at Albany, June 19, 1754. After concluding the treaty with the Six Nations, the following plan of Union, largely drawn by Franklin, was adopted for recommendation to colonial assemblies. The plan was, as Frothingham tersely says, "rejected in America because it had too much of the prerogative, and in England because it was too democratic." The plan is here given with the interesting comments of Franklin, which are distinguished by italics.

— Note by Howard W. Preston

PLAN OF A proposed Union of the several Colonies of Massachusetts-Bay, New Hampshire, Connecticut, Rhode Island, New-York, New-Jersey, Pennsylvania, Maryland, Virginia, North Carolina, and South Carolina for their mutual Defence and Security, and for the extending the British Settlements in North America.

That humble application be made for an act of Parliament of Great Britain, by virtue of which one general government may be formed in America, including all the said Colonies, within and under which government each Colony may retain its present constitution, except in the particulars wherein a change may be directed by the said act, as hereafter follows.

PRESIDENT-GENERAL
AND GRAND COUNCIL.

That the said general government be administered by a President-General, to be appointed and supported by the crown; and a Grand Council to be chosen by the representatives of the people of the several Colonies met in their respective assemblies.

It was thought that it would be best the President-General should be supported as well as appointed by the crown, that so all disputes between him and the Grand-Council concerning his salary might be prevented; as such disputes have been frequently of mischievous consequence in particular Colonies, especially in time of public danger. The quitrents of crown lands in America might in a short time be sufficient for this purpose. The choice of members for the Grand-Council is placed in the House of Representatives of each government, in order to give the people a share in this new general government, as the crown has its share by the appointment of the President-General.

But it being proposed by the gentlemen of the Council of New York, and some other counsellors among the commissioners, to alter the plan in this particular, and to give the governors and councils of the several Provinces a share in the choice of the Grand-Council, or at least a power of approving and confirming, or of disallowing, the choice made by the House of Representatives, it was said,— "That the government or constitution, proposed to be formed by the plan, consists of two branches: a President-General appointed by the crown, and a Council chosen by the people, or by the people's representatives, which is the same thing.

"That, by a subsequent article, the council chosen by the people can effect nothing without the consent of the President-General appointed by the crown; the crown possesses, therefore, full one half of the power of this constitution.

"That in the British constitution, the crown is supposed to possess but one third, the Lords having their share.

"That the constitution seemed rather more favorable for the crown.

"That it is essential to English liberty that the subject should not be taxed but by his own consent, or the consent of his elected representatives.

"That taxes to be laid and levied by this proposed constitution will be proposed and agreed to by the representatives of the people, if the plan in this particular be preserved.

"But if the proposed alteration should take place, it seemed as if matters may be so managed, as that the crown shall finally have the

appointment, not only of the President-General, but of a majority of the Grand-Council; for seven out of eleven governors and councils are appointed by the crown.

"And so the people in all the Colonies would in effect be taxed by their governors.

"It was therefore apprehended, that such alterations of the plan would give great dissatisfaction, and that the Colonies could not be easy under such a power in governors, and such an infringement of what they take to be English liberty.

"Besides, the giving a share in the choice of the Grand Council would not be equal with respect to all the Colonies, as their constitutions differ. In some, both governor and council are appointed by the crown. In others, they are both appointed by the proprietors. In some, the people have a share in the choice of the council; in others, both government and council are wholly chosen by the people. But the House of Representatives is everywhere chosen by the people; and, therefore, placing the right of choosing the Grand Council in the representatives is equal with respect to all.

"That the Grand Council is intended to represent all the several Houses of Representatives of the Colonies, as a House of Representatives doth the several towns or counties of a Colony. Could all the people of a Colony be consulted and unite in public measures, a House of Representatives would be needless, and could all the Assemblies consult and unite in general measures, the Grand Council would be unnecessary.

"That a House of Commons or the House of Representatives, and the Grand Council are alike in their nature and intention. And, as it would seem improper that the King or House of Lords should have a power of disallowing or appointing Members of the House of Commons; so, likewise, that a governor and council appointed by the crown should have a power of disallowing or appointing members of the Grand Council, who, in this constitution, are to be the representatives of the people.

"If the governor and councils therefore were to have a share in the choice of any that are to conduct this general government, it should seem more proper that they should choose the President-General. But this being an office of great trust and importance to the nation, it was thought better to be filled by the immediate appointment of the crown.

"The power proposed to be given by the plan to the Grand Council is only a concentration of the powers of the several assemblies in certain points for the general welfare; as the power of the President-General is of the several governors in the same point.

"And as the choice therefore of the Grand Council, by the representatives of the people, neither gives the people any new powers, nor diminishes the power of the crown, it was thought and hoped the crown would not disapprove of it."

Upon the whole, the commissioners were of opinion, that the choice was most properly placed in the representatives of the people.

ELECTION OF MEMBERS.

That within   months after the passing such act, the House of Representatives that happens to be sitting within that time, or that shall be especially for that purpose convened, may and shall choose members for the Grand Council, in the following proportion, that is to say,

Massachusetts Bay	7
New Hampshire	2
Connecticut	5
Rhode Island	2
New York	4
New Jersey	3
Pennsylvania	6
Maryland	4
Virginia	7
North Carolina	4
South Carolina	4
	48

It was thought, that if the least Colony was allowed two, and the others in proportion, the number would be very great, and the expense heavy; and that less than two would not be convenient, as, a single person being by any accident prevented appearing at the meeting, the Colony he ought appear for would not be represented. That, as the choice was not immediately popular, they would be generally men of good abilities for business, and men of reputation for integrity, and that forty-eight such men might be a number sufficient. But, though it was thought reasonable that each Colony should have a share in the representative body in some degree according to the proportion it contributed to the general treasury, yet the proportion of wealth or power of the Colonies is not to be judged by the proportion here fixed: because it was at first agreed, that the greatest Colony should not have more than seven members, nor the least less than two; and the setting these proportions between these two extremes was not nicely attended to, as it would find itself, after the first election, from the sum brought into the treasury by a subsequent article.

PLACE OF FIRST MEETING.

—Who shall meet for the first time at the city of Philadelphia in Pennsylvania, being called by the President-General as soon as conveniently may be after his appointment.

Philadelphia was named as being nearer the centre of the Colonies, where the commissioners would be well and cheaply accommodated. The high roads, through the whole extent, are for the most part very good, in which forty or fifty miles a day may very well be, and frequently are, travelled. Great part of the way may likewise be gone by water. In summer time, the passages are frequently performed in a week from Charleston to Philadelphia and New York, and from Rhode Island to New York through the Sound, in two or three days, and from New York to Philadelphia, by water and land, in two days, by stage boats, and street carriages that set out every other day. The journey from Charleston to Philadelphia may likewise be facilitated by boats running up Chesapeake Bay three hundred miles. But if the whole journey be performed on horseback, the most distant members, viz., the two from New Hampshire and from South Carolina, may probably render themselves at Philadelphia in fifteen or twenty days; the majority may be there in much less time.

NEW ELECTION.

That there shall be a new election of the members of the Grand Council every three years and, on the death or resignation of any member, his place should be supplied by a new choice at the next sitting of the Assembly of the Colony he represented.

Some Colonies have annual assemblies, some continue during a governor's pleasure; three years was thought a reasonable medium as affording a new member time to improve himself in the business, and to act after such improvement, and yet giving opportunities, frequently enough, to change him if he has misbehaved.

PROPORTION OF MEMBERS AFTER THE FIRST THREE YEARS.

That after the first three years, when the proportion of money arising out of each Colony to the general treasury can be known, the number of members to be chosen for each Colony shall, from time to time, in all ensuing elections, be regulated by that proportion, yet so as that the number to be chosen by any one Province be not more than seven, nor less than two.

By a subsequent article, it is proposed that the General Council shall lay and levy such general duties as to them may appear most equal and least burdensome, etc. Suppose, for instance, they lay a small duty or excise on some commodity imported into or made in the Colonies, and pretty generally and equally used in all of them, as rum, perhaps, or wine; the yearly produce of this duty or excise, if fairly collected, would be in some Colonies greater, in others less, as the Colonies are greater or smaller. When the collector's accounts are brought in, the proportions will appear; and from them it is proposed to regulate the proportion of the representatives to be chosen at the next general election, within the limits, however, of seven and two. These numbers may therefore vary in the course of years, as the Colonies may in the growth and increase of people. And thus the quota of tax from each Colony would naturally vary with its circumstances, thereby preventing all disputes and dissatisfaction about the just proportions due from each, which might otherwise produce penicious consequences, and destroy the harmony and good agreement that ought to subsist between the several parts of the Union.

MEETINGS OF THE GRAND COUNCIL AND CALL.

That the Grand Council shall meet once in every year, and oftener if occasion require, at such time and place as they shall adjourn to at the last preceding meeting, or as they shall be called to meet at by the President-General on any emergency; he having first obtained in writing the consent of seven of the members to such call, and sent due and timely notice to the whole.

It was thought, in establishing and governing new Colonies or settlements, or regulating Indian trade, Indian treaties, etc., there would, every year, sufficient business arise to require at least one meeting, and at such meeting many things might be suggested for the benefit of all the Colonies.

This annual meeting may either be at a time and place certain, to be fixed by the President-General and Grand Council at their first meeting; or left at liberty, to be at such time and place as they shall adjourn to, or be called to meet at, by the President-General.

In time of war, it seems convenient that the meeting should be in that colony which is nearest the seat of action.

The power of calling them on any emergency seemed necessary to be vested in the President-General; but, that such power might not be wantonly used to harass the members, and oblige them to make frequent long journeys to little purpose, the consent of seven at least to such call was supposed a convenient guard.

CONTINUANCE.

That the Grand Council have power to choose their speaker; and shall neither be dissolved, prorogued, nor continued sitting longer than six weeks at one time, without their own consent or the special command of the crown.

The speaker should be presented for approbation; it being convenient, to prevent misunderstandings and disgusts, that the mouth of the Council should be a person agreeable, if possible, to the Council and President-General.

Governors have sometimes wantonly exercised the power of proroguing or continuing the sessions of assemblies, merely to harass the members and compel a compliance; and sometimes dissolve them on slight disgusts. This it was feared might be done by the President-General, if not provided against; and the inconvenience and hardship would be greater in the general government than in particular Colonies, in proportion to the distance the members must be from home during sittings, and the long journeys some of them must necessarily take.

MEMBERS' ALLOWANCE.

That the members of the Grand Council shall be allowed for their service ten shillings per diem, during their session and journey to and from the place of meeting; twenty miles to be reckoned a day's journey.

It was thought proper to allow some wages, lest the expense might deter some suitable persons from the service; and not to allow too great wages, lest unsuitable persons should be tempted to cabal for the employment, for the sake of gain. Twenty miles were set down as a day's journey, to allow for accidental hindrances on the road, and the greater expenses of travelling than residing at the place of meeting.

ASSENT OF PRESIDENT-GENERAL AND HIS DUTY.

That the assent of the President-General be requisite to all acts of the Grand Council, and that it be his office and duty to cause them to be carried into execution.

The assent of the President-General to all acts of the Grand Council was made necessary in order to give the crown its due share of influence in this government, and connect it with that of Great Britain. The President-General, besides one half of the legislative power, hath in his hands the whole executive power.

POWER OF PRESIDENT-GENERAL AND GRAND COUNCIL, TREATIES OF PEACE AND WAR.

That the President-General, with the advice of the Grand Council, hold or direct all Indian treaties, in which the general interest of the Colonies may be concerned, and make peace or declare war with Indian nations.

The power of making peace or war with Indian nations is at present supposed to be in every Colony, and is expressly granted to some by charter, so that no new power is hereby intended to be granted to the Colonies. But as, in consequence of this power, one Colony might make peace with a nation that another was justly engaged in war with; or make war on slight occasion without the concurrence or approbation of neighboring Colonies, greatly endangered by it; or make particular treaties of neutrality in case of a general war, to their own private advantage in trade, by supplying the common enemy, of all which there have been instances, it was thought better to have all treaties of a general nature under a general direction, that so the good of the whole may be consulted and provided for.

INDIAN TRADE.

That they make such laws as they judge necessary for regulating all Indian trade.

Many quarrels and wars have arisen between the colonies and Indian nations, through the bad conduct of traders, who cheat the Indians after making them drunk, etc., to the great expense of the colonies, both in blood and treasure. Particular colonies are so interested in the trade, as not to be willing to admit such a regulation as might be best for the whole; and therefore it was thought best under a general direction.

INDIAN PURCHASES.

That they make all purchases from Indians, for the crown, of lands not now within the bounds of particular colonies, or that shall not be within their bounds when some of them are reduced to more convenient dimensions.

Purchases from the Indians, made by private persons, have been attended with many inconveniences. They have frequently interfered and occasioned uncertainty of titles, many disputes and expensive lawsuits, and hindered the settlement of the land so disputed. Then the Indians have been cheated by such private purchases, and discontent and wars have been the consequence. These would be prevented by public fair purchases.

Several of the Colony charters in America extend their bounds to the South Sea, which may perhaps be three or four thousand miles in length to one or two hundred miles in breadth. It is supposed they must in time be reduced to dimensions more convenient for the common purposes of government.

Very little of the land in these grants is yet purchased of the Indians.

It is much cheaper to purchase of them, than to take and maintain the possession by force; for they are generally very reasonable in their demands for land; and the expense of guarding a large frontier against their incursions is vastly great; because all must be guarded, and always guarded, as we know not where or when to expect them.

NEW SETTLEMENTS.

That they make new settlements on such purchases by granting lands in the King's name, reserving a quit-rent to the crown for the use of the general treasury.

It is supposed better that there should be one purchaser than many; and that the crown should be that purchaser, or the Union in the name of the crown. By this means the bargains may be more easily made, the price not enhanced by numerous bidders, future disputes about private Indian purchases, and monopolies of vast tracts to particular persons (which are prejudicial to the settlement and peopling of the country), prevented; and, the land being again granted in small tracts to the settlers, the quit-rents reserved may in time become a fund for support of government, for defence of the country, ease of taxes, etc.

Strong forts on the Lakes, the Ohio, etc., may, at the same time they secure our present frontiers, serve to defend new colonies settled under their protection; and such colonies would also mutually defend and support such forts, and better secure the friendship of the far Indians.

A particular colony has scarce strength enough to exert itself by new settlements, at so great a distance from the old; but the joint force of the Union might suddenly establish a new colony or two in those parts, or extend an old colony to particular passes, greatly to the security of our present frontiers, increase of trade and people, breaking off the French communication between Canada and Louisiana, and speedy settlement of the intermediate lands.

The power of settling new colonies is therefore thought a valuable part of the plan, and what cannot so well be executed by two unions as by one.

LAWS TO GOVERN THEM.

That they make laws for regulating and governing such new settlements, till the crown shall think fit to form them into particular governments.

The making of laws suitable for the new colonies, it was thought, would be properly vested in the president-general and grand council; under whose protection they must at first necessarily be, and who would be well acquainted with their circumstances, as having settled them. When they are become sufficiently populous, they may by the crown be formed into complete and distinct governments.

The appointment of a sub-president by the crown, to take place in case of the death or absence of the president-general, would perhaps be an improvement of the plan; and if all the governors of particular provinces were to be formed into a standing council of state, for the advice and assistance of the president-general, it might be another considerable improvement.

RAISE SOLDIERS, AND
EQUIP VESSELS, ETC.

That they raise and pay soldiers and build forts for the defence of any of the colonies, and equip vessels of force to guard the coasts and protect the trade on the ocean, lakes, or great rivers; but they shall not impress men in any colony, without the consent of the legislature.

It was thought, that quotas of men, to be raised and paid by the several colonies, and joined for any public service, could not always be got together with the necessary expedition. For instance, suppose one thousand men should be wanted in New Hampshire on any emergency. To fetch them by fifties and hundreds out of every colony, as far as South Carolina, would be inconvenient, the transportation chargeable, and the occasion perhaps passed before they could be assembled; and therefore it would be best to raise them (by offering bounty money and pay) near the place where they would be wanted, to be discharged again when the service should be over.

Particular colonies are at present backward to build forts at their own expense, which they say will be equally useful to their neighboring colonies, who refuse to join, on a presumption that such forts will be built and kept up, though they contribute nothing. This unjust conduct weakens the whole; but, the forts being for the good of the whole, it was thought best they should be built and maintained by the whole, out of the common treasury.

In the time of war, small vessels of force are sometimes necessary in the colonies to scour the coasts of small privateers. These being provided by the Union will be an advantage in turn to the colonies which are situated on the sea, and whose frontiers on the land-side, being covered by other colonies, reap but little immediate benefit from the advanced forts.

POWER TO MAKE LAWS, LAY DUTIES, ETC.

That for these purposes they have power to make laws and lay and levy such general duties, imposts or taxes, as to them shall appear most equal and just (considering the ability and other circumstances of the inhabitants in the several colonies), and such as may be collected with the least inconvenience to the people; rather discouraging luxury, than loading industry with unnecessary burdens.

The laws which the president-general and grand council are empowered to make are such only as shall be necessary for the government of the settlements; the raising, regulating, and paying soldiers for the general service; the regulating of Indian trade; and laying and collecting the general duties and taxes. They should also have a power to restrain the exportation of provisions to the enemy from any of the colonies, on particular occasions, in time of war. But it is not intended that they may interfere with the constitution or government of the particular colonies, who are to be left to their own laws, and to lay, levy and apply their own taxes as before.

GENERAL TREASURER AND PARTICULAR TREASURER.

That they may appoint a General Treasurer, and Particular Treasurer in government when necessary; and, from time to time, may order the sums in the treasuries of each government into the general treasury, or draw on them for special payments, as they find most convenient.

The treasurers here meant are only for the general funds and not for the particular funds of each colony, which remain in the hands of their own treasurers at their own disposal.

MONEY, HOW TO ISSUE.

Yet no money to issue but by joint orders of the President-General and Grand Council, except where sums have been appointed to particular purposes, and the President-General is previously empowered by an act to draw such sums.

To prevent misapplication of the money, or even application that might be dissatisfactory to the crown or the people, it was thought necessary to join the president-general and grand council in all issues of money

ACCOUNTS.

That the general accounts shall be yearly settled and reported to the several Assemblies.

By communicating the accounts yearly to each Assembly, they will be satisfied of the prudent and honest conduct of their representatives in the grand council.

QUORUM.

That a quorum of the Grand Council, empowered to act with the President-General, do consist of twenty-five members; among whom there shall be one or more from a majority of the Colonies.

The quorum seems large, but it was thought it would not be satisfactory to the colonies in general, to have matters of importance to the whole transacted by a smaller number, or even by this number of twenty-five, unless there were among them one at least from a majority of the colonies, because otherwise, the whole quorum being made up of numbers from three or four colonies at one end of the union, something might be done that would not be equal with respect to the rest, and thence dissatisfaction and discords might rise to the prejudice of the whole.

LAWS TO BE TRANSMITTED.

That the laws made by them for the purposes aforesaid shall not be repugnant, but, as near as may be, agreeable to the laws of England, and shall be transmitted to the King in Council for approbation, as soon as may be after their passing; and if not disapproved within three years after presentation, to remain in force.

This was thought necessary for the satisfaction of the crown, to preserve the connection of the parts of the British empire with the whole, of the members with the head, and to induce greater care and circumspection in making of the laws, that they be good in themselves and for the general benefit.

DEATH OF THE PRESIDENT-GENERAL.

That, in case of the death of the President-General, the Speaker of the Grand Council for the time being shall succeed, and be vested with the same powers and authorities, to continue till the King's pleasure be known.

It might be better, perhaps, as was said before, if the crown appointed a vice-president, to take place on the death or absence of the president-general; for so we should be more sure of a suitable person at the head of the colonies. On the death or absence of both, the speaker to take place (or rather the eldest King's governor) till his Majesty's pleasure be known.

OFFICERS, HOW APPOINTED.

That all military commission officers, whether for land or sea service, to act under this general constitution, shall be nominated by the President-General; but the approbation of the Grand Council is to be obtained, before they receive their commissions. And all civil officers are to be nominated by the Grand Council, and to receive the President-General's approbation before they officiate.

It was thought it might be very prejudicial to the service, to have officers appointed unknown to the people or unacceptable, the generality of Americans serving willingly under officers they know; and not caring to engage in the service under strangers, or such as are often appointed by governors through favor or interest. The service here meant, is not the stated, settled service in standing troops; but any sudden and short service, either for defence of our colonies, or invading the enemy's country (such as the expedition to Cape Breton in the last war; in which many substantial farmers and tradesmen engaged as common soldiers, under officers of their own country, for whom they had an esteem and affection; who would not have engaged in a standing army, or under officers from England). It was therefore thought best to give the Council the power of approving the officers, which the people will look on as a great security of their being good men. And without some such provision as this, it was thought the expense of engaging men in the service on any emergency would be much greater, and the number who could be induced to engage much less; and that therefore it would be most for the King's service and the general benefit of the nation, that the prerogative should relax a little in this particular throughout all the colonies in America; as it had already done much more in the charters of some particular colonies, viz.: Connecticut and Rhode Island.

The civil officers will be chiefly treasurers and collectors of taxes; and the suitable persons are most likely to be known by the council.

VACANCIES, HOW SUPPLIED.

But, in case of vacancy by death or removal of any officer civil or military, under this constitution, the Governor of the province in which such vacancy happens, may appoint, till the pleasure of the President-General and Grand Council can be known.

The vacancies were thought best supplied by the governors in each province, till a new appointment can be regularly made; otherwise the service might suffer before the meeting of the president-general and grand council.

EACH COLONY MAY DEFEND ITSELF IN EMERGENCY, ETC.

That the particular military as well as civil establishments in each colony remain in their present state, the general constitution notwithstanding; and that on sudden emergencies any colony may defend itself, and lay the accounts of expense thence arising before the president-general and general council, who may allow and order payment of the same, as far as they judge such accounts just and reasonable.

Otherwise the union of the whole would weaken the parts, contrary to the design of the union. The accounts are to be judged of by the president-general and grand council, and allowed if found reasonable. This was thought necessary to encourage colonies to defend themselves, as the expense would be light when borne by the whole; and also to check imprudent and lavish expense in such defences.

[DIH]

The Stamp Act

March 22, 1765

A stamp act formed part of the plan of colonial taxation outlined by [Charles] Townshend in 1763, and adopted by George Grenville when the latter became prime minister. In September, 1763, the commissioners of stamp duties were requested to draft provisions for the extension of those duties to America. In March, 1764, shortly before the passage of the Sugar Act, Grenville announced his intention of introducing, at the next session, a stamp bill; and the plan received the approval of Parliament. In the meantime, opportunity was given the colonial agents to communicate with their respective governments, in order that the colonies, in case the stamp tax were deemed objectionable, might agree upon some other method of raising the desired revenue. The prospect of parliamentary taxation was viewed with alarm in America, where a stricter enforcement of the acts of trade was already thought to threaten disaster to commerce. When, however, the subject was again brought before Parliament by Grenville, in February, 1765, the colonial agents, although remonstrating against the proposed measure, were unable to recommend any substitute; while petitions from the colonial assemblies, and from London merchants interested in the American trade, were refused consideration, under a rule of the House of Commons forbidding the reception of petitions on money bills. There was little opposition in Parliament, and the bill passed the Commons by a vote of 205 to 49, and the Lords without a division. George III. was at the time insane, and the act received the royal assent, March 22, by commission.

– Note by William MacDonald

AN ACT FOR *granting and applying certain stamp duties, and other duties, in the* British *colonies and plantations in* America, *towards further defraying the expences of defending, protecting, and securing the same; and for amending such parts of the several acts of parliament relating to the trade* and revenues of the said colonies and plantations, as direct the manner of determining and recovering the penalties and forfeitures therein mentioned.

Whereas by an act made in the last session of parliament, several duties were granted, continued, and appropriated, towards defraying the expences of defending, protecting, and securing, the British colonies and plantations in America: and whereas it is just and necessary, that provision be made for raising a further revenue within your Majesty's dominions in America, towards defraying the said expences: we, your Majesty's most dutiful and loyal subjects, the commons of Great Britain in parliament assembled, have therefore resolved to give and grant unto your Majesty the several rates and duties here in after mentioned; and do most humbly beseech your Majesty that it may be enacted, and be it enacted . . . , That from and after the first day of November, one thousand seven hundred and sixty five, there shall be raised, levied, collected, and paid unto his Majesty, his heirs, and successors, throughout the colonies and plantations in America which now are, or hereafter may be, under the dominion of his Majesty, his heirs and successors,

For every skin or piece of vellum or parchment, or sheet or piece of paper, on which shall be ingrossed, written or printed, any declaration, plea, replication, rejoinder, demurrer, or other pleading, or any copy thereof, in any court of law within the British colonies and plantations in America, a stamp duty of three pence.

[...]

For every skin . . . on which shall be ingrossed . . . any register, . . . not herein before charged, within the said colonies and plantations, a stamp duty of two shillings.

And for and upon every pack of playing cards, and all dice, which shall be sold or used within the said colonies and plantations, the several stamp duties following (that is to say)

For every pack of such cards, the sum of one shilling.

And for every pair of such dice, the sum of ten shillings.

And for and upon every paper, commonly called a pamphlet, and upon every news paper, containing publick news, intelligence, or occurrences, which shall be printed, dispersed, and made publick, within any of the said colonies and plantations, and for and upon such advertisements as are herein after mentioned, the respective duties following (that is to say)

For every such pamphlet and paper contained in half a sheet, or any lesser piece of paper, which shall be so printed, a stamp duty of one halfpenny, for every printed copy thereof.

For every such pamphlet and paper (being larger than half a sheet, and not exceeding one whole sheet) which shall be so printed, a stamp duty of one penny, for every printed copy thereof.

For every pamphlet and paper being larger than one whole sheet, and not exceeding six sheets in octavo, or in a lesser page, or not exceeding twelve sheets in quarto, or twenty sheets in folio, which shall be so printed, a duty after the rate of one shilling for every sheet of any kind of paper which shall be contained in one printed copy thereof.

For every advertisement to be contained in any gazette, news paper, or other paper, or any pamphlet which shall be so printed, a duty of two shillings.

For every almanack or calendar, for any one particular year, or for any time less than a year, which shall be written or printed on one side only of any one sheet, skin, or piece of paper parchment, or vellum, within the said colonies and plantations, a stamp duty of two pence.

For every other almanack or calendar for any one particular year, which shall be written or printed within the said colonies and plantations, a stamp duty of four pence.

And for every almanack or calendar written or printed within the said colonies and plantations, to serve for several years, duties to the same amount respectively shall be paid for every such year.

For every skin . . . on which any instrument, proceeding, or other matter or thing aforesaid, shall be ingrossed . . . within the said colonies and plantations, in any other than the *English* language, a stamp duty of double the amount of the respective duties before charged thereon.

And there shall be also paid in the said colonies and plantations, a duty of six pence for every twenty shillings, in any sum not exceeding fifty pounds sterling money, which shall be given, paid, contracted, or agreed for, with or in relation to any clerk or apprentice, which shall be put or placed to or with any master or mistress to learn any profession, trade, or employment.

II. And also a duty of one shilling for every twenty shillings, in any sum exceeding fifty pounds, which shall be given, paid, contracted, or agreed, for, with, or in relation to any such clerk or apprentice. [...]

IX. Provided always, That nothing in this act contained shall extend to charge with any duty, any deed, or other instrument, which shall be made between any *Indian* nation and the governor, proprietor of any colony, lieutenant governor, or commander in chief alone, or in conjunction with any other person or persons, or with any council, or any council and assembly of any of the said colonies or plantations, for or relating to the granting, surrendering, or conveying, any lands belonging to such nation, to, for, or on behalf of his Majesty, or any such proprietor, or to any colony or plantation.

X. Provided always, That this act shall not extend to charge any proclamation, forms of prayer and thanksgiving, or any printed votes of any house of assembly in any of the said colonies and plantations, with any of the said duties on pamphlets or news papers; or to charge any books commonly used in any of the schools within the said colonies and plantations, or any books containing only matters of devotion or piety; or to charge any single advertisement printed by itself, or the daily accounts or bills of goods imported and exported, so as such accounts or bills do contain no other matters than what have been usually comprized therein; any thing herein contained to the contrary not withstanding. [...]

XXVI. And, for the better collecting and securing the duties hereby charged on pamphlets containing more than one sheet of paper as aforesaid, be it further enacted . . . , That from and after . . . [Nov. 1, 1765] . . . one printed copy of every pamphlet which shall be printed or published within any of the said colonies . . . , shall within the space of fourteen days after the printing thereof, be brought to the chief distributor in the colony . . . where such pamphlet shall be printed, and the title thereof, with the number of the sheets contained therein, and the duty hereby charged thereon, shall be registered or entered in a book to be there kept for that purpose; which duty shall be thereupon paid to the proper officer or officers appointed to receive the same, or his or their deputy or clerk, who shall thereupon forthwith give a receipt for the same on such printed copy, to denote the payment of the duty hereby charged on such pamphlet; and if any such pamphlet shall be printed or published, and the duty hereby charged thereon shall not be duly paid, and the title and number of sheets shall not be registered, and a receipt for such duty given on one copy, where required so to be, within the time herein before for that purpose limited; that then the author, printer, and publisher, and all other persons concerned in or about the printing or publishing of such pamphlet, shall, for every such offence, forfeit the sum of ten pounds, and shall lose all property therein, and in every other copy thereof, so as any person may freely print and publish the same, paying the duty payable in respect thereof by virtue of this act, without being liable to any action, prosecution, or penalty for so doing.

XXVII. And it is hereby further enacted . . . , That no person whatsoever shall sell or expose to sale any such pamphlet, or any news paper, without the true respective name or names, and place or places of abode, of some known person or persons by or for whom the same was really and truly printed or published, shall be written or printed thereon; upon pain that every person offending therein shall, for every such offence, forfeit the sum of twenty pounds. [...]

[SDIA]

Declarations of the Rights
and Grievances of the Colonists

October 19, 1765

THE New York Congress, "the Day Star of the American Union," summoned by the Massachusetts legislature, met at the City Hall in New York, Oct. 7, 1765. It consisted of twenty-eight delegates from nine colonies, Virginia, New Hampshire, Georgia, and North Carolina being unrepresented. It was much debated whether to found American liberties on natural rights or on royal charters, but the former ground was finally taken. On the 25th the delegates who were so authorized (viz., those from Massachusetts, New Jersey, Rhode Island, Pennsylvania, Delaware and Maryland), signed the Declaration of Rights, and the Congress adjourned. "Perhaps the best general summary of the rights and liberties asserted by all the colonies, is contained in the celebrated declaration drawn up by the Congress of the nine colonies assembled at New York, October, 1765," wrote Judge Story.
— Note by Charles W. Eliot

RESOLVES OF THE CONVENTION
OF THE ENGLISH COLONIES AT
NEW YORK, OCTOBER 19, 1765.

THE CONGRESS UPON mature deliberation, agreed to the following declarations of the rights and grievances of the colonists in America:

The members of this congress, sincerely devoted, with the warmest sentiments of affection and duty, to His Majesty's person and government, inviolably attached to the present happy establishment of the Protestant succession, and with minds deeply impressed by a sense of the present and impending misfortunes of the British colonies on this continent; having considered as maturely as time will permit, the circumstances of the said colonies, esteem it our indispensable duty to make the following declarations of our humble opinion respecting the most essential rights and liberties of the colonists and of the grievances under which they labor by reason of the several late acts of Parliament.

1. That His Majesty's subjects in these colonies, owe the same allegiance to the crown of Great Britain, that is owing from his subjects born within the realm; and all due subordination to that august body, the Parliament of Great Britain.

2. That His Majesty's liege subjects, in these colonies, are entitled to all the inherent rights and liberties of his natural born subjects within the kingdom of Great Britain.

3. That it is inseparably essential to the freedom of a people, and the undoubted right of Englishmen, that no taxes be imposed on them but with their own consent, given personally, or by their representatives.

4. That the people of these colonies are not, and from their local circumstances cannot be, represented in the House of Commons, in Great Britain.

5. That the only representatives of the people of these colonies, are persons chosen therein by themselves; and that no taxes ever have been, or can be constitutionally imposed on them, but by their respective legislatures.

6. That all supplies to the crown, being the free gifts of the people, it is unreasonable and inconsistent with the principles and spirit of the British constitution, for the people of Great Britain to grant to His Majesty, the property of the colonists.

7. That trial by jury is the inherent and invaluable right of every British subject in these colonies.

8. That the late act of Parliament, entitled "An act for granting and applying certain stamp duties, and other duties in the British colonies and plantations, in America, etc.," by imposing taxes on the inhabitants of these colonies, and the said act, and several other acts, by extending the jurisdiction of the courts of admiralty beyond its ancient limits, have a manifest tendency to subvert the rights and liberties of the colonists.

9. That the duties imposed by several late acts of Parliament, from the peculiar circumstances of these colonies, will be extremely burthensome and grievous, and from the scarcity of specie, the payment of them absolutely impracticable.

10. That as the profits of the trade of these colonies ultimately centre in Great Britain, to pay for the manufactures which they are obliged to take from thence, they eventually contribute very largely to all supplies granted there to the crown.

11. That the restrictions imposed by several late acts of Parliament on the trade of these colonies, will render them unable to purchase the manufactures of Great Britain.

12. That the increase, prosperity, and happiness of these colonies depend on the full and free enjoyments of their rights and liberties, and an intercourse with Great Britain, mutually affectionate and advantageous.

13. That it is the right of the British subjects in these colonies to petition the King, or either house of Parliament.

Lastly. That it is the indispensable duty of these colonies, to the best of sovereigns, to the mother country, and to themselves, to endeavour by a loyal and dutiful address to His Majesty, and humble applications to both houses of Parliament, to procure the repeal of the act for granting and applying certain stamp duties, of all clauses of any other acts of Parliament, whereby the jurisdiction of the admiralty is extended, as aforesaid, and of the other late acts for the restriction of American commerce.

[DIH]

Benjamin Franklin and a Committee of the House of Commons, Examination on the State of the Colonies during the Stamp Act Controversy

1766

The examination was conducted in great part by the friends of the colonies, and the answers were prepared beforehand.

— Note by Albert Bushnell Hart

Q. WHAT IS YOUR Name, and Place of abode?

A. Franklin, of Philadelphia.

Q. Do the Americans pay any considerable taxes among themselves?

A. Certainly many, and very heavy taxes.

Q. What are the present taxes in Pennsylvania, laid by the laws of the Colony?

A. There are taxes on all estates real and personal, a poll-tax, a tax on all offices, professions, trades and businesses, according to their profits; an excise upon all wine, rum and other spirits; and a duty of ten pounds per head on all negroes imported, with some other duties. . . .

Q. Are not the Colonies, from their circumstances, very able to pay the stamp-duty?

A. In my opinion, there is not gold and silver enough in the Colonies to pay the stamp duty for one year.

Q. Don't you know that the money arising from the stamps was all to be laid out in America?

A. I know it is appropriated by the act to the American service; but it will be spent in the conquered Colonies, where the soldiers are, not in the Colonies that pay it.

Q. Is there not a ballance of trade due from the Colonies where the troops are posted, that will bring back the money to the old Colonies.

A. I think not. I believe very little would come back. I know of no trade likely to bring it back. I think it would come from the Colonies where it was spent directly to England; for I have always observed, that in every Colony the more plenty the means of remittance to England the more goods are sent for, and the more trade with England carried on. . . .

Q. How many white men do you suppose there are in North America?

A. About 300,000 from sixteen to sixty years of age.

Q. What may be the amount of one year's imports into Pennsylvania from Britain?

A. I have been informed that our merchants compute the imports from Britain to be above 500,000 Pounds.

Q. What may be the amount of the produce of your province exported to Britain?

A. It must be small, as we produce little that is wanted in Britain. I suppose it cannot exceed 40,000 Pounds.

Q. How then do you pay the ballance?

A. The ballance is paid by our produce carried to the West-Indies, and sold in our own islands, or to the French, Spanian[r]ds, Danes and Dutch; by the same carried to other colonies in North-America, as to New-England, Nova-Scotia, Newfoundland, Carolina and Georgia; by the same carried to different parts of Europe, as Spain, Portugal and Italy: In all which places we receive either money, bills of exchange, or commodities that suit for remittance to Britain; which, together with all the profits on the industry of our merchants and mariners, arising in those circuitous voyages, and the freights made by their ships, center finally in Britain, to discharge the ballance, and pay for British manufactures continually used in the province, or sold to foreigners by our traders.

Q. Have you heard of any difficulties lately laid on the Spanish trade?

A. Yes, I have heard that it has been greatly obstructed by some new regulations, and by the English men of war and cutters stationed all along the coast of America.

Q. Do you think it right America should be protected by this country, and pay no part of the expence.

A. That is not the case. The colonies raised, cloathed and paid, during the last war, near 25,000 men, and spent many millions.

Q. Were you not reimbursed by parliament?

A. We were reimbursed what, in your opinion, we had advanced beyond our proportion, or beyond what might be reasonably expected from us; and it was a very small part of what we spent. Pennsylvania, in particular, disbursed about 500,000 pounds, and the reimbursements, in the whole, did not exceed 60,000 pounds. . . .

Q. Do not you think the people of America would submit to pay the stamp duty, if it was moderated?

A. No, never, unless compelled by force of arms. . . .

Q. What was the temper of America towards Great Britain before the year 1763?

A. The best in the world. They submitted willingly to the government of the Crown, and paid, in all their courts, obedience to acts of parliament. Numerous as the people are in the several old provinces, they cost you nothing in forts, citadels, garrisons or armies, to keep them in subjection. They were governed by this country at the expence only of a little pen, ink and paper. They were led by a thread. They had not only a respect, but an affection, for Great Britain, for its laws, its customs and manners, and even a fondness for its fashions, that greatly increased the commerce. Natives of Britain were always treated with particular regard; to be an Old England-man, was, of itself, a character of some respect, and gave a kind of rank among us.

Q. And what is their temper now?

A. O, very much altered.

Q. Did you ever hear the authority of parliament to make laws for America questioned till lately?

A. The authority of parliament was allowed to be valid in all laws, except such as should lay internal taxes. It was never disputed in laying duties to regulate commerce. . . .

Q. In what light did the people of America use to consider the parliament of Great Britain?

A. They considered the parliament as the great bulwark & security of their liberties and privileges, and always spoke of it with the utmost respect and veneration: arbitrary ministers, they thought, might possibly, at times, attempt to oppress them, but they relied on it, that the parliament, on application, would always give redress. They remembered, with gratitude, a strong instance of this, when a bill was brought into parliament, with a clause to make royal instructions laws in the colonies, which the house of commons would not pass, and it was thrown out.

Q. And have they not still the same respect for parliament?

A. No; it is greatly lessened.

Q. To what cause does that owe?

A. To a concurrence of causes; the restraints lately laid on their trade, by which the bringing of foreign gold and silver into the colonies was prevented; the prohibition of making paper money among themselves; and then demanding a new and heavy tax by stamps; taking away at the same time, trials by juries, and refusing to receive & hear their humble petitions.

Q. Don't you think they would submit to the stamp-act, if it was modified, the obnoxious parts taken out, and the duties reduced to some particulars, of small moment?

A. No; they will never submit to it. . . .

Q. Was it an opinion in America before 1763, that the parliament had no right to lay taxes and duties there?

A. I never heard any objection to the right of laying duties to regulate commerce; but a right to lay internal taxes was never supposed to be in parliament, as we are not represented there. . . .

Q. Would the repeal of the stamp-act be any discouragement of your manufactures? Will the people that have begun the manufacture decline it?

A. Yes, I think they will; especially, if, at the same time, the trade is opened again, so that remittances can be easily made. I have known several instances that make it probable. In the war before last, tobacco being low, and making little remittance, the people of Virginia went generally into family manufactures. Afterwards, when tobacco bore a better price, they returned to the use of British manufactures. So fulling mills were very much disused in the last war in Pennsylvania, because bills were then plenty, and remittance could easily be made to Britain for English cloth and other goods.

Q. If the stamp-act should be repealed, would it induce the assemblies of America to acknowledge the rights of parliament to tax them, and would they erase their resolutions?

A. No, never.

Q. Is there no means of obliging them to erase those resolutions?

A. None that I know of; they will never do it unless compelled by force of arms.

Q. Is there no power on earth that can force them to erase them?

A. No power, how great soever, can force men to change their opinions. . . .

Q. Would it be most for the interest of Great-Britain, to employ the hands of Virginia in tobacco, or in manufactures?

A. In tobacco to be sure.

Q. What used to be the pride of the Americans?

A. To indulge in the fashions and manufactures of G. Britain.

Q. What is now their pride?

A. To wear their old cloths over again, till they can make new ones.

Withdrew.

[AHC]

The Fight for
Independence

First Continental Congress, Declaration and Resolves

October 14, 1774

JUNE 17, 1774, *the Massachusetts House of Representatives, under the leadership of Samuel Adams, resolved: "That a meeting of committees from the several colonies on this continent is highly expedient and necessary, to consult upon the present state of the colonies, and the miseries to which they are and must be reduced by the operation of certain acts of Parliament respecting America, and to deliberate and determine upon wise and proper measures, to be by them recommended to all the colonies, for the recovery and establishment of their just rights and liberties, civil and religious, and the restoration of union and harmony between Great Britain and the colonies, most ardently desired by all good men: Therefore, resolved, that the Hon. James Bowdoin, Esq., the Hon. Thomas Cushing, Esq., Mr. Samuel Adams, John Adams and Robert Treat Paine, Esqrs., be, and they are hereby appointed a committee on the part of this province, for the purposes aforesaid, any three of whom to be a quorum, to meet such committees or delegates from the other colonies as have been or may be appointed, either by their respective houses of burgesses or representatives, or by convention, or by the committees of correspondence appointed by the respective houses of assembly, in the city of Philadelphia, or any other place that shall be judged most suitable by the committee, on the 1st day of September next; and that the speaker of the house be directed, in a letter to the speakers of the houses of burgesses or representatives in the several colonies, to inform them of the substance of these resolves."*

In accordance with this call, delegates from all the colonies except North Carolina and Georgia met at Philadelphia September 5; representatives from North Carolina appearing on the 14th. On the 7th, a committee of two from each colony was appointed "to state the rights of the colonies in general, the several instances in which those rights are violated or infringed, and the means most proper to be pursued for obtaining a restoration of them." A report under this resolution was brought in on the 22d, and read. On the 24th, however, it was voted "that the Congress do confine themselves, at present, to the consideration of such rights as have been infringed by acts of the British Parliament since the year 1763." A report in accordance with this vote being brought in and read, further consideration was postponed while the Congress deliberated "on the means most proper to be used for a restoration" of colonial rights. The report on the rights and grievances of the colonies was finally taken up October 12, and on the 14th agreed to in the form following.

— Note by William MacDonald

WHEREAS, SINCE THE close of the last war, the British parliament, claiming a power, of right, to bind the people of America by statutes in all cases whatsoever, hath, in some acts, expressly imposed taxes on them, and in others, under various pretenses, but in fact for the purpose of raising a revenue, hath imposed rates and duties payable in these colonies, established a board of commissioners, with unconstitutional powers, and extended the jurisdiction of courts of admiralty, not only for collecting the said duties, but for the trial of causes merely arising within the body of a county.

And whereas, in consequence of other statutes, judges, who before held only estates at will in their offices, have been made dependent on the crown alone for their salaries, and standing armies kept in times of peace: And whereas it has lately been resolved in parliament, that by force of a statute, made in the thirty-fifth year of the reign of King Henry the Eighth, colonists may be transported to England, and tried there upon accusations for treasons and misprisions, or concealments of treasons committed in the colonies, and by a late statute, such trials have been directed in cases therein mentioned:

And whereas, in the last session of parliament, three statutes were made; one entitled, "An act to discontinue, in such manner and for such time as are therein mentioned, the landing and discharging, lading, or shipping of goods, wares and merchandize, at the town, and within the harbour of Boston, in the province of Massachusetts-Bay in North-America;" another entitled, "An act for the better regulating the government of the province of Massachusetts-Bay in New England;" and another entitled, "An act for the impartial administration of justice, in the cases of persons questioned for any act done by them in the execution of the law, or for the suppression of riots and tumults, in the province of the Massachusetts-Bay in New England;" and another statute was then made, "for making more effectual provision for the government of the province of Quebec, &c." All which statutes are impolitic, unjust, and cruel, as well as unconstitutional, and most dangerous and destructive of American rights:

And whereas, assemblies have been frequently dissolved, contrary to the rights of the people, when they attempted to deliberate on grievances; and their dutiful, humble, loyal, and reasonable petitions to the crown for redress, have been repeatedly treated with contempt, by his Majesty's ministers of state:

The good people of the several colonies of New-Hampshire, Massachusetts-Bay, Rhode-Island and Providence Plantations, Connecticut, New-York, New-Jersey, Pennsylvania, Newcastle, Kent, and Sussex on Delaware, Maryland, Virginia, North-Carolina, and South-Carolina, justly alarmed at these arbitrary proceedings of parliament and administration, have severally elected, constituted, and appointed deputies to meet, and sit in general Congress, in the city of Philadelphia, in order to obtain such establishment, as that their religion, laws, and liberties, may not be subverted: Whereupon the deputies so appointed being now assembled, in a full and free representation of these colonies, taking into their most serious consideration, the best means of attaining the ends aforesaid, do, in the first place, as Englishmen, their ancestors in like cases have usually done, for asserting and vindicating their rights and liberties, DECLARE,

That the inhabitants of the English colonies in North-America, by the immutable laws of nature, the principles of the English constitution, and the several charters or compacts, have the following RIGHTS:

Resolved, N. C. D. 1. That they are entitled to life, liberty and property: and they have never ceded to any foreign power whatever, a right to dispose of either without their consent.

Resolved, N. C. D. 2. That our ancestors, who first settled these colonies, were at the time of their emigration from the mother country, entitled to all the rights, liberties, and immunities of free and natural-born subjects, within the realm of England.

Resolved, N. C. D. 3. That by such emigration they by no means forfeited, surrendered, or lost any of those rights, but that they were, and their descendants now are, entitled to the exercise and enjoyment of all such of them, as their local and other circumstances enable them to exercise and enjoy.

Resolved, 4. That the foundation of English liberty, and of all free government, is a right in the people to participate in their legislative council: and as the English colonists are not represented, and from their local and other circumstances, cannot properly be represented in the British parliament, they are entitled to a free and exclusive power of legislation in their several provincial legislatures, where their right of representation can alone be preserved, in all cases of taxation and internal polity, subject only to the negative of their sovereign, in such manner as has been heretofore used and accustomed: But, from the necessity of the case, and a regard to the mutual interest of both countries, we cheerfully consent to the operation of such acts of the British parliament, as are bona fide, restrained to the regulation of our external commerce, for the purpose of securing the commercial advantages of the whole empire to the mother country, and the commercial benefits of its respective members; excluding every idea of taxation internal or external, for raising a revenue on the subjects, in America, without their consent.

Resolved, N. C. D. 5. That the respective colonies are entitled to the common law of England, and more especially to the great and inestimable privilege of being tried by their peers of the vicinage, according to the course of that law.

Resolved, 6. That they are entitled to the benefit of such of the English statutes, as existed at the time of their colonization; and which they have, by experience, respectively found to be applicable to their several local and other circumstances.

Resolved, N. C. D. 7. That these, his majesty's colonies, are likewise entitled to all the immunities and privileges granted and confirmed to them by royal charters, or secured by their several codes of provincial laws.

Resolved, N. C. D. 8. That they have a right peaceably to assemble, consider of their grievances, and petition the king; and that all prosecutions, prohibitory proclamations, and commitments for the same, are illegal.

Resolved, N. C. D. 9. That the keeping a standing army in these colonies, in times of peace, without the consent of the legislature of that colony, in which such army is kept, is against law.

Resolved, N. C. D. 10. It is indispensably necessary to good government, and rendered essential by the English constitution, that the constituent branches of the legislature be independent of each other; that, therefore, the exercise of legislative power in several colonies, by a council appointed, during pleasure, by the crown, is unconstitutional, dangerous and destructive to the freedom of American legislation.

All and each of which the aforesaid deputies, in behalf of themselves, and their constituents, do claim, demand, and insist on, as their indubitable rights and liberties; which cannot be legally taken from them, altered or abridged by any power whatever, without their own consent, by their representatives in their several provincial legislatures.

In the course of our inquiry, we find many infringements and violations of the foregoing rights, which, from an ardent desire, that harmony and mutual intercourse of affection and interest may be restored, we pass over for the present, and proceed to state such acts and measures as have been adopted since the last war, which demonstrate a system formed to enslave America.

Resolved, N. C. D. That the following acts of parliament are infringements and violations of the rights of the colonists; and that the repeal of them is essentially necessary, in order to restore harmony between Great-Britain and the American colonies, viz.

The several acts of 4 Geo. III. ch. 15. and ch. 34.—5 Geo. III. ch. 25.—6 Geo. III. ch. 52.—7 Geo. III. ch. 41. and ch. 46—8 Geo. III. ch. 22. which impose duties for the purpose of raising a revenue in America, extend the power of the admiralty courts beyond their ancient limits, deprive the American subject of trial by jury, authorize the judges certificate to indemnify the prosecutor from damages, that he might otherwise be liable to, requiring oppressive security from a claimant of ships and goods seized, before he shall be allowed to defend his property, and are subversive of American rights.

Also 12 Geo. III. ch. 24. intituled, "An act for the better securing his majesty's dockyards, magazines, ships, ammunition, and stores," which declares a new offence in America, and deprives the American subject of a constitutional trial by jury of the vicinage, by authorizing the trial of any person, charged with the committing any offence described in the said act, out of the realm, to be indicted and tried for the same in any shire or county within the realm.

Also the three acts passed in the last session of parliament, for stopping the port and blocking up the harbour of Boston, for altering the charter and government of Massachusetts-Bay, and that which is entitled, "An act for the better administration of justice, &c."

Also the act passed in the same session for establishing the Roman Catholic religion, in the province of Quebec, abolishing the equitable system of English laws, and erecting a tyranny there, to the great danger, (from so total a dissimilarity of religion, law and government) of the neighbouring British colonies, by the assistance of whose blood and treasure the said country was conquered from France.

Also the act passed in the same session, for the better providing suitable quarters for officers and soldiers in his majesty's service, in North-America.

Also, that the keeping a standing army in several of these colonies, in time of peace, without the consent of the legislature of that colony, in which such array is kept, is against law.

To these grievous acts and measures, Americans cannot submit, but in hopes their fellow subjects in Great-Britain will, on a revision of them, restore us to that state, in which both countries found happiness and prosperity, we have for the present, only resolved to pursue the following peaceable measures: 1. To enter into a non-importation, non-consumption, and non-exportation agreement or association. 2. To prepare an address to the people of Great-Britain, and a memorial to the inhabitants of British America: and 3. To prepare a loyal address to his majesty, agreeable to resolutions already entered into.

[SDIA]

Patrick Henry, Speech, "Give Me Liberty or Give Me Death"

March 23, 1775

Patrick Henry's reputation as the greatest orator of the revolutionary period dates from his 1765 speech that contained the resounding phrase, "If this be treason, make the most of it," delivered in the Virginia House of Burgesses during the Stamp Act crisis. Ten years later on March 23, 1775, with revolutionary fervor sweeping the colonies less than a month before the battles of Lexington and Concord, Henry solidified his position with the words reprinted here—sometimes called "The War Inevitable" speech. In this address before the Virginia Revolutionary Committee in St. John's Church, Richmond, speaking in favor of resolutions for arming the Virginia militia, Henry electrified his audience with his fervent call to action. The militia resolutions passed.
– Note by John Grafton

NO MAN THINKS more highly than I do of the patriotism, as well as abilities, of the very worthy gentlemen who have just addressed the House. But different men often see the same subject in different lights; and therefore, I hope it will not be thought disrespectful to those gentlemen if, entertaining as I do opinions of a character very opposite to theirs, I shall speak forth my sentiments freely and without reserve. This is no time for ceremony. The question before the House is one of awful moment to this country. For my own part, I consider it as nothing less than a question of freedom or slavery; and in proportion to the magnitude of the subject ought to be the freedom of the debate. It is only in this way that we can hope to arrive at truth, and fulfill the great responsibility which we hold to God and our country. Should I keep back my opinions at such a time, through fear of giving offense, I should consider myself as guilty of treason towards my country, and of an act of disloyalty toward the Majesty of Heaven, which I revere above all earthly kings.

Mr. President it is natural to man to indulge in the illusions of hope. We are apt to shut our eyes against a painful truth, and listen to the song of that siren till she transforms us into beasts. Is this the part of wise men, engaged in a great and arduous struggle for liberty? Are we disposed to be of the number of those who, having eyes, see not, and having ears hear not, the things which so nearly concern their temporal salvation? For my part, whatever anguish of spirit it may cost, I am willing to know the whole truth; to know the worst, and to provide for it.

I have but one lamp by which my feet are guided, and that is the lamp of experience. I know of no way of judging of the future but by the past. And judging by the past, I wish to know what there has been in the conduct of the British ministry for the last ten years to justify those hopes with which gentlemen have been pleased to solace themselves and the House. Is it that insidious smile with which our petition has been lately received? Trust it not, sir; it will prove a snare to your feet. Suffer not yourselves to be betrayed with a kiss. Ask yourselves how this gracious reception of our petition comports with those warlike preparations which cover our waters and darken our land. Are fleets and armies necessary to a work of love and reconciliation? Have we shown ourselves so unwilling to be reconciled that force must be called in to win back our love? Let us not deceive ourselves, sir. These are the implements of war and subjugation; the last arguments to which kings resort. I ask gentlemen, sir, what means this martial array, if its purpose be not to force us to submission? Can gentlemen assign any other possible motive for it? Has Great Britain any enemy, in this quarter of the world, to call for all this accumulation of navies and armies? No, sir, she has none. They are meant for us: they can be meant for no other. They are sent over to bind and rivet upon us those chains which the British ministry have been so long forging. And what have we to oppose to them? Shall we try argument? Sir, we have been trying that for the last ten years. Have we anything new to offer upon the subject? Nothing. We have held the subject up in every light of which it is capable; but it has been all in vain. Shall we resort to entreaty and humble supplication? What terms shall we find which have not been already exhausted? Let us not, I beseech you, sir, deceive ourselves. Sir, we have done everything that could be done to avert the storm which is now coming on. We have petitioned; we have remonstrated; we have supplicated; we have prostrated ourselves before the throne, and have implored its interposition to arrest the tyrannical hands of the ministry and parliament. Our petitions have been slighted; our remonstrances have produced additional violence and insult; our supplications have been disregarded; and we have been spurned, with contempt from the foot of the throne! In vain after these things may we indulge the fond hope of peace and reconciliation. There is no longer any room for hope. If we wish to be free—if we mean to preserve inviolate those inestimable privileges for which we have been so long contending—if we mean not basely to abandon the noble struggle in which we have been so long engaged and which we have pledged ourselves never to abandon until the glorious object of our contest shall be obtained—we must fight! I repeat it, sir, we must fight! An appeal to arms and to the God of hosts is all that is left us!

They tell us, sir, that we are weak; unable to cope with so formidable an adversary. But when shall we be stronger? Will it be the next week or the next year? Will it be when we are totally disarmed, and when a British guard shall be stationed in every house? Shall we gather strength by irresolution and inaction? Shall we acquire the means of effectual resistance by lying supinely on our backs and hugging the delusive phantom of hope, until our enemies shall have bound us hand and foot? Sir, we are not weak if we make a proper use of those means which the god of nature hath placed in our power. The millions of people, armed in the holy cause of liberty, and in such a country as that which we possess, are invincible by any force which our enemy can send against us. Besides, sir, we shall not fight our battles alone. There is a just God who presides over the destinies of nations, and who will raise up friends to fight our battles for us. The battle, sir, is not to the strong alone; it is to the vigilant, the active, the brave. Besides, sir, we have no election. If we were base enough to desire it, it is now too late to retire from the contest. There is no retreat but in submission and slavery! Our chains are forged! Their clanking may be heard on the plains of Boston! The war is inevitable—and let it come! I repeat it, sir, let it come.

It is in vain, sir, to extenuate the matter. Gentlemen may cry, Peace, Peace—but there is no peace. The war is actually begun! The next gale that sweeps from the north will bring to our ears the

clash of resounding arms! Our brethren are already in the field!
Why stand we here idle? What is it that gentlemen wish? What
would they have? Is life so dear, or peace so sweet, as to be purchased at the price of chains and slavery? Forbid it, Almighty God!
I know not what course others may take; but as for me, give me
liberty or give me death!

[DI]

Continental Congress, Declaration of the Causes and Necessity of Taking Up Arms

July 6, 1775

June 23, 1775, John Rutledge of South Carolina, William Livingston of New Jersey, Franklin, Jay, and Thomas Johnson of Maryland, were appointed a committee "to draw up a declaration, to be published by General Washington, upon his arrival at the camp before Boston." The report was brought in the next day, and on the 26th, after debate, was recommitted, and Dickinson and Jefferson added to the committee. A draft prepared by Jefferson being thought by Dickinson too outspoken, the latter prepared a new one, retaining, however, the closing paragraphs as drawn by Jefferson. In this form the declaration was reported June 27, and agreed to July 6.

— Note by William MacDonald

A declaration by the Representatives of the United Colonies of North-America, now met in Congress at Philadelphia, setting forth the causes and necessity of their taking up arms.

IF IT WAS possible for men, who exercise their reason to believe, that the divine Author of our existence intended a part of the human race to hold an absolute property in, and an unbounded power over others, marked out by his infinite goodness and wisdom, as the objects of a legal domination never rightfully resistible, however severe and oppressive, the inhabitants of these colonies might at least require from the parliament of Great-Britain some evidence, that this dreadful authority over them, has been granted to that body. But a reverence for our great Creator, principles of humanity, and the dictates of common sense, must convince all those who reflect upon the subject, that government was instituted to promote the welfare of mankind, and ought to be administered for the attainment of that end. The legislature of Great-Britain, however, stimulated by an inordinate passion for a power not only unjustifiable, but which they know to be peculiarly reprobated by the very constitution of that kingdom, and desperate of success in any mode of contest, where regard should be had to truth, law, or right, have at length, deserting those, attempted to effect their cruel and impolitic purpose of enslaving these colonies by violence, and have thereby rendered it necessary for us to close with their last appeal from reason to arms. — Yet, however blinded that assembly may be, by their intemperate rage for unlimited domination, so to slight justice and the opinion of mankind, we esteem ourselves bound by obligations of respect to the rest of the world, to make known the justice of our cause.

Our forefathers, inhabitants of the island of Great-Britain, left their native land, to seek on these shores a residence for civil and religious freedom. At the expense of their blood, at the hazard of their fortunes, without the least charge to the country from which they removed, by unceasing labour, and an unconquerable spirit, they effected settlements in the distant and inhospitable wilds of America, then filled with numerous and warlike nations of barbarians. — Societies or governments, vested with perfect legislatures, were formed under charters from the crown, and a harmonious intercourse was established between the colonies and the kingdom from which they derived their origin. The mutual benefits of this union became in a short time so extraordinary, as to excite astonishment. It is universally confessed, that the amazing increase of the wealth, strength, and navigation of the realm, arose from this source; and the minister, who so wisely and successfully directed the measures of Great-Britain in the late war, publicly declared, that these colonies enabled her to triumph over her enemies. — Towards the conclusion of that war, it pleased our sovereign to make a change in his counsels. — From that fatal moment, the affairs of the British Empire began to fall into confusion, and gradually sliding from the summit of glorious prosperity, to which they had been advanced by the virtues and abilities of one man, are at length distracted by the convulsions, that now shake it to its deepest foundations. — The new ministry finding the brave foes of Britain, though frequently defeated, yet still contending, took up the unfortunate idea of granting them a hasty peace, and of then subduing her faithful friends.

These devoted colonies were judged to be in such a state, as to present victories without bloodshed, and all the easy emoluments of statuteable plunder. — The uninterrupted tenor of their peaceable and respectful behaviour from the beginning of colonization, their dutiful, zealous, and useful services during the war, though so recently and amply acknowledged in the most honourable manner by his majesty, by the late king, and by parliament, could not save them from the meditated innovations. — Parliament was influenced to adopt the pernicious project, and assuming a new power over them, have in the course of eleven years, given such decisive specimens of the spirit and consequences attending this power, as to leave no doubt concerning the effects of acquiescence under it. They have undertaken to give and grant our money without our consent, though we have ever exercised an exclusive right to dispose of our own property; statutes have been passed for extending the jurisdiction of courts of admiralty and vice-admiralty beyond their ancient limits; for depriving us of the accustomed and inestimable privilege of trial by jury, in cases affecting both life and property; for suspending the legislature of one of the colonies; for interdicting all commerce to the capital of another; and for altering fundamentally the form of government established by charter, and secured by acts of its own legislature solemnly confirmed by the crown; for exempting the "murderers" of colonists from legal trial, and in effect, from punishment; for erecting in a neighbouring province, acquired by the joint arms of Great-Britain and America, a despotism dangerous to our very existence; and for quartering soldiers upon the colonists in time of profound peace. It has also been resolved in parliament, that colonists charged with committing certain offences, shall be transported to England to be tried.

But why should we enumerate our injuries in detail? By one statute it is declared, that parliament can "of right make laws to bind us in all cases whatsoever." What is to defend us against so enormous, so unlimited a power? Not a single man of those who assume it, is chosen by us; or is subject to our controul or influence; but, on the contrary, they are all of them exempt from the operation of such laws, and an American revenue, if not diverted from the ostensible purposes for which it is raised, would actually lighten their own burdens in proportion, as they increase ours. We saw the misery to which such despotism would reduce us. We for ten years incessantly and

ineffectually besieged the throne as supplicants; we reasoned, we remonstrated with parliament, in the most mild and decent language.

Administration sensible that we should regard these oppressive
measures as freemen ought to do, sent over fleets and armies to
enforce them. The indignation of the Americans was roused, it is
true; but it was the indignation of a virtuous, loyal, and affectionate
people. A Congress of delegates from the United Colonies was assembled at Philadelphia, on the fifth day of last September. We
resolved again to offer an humble and dutiful petition to the king,
and also addressed our fellow-subjects of Great-Britain. We have
pursued every temperate, every respectful measure: we have even
proceeded to break off our commercial intercourse with our
fellow-subjects, as the last peaceable admonition, that our attachment to no nation upon earth should supplant our attachment to
liberty. — This, we flattered ourselves, was the ultimate step of the
controversy: but subsequent events have shewn, how vain was this
hope of finding moderation in our enemies.

Several threatening expressions against the colonies were inserted
in his majesty's speech; our petition, tho' we were told it was a
decent one, and that his majesty had been pleased to receive it graciously, and to promise laying it before his parliament, was huddled
into both houses among a bundle of American papers, and there
neglected. The lords and commons in their address, in the month
of February, said, that "a rebellion at that time actually existed
within the province of Massachusetts-Bay; and that those concerned in it, had been countenanced and encouraged by unlawful
combinations and engagements, entered into by his majesty's subjects in several of the other colonies; and therefore they besought
his majesty, that he would take the most effectual measures to enforce due obedience to the laws and authority of the supreme legislature." — Soon after, the commercial intercourse of whole
colonies, with foreign countries, and with each other, was cut off
by an act of parliament; by another several of them were intirely
prohibited from the fisheries in the seas near their co[a]sts, on
which they always depended for their sustenance; and large rein-
forcements of ships and troops were immediately sent over to general Gage.

Fruitless were all the entreaties, arguments, and eloquence of an
illustrious band of the most distinguished peers, and commoners,
who nobly and stren[u]ously asserted the justice of our cause, to

stay, or even to mitigate the heedless fury with which these accumulated and unexampled outrages were hurried on. — Equally fruitless was the interference of the city of London, of Bristol, and many other respectable towns in our favour. Parliament adopted an insidious manœvre calculated to divide us, to establish a perpetual auction of taxations where colony should bid against colony, all of them uninformed what ransom would redeem their lives; and thus to extort from us, at the point of the bayonet, the unknown sums that should be sufficient to gratify, if possible to gratify, ministerial rapacity, with the miserable indulgence left to us of raising, in our own mode, the prescribed tribute. What terms more rigid and humiliating could have been dictated by remorseless victors to conquered enemies? in our circumstances to accept them, would be to deserve them.

Soon after the intelligence of these proceedings arrived on this continent, general Gage, who in the course of the last year had taken possession of the town of Boston, in the province of Massachusetts-Bay, and still occupied it is [as] a garrison, on the 19th day of April, sent out from that place a large detachment of his army, who made an unprovoked assault on the inhabitants of the said province, at the town of Lexington, as appears by the affidavits of a great number of persons, some of whom were officers and soldiers of that detachment, murdered eight of the inhabitants, and wounded many others. From thence the troops proceeded in warlike array to the town of Concord, where they set upon another party of the inhabitants of the same province, killing several and wounding more, until compelled to retreat by the country people suddenly assembled to repel this cruel aggression. Hostilities, thus commenced by the British troops, have been since prosecuted by them without regard to faith or reputation. — The inhabitants of Boston being confined within that town by the general their governor, and having, in order to procure their dismission, entered into a treaty with him, it was stipulated that the said inhabitants having deposited their arms with their own magistrates, should have liberty to depart, taking with them their other effects. They accordingly delivered up their arms, but in open violation of honour, in defiance of the obligation of treaties, which even savage nations esteemed sacred, the governor ordered the arms deposited as aforesaid, that they might be preserved for their owners, to be seized by a body of soldiers; detained the greatest part of the inhabitants in the town, and compelled the few who were permitted to retire, to leave their most valuable effects behind.

By this perfidy wives are separated from their husbands, children from their parents, the aged and the sick from their relations and friends, who wish to attend and comfort them; and those who have been used to live in plenty and even elegance, are reduced to deplorable distress.

The general, further emulating his ministerial masters, by a proclamation bearing date on the 12th day of June, after venting the grossest falsehoods and calumnies against the good people of these colonies, proceeds to "declare them all, either by name or description, to be rebels and traitors, to supersede the course of the common law, and instead thereof to publish and order the use and exercise of the law martial." — His troops have butchered our countrymen, have wantonly burnt Charlestown, besides a considerable number of houses in other places; our ships and vessels are seized; the necessary supplies of provisions are intercepted, and he is exerting his utmost power to spread destruction and devastation around him.

We have received certain intelligence, that general Carelton [*Carleton*], the governor of Canada, is instigating the people of that province and the Indians to fall upon us; and we have but too much reason to apprehend, that schemes have been formed to excite domestic enemies against us. In brief, a part of these colonies now feel and all of them are sure of feeling, as far as the vengeance of administration can inflict them, the complicated calamities of fire, sword, and famine. We★ are reduced to the alternative of chusing an unconditional submission to the tyranny of irritated ministers, or resistance by force. — The latter is our choice. — We have counted the cost of this contest, and find nothing so dreadful as voluntary slavery. — Honour, justice, and humanity, forbid us tamely to surrender that freedom which we received from our gallant ancestors, and which our innocent posterity have a right to receive from us. We cannot endure the infamy and guilt of resigning succeeding generations to that wretchedness which inevitably awaits them, if we basely entail hereditary bondage upon them.

Our cause is just. Our union is perfect. Our internal resources are great, and, if necessary, foreign assistance is undoubtedly

---

★From this point the declaration follows Jefferson's draft. [Note by William MacDonald]

attainable. — We gratefully acknowledge, as signal instances of the Divine favour towards us, that his Providence would not permit us to be called into this severe controversy, until we were grown up to our present strength, had been previously exercised in warlike operation, and possessed of the means of defending ourselves. With hearts fortified with these animating reflections, we most solemnly, before God and the world, *declare,* that, exerting the utmost energy of those powers, which our beneficent Creator hath graciously bestowed upon us, the arms we have been compelled by our enemies to assume, we will, in defiance of every hazard, with unabating firmness and perseverance, employ for the preservation of our liberties; being with one mind resolved to die freemen rather then to live slaves.

Lest this declaration should disquiet the minds of our friends and fellow-subjects in any part of the empire, we assure them that we mean not to dissolve that union which has so long and so happily subsisted between us, and which we sincerely wish to see restored. — Necessity has not yet driven us into that desperate measure, or induced us to excite any other nation to war against them. — We have not raised armies with ambitious designs of separating from Great-Britain, and establishing independent states. We fight not for glory or for conquest. We exhibit to mankind the remarkable spectacle of a people attacked by unprovoked enemies, without any imputation or even suspicion of offence. They boast of their privileges and civilization, and yet proffer no milder conditions than servitude or death.

In our own native land, in defence of the freedom that is our birth-right, and which we ever enjoyed till the late violation of it — for the protection of our property, acquired solely by the honest industry of our fore-fathers and ourselves, against violence actually offered, we have taken up arms. We shall lay them down when hostilities shall cease on the part of the aggressors, and all danger of their being renewed shall be removed, and not before.

With an humble confidence in the mercies of the supreme and impartial Judge and Ruler of the Universe, we most devoutly implore his divine goodness to protect us happily through this great conflict, to dispose our adversaries to reconciliation on reasonable terms, and thereby to relieve the empire from the calamities of civil war.

[SDIA]

Thomas Paine,
Selections from *Common Sense*

February 14, 1776

We present the introduction to and first part of the second edition of Thomas Paine's pamphlet Common Sense *(the first edition was published only a month before). When he wrote the manifesto that helped inspire the successful revolution against Great Britain, the British-born author (1737–1809) had been in America only a year and a half (he had been encouraged to emigrate from England by Benjamin Franklin). "Writing, for him," his twentieth-century admirer John Dos Passos reminds us, "was the direct putting down of plain speech."[1]*

ADDRESSED TO THE INHABITANTS OF AMERICA

"Man knows no Master save creating HEAVEN,
Or those whom Choice and common Good ordain."
—THOMSON.[2]

INTRODUCTION

PERHAPS THE SENTIMENTS contained in the following pages, are not *yet* sufficiently fashionable to procure them general favor; a long habit of not thinking a thing *wrong,* gives it a superficial appearance of being *right,* and raises at first a formidable outcry in defence of custom. But the tumult soon subsides. Time makes more converts than reason.

---

[1]John Dos Passos. *The Essential Thomas Paine.* Mineola, New York: Dover Publications, 2008. p. 156. [This edition was originally published as *The Living Thoughts of Tom Paine* in 1940.]

[2]James Thomson, from *Liberty: A Poem,* 1736

As a long and violent abuse of power, is generally the Means of calling the right of it in question (and in Matters too which might never have been thought of, had not the Sufferers been aggravated into the inquiry) and as the King of England hath undertaken in his *own Right,* to support the Parliament in what he calls *Theirs,* and as the good people of this country are grievously oppressed by the combination, they have an undoubted privilege to inquire into the pretensions of both, and equally to reject the usurpation of either.

In the following sheets, the author hath studiously avoided every thing which is personal among ourselves. Compliments as well as censure to individuals make no part thereof. The wise, and the worthy, need not the triumph of a pamphlet; and those whose sentiments are injudicious, or unfriendly, will cease of themselves unless too much pains is bestowed upon their conversion.

The cause of America is in a great measure the cause of all mankind. Many circumstances hath, and will arise, which are not local, but universal, and through which the principles of all Lovers of Mankind are affected, and in the Event of which, their Affections are interested. The laying a Country desolate with Fire and Sword, declaring War against the natural rights of all Mankind, and extirpating the Defenders thereof from the Face of the Earth, is the Concern of every Man to whom Nature hath given the Power of feeling; of which Class, regardless of Party Censure, is the

AUTHOR

P.S. . . . Who the Author of this Production is, is wholly unnecessary to the Public, as the Object for Attention is the *Doctrine itself,* not the *Man.* Yet it may not be unnecessary to say, That he is unconnected with any Party, and under no sort of Influence public or private, but the influence of reason and principle.

Philadelphia, February 14, 1776.

COMMON SENSE

Of the Origin and Design of
Government in General. With concise
Remarks on the English Constitution

Some writers have so confounded society with government, as to leave little or no distinction between them; whereas they are not only different, but have different origins. Society is produced by our wants, and government by our wickedness; the former promotes our happiness *positively* by uniting our affections, the latter *negatively* by restraining our vices. The one encourages intercourse, the other creates distinctions. The first is a patron, the last a punisher.

Society in every state is a blessing, but government even in its best state is but a necessary evil; in its worst state an intolerable one; for when we suffer, or are exposed to the same miseries *by a government,* which we might expect in a country *without government,* our calamity is heightened by reflecting that we furnish the means by which we suffer. Government, like dress, is the badge of lost innocence; the palaces of kings are built on the ruins of the bowers of paradise. For were the impulses of conscience clear, uniform, and irresistibly obeyed, man would need no other lawgiver; but that not being the case, he finds it necessary to surrender up a part of his property to furnish means for the protection of the rest; and this he is induced to do by the same prudence which in every other case advises him out of two evils to choose the least. *Wherefore,* security being the true design and end of government, it unanswerably follows that whatever *form* thereof appears most likely to ensure it to us, with the least expense and greatest benefit, is preferable to all others.

In order to gain a clear and just idea of the design and end of government, let us suppose a small number of persons settled in some sequestered part of the earth, unconnected with the rest, they will then represent the first peopling of any country, or of the world. In this state of natural liberty, society will be their first thought. A thousand motives will excite them thereto; the strength of one man is so unequal to his wants, and his mind so unfitted for perpetual solitude, that he is soon obliged to seek assistance and relief of another, who in his turn requires the same. Four or five united would be able to raise a tolerable dwelling in the midst of a wilderness, but *one* man might labour out the common period of life without accomplishing any thing; when he had felled his timber he could not remove it, nor erect it after it was removed; hunger in the mean time would urge him from his work, and every different want call him a different way. Disease, nay even misfortune would be death, for though neither might be mortal, yet either would disable him from living, and reduce him to a state in which he might rather be said to perish than to die.

Thus necessity, like a gravitating power, would soon form our newly arrived emigrants into society, the reciprocal blessings of which, would supersede, and render the obligations of law and government unnecessary while they remained perfectly just to each other; but as nothing but heaven is impregnable to vice, it will unavoidably happen, that in proportion as they surmount the first difficulties of emigration, which bound them together in a common cause, they will begin to relax in their duty and attachment to each other; and this remissness, will point out the necessity, of establishing some form of government to supply the defect of moral virtue.

Some convenient tree will afford them a State-House, under the branches of which, the whole colony may assemble to deliberate on public matters. It is more than probable that their first laws will have the title only of REGULATIONS, and be enforced by no other penalty than public disesteem. In this first parliament every man, by natural right, will have a seat.

But as the colony increases, the public concerns will increase likewise, and the distance at which the members may be separated, will render it too inconvenient for all of them to meet on every occasion as at first, when their number was small, their habitations near, and the public concerns few and trifling. This will point out the convenience of their consenting to leave the legislative part to be managed by a select number chosen from the whole body, who are supposed to have the same concerns at stake which those have who appointed them, and who will act in the same manner as the whole body would act were they present. If the colony continue increasing, it will become necessary to augment the number of the representatives, and that the interest of every part of the colony may be attended to, it will be found best to divide the whole into convenient parts, each part sending its proper number; and that the *elected* might never form to themselves an interest separate from the *electors,* prudence will point out the propriety of having elections often; because as the *elected* might by that means return and mix again with the general body of the *electors* in a few months, their fidelity to the public will be secured by the prudent reflexion of not making a rod for themselves. And as this frequent interchange will establish a common interest with every part of the community, they will mutually and naturally support each other, and on this (not on the unmeaning name of king) depends the *strength of government, and the happiness of the governed.*

Here then is the origin and rise of government; namely, a model rendered necessary by the inability of moral virtue to govern the world; here too is the design and end of government, viz. freedom and security. And however our eyes may be dazzled with show, or our ears deceived by sound; however prejudice may warp our wills, or interest darken our understanding, the simple voice of nature and of reason will say, it is right.

I draw my idea of the form of government from a principle in nature, which no art can overturn, viz. that the more simple any thing is, the less liable it is to be disordered, and the easier repaired when disordered; and with this maxim in view, I offer a few remarks on the so much boasted constitution of England. That it was noble for the dark and slavish times in which it was erected, is granted. When the world was over run with tyranny the least remove therefrom was a glorious rescue. But that it is imperfect, subject to convulsions, and incapable of producing what it seems to promise, is easily demonstrated.

Absolute governments (tho' the disgrace of human nature) have this advantage with them, that they are simple; if the people suffer, they know the head from which their suffering springs, know likewise the remedy, and are not bewildered by a variety of causes and cures. But the constitution of England is so exceedingly complex, that the nation may suffer for years together without being able to discover in which part the fault lies, some will say in one and some in another, and every political physician will advise a different medicine.

I know it is difficult to get over local or long standing prejudices, yet if we will suffer ourselves to examine the component parts of the English constitution, we shall find them to be the base remains of two ancient tyrannies, compounded with some new republican materials.

First.—The remains of monarchical tyranny in the person of the king.

Secondly.—The remains of aristocratical tyranny in the persons of the peers.

Thirdly.—The new republican materials, in the persons of the commons, on whose virtue depends the freedom of England.

The two first, by being hereditary, are independent of the people; wherefore in a *constitutional sense* they contribute nothing towards the freedom of the state.

To say that the constitution of England is a *union* of three powers reciprocally *checking* each other, is farcical, either the words have no meaning, or they are flat contradictions.

To say that the commons is a check upon the king, presupposes two things.

First.—That the king is not to be trusted without being looked after, or in other words, that a thirst for absolute power is the natural disease of monarchy.

Secondly.—That the commons, by being appointed for that purpose, are either wiser or more worthy of confidence than the crown.

But as the same constitution which gives the commons a power to check the king by withholding the supplies, gives afterwards the king a power to check the commons, by empowering him to reject their other bills; it again supposes that the king is wiser than those whom it has already supposed to be wiser than him. A mere absurdity!

There is something exceedingly ridiculous in the composition of monarchy; it first excludes a man from the means of information, yet empowers him to act in cases where the highest judgment is required. The state of a king shuts him from the world, yet the business of a king requires him to know it thoroughly; wherefore the different parts, by unnaturally opposing and destroying each other, prove the whole character to be absurd and useless.

Some writers have explained the English constitution thus; the king, say they, is one, the people another; the peers are an house in behalf of the king; the commons in behalf of the people; but this hath all the distinctions of an house divided against itself; and though the expressions be pleasantly arranged, yet when examined they appear idle and ambiguous; and it will always happen, that the nicest construction that words are capable of, when applied to the description of something which either cannot exist, or is too incomprehensible to be within the compass of description, will be words of sound only, and though they may amuse the ear, they cannot inform the mind, for this explanation includes a previous question, viz. *How came the king by a power which the people are afraid to trust, and always obliged to check?* Such a power could not be the gift of a wise people, neither can any power, *which needs checking,* be from God; yet the provision, which the constitution makes, supposes such a power to exist.

But the provision is unequal to the task; the means either cannot or will not accomplish the end, and the whole affair is a felo de se[3]; for as the greater weight will always carry up the less, and as all the wheels of a machine are put in motion by one, it only remains to know

---

[3] *felo de se*: an act of deliberate self-destruction.

which power in the constitution has the most weight, for that will govern; and though the others, or a part of them, may clog, or, as the phrase is, check the rapidity of its motion, yet so long as they cannot stop it, their endeavors will be ineffectual; the first moving power will at last have its way, and what it wants in speed is supplied by time.

That the crown is this overbearing part in the English constitution needs not be mentioned, and that it derives its whole consequence merely from being the giver of places and pensions is self-evident, wherefore, though we have been wise enough to shut and lock a door against absolute monarchy, we at the same time have been foolish enough to put the crown in possession of the key.

The prejudice of Englishmen, in favour of their own government by king, lords and commons, arises as much or more from national pride than reason. Individuals are undoubtedly safer in England than in some other countries, but the *will* of the king is as much the *law* of the land in Britain as in France, with this difference, that instead of proceeding directly from his mouth, it is handed to the people under the most formidable shape of an act of parliament. For the fate of Charles the first, hath only made kings more subtle—not more just.

Wherefore, laying aside all national pride and prejudice in favour of modes and forms, the plain truth is, that *it is wholly owing to the constitution of the people, and not to the constitution of the government* that the crown is not as oppressive in England as in Turkey.

An inquiry into the *constitutional errors* in the English form of government is at this time highly necessary, for as we are never in a proper condition of doing justice to others, while we continue under the influence of some leading partiality, so neither are we capable of doing it to ourselves while we remain fettered by any obstinate prejudice. And as a man, who is attached to a prostitute, is unfitted to choose or judge of a wife, so any prepossession in favour of a rotten constitution of government will disable us from discerning a good one.

[DAAL]

Virginia Bill of Rights

June 12, 1776

When, on the 15th of May 1776, the Convention of Virginia instructed their delegates in Congress to propose to that body to declare the United Colonies free and independent States, it, at the same time, appointed a committee to prepare a declaration of rights and such a plan of government as would be most likely to maintain peace and order in the Colony and secure substantial and equal liberty to the people. On subsequent days the committee was enlarged; Mr. George Mason was added to it on the 18th. The declaration of rights was on the 27th reported by Mr. Archibald Cary, the chairman of the committee, and, after being twice read, was ordered to be printed for the perusal of members. It was considered in committee of the whole on the 29th of May and the 3d, 4th, 5th and 10th of June. It was then reported to the house with amendments. On the 11th the Convention considered the amendments, and having agreed thereto, ordered that the declaration (with the amendments) be fairly transcribed and read a third time. This having been done on the 12th, the declaration was then read a third time and passed nem. con. A manuscript copy of the first draft of the declaration, just as it was drawn by Mr. Mason, is in the library of Virginia.

— Note by John M. Patton

A Declaration of Rights made by the Representatives of the good people of VIRGINIA, *assembled in full and free Convention, which rights do pertain to them and their posterity as the basis and foundation of government.*

1. THAT ALL MEN are by nature equally free and independent, and have certain inherent rights, of which, when they enter into a state of society, they cannot, by any compact, deprive or divest their posterity; namely, the enjoyment of life and liberty, with the means

of acquiring and possessing property, and pursuing and obtaining happiness and safety.

2. That all power is vested in, and consequently derived from, the people; that Magistrates are their trustees and servants, and at all times amenable to them.

3. That government is, or ought to be, instituted for the common benefit, protection and security of the people, nation, or community: of all the various modes and forms of government, that is best, which is capable of producing the greatest degree of happiness and safety, and is most effectually secured against the danger of mal-administration; and that, when any government shall be found inadequate or contrary to these purposes, a majority of the community hath an indubitable, unalienable, and indefeasible right, to reform, alter, or abolish it, in such manner as shall be judged most conducive to the public weal.

4. That no man, or set of men, are entitled to exclusive or separate emoluments or privileges from the community, but in consideration of public services; which not being descendible, neither ought the offices of Magistrate, Legislator, or Judge, to be hereditary.

5. That the legislative and executive powers of the state should be separate and distinct from the judiciary; and that the members of the two first may be restrained from oppression, by feeling and participating the burthens of the people, they should, at fixed periods, be reduced to a private station, return into that body from which they were originally taken, and the vacancies be supplied by frequent, certain, and regular elections, in which all, or any part of the former members, to be again eligible, or ineligible, as the laws shall direct.

6. That elections of members to serve as representatives of the people, in Assembly, ought to be free; and that all men, having sufficient evidence of permanent common interest with, and attachment to, the community, have the right of suffrage and cannot be taxed or deprived of their property for public uses, without their own consent, or that of their representatives so elected, nor bound by any law to which they have not, in like manner, assented, for the public good.

7. That all power of suspending laws, or the execution of laws, by any authority, without consent of the representatives of the people, is injurious to their rights, and ought not to be exercised.

8. That, in all capital or criminal prosecutions, a man hath a right to demand the cause and nature of his accusation, to be confronted with the accusers and witnesses, to call for evidence in his favour,

and to a speedy trial by an impartial jury of his vicinage, without whose unanimous consent he cannot be found guilty; nor can he be compelled to give evidence against himself; that no man be deprived of his liberty, except by the law of the land or the judgment of his peers.

9. That excessive bail ought not to be required, nor excessive fines imposed, nor cruel and unusual punishments inflicted.

10. That general warrants, whereby an officer or messenger may be commanded to search suspected places without evidence of a fact committed, or to seize any person or persons not named, or whose offence is not particularly described and supported by evidence, are grievous and oppressive, and ought not to be granted.

11. That, in controversies respecting property, and in suits between man and man, the ancient trial by jury is preferable to any other, and ought to be held sacred.

12. That the freedom of the press is one of the great bulwarks of liberty, and can never be restrained but by despotic governments.

13. That a well regulated militia, composed of the body of the people, trained to arms, is the proper, natural and safe defence of a free state; that standing armies, in time of peace, should be avoided, as dangerous to liberty; and that in all cases, the military should be under strict subordination to, and governed by, the civil power.

14. That the people have a right to uniform government; and therefore, that no government separate from, or independent of, the government of *Virginia,* ought to be erected or established within the limits thereof.

15. That no free government, or the blessing of liberty, can be preserved to any people, but by a firm adherence to justice, moderation, temperance, frugality, and virtue, and by a frequent recurrence to fundamental principles.

16. That religion, or the duty which we owe to our Creator, and the manner of discharging it, can be directed only by reason and conviction, not by force or violence; and therefore all men are equally entitled to the free exercise of religion, according to the dictates of conscience; and that it is the mutual duty of all to practise Christian forbearance, love, and charity towards each other.

[COV]

Declaration of Independence

July 4, 1776

The second Continental Congress convened in Philadelphia on May 10, 1775, three weeks after the battles of Lexington and Concord. On June 7th, delegate Richard Henry Lee of Virginia introduced the resolution, "That these United Colonies are, and of right ought to be, free and independent States, that they are absolved from all allegiance to the British Crown, and that all political connection between them and the State of Great Britain is, and ought to be, totally dissolved." On June 11th, in anticipation of an imminent vote on independence, a committee consisting of Thomas Jefferson, John Adams, Benjamin Franklin, Roger Sherman, and Robert R. Livingston was appointed by the Congress as a whole to draft a declaration embodying Lee's resolution. The task of writing the Declaration was turned over to Jefferson by his fellow committee members in deference to his well-known and unmatched literary talent. In about two weeks, Jefferson produced his draft.

The Declaration reflected the political philosophy informed by John Locke's central idea that governments derive their power from the consent of the governed, a concept to which Jefferson's public life was dedicated. Adams and Franklin reviewed Jefferson's draft and produced forty-seven distinct amendments to it before the document was presented to the whole Congress by the Committee on June 28th. On July 2, 1776, while the Declaration was under review by the whole body, Congress adopted Lee's resolution declaring independence from Great Britain. Congress as a whole then produced thirty-nine additional changes in style and substance to the Declaration, most importantly removing both a reproach directed at the British people (instead of just at the crown and government), and a condemnation of slavery. On July 4, 1776, the actual Declaration as finally drafted and amended — distinct from the abstract idea of independence from Great

Britain — was formally adopted by the Congress. At the order of John Hancock, it was printed by Philadelphia printer John Dunlap, and sent in Dunlap's printed broadside version to the various state legislatures, the first to receive it being New Jersey and Delaware. The Pennsylvania Evening Post printed it on July 6th, the first appearance of the Declaration of Independence before the public. On July 9th, Washington ordered that it be read to his army in New York, his personal copy of the Dunlap broadside being used for that purpose. Later that night, a mob of angry New Yorkers demolished the bronze statue of George III that stood on the Bowling Green at the foot of Broadway.

On July 19th, Congress ordered the Declaration engrossed (officially inscribed) and signed by the members. The engrossed copy was signed by most of the members on August 2nd. Partly because of the lapse of time between its adoption on July 4th and the general signing on August 2nd, some of the delegates who voted for it on July 4th never signed it; and some who later signed it weren't present earlier when it was adopted. The engrossed, signed copy — bearing John Hancock's familiar and prominent signature — among all the others survived many vicissitudes in its long life, narrowly avoiding destruction a number of times. It is now in the National Archives in Washington, D.C. There remain twenty-four surviving copies of the Dunlap broadside version. Only a small fragment of an early draft by Jefferson survives in his own handwriting.

Fifty years after the signing of the Declaration of Independence, the eighty-three-year-old Jefferson was invited to Washington to participate in a commemorative celebration. Too ill to attend, Jefferson reflected on the events of the summer of 1776 and the Declaration in his gracious and regretful letter of refusal to Roger C. Weightman: "May it be to the world, what I believe it will be (to some parts sooner, to others later, but finally to all), the signal of arousing men to burst the chains under which monkish ignorance and superstition had persuaded them to bind themselves, and to assume the blessings and security of self-government. That form, which we have substituted, restores the free right to the unbounded exercise of reason and freedom of opinion." This eloquent memorial was Jefferson's last letter: he died at Monticello ten days later, on July 4, 1826, fifty years to the day from the adoption of the Declaration of Independence by the Continental Congress. And, in one of history's more resonant coincidences, on the same day his old colleague John Adams passed away at his home in Quincy, Massachusetts. The last surviving signer of the Declaration of Independence, Charles Carroll of Maryland, died at age ninety-five in 1832.

— Note by John Grafton

IN CONGRESS, JULY 4, 1776

THE UNANIMOUS DECLARATION of the thirteen united STATES OF AMERICA.

When in the Course of human events it becomes necessary for one people to dissolve the political bands which have connected them with another, and to assume among the powers of the earth, the separate and equal station to which the Laws of Nature and of Nature's God entitle them, a decent respect to the opinions of mankind requires that they should declare the causes which impel them to the separation. – We hold these truths to be self-evident, that all men are created equal, that they are endowed by their Creator with certain unalienable Rights, that among these are Life, Liberty and the pursuit of Happiness. – That to secure these rights, Governments are instituted among Men, deriving their just powers from the consent of the governed, – That whenever any Form of Government becomes destructive of these ends, it is the Right of the People to alter or to abolish it, and to institute new Government, laying its foundation on such principles and organizing its powers in such form, as to them shall seem most likely to effect their Safety and Happiness. Prudence, indeed, will dictate that Governments long established should not be changed for light and transient causes; and accordingly all experience hath shewn that mankind are more disposed to suffer, while evils are sufferable, than to right themselves by abolishing the forms to which they are accustomed. But when a long train of abuses and usurpations, pursuing invariably the same Object evinces a design to reduce them under absolute Despotism, it is their right, it is their duty, to throw off such Government, and to provide new Guards for their future security. – Such has been the patient sufferance of these Colonies; and such is now the necessity which constrains them to alter their former Systems of Government. The history of the present King of Great Britain is a history of repeated injuries and usurpations, all having in direct object the establishment of an absolute Tyranny over these States. To prove this, let Facts be submitted to a candid world. – He has refused his Assent to Laws, the most wholesome and necessary for the public good. – He has forbidden his Governors to pass Laws of immediate and pressing importance, unless suspended in their operation till his Assent should be obtained; and when so suspended, he has utterly neglected to attend to them. – He has refused to pass other Laws for the accommodation of large districts of people, unless those people would relinquish the right of Representation in the Legislature, a right inestimable to them and formidable to tyrants only. – He has called together legislative bodies at places unusual, uncomfortable, and distant from the depository of their public Records, for the sole purpose of fatiguing them into compliance with his measures. – He has dissolved Representative Houses repeatedly, for opposing with manly firmness his invasions on the rights of the people. – He has refused for a long time, after such dissolutions, to cause others to be elected; whereby the Legislative powers, incapable of Annihilation, have returned to the People at large for their exercise; the State remaining in the mean time exposed to all the dangers of invasion from without, and convulsions within. – He has endeavoured to prevent the population of these States; for that purpose obstructing the Laws for Naturalization of Foreigners; refusing to pass others to encourage their migrations hither, and raising the conditions of new Appropriations of Lands. – He has obstructed the Administration of Justice, by refusing his Assent to Laws for establishing Judiciary powers. – He has made Judges dependent on his Will alone, for the tenure of their offices, and the amount and payment of their salaries. – He has erected a multitude of New Offices, and sent hither swarms of Officers to harass our people, and eat out their substance. He has kept among us, in times of peace, Standing Armies without the Consent of our legislatures. – He has affected to render the Military independent of and superior to the civil power. – He has combined with others to subject us to a jurisdiction foreign to our constitution, and unacknowledged by our laws; giving his Assent to their Acts of pretended Legislation: – For quartering large bodies of armed troops among us: – For protecting them, by a mock Trial, from punishment for any Murders which they should commit on the Inhabitants of these States: – For cutting off our Trade with all parts of the world: – For imposing Taxes on us without our Consent: – For depriving us in many cases, of the benefits of Trial by Jury: – For transporting us beyond Seas to be tried for pretended offences: – For abolishing the free System of English Laws in a neighboring Province, establishing therein an Arbitrary government, and enlarging its Boundaries so as to render it at once an example and fit instrument for introducing the same absolute rule into these Colonies: – For taking away our Charters, abolishing our most valuable Laws and altering fundamentally the Forms of our Governments: – For suspending our own Legislatures, and declaring themselves invested with power to legislate for us in all cases whatsoever. – He has abdicated Government here, by declaring us out of his Protection and waging War against us. – He has plundered our seas, ravaged our Coasts, burnt our towns, and destroyed the lives of our people. – He is at this time transporting large Armies of foreign Mercenaries to compleat the works of death, desolation and tyranny, already begun with circumstances of Cruelty & perfidy scarcely paralleled in the most barbarous ages, and totally unworthy the Head of a civilized nation. – He has constrained our fellow Citizens taken Captive on the high Seas to bear Arms against their Country, to become the executioners of their friends and Brethren, or to fall themselves by their Hands. – He has excited domestic insurrections amongst us, and has endeavoured to bring on the inhabitants of our frontiers, the merciless Indian Savages, whose known rule of warfare, is an undistinguished destruction of all ages, sexes and conditions. In every stage of these Oppressions We have Petitioned for Redress in the most humble terms: Our repeated Petitions have been answered only by repeated injury. A Prince, whose character is thus marked by every act which may define a Tyrant, is unfit to be the ruler of a free people. Nor have We been wanting in attentions to our British brethren. We have warned them from time to time of attempts by their legislature to extend an unwarrantable jurisdiction over us. We have reminded them of the circumstances of our emigration and settlement here. We have appealed to their native justice and magnanimity, and we have conjured them by the ties of our common kindred to disavow these usurpations, which would inevitably interrupt our connections and correspondence. They too have been deaf to the voice of justice and of consanguinity. We must, therefore, acquiesce in the necessity, which denounces our Separation, and hold them, as we hold the rest of mankind, Enemies in War, in Peace Friends. –

WE, THEREFORE, the Representatives of the UNITED STATES OF AMERICA, in General Congress, Assembled, appealing to the Supreme Judge of the world for the rectitude of our intentions, do, in the Name, and by Authority of the good People of these Colonies, solemnly publish and declare, That these United Colonies are, and of Right ought to be FREE AND INDEPENDENT STATES; that they are

Absolved from all Allegiance to the British Crown, and that all political connection between them and the State of Great Britain, is and ought to be totally dissolved; and that as Free and Independent States, they have full Power to levy War, conclude Peace, contract Alliances, establish Commerce, and to do all other Acts and Things which Independent States may of right do. – And for the support of this Declaration, with a firm reliance on the protection of divine Providence, we mutually pledge to each other our Lives, our Fortunes and our sacred Honor.

John Hancock
Button Gwinnett
Lyman Hall
Geo. Walton
Wm. Hooper
Joseph Hewes
John Penn
Edward Rutledge
Thos. Heyward, Jr.
Thomas Lynch, Jr.
Arthur Middleton
Samuel Chase
Wm. Paca
Thos. Stone
Charles Carroll of
    Carrollton
George Wythe
Richard Henry Lee
Th. Jefferson

Benj. Harrison
Thos. Nelson, Jr.
Francis Lightfoot Lee
Carter Braxton
Robt. Morris
Benjamin Rush
Benj. Franklin
John Morton
Geo. Clymer
Jas. Smith
Geo. Taylor
James Wilson
Geo. Ross
Caesar Rodney
Geo. Read
Tho. M:Kean
Wm. Floyd
Phil. Livingston
Frans. Lewis

Lewis Morris
Richd. Stockton
Jno. Witherspoon
Fras. Hopkinson
John Hart
Abra. Clark
Josiah Bartlett
Wm. Whipple
Saml. Adams
John Adams
Robt. Treat Paine
Elbridge Gerry
Step. Hopkins
William Ellery
Roger Sherman
Sam. Huntington
Wm. Williams
Oliver Wolcott
Matthew Thornton

[DI]

Samuel Adams, Speech, American Independence

August 1, 1776

Samuel Adams (1722–1803), great American patriot, was one of the ablest leaders of the revolutionaries of Massachusetts and later of the Continental Congress. Here are portions of an eloquent address on American independence which he delivered at the State House in Philadelphia, on August 1, 1776, a month after the signing of the Declaration of Independence.

— Note by Lewis Copeland.

WE ARE NOW on this continent, to the astonishment of the world, three millions of souls united in one cause. We have large armies, well disciplined and appointed, with commanders inferior to none in military skill, and superior in activity and zeal. We are furnished with arsenals and stores beyond our most sanguine expectations, and foreign nations are waiting to crown our success by their alliances. There are instances of, I would say, an almost astonishing Providence in our favor; our success has staggered our enemies, and almost given faith to infidels; so we may truly say it is not our own arm which has saved us.

The hand of Heaven appears to have led us on to be, perhaps, humble instruments and means in the great providential dispensation which is completing. We have fled from the political Sodom; let us not look back, lest we perish and become a monument of infamy and derision to the world. For can we ever expect more unanimity and a better preparation for defense; more infatuation of counsel among our enemies, and more valor and zeal among ourselves? The same force and resistance which are sufficient to procure us our liberties will secure us a glorious independence and support us in the dignity of free, imperial states. We cannot suppose that our opposition has made a corrupt and dissipated nation more friendly to America, or created in them a greater respect for the rights of mankind. We can therefore expect a restoration and establishment of our privileges, and a compensation for the injuries we have received, from their want of power, from their fears, and not from their virtues. The unanimity and valor which will affect an honorable peace can render a future contest for our liberties unnecessary. He who has strength to chain down the wolf is a madman if he let him loose without drawing his teeth and paring his nails.

We have no other alternative than independence, or the most ignominious and galling servitude. The legions of our enemies thicken on our plains; desolation and death mark their bloody career; whilst the mangled corpses of our countrymen seem to cry out to us as a voice from Heaven.

Our union is now complete; our constitution composed, established, and approved. You are now the guardians of your own liberties. We may justly address you, as the *decemviri* did the Romans, and say: "Nothing that we propose can pass into a law without your consent. Be yourselves, O Americans, the authors of those laws on which your happiness depends."

You have now in the field armies sufficient to repel the whole force of your enemies and their base and mercenary auxiliaries. The hearts of your soldiers beat high with the spirit of freedom; they are animated with the justice of their cause, and while they grasp their swords can look up to Heaven for assistance. Your adversaries are composed of wretches who laugh at the rights of humanity, who turn religion into derision, and would, for higher wages, direct their swords against their leaders or their country. Go on, then, in your generous enterprise, with gratitude to Heaven for past success, and confidence of it in the future. For my own part, I ask no greater blessing than to share with you the common danger and common glory. If I have a wish dearer to my soul than that my ashes may be mingled with those of a Warren and a Montgomery, it is that these American States may never cease to be free and independent.

[WGS]

Thomas Paine, Essay from *The American Crisis*, "These are the times that try men's souls"

December 23, 1776

The most inspirational of the writers for independence from Great Britain, Thomas Paine was himself born in England and moved to America in 1774. As a result of the Revolutionary War that followed the signing of the Declaration of Independence, Paine in this essay tries to rally the support of Pennsylvanians for General George Washington's hard-pressed army: "Not all the treasures of the world, so far as I believe, could have induced me to support an offensive war, for I think it murder [Paine was born a Quaker]; but if a thief breaks into my house, burns and destroys my property, and kills or threatens to kill me, or those that are in it, and to 'bind me in all cases whatsoever' to his absolute will, am I to suffer it?"

THE AMERICAN CRISIS

THESE ARE THE times that try men's souls. The summer soldier and the sunshine patriot will, in this crisis, shrink from the service of their country; but he that stands it *now*, deserves the love and thanks of man and woman. Tyranny, like hell, is not easily conquered; yet we have this consolation with us, that the harder the conflict, the more glorious the triumph. What we obtain too cheap, we esteem too lightly: it is dearness only that gives every thing its value. Heaven knows how to put a proper price upon its goods; and it would be strange indeed if so celestial an article as FREEDOM should not be highly rated. Britain, with an army to enforce her tyranny, has declared that she has a right *(not only to* TAX) but "to BIND *us in* ALL CASES WHATSOEVER," and if being *bound in that manner,* is not slavery, then is there not such a thing as slavery upon earth. Even the expression is impious; for so unlimited a power can belong only to God.

Whether the independence of the continent was declared too soon, or delayed too long, I will not now enter into as an argument; my own simple opinion is, that had it been eight months earlier, it would have been much better. We did not make a proper use of last winter, neither could we, while we were in a dependent state. However, the fault, if it were one, was all our own; we have none to blame but ourselves. But no great deal is lost yet. All that Howe has been doing for this month past, is rather a ravage than a conquest, which the spirit of the Jerseys, a year ago, would have quickly repulsed, and which time and a little resolution will soon recover.

I have as little superstition in me as any man living, but my secret opinion has ever been, and still is, that God Almighty will not give up a people to military destruction, or leave them unsupportedly to perish, who have so earnestly and so repeatedly sought to avoid the calamities of war, by every decent method which wisdom could invent. Neither have I so much of the infidel in me, as to suppose that He has relinquished the government of the world, and given us up to the care of devils; and as I do not, I cannot see on what grounds the king of Britain can look up to heaven for help against us: a common murderer, a highwayman, or a house-breaker, has as good a pretence as he.

'Tis surprising to see how rapidly a panic will sometimes run through a country. All nations and ages have been subject to them. Britain has trembled like an ague at the report of a French fleet of flat-bottomed boats; and in the fifteenth century the whole English army, after ravaging the kingdom of France, was driven back like men petrified with fear; and this brave exploit was performed by a few broken forces collected and headed by a woman, Joan of Arc. Would that heaven might inspire some Jersey maid to spirit up her countrymen, and save her fair fellow sufferers from ravage and ravishment! Yet panics, in some cases, have their uses; they produce as much good as hurt. Their duration is always short; the mind soon grows through them, and acquires a firmer habit than before. But their peculiar advantage is, that they are the touchstones of sincerity and hypocrisy, and bring things and men to light, which might otherwise have lain for ever undiscovered. In fact, they have the same effect on secret traitors, which an imaginary apparition would have upon a private murderer. They sift out the hidden thoughts of man, and hold them up in public to the world. Many a disguised Tory has lately shown his head, that shall penitentally solemnize with curses the day on which Howe arrived upon the Delaware.

As I was with the troops at Fort Lee, and marched with them to the edge of Pennsylvania, I am well acquainted with many circumstances, which those who live at a distance know but little or nothing of. Our situation there was exceedingly cramped, the place being a narrow neck of land between the North River and the Hackensack. Our force was inconsiderable, being not one-fourth so great as Howe could bring against us. We had no army at hand to have relieved the garrison, had we shut ourselves up and stood on our defence. Our ammunition, light artillery, and the best part of our stores, had been removed, on the apprehension that Howe would endeavor to penetrate the Jerseys, in which case Fort Lee could be of no use to us; for it must occur to every thinking man, whether in the army or not, that these kind of field forts are only for temporary purposes, and last in use no longer than the enemy directs his force against the particular object which such forts are raised to defend. Such was our situation and condition at Fort Lee on the morning of the 20th of November, when an officer arrived with information that the enemy with 200 boats had landed about seven miles above; Major General Nathaniel Green, who commanded the garrison, immediately ordered them under arms, and sent express to General Washington at the town of Hackensack, distant by the way of the ferry – six miles. Our first object was to secure the bridge over the Hackensack, which laid up the river between the enemy and us, about six miles from us, and three from them. General Washington arrived in about three-quarters of an hour, and marched at the head of the troops towards the bridge, which place I expected we should have a brush for; however, they did not choose to dispute it with us, and the greatest part of our troops went over the bridge, the rest over the ferry, except some which passed at a mill on a small creek, between the bridge and the ferry, and made their way through some marshy grounds up to the town of Hackensack, and there passed the river. We brought off as much baggage as the wagons could contain, the rest was lost. The simple object was to bring off the garrison, and march them on till they could be strengthened by the Jersey or Pennsylvania militia, so as to be enabled to make a stand. We staid four days at Newark, collected our out-posts with some of the Jersey militia, and marched out twice to meet the enemy, on being informed that they were advancing, though our numbers were greatly inferior to theirs. Howe, in my little opinion, committed a great error in generalship in not throwing a body of forces off from Staten Island through Amboy, by which means he might have seized all our stores at Brunswick, and intercepted our march into Pennsylvania; but if we believe the power of hell to be limited, we must likewise believe that their agents are under some providential control.

I shall not now attempt to give all the particulars of our retreat to the Delaware; suffice it for the present to say, that both officers and men, though greatly harassed and fatigued, frequently without rest, covering, or provision, the inevitable consequences of a long retreat, bore it with a manly and martial spirit. All their wishes centered in one, which was, that the country would turn out and help them to drive the enemy back. Voltaire has remarked that King William never appeared to full advantage but in difficulties and in action; the same remark may be made on General Washington, for the character fits him. There is a natural firmness in some minds which cannot be unlocked by trifles, but which, when unlocked, discovers a cabinet of fortitude; and I reckon it among those kind of public blessings, which we do not immediately see, that God hath blessed him with uninterrupted health, and given him a mind that can even flourish upon care.

I love the man that can smile in trouble that can gather strength from distress, and grow brave by reflection. 'Tis the business of little minds to shrink; but he whose heart is firm, and whose conscience approves his conduct, will pursue his principles unto death. My own line of reasoning is to myself as straight and clear as a ray of light. Not all the treasures of the world, so far as I believe, could have induced me to support an offensive war, for I think it murder; but if a thief breaks into my house, burns and destroys my property, and kills or threatens to kill me, or those that are in it, and to *"bind me in all cases whatsoever"* to his absolute will, am I to suffer it? What signifies it to me, whether he who does it is a king or a common man; my countryman or not my countryman; whether it be done by an individual villain, or an army of them? If we reason to the root of things we shall find no difference; neither can any just cause be assigned why we should punish in the one case and pardon in the other. Let them call me rebel and welcome, I feel no concern from it; but I should suffer the misery of devils, were I to make a whore of my soul by swearing allegiance to one whose character is that of a sottish, stupid, stubborn, worthless, brutish man. I conceive likewise a horrid idea in receiving mercy from a being, who at the last day shall be shrieking to the rocks and mountains to cover him, and fleeing, with terror from the orphan, the widow, and the slain of America.

There are cases which cannot be overdone by language, and this is one. There are persons, too, who see not the full extent of the evil which threatens them; they solace themselves with hopes that the enemy, if he succeed, will be merciful. It is the madness of folly, to expect mercy from those who have refused to do justice; and even mercy, where conquest is the object, is only a trick of war; the cunning of the fox is as murderous as the violence of the wolf, and we ought to guard equally against both. Howe's first object is, partly by threats and partly by promises, to terrify or seduce the people to deliver up their arms and receive mercy. The ministry recommended the same plan to Gage, and this is what the tories call making their peace, *"a peace which passeth all understanding"* indeed! A peace which would be the immediate forerunner of a worse ruin than any we have yet thought of. Ye men of Pennsylvania, do reason upon these things! Were the back counties to give up their arms, they would fall an easy prey to the Indians, who are all armed: this perhaps is what some Tories would not be sorry for. Were the home counties to deliver up their arms, they would be exposed to the resentment of the back counties, who would then have it in their power to chastise their defection at pleasure. And were any one state to give up its arms, *that* state must be garrisoned by all Howe's army of Britons and Hessians to preserve it from the anger of the rest. Mutual fear is the principal link in the chain of mutual love, and woe be to that state that breaks the compact. Howe is mercifully inviting you to barbarous destruction, and men must be either rogues or fools that will not see it. I dwell not upon the vapors of imagination; I bring reason to your ears, and, in language as plain as A, B, C, hold up truth to your eyes.

I thank God, that I fear not. I see no real cause for fear. I know our situation well, and can see the way out of it. While our army was collected, Howe dared not risk a battle; and it is no credit to him that he decamped from the White Plains, and waited a mean opportunity to ravage the defenseless Jerseys; but it is great credit to us, that, with a handful of men, we sustained an orderly retreat for near an hundred miles, brought off our ammunition, all our field pieces, the greatest part of our stores, and had four rivers to pass. None can say that our retreat was precipitate, for we were near three weeks in performing it, that the country might have time to come in. Twice we marched back to meet the enemy, and remained out till dark. The sign of fear was not seen in our camp, and had not some of the cowardly and disaffected inhabitants spread false alarms through the country, the Jerseys had never been ravaged. Once more we are again collected and collecting; our new army at both ends of the continent is recruiting fast, and we shall be able to open the next campaign with sixty thousand men, well armed and clothed. This is our situation, and who will may know it. By perseverance and fortitude we have the prospect of a glorious issue; by cowardice and submission, the sad choice of a variety of evils – a ravaged country – a depopulated city – habitations without safety, and slavery without hope – our homes turned into barracks and bawdy-houses for Hessians, and a future race to provide for, whose fathers we shall doubt of. Look on this picture and weep over it! and if there yet remains one thoughtless wretch who believes it not, let him suffer it unlamented.

COMMON SENSE
December 23, 1776

[ETP]

Articles of Confederation

November 15, 1777

The necessity of some provision for a general government was early felt. A committee, appointed by Congress June 11, 1776, "to prepare and digest the form of a confederation to be entered into between these colonies," reported July 12, articles drawn up by John Dickinson. These were not approved, and the matter dropped for the time. At length, Nov. 15, 1777, Congress agreed upon the Articles of Confederation, and ordered them forwarded to the several states that they might instruct their delegates to ratify them in congress. The dates of ratification were—Massachusetts, Rhode Island, Connecticut, New York, Pennsylvania, Virginia, and South Carolina, July 9, 1778—North Carolina, July 21, 1778—Georgia, July 24, 1778—New Jersey, Nov. 26, 1778—Delaware, Feb. 22, 1779—Maryland, March 1, 1781. The principal defects are well summarized by [the historian, James] Schouler. I. Want of power to enforce obedience. II. Operation of the fundamental law not upon individuals but upon states. III. Large vote requisite in congress for passage of important measures. IV. Want of right to regulate foreign Commerce. V. Virtual omission of power to alter the existing articles.

— Note by Howard W. Preston

To all to whom these Presents shall come, we the undersigned Delegates of the States affixed to our Names, send greeting.

WHEREAS THE DELEGATES of the United States of America in Congress assembled did on the fifteenth day of November in the Year of our Lord One Thousand Seven Hundred and Seventyseven, and in the Second Year of the Independence of America agree to certain articles of Confederation and perpetual Union between the States of Newhampshire, Massachusetts-bay, Rhodeisland and Providence Plantations, Connecticut, New York, New Jersey, Pennsylvania, Delaware, Maryland, Virginia, North-Carolina, South-Carolina and Georgia in the Words following, viz.

"Articles of Confederation and perpetual Union between the States of Newhampshire, Massachusetts-bay, Rhodeisland and Providence Plantations, Connecticut, New-York, New-Jersey, Pennsylvania, Delaware, Maryland, Virginia, North-Carolina, South-Carolina and Georgia.

ARTICLE I. The stile of this confederacy shall be "The United States of America."

ARTICLE II. Each State retains its sovereignty, freedom and independence, and every power, jurisdiction and right, which is not by this confederation expressly delegated to the United States, in Congress assembled.

ARTICLE III. The said States hereby severally enter into a firm league of friendship with each other, for their common defence, the security of their liberties, and their mutual and general welfare, binding themselves to assist each other, against all force offered to, or attacks made upon them, or any of them, on account of religion, sovereignty, trade, or any other pretence whatever.

ARTICLE IV. The better to secure and perpetuate mutual friendship and intercourse among the people of the different States in this Union, the free inhabitants of each of these States, paupers, vagabonds and fugitives from justice excepted, shall be entitled to all privileges and immunities of free citizens in the several States; and the people of each State shall have free ingress and regress to and from any other State, and shall enjoy therein all the privileges of trade and commerce, subject to the same duties, impositions and restrictions as the inhabitants thereof respectively, provided that such restrictions shall not extend so far as to prevent the removal of property imported into any State, to any other State of which the owner is an inhabitant; provided also that no imposition, duties or restriction shall be laid by any State, on the property of the United States, or either of them.

If any person guilty of, or charged with treason, felony, or other high misdemeanor in any State, shall flee from justice, and be found in any of the United States, he shall upon demand of the Governor or Executive power, of the State from which he fled, be delivered up and removed to the State having jurisdiction of his offence.

Full faith and credit shall be given in each of these States to the records, acts and judicial proceedings of the courts and magistrates of every other State.

ARTICLE V. For the more convenient management of the general interests of the United States, delegates shall be annually appointed in such manner as the legislature of each State shall direct, to meet in Congress on the first Monday in November, in every year, with a power reserved to each State, to recall its delegates, or any of them, at any time within the year, and to send others in their stead, for the remainder of the year.

No State shall be represented in Congress by less than two, nor by more than seven members; and no person shall be capable of being a delegate for more than three years in any term of six years; nor shall any person, being a delegate, be capable of holding any office under the United States, for which he, or another for his benefit receives any salary, fees or emolument of any kind.

Each State shall maintain its own delegates in a meeting of the States, and while they act as members of the committee of the States.

In determining questions in the United States, in Congress assembled, each State shall have one vote.

Freedom of speech and debate in Congress shall not be impeached or questioned in any court, or place out of Congress, and the members of Congress shall be protected in their persons from arrests and imprisonments, during the time of their going to and from, and attendance on Congress, except for treason, felony, or breach of the peace.

ARTICLE VI. No State without the consent of the United States in Congress assembled, shall send any embassy to, or receive any embassy from, or enter into any conferrence, agreement, alliance or treaty with any king prince or state; nor shall any person holding any office of profit or trust under the United States, or any of them, accept of any present, emolument, office or title of any kind whatever from any king, prince or foreign state; nor shall the United States in Congress assembled, or any of them, grant any title of nobility.

No two or more States shall enter into any treaty, confederation or alliance whatever between them, without the consent of the United States in Congress assembled, specifying accurately the purposes for which the same is to be entered into, and how long it shall continue.

No State shall lay any imposts or duties, which may interfere with any stipulations in treaties, entered into by the United States in Congress assembled, with any king, prince or state, in pursuance of any treaties already proposed by Congress, to the courts of France and Spain.

No vessels of war shall be kept up in time of peace by any State, except such number only, as shall be deemed necessary by the United States in Congress assembled, for the defence of such State, or its trade; nor shall any body of forces be kept up by any State, in time of peace, except such number only, as in the judgment of the United States, in Congress assembled, shall be deemed requisite to garrison the forts necessary for the defence of such State; but every State shall always keep up a well regulated and disciplined militia, sufficiently armed and accoutred, and shall provide and constantly have ready for use, in public stores, a due number of field pieces and tents, and a proper quantity of arms, ammunition and camp equipage.

No State shall engage in any war without the consent of the United States in Congress assembled, unless such State be actually invaded by enemies, or shall have received certain advice of a resolution being formed by some nation of Indians to invade such State, and the danger is so imminent as not to admit of a delay, till the United States in Congress assembled can be consulted: nor shall any State grant commissions to any ships or vessels of war, nor letters of marque or reprisal, except it be after a declaration of war by the United States in Congress assembled, and then only against the kingdom or state and the subjects thereof, against which war has been so declared, and under such regulations as shall be established by the United States in Congress assembled, unless such State be infested by pirates, in which case vessels of war may be fitted out for that occasion, and kept so long as the danger shall continue, or until the United States in Congress assembled shall determine otherwise.

ARTICLE VII. When land-forces are raised by any State for the common defence, all officers of or under the rank of colonel, shall be appointed by the Legislature of each State respectively by whom such forces shall be raised, or in such manner as such State shall direct, and all vacancies shall be filled up by the State which first made the appointment.

ARTICLE VIII. All charges of war, and all other expenses that shall be incurred for the common defence or general welfare, and allowed by the United States in Congress assembled, shall be defrayed out of a common treasury, which shall be supplied by the several States, in proportion to the value of all land within each State, granted to or surveyed for any person, as such land and the buildings and improvements thereon shall be estimated according to such mode as the United States in Congress assembled, shall from time to time direct and appoint.

The taxes for paying that proportion shall be laid and levied by the authority and direction of the Legislatures of the several States within the time agreed upon by the United States in Congress assembled.

ARTICLE IX. The United States in Congress assembled, shall have the sole and exclusive right and power of determining on peace and war, except in the cases mentioned in the sixth article—of sending and receiving ambassadors—entering into treaties and alliances, provided that no treaty of commerce shall be made whereby the legislative power of the respective States shall be restrained from imposing such imposts and duties on foreigners, as their own people are subjected to, or from prohibiting the exportation or importation of any species of goods or commodities whatsoever—of establishing rules for deciding in all cases, what captures on land or water shall be legal, and in what manner prizes taken by land or naval forces in the service of the United States shall be divided or appropriated—of granting letters of marque and reprisal in times of peace—appointing courts for the trial of piracies and felonies committed on the high seas and establishing courts for receiving and determining finally appeals in all cases of captures, provided that no member of Congress shall be appointed a judge of any of the said courts.

The United States in Congress assembled shall also be the last resort on appeal in all disputes and differences now subsisting or that hereafter may arise between two or more States concerning boundary, jurisdiction or any other cause whatever; which authority shall always be exercised in the manner following. Whenever the legislative or executive authority or lawful agent of any State in controversy with another shall present a petition to Congress, stating the matter in question and praying for a hearing, notice thereof shall be given by order of Congress to the legislative or executive authority of the other State in controversy, and a day assigned for the appearance of the parties by their lawful agents, who shall then be directed to appoint by joint consent, commissioners or judges to constitute a court for hearing and determining the matter in question: but if they cannot agree, Congress shall name three persons out of each of the United States, and from the list of such persons each party shall alternately strike out one, the petitioners beginning, until the number shall be reduced to thirteen; and from that number not less than seven, nor more than nine names as Congress shall direct, shall in the presence of Congress be drawn out by lot, and the persons whose names shall be so drawn or any five of them, shall be commissioners or judges, to hear and finally determine the controversy, so always as a major part of the judges who shall hear the cause shall agree in the determination: and if either party shall neglect to attend at the day appointed, without showing reasons, which Congress shall judge sufficient, or being present shall refuse to strike, the Congress shall proceed to nominate three persons out of each State, and the Secretary of Congress shall strike in behalf of such party absent or refusing; and the judgment and sentence of the court to be appointed, in the manner before prescribed, shall be final and conclusive; and if any of the parties shall refuse to submit to the authority of such court, or to appear or defend their claim or cause, the court shall nevertheless proceed to pronounce sentence, or judgment, which shall in like manner be final and decisive, the judgment or sentence and other proceedings being in either case transmitted to Congress, and lodged among the acts of Congress for the security of the parties concerned: provided that every commissioner, before he sits in judgment, shall take an oath to be administered by one of the judges of the supreme or superior court of the State where the cause shall be tried, "well and truly to hear and determine the matter in question, according to the best of his judgment, without favour, affection or hope of reward:" provided also that no State shall be deprived of territory for the benefit of the United States.

All controversies concerning the private right of soil claimed under different grants of two or more States, whose jurisdiction as they may respect such lands, and the States which passed such grants are adjusted, the said grants or either of them being at the same time claimed to have originated antecedent to such settlement of jurisdiction, shall on the petition of either party to the Congress of the

United States, be finally determined as near as may be in the same manner as is before prescribed for deciding disputes respecting territorial jurisdiction between different States.

The United States in Congress assembled shall also have the sole and exclusive right and power of regulating the alloy and value of coin struck by their own authority, or by that of the respective States.—fixing the standard of weights and measures throughout the United States—regulating the trade and managing all affairs with the Indians, not members of any of the States, provided that the legislative right of any State within its own limits be not infringed or violated—reestablishing and regulating post-offices from one State to another, throughout all the United States, and exacting such postage on the papers passing thro' the same as may be requisite to defray the expenses of the said office—appointing all officers of the land forces, in the service of the United States, excepting regimental officers—appointing all the officers of the naval forces, and commissioning all officers whatever in the service of the United States—making rules for the government and regulation of the said land and naval forces, and directing their operations.

The United States in Congress assembled shall have authority to appoint a committee, to sit in the recess of Congress, to be denominated "a Committee of the States," and to consist of one delegate from each State; and to appoint such other committees and civil officers as may be necessary for managing the general affairs of the United States under their direction—to appoint one of their number to preside, provided that no person be allowed to serve in the office of president more than one year in any term of three years; to ascertain the necessary sums of money to be raised for the service of the United States, and to appropriate and apply the same for defraying the public expenses—to borrow money, or emit bills on the credit of the United States, transmitting every half year to the respective States an account of the sums of money so borrowed or emitted,—to build and equip a navy—to agree upon the number of land forces, and to make requisitions from each State for its quota, in proportion to the number of white inhabitants in such State; which requisition shall be binding, and thereupon the Legislature of each State shall appoint the regimental officers, raise the men and cloath, arm and equip them in a soldier like manner, at the expense of the United States; and the officers and men so cloathed, armed and equipped shall march to the place appointed, and within the time agreed on by the United States in Congress assembled: but if the United States in Congress assembled shall, on consideration of circumstances judge proper that any State should not raise men, or should raise a smaller number than its quota, and that any other State should raise a greater number of men than the quota thereof, such extra number shall be raised, officered, cloathed, armed and equipped in the same manner as the quota of such State, unless the legislature of such State shall judge that such extra number cannot be safely spared out of the same, in which case they shall raise officer, cloath, arm and equip as many of such extra number as they judge can be safely spared. And the officers and men so cloathed, armed and equipped, shall march to the place appointed, and within the time agreed on by the United States in Congress assembled.

The United States in Congress assembled shall never engage in a war, nor grant letters of marque and reprisal in time of peace, nor enter into any treaties or alliances, nor coin money, nor regulate the value thereof, nor ascertain the sums and expenses necessary for the defence and welfare of the United States, or any of them, nor emit bills, nor borrow money on the credit of the United States, nor appropriate money, nor agree upon the number of vessels of war, to be built or purchased, or the number of land or sea forces to be raised, nor appoint a commander in chief of the army or navy, unless nine States assent to the same: nor shall a question on any other point, except for adjourning from day to day be determined, unless by the votes of a majority of the United States in Congress assembled.

The Congress of the United States shall have power to adjourn to any time within the year, and to any place within the United States, so that no period of adjournment be for a longer duration than the space of six months, and shall publish the journal of their proceedings monthly, except such parts thereof relating to treaties, alliances or military operations, as in their judgment require secrecy; and the yeas and nays of the delegates of each State on any question shall be entered on the journal, when it is desired by any delegate; and the delegates of a State, or any of them, at his or their request shall be furnished with a transcript of the said journal, except such parts as are above excepted, to lay before the Legislatures of the several States.

ARTICLE X. The committee of the States, or any nine of them, shall be authorized to execute, in the recess of Congress, such of the powers of Congress as the United States in Congress assembled, by the consent of nine States, shall from time to time think expedient to vest them with; provided that no power be delegated to the said committee, for the exercise of which, by the articles of confederation, the voice of nine States in the Congress of the United States assembled is requisite.

ARTICLE XI. Canada acceding to this confederation, and joining in the measures of the United States, shall be admitted into, and entitled to all the advantages of this Union: but no other colony shall be admitted into the same, unless such admission be agreed to by nine States.

ARTICLE XII. All bills of credit emitted, monies borrowed and debts contracted by, or under the authority of Congress, before the assembling of the United States, in pursuance of the present confederation, shall be deemed and considered as a charge against the United States, for payment and satisfaction whereof the said United States, and the public faith are hereby solemnly pledged.

ARTICLE XIII. Every State shall abide by the determinations of the United States in Congress assembled, on all questions which by this confederation are submitted to them. And the articles of this confederation shall be inviolably observed by every State, and the Union shall be perpetual; nor shall any alteration at any time hereafter be made in any of them; unless such alteration be agreed to in a Congress of the United States, and be afterwards confirmed by the Legislatures of every State.

And whereas it has pleased the Great Governor of the world to incline the hearts of the Legislatures we respectively represent in Congress, to approve of, and to authorize us to ratify the said articles of confederation and perpetual union. Know ye that we the undersigned delegates, by virtue of the power and authority to us given for that purpose, do by these presents, in the name and in behalf of our respective constituents, fully and entirely ratify and confirm each and every of the said articles of confederation and perpetual union, and all and singular the matters and things therein contained: and we do further solemnly plight and engage the faith of our respective constituents, that they shall abide by the determinations of the United States in Congress assembled, on all questions, which by the said confederation are submitted to them. And that the articles thereof shall be inviolably observed by the States we respectively represent, and that the Union shall be perpetual.

In witness whereof we have hereunto set our hands in Congress. Done at Philadelphia in the State of Pennsylvania the ninth day of

July in the year of our Lord one thousand seven hundred and seventy-eight, and in the third year of the independence of America.

On the part & behalf of the State of New Hampshire.

JOSIAH BARTLETT,   JOHN WENTWORTH, Junr.,
                                     August 8th, 1778.

On the part and behalf of the State of Massachusetts Bay.

JOHN HANCOCK,   FRANCIS DANA,
SAMUEL ADAMS,   JAMES LOVELL,
ELBRIDGE GERRY,   SAMUEL HOLTEN.

On the part and behalf of the State of Rhode Island and Providence Plantations.

WILLIAM ELLERY,   JOHN COLLINS.
HENRY MARCHANT,

On the part and behalf of the State of Connecticut.

ROGER SHERMAN,   TITUS HOSMER,
SAMUEL HUNTINGTON,   ANDREW ADAMS.
OLIVER WOLCOTT,

On the part and behalf of the State of New York.

JAS. DUANE,   WM. DUER,
FRA. LEWIS,   GOUV. MORRIS.

On the part and in behalf of the State of New Jersey, Novr. 26, 1778.

JNO. WITHERSPOON,   NATH. SCUDDER.

On the part and behalf of the State of Pennsylvania.

ROBT. MORRIS,   WILLIAM CLINGAN,
DANIEL ROBERDEAU,   JOSEPH REED,
JONA. BAYARD SMITH,   22d July, 1778.

On the part & behalf of the State of Delaware.

THO. M'KEAN,   NICHOLAS VAN DYKE.
    Feby. 12, 1779.
JOHN DICKINSON, May 5th, 1779.

On the part and behalf of the State of Maryland,
JOHN HANSON,   DANIEL CARROLL,
   March 1, 1781.   Mar. 1, 1781.

On the part and behalf of the State of Virginia.
RICHARD HENRY LEE,   JNO. HARVIE,
JOHN BANISTER,   FRANCIS LIGHTFOOT LEE.
THOMAS ADAMS,

On the part and behalf of the State of No. Carolina.
JOHN PENN, July 21, 1778.   JNO. WILLIAMS.
CORNS. HARNETT,

On the part & behalf of the State of South Carolina.
HENRY LAURENS,   RICHD. HUTSON.
WILLIAM HENRY DRAYTON,   THOS. HEYWARD, Junr.
JNO. MATHEWS,

On the part & behalf of the State of Georgia.
JNO. WALTON,   EDWD. LANGWORTHY.
   24th July, 1778.
EDWD. TELFAIR,

[DIH]

Articles of Capitulation, Yorktown

October 19, 1781

The surrender of Cornwallis, arranged in these articles, virtually brought to a close the hostilities in the war between Great Britain and her American colonies, and assured the independence of the United States.

— Note by Charles W. Eliot

SETTLED BETWEEN HIS *Excellency General Washington, Commander-in-chief of the combined Forces of America and France; his Excellency the Count de Rochambeau, Lieutenant-General of the Armies of the King of France, Great Cross of the royal and military Order of St. Louis, commanding the auxiliary Troops of his Most Christian Majesty in America; and his Excellency the Count de Grasse, Lieutenant-General of the Naval Armies of his Most Christian Majesty, Commander of the Order of St. Louis, Commander-in-Chief of the Naval Army of France in the Chesapeake, on the one Part; and the Right Honorable Earl Cornwallis, Lieutenant-General of his Britannic Majesty's Forces, commanding the Garrisons of York and Gloucester; and Thomas Symonds, Esquire, commanding his Britannic Majesty's Naval Forces in York River in Virginia, on the other Part.*

ARTICLE I. The garrisons of York and Gloucester, including the officers and seamen of his Britannic Majesty's ships, as well as other mariners, to surrender them prisoners of war to the combined forces of America and France. The land troops to remain prisoners to the United States, the navy to the naval army of his Most Christian Majesty.

Granted.

ARTICLE II. The artillery, arms, accoutrements, military chest, and public stores of every denomination, shall be delivered unimpaired to the heads of departments appointed to receive them.
Granted.

ARTICLE III. At twelve o'clock this day the two redoubts on the left flank of York to be delivered, the one to a detachment of American infantry, the other to a detachment of French grenadiers.
Granted.

The garrison of York will march out to a place to be appointed in front of the posts, at two o'clock precisely, with shouldered arms, colors cased, and drums beating a British or German march. They are then to ground their arms, and return to their encampments, where they will remain until they are despatched to the places of their destination. Two works on the Gloucester side will be delivered at one o'clock to a detachment of French and American troops appointed to possess them. The garrison will march out at three o'clock in the afternoon; the cavalry with their swords drawn, trumpets sounding, and the infantry in the manner prescribed for the garrison of York. They are likewise to return to their encampments until they can be finally marched off.

ARTICLE IV. Officers are to retain their side-arms. Both officers and soldiers to keep their private property of every kind; and no part of their baggage or papers to be at any time subject to search or inspection. The baggage and papers of officers and soldiers taken during the siege to be likewise preserved for them.
Granted.

It is understood that any property obviously belonging to the inhabitants of these States, in the possession of the garrison, shall be subject to be reclaimed.

ARTICLE V. The soldiers to be kept in Virginia, Maryland, or Pennsylvania, and as much by regiments as possible, and supplied with the same rations of provisions as are allowed to soldiers in the service of America. A field-officer from each nation, to wit, British, Anspach, and Hessian, and other officers on parole, in the proportion of one to fifty men to be allowed to reside near their respective regiments, to visit them frequently, and be witnesses of their treatment; and that their officers may receive and deliver clothing and other necessaries for them, for which passports are to be granted when applied for.

Granted.

ARTICLE VI. The general, staff, and other officers not employed as mentioned in the above articles, and who choose it, to be permitted to go on parole to Europe, to New York, or to any other American maritime posts at present in the possession of the British forces, at their own option; and proper vessels to be granted by the Count de Grasse to carry them under flags of truce to New York within ten days from this date, if possible, and they to reside in a district to be agreed upon hereafter, until they embark. The officers of the civil department of the army and navy to be included in this article. Passports to go by land to be granted to those to whom vessels cannot be furnished.

Granted.

ARTICLE VII. Officers to be allowed to keep soldiers as servants, according to the common practice of the service. Servants not soldiers are not to be considered as prisoners, and are to be allowed to attend their masters.

Granted.

ARTICLE VIII. The Bonetta sloop-of-war to be equipped, and navigated by its present captain and crew, and left entirely at the disposal of Lord Cornwallis from the hour that the capitulation is signed, to receive an aid-de-camp to carry despatches to Sir Henry Clinton; and such soldiers as he may think proper to send to New York, to be permitted to sail without examination. When his despatches are ready, his Lordship engages on his part, that the ship shall be delivered to the order of the Count de Grasse, if she escapes the dangers of the sea. That she shall not carry off any public stores. Any part of the crew that may be deficient on her return, and the soldiers passengers, to be accounted for on her delivery.

ARTICLE IX. The traders are to preserve their property and to be allowed three months to dispose of or remove them; and those traders are not to be considered as prisoners of war.

The traders will be allowed to dispose of their effects, the allied army having the right of preemption. The traders to be considered as prisoners of war upon parole.

ARTICLE X. Natives or inhabitants of different parts of this country, at present in York or Gloucester, are not to be punished on account of having joined the British army.

This article cannot be assented to, being altogether of civil resort.

ARTICLE XI. Proper hospitals to be furnished for the sick and wounded. They are to be attended by their own surgeons on parole; and they are to be furnished with medicines and stores from the American hospitals.

The hospital stores now at York and Gloucester shall be delivered for the use of the British sick and wounded. Passports will be granted for procuring them further supplies from New York, as occasion may require; and proper hospitals will be furnished for the reception of the sick and wounded of the two garrisons.

ARTICLE XII. Wagons to be furnished to carry the baggage of the officers attending the soldiers, and to surgeons when travelling on account of the sick, attending the hospitals at public expense.

They are to be furnished if possible.

ARTICLE XIII. The shipping and boats in the two harbours, with all their stores, guns, tackling, and apparel, shall be delivered up in their present state to an officer of the navy appointed to take possession of them, previously unloading the private property, part of which had been on board for security during the siege.

Granted.

ARTICLE XIV. No article of capitulation to be infringed on pretence of reprisals; and if there be any doubtful expressions in it, they are to be interpreted according to the common meaning and acceptation of the words.

Granted.

Done at Yorktown, in Virginia, October 19th, 1781.

> CORNWALLIS,
> THOMAS SYMONDS.

Done in the Trenches before Yorktown, in Virginia, October 19th, 1781.

> GEORGE WASHINGTON,
> LE COMTE DE ROCHAMBEAU,
> LE COMTE DE BARRAS,
> *En mon nom & celui du*
> COMTE DE GRASSE.

[AHD]

Hector St. John De Crevecoeur
Letters from an American Farmer, "What Is an American?"

1782

These excerpts are taken from Letter III of Crevecoeur's famous account,
Letters from an American Farmer. *Crevecoeur (1735–1813) moved to*
America in 1754, where he married and then cultivated his farm in New
York along the Hudson River. His book inspired many Americans, and in
his own time inspired many emigrants in his home country of France.
Unfortunately, shortly after its publication, while he was traveling abroad,
Crevecoeur's farm was destroyed by Native Americans and in that calamity
his wife died. In 1790 he returned to France, where he lived until his death.

I wish I could be acquainted with the feelings and thoughts which
must agitate the heart and present themselves to the mind of an
enlightened Englishman, when he first lands on this continent. He
must greatly rejoice that he lived at a time to see this fair country
discovered and settled; he must necessarily feel a share of national
pride, when he views the chain of settlements which embellishes
these extended shores. When he says to himself, this is the work of
my countrymen, who, when convulsed by factions, afflicted by a
variety of miseries and wants, restless and impatient, took refuge
here. They brought along with them their national genius, to
which they principally owe what liberty they enjoy, and what substance they possess. Here he sees the industry of his native country
displayed in a new manner, and traces in their works the embrios

of all the arts, sciences, and ingenuity which flourish in Europe. Here he beholds fair cities, substantial villages, extensive fields, an immense country filled with decent houses, good roads, orchards, meadows, and bridges, where an hundred years ago all was wild, woody and uncultivated! What a train of pleasing ideas this fair spectacle must suggest; it is a prospect which must inspire a good citizen with the most heartfelt pleasure.

The difficulty consists in the manner of viewing so extensive a scene. He is arrived on a new continent; a modern society offers itself to his contemplation, different from what he had hitherto seen. It is not composed, as in Europe, of great lords who possess everything and of a herd of people who have nothing. Here are no aristocratical families, no courts, no kings, no bishops, no ecclesiastical dominion, no invisible power giving to a few a very visible one; no great manufacturers employing thousands, no great refinements of luxury. The rich and the poor are not so far removed from each other as they are in Europe. Some few towns excepted, we are all tillers of the earth, from Nova Scotia to West Florida. We are a people of cultivators, scattered over an immense territory communicating with each other by means of good roads and navigable rivers, united by the silken bands of mild government, all respecting the laws, without dreading their power, because they are equitable. We are all animated with the spirit of an industry which is unfettered and unrestrained, because each person works for himself. If he travels through our rural districts he views not the hostile castle, and the haughty mansion, contrasted with the clay-built hut and miserable cabin, where cattle and men help to keep each other warm, and dwell in meanness, smoke, and indigence. A pleasing uniformity of decent competence appears throughout our habitations. The meanest of our log-houses is a dry and comfortable habitation. Lawyer or merchant are the fairest titles our towns afford; that of a farmer is the only appellation of the rural inhabitants of our country.

It must take some time ere he can reconcile himself to our dictionary, which is but short in words of dignity, and names of honor. There, on a Sunday, he sees a congregation of respectable farmers and their wives, all clad in neat homespun, well mounted, or riding in their own humble wagons. There is not among them an esquire, saving the unlettered magistrate. There he sees a parson as simple as his flock, a farmer who does not riot on the labor of others. We have no princes, for whom we toil, starve, and bleed: we are the most perfect society now existing in the world. Here man is free; as he ought to be; nor is this pleasing equality so transitory as many others are. Many ages will not see the shores of our great lakes replenished with inland nations, nor the unknown bounds of North America entirely peopled. Who can tell how far it extends? Who can tell the millions of men whom it will feed and contain? for no European foot has as yet traveled half the extent of this mighty continent!

The next wish of this traveler will be to know whence came all these people? They are mixture of English, Scotch, Irish, French, Dutch, Germans, and Swedes. From this promiscuous breed, that race now called Americans have arisen. The eastern provinces must indeed be excepted, as being the unmixed descendants of Englishmen. I have heard many wish that they had been more intermixed also: for my part, I am no wisher, and think it much better as it has happened. They exhibit a most conspicuous figure in this great and variegated picture; they too enter for a great share in the pleasing perspective displayed in these thirteen provinces. 1 know it is fashionable to reflect on them, but I respect them for what they have done; for the accuracy and wisdom with which they have settled their territory; for the decency of their manners; for their early love of letters; their ancient college, the first in this hemisphere; for their industry; which to me who am but a farmer, is the criterion of everything. There never was a people, situated as they are, who with so ungrateful a soil have done more in so short a time. Do you think that the monarchical ingredients which are more prevalent in other governments have purged them from all foul stains? Their histories assert the contrary.

In this great American asylum, the poor of Europe have by some means met together, and in consequence of various causes; to what purpose should they ask one another what countrymen they are? Alas, two thirds of them had no country. Can a wretch who wanders about, who works and starves, whose life is a continual scene of sore affliction or pinching penury; can that man call England or any other kingdom his country? A country that had no bread for him, whose fields procured him no harvest, who met with nothing but the frowns of the rich, the severity of the laws, with jails and punishments; who owned not a single foot of the extensive surface of this planet? No! urged by a variety of motives, here they came. Everything has tended to regenerate them; new laws, a new mode of living, a new social system; here they are become men: in Europe they were as so many useless plants, wanting vegetative mold, and refreshing showers; they withered, and were mowed

down by want, hunger, and war; but now by the power of transplantation, like all other plants they have taken root and flourished!
Formerly they were not numbered in any civil lists of their country,
except in those of the poor; here they rank as citizens.

By what invisible power has this surprising metamorphosis been
performed? By that of the laws and that of their industry. The laws,
the indulgent laws, protect them as they arrive, stamping on them the
symbol of adoption; they receive ample rewards for their labors; these
accumulated rewards procure them lands; those lands confer on them
the title of freemen, and to that title every benefit is affixed which
men can possibly require. This is the great operation daily performed
by our laws. From whence proceed these laws? From our government. Whence the government? It is derived from the original genius
and strong desire of the people ratified and confirmed by the crown.
This is the great chain which links us all, this is the picture which
every province exhibits, Nova Scotia excepted. There the crown has
done all; either there were no people who had genius, or it was not
much attended to: the consequence is, that the province is very thinly
inhabited indeed; the power of the crown in conjunction with the
muskets has prevented men from settling there. Yet some parts of it
flourished once, and it contained a mild harmless set of people. But
for the fault of a few leaders, the whole were banished. The greatest
political error the crown ever committed in America was to cut off
men from a country which wanted nothing but men!

What attachment can a poor European emigrant have for a
country where he had nothing? The knowledge of the language,
the love of a few kindred as poor as himself, were the only cords
that tied him: his country is now that which gives him land, bread,
protection, and consequence: *Ubi panis ibi patria,*[1] is the motto of
all emigrants. What then is the American, this new man? He is
either an European, or the descendant of an European, hence that
strange mixture of blood, which you will find in no other country.
I could point out to you a family whose grandfather was an
Englishman, whose wife was Dutch, whose son married a French
woman, and whose present four sons have now four wives of different nations. He is an American, who leaving behind him all his
ancient prejudices and manners, receives new ones from the new

---

[1] *Ubi panis ibi patria,* Latin for "Where the bread is is where my country is."

mode of life he has embraced, the new government he obeys, and the new rank he holds.

He becomes an American by being received in the broad lap of our great Alma Mater. Here individuals of all nations are melted into a new race of men, whose labors and posterity will one day cause great changes in the world. Americans are the western pilgrims, who are carrying along with them that great mass of arts, sciences, vigor, and industry which began long since in the east; they will finish the great circle. The Americans were once scattered all over Europe; here they are incorporated into one of the finest systems of population which has ever appeared, and which will hereafter become distinct by the power of the different climates they inhabit. The American ought therefore to love this country much better than that wherein either he or his forefathers were born. Here the rewards of his industry follow with equal steps the progress of his labor; his labor is founded on the basis of nature, self-interest; can it want a stronger allurement? Wives and children, who before in vain demanded of him a morsel of bread, now, fat and frolicsome, gladly help their father to clear those fields whence exuberant crops are to arise to feed and to clothe them all; without any part being claimed, either by a despotic prince, a rich abbot, or a mighty lord. Here religion demands but little of him; a small voluntary salary to the minister, and gratitude to God; can he refuse these? The American is a new man, who acts upon new principles; he must therefore entertain new ideas, and form new opinions. From involuntary idleness, servile dependence, penury, and useless labor, he has passed to toils of a very different nature, rewarded by ample subsistence.—This is an American.

[...]

As I have endeavoured to shew you how Europeans become Americans; it may not be disagreeable to shew you likewise how the various Christian sects introduced, wear out, and how religious indifference becomes prevalent. When any considerable number of a particular sect happen to dwell contiguous to each other, they immediately erect a temple, and there worship the Divinity agreeably to their own peculiar ideas. Nobody disturbs them. If any new sect springs up in Europe, it may happen that many of its professors will come and settle in America. As they bring their zeal with them, they are at liberty to make proselytes if they can, and to build a meeting and to follow the dictates of their consciences; for neither the government nor any other power interferes. If they are peaceable subjects, and are industrious, what is it to their neighbors how and in what manner they think fit to address their prayers to the Supreme Being? But if the sectaries are not settled close together, if they are mixed with other denominations, their zeal will cool for want of fuel, and will be extinguished in a little time. Then the Americans become as to religion, what they are as to country, allied to all. In them the name of Englishman, Frenchman, and European is lost, and in like manner, the strict modes of Christianity as practised in Europe are lost also. This effect will extend itself still farther hereafter, and though this may appear to you as a strange idea, yet it is a very true one. I shall be able perhaps hereafter to explain myself better, in the meanwhile, let the following example serve as my first justification.

Let us suppose you and I to be traveling; we observe that in this house, to the right, lives a Catholic, who prays to God as he has been taught, and believes in transubstantion; he works and raises wheat, he has a large family of children, all hale and robust; his belief, his prayers offend nobody. About one mile farther on the same road, his next neighbor may be a good honest plodding German Lutheran, who addresses himself to the same God, the God of all, agreeably to the modes he has been educated in, and believes in consubstantiation; by so doing he scandalizes nobody; he also works in his fields, embellishes the earth, clears swamps, &c. What has the world to do with his Lutheran principles? He persecutes nobody, and nobody persecutes him, he visits his neighbors, and his neighbors visit him. Next to him lives a seceder, the most enthusiastic of all sectaries; his zeal is hot and fiery, but separated as he is from others of the same complexion, he has no congregation of his own to resort to, where he might cabal and mingle religious pride with worldly obstinacy. He likewise raises good crops, his house is handsomely painted, his orchard is one of the fairest in the neighborhood.

How does it concern the welfare of the country, or of the province at large, what this man's religious sentiments are, or really whether he has any at all? He is a good farmer, he is a sober, peaceable, good citizen: William Penn himself would not wish for more. This is the visible character, the invisible one is only guessed at, and is nobody's business. Next again lives a Low Dutchman, who implicitly believes the rules laid down by the synod of Dort. He conceives no other idea of a clergyman than that of an hired man; if he does his work well he will pay him the stipulated sum; if not he will dismiss him, and do without his sermons, and let his church be shut up for years. But notwithstanding this coarse idea, you will find his house and farm to be the neatest in all the country; and you will judge by his wagon and fat horses, that he thinks more of the affairs of this world than of those of the next. He is sober and laborious; therefore he is all he ought to be as to the affairs of this life; as for those of the next, he must trust to the great Creator. Each of these people instruct their children as well as they can, but these instructions are feeble compared to those which are given to the youth of the poorest class in Europe. Their children will therefore grow up less zealous and more indifferent in matters of religion than their parents. The foolish vanity, or rather the fury of making Proselytes, is unknown here; they have no time. The seasons call for all their attention, and thus in a few years, this mixed neighborhood will exhibit a strange religious medley, that will be neither pure Catholicism nor pure Calvinism. A very perceptible indifference even in the first generation will become apparent; and it may happen that the daughter of the Catholic will marry the son of the secede, and settle by themselves at a distance from their parents. What religious education will they give their children? A very imperfect one. If there happens to be in the neighborhood any place of worship, we will suppose a Quaker's meeting; rather than not shew their fine clothes, they will go to it, and some of them may perhaps attach themselves to that society. Others will remain in a perfect state of indifference; the children of these zealous parents will not be able to tell what their religious principles are and their grandchildren still less. The neighborhood of a place of worship generally leads them to it, and the action of going thither, is the strongest evidence they can give of their attachment to any sect.

The Quakers are the only people who retain a fondness for their own mode of worship; for be they ever so far separated from each other, they hold a sort of communion with the society, and seldom depart from its rules, at least in this country. Thus all sects are mixed as well as all nations; thus religious indifference is imperceptibly disseminated from one end of the continent to the other; which is at present one of the strongest characteristics of the Americans. Where this will reach no one can tell, perhaps it may leave a vacuum fit to receive other systems. Persecution, religious pride, the love of contradiction, are the food of what the world commonly calls religion. These motives have ceased here: zeal in Europe is confined; here it evaporates in the great distance it has to travel;

there it is a grain of powder enclosed, here it burns away in the open air, and consumes without effect.

[. . .]

It is no wonder that this country has so many charms, and presents to Europeans so many temptations to remain in it. A traveler in Europe becomes a stranger as soon as he quits his own kingdom; but it is otherwise here. We know, properly speaking, no strangers; this is every person's country; the variety of our soils, situations, climates, governments, and produce, hath something which must please every body. No sooner does an European arrive, no matter of what condition, than his eyes are opened upon the fair prospect; he hears his language spoke, he retraces many of his own country manners, he perpetually hears the names of families and towns with which he is acquainted; he sees happiness and prosperity in all places disseminated; he meets with hospitality, kindness, and plenty everywhere; he beholds hardly any poor, he seldom hears of punishments and executions; and he wonders at the elegance of our towns, those miracles of industry and freedom. He cannot admire enough our rural districts, our convenient roads, good taverns, and our many accommodations; he involuntarily loves a country where everything is so lovely. When in England, he was a mere Englishman; here he stands on a larger portion of the globe, not less than its fourth part, and may see the productions of the north, in iron and naval stores; the provisions of Ireland, the grain of Egypt, the indigo, the rice of China. He does not find, as in Europe, a crowded society, where every place is over-stocked; he does not feel that perpetual collision of parties, that difficulty of beginning, that contention which oversets so many. There is room for every body in America; has he any particular talent, or industry? he exerts it in order to procure a livelihood, and it succeeds. Is he a merchant? The avenues of trade are infinite; is he eminent in any respect? He will be employed and respected. Does he love a country life? Pleasant farms present themselves; he may purchase what he wants, and thereby become an American tanner. Is he a laborer, sober and industrious? He need not go many miles, nor receive many information before he will be hired, well fed at the table of his employer, and paid four or five times more than he can get in Europe. Does he want uncultivated lands? Thousands of acres present themselves, which he may purchase cheap. Whatever be his talents or inclinations, if they are moderate, he may satisfy them.

I do not mean that everyone who comes will grow rich in a little time; no, but he may procure an easy, decent maintenance, by his industry. Instead of starving he will be fed, instead of being idle he will have employment; and these are riches enough for such men as come over here. The rich stay in Europe; it is only the middling and the poor that emigrate. Would you wish to travel in independent idleness, from north to south, you will find easy access, and the most cheerful reception at every house; society without ostentation, good cheer without pride, and every decent diversion which the country affords, with little expense. It is no wonder that the European who has lived here a few years, is desirous to remain; Europe with all its pomp, is not to be compared to this continent, for men of middle stations, or laborers.

An European, when he first arrives, seems limited in his intentions, as well as in his views; but he very suddenly alters his scale; two hundred miles formerly appeared a very great distance, it is now but a trifle; he no sooner breathes our air than he forms schemes, and embarks in designs he never would have thought of in his own country. There the plenitude of society confines many useful ideas, and often extinguishes the most laudable schemes which here ripen into maturity. Thus Europeans become Americans.

But how is this accomplished in that crowd of low, indigent people, who flock here every year from all parts of Europe? I will tell you; they no sooner arrive than they immediately feel the good effects of that plenty of provisions we possess: they fare on our best food, and they are kindly entertained; their talents, character, and peculiar industry are immediately inquired into; they find countrymen everywhere disseminated, let them come from whatever part of Europe. Let me select one as an epitome of the rest; he is hired, he goes to work, and works moderately; instead of being employed by a haughty person, he finds himself with his equal, placed at the substantial table of the farmer, or else at an inferior one as good; his wages are high, his bed is not like that bed of sorrow on which he used to lie: if he behaves with propriety, and is faithful, he is caressed, and becomes as it were a member of the family. He begins to feel the effects of a sort of resurrection; hitherto he had not lived, but simply vegetated; he now feels himself a man, because he is treated as such; the laws of his own country had overlooked him in his insignificancy; the laws of this cover him with their mantle.

Judge what an alteration there must arise in the mind and thoughts of this man; he begins to forget his former servitude and dependence, his heart involuntarily swells and glows; this first swell inspires him with those new thoughts which constitute an American. What love can he entertain for a country where his existence was a burthen to him; if he s a generous good man, the love of this new adoptive parent will sink deep into his heart. He looks around, and sees many a prosperous person, who but a few years before was as poor as himself. This encourages him much, he begins to form some little scheme, the first, alas, he ever formed in his life. If he is wise he thus spends two or three years, in which time he acquires knowledge, the use of tools, the modes of working the lands, felling trees, &c. This prepares the foundation of a good name, the most useful acquisition he can make. He is encouraged, he has gained friends; he is advised and directed, he feels bold, he purchases some land; he gives all the money he has brought over, as well as what he has earned, and trusts to the God of harvests for the discharge of the rest. His good name procures him credit. He is now possessed of the deed, conveying to him and his posterity the fee simple and absolute property of two hundred acres of land, situated on such a river.

What an epocha in this man's life! He is become a freeholder, from perhaps a German boor—he is now an American, a Pennsylvanian, an English subject. He is naturalized, his name is enrolled with those of the other citizens of the province. Instead of being a vagrant, he has a place of residence; he is called the inhabitant of such a county, or of such a district, and for the first time in his life counts for something; for hitherto he has been a cypher. I only repeat what I have heard man say, and no wonder their hearts should glow, and be agitated with a multitude of feelings, not easy to describe. From nothing to start into being; from a servant to the rank of a master; from being the slave of some despotic prince, to become a free man, invested with lands, to which every municipal blessing is annexed! What a change indeed! It is in consequence of that change that he becomes an American. This great metamorphosis has a double effect, it extinguishes all his European prejudices, he forgets that mechanism of subordination, that servility of disposition which poverty had taught him; and sometimes he is apt to forget too much, often passing from one extreme to the other. If he is a good man, he forms schemes of future prosperity, he proposes to educate his children better than he has been educated himself; he thinks of future modes of conduct, feels an ardor to labor he never felt before. Pride steps in and leads him to everything that the laws do not forbid: he respects them; with a heartfelt gratitude he looks toward the east, toward that insular government from whose wisdom all his new felicity is derived, and under whose wings and protection he now lives. These reflections constitute him the good man and the good subject....

SOURCE: J. Hector St. John Crevecoeur. *Letters from an American Farmer*. New York: Fox, Duffield. 1904.

[EI]

Thomas Paine, *The American Crisis*, "Thoughts on the Peace, and the Probable Advantages Thereof"

April 19, 1783

On the occasion of the successful conclusion of the war against Great Britain, Thomas Paine, in his continued inspiring role as the author of "Common Sense," announces his retirement from that role: "It was the cause of America that made me an author. The force with which it struck my mind, and the dangerous condition the country appeared to me in, by courting an impossible and an unnatural reconciliation with those who were determined to reduce her, instead of striking out into the only line that could cement and save her, a DECLARATION OF INDEPENDENCE, made it impossible for me, feeling as I did, to be silent: and if, in the course of more than seven years, I have rendered her any service, I have likewise added something to the reputation of literature, by freely and disinterestedly employing it in the great cause of mankind ..."

"THE TIMES THAT tried men's souls," are over – and the greatest and completest revolution the world ever knew, gloriously and happily accomplished.

But to pass from the extremes of danger to safety – from the tumult of war to the tranquility of peace, though sweet in contemplation, requires a gradual exposure of the senses to receive it. Even calmness has the power of stunning, when it opens too instantly upon us. The long and raging hurricane that should cease in a moment would leave us in a state rather of wonder than enjoyment; and some moments of recollection must pass, before we could be capable of tasting the felicity of repose. There are but few instances, in which the mind is fitted for sudden transitions: it takes in its pleasures by reflection and comparison and those must have time to act, before the relish for new scenes is complete.

In the present case – the mighty magnitude of the object – the various uncertainties of fate it has undergone – the numerous and complicated dangers we have suffered or escaped – the eminence we now stand on, and the vast prospect before us, must all conspire to impress us with contemplation.

To see it in our power to make a world happy – to teach mankind the art of being so – to exhibit on the theatre of the universe a character hitherto unknown – and to have, as it were, a new creation entrusted to our hands, are honors that command reflection, and can neither be too highly estimated, nor too gratefully received.

In this pause then of recollection – while the storm is ceasing, and the long agitated mind vibrating to a rest, let us look back on the scenes we have passed, and learn from experience what is yet to be done.

Never, I say, had a country so many openings to happiness as this. Her setting out in life, like the rising of a fair morning, was unclouded and promising. Her cause was good. Her principles just and liberal. Her temper serene and firm. Her conduct regulated by the nicest steps, and everything about her wore the mark of honor. It is not every country (perhaps there is not another in the world) that can boast so fair an origin. Even the first settlement of America corresponds with the character of the revolution. Rome, once the proud mistress of the universe, was originally a band of ruffians. Plunder and rapine made her rich, and her oppression of millions made her great. But America need never be ashamed to tell her birth, nor relate the stages by which she rose to empire.

The remembrance, then, of what is past, if it operates rightly, must inspire her with the most laudable of all ambition, that of adding to the fair fame she began with. The world has seen her great in adversity; struggling, without a thought of yielding, beneath accumulated difficulties, bravely, nay proudly, encountering distress, and rising in resolution as the storm increased. All this is justly due to her, for her fortitude has merited the character. Let, then, the world see that she can bear prosperity: and that her honest virtue in time of peace, is equal to the bravest virtue in time of war.

She is now descending to the scenes of quiet and domestic life. Not beneath the cypress shade of disappointment, but to enjoy in her own land, and under her own vine, the sweet of her labors, and the reward of her toil. – In this situation, may she never forget that a fair national reputation is of as much importance as independence. That it possesses a charm that wins upon the world, and makes even enemies civil. That it gives a dignity which is often superior to power, and commands reverence where pomp and splendor fail.

It would be a circumstance ever to be lamented and never to be forgotten, were a single blot, from any cause whatever, suffered to fall on a revolution, which to the end of time must be an honor to the age that accomplished it: and which has contributed more to enlighten the world, and diffuse a spirit of freedom and liberality among mankind, than any human event (if this may be called one) that ever preceded it.

It is not among the least of the calamities of a long continued war, that it unhinges the mind from those nice sensations which at other times appear so amiable. The continual spectacle of woe blunts the finer feelings, and the necessity of bearing with the sight, renders it familiar. In like manner, are many of the moral obligations of society weakened, till the custom of acting by necessity becomes an apology, where it is truly a crime. Yet let but a nation conceive rightly of its character, and it will be chastely just in protecting it. None ever began with a fairer than America and none can be under a greater obligation to preserve it.

The debt which America has contracted, compared with the cause she has gained, and the advantages to flow from it, ought scarcely to be mentioned. She has it in her choice to do, and to live as happily as she pleases. The world is in her hands. She has no foreign power to monopolize her commerce, perplex her legislation, or control her prosperity. The struggle is over, which must one day have happened, and, perhaps, never could have happened at a better time.[*] And instead of a domineering master, she has

---

[*] That the revolution began at the exact period of time best fitted to the purpose, is sufficiently proved by the event. – But the great hinge on which the whole machine turned, is the *Union of the States:* and this union was naturally produced by the inability of any one state to support itself against any foreign enemy without the assistance of the rest.

gained an *ally* whose exemplary greatness, and universal liberality, have extorted a confession even from her enemies.

With the blessings of peace, independence, and an universal commerce, the states, individually and collectively, will have leisure and opportunity to regulate and establish their domestic concerns, and to put it beyond the power of calumny to throw the least reflection on their honor. Character is much easier kept than recovered, and that man, if any such there be, who, from sinister views, or littleness of soul, lends unseen his hand to injure it, contrives a wound it will never be in his power to heal.

As we have established an inheritance for posterity, let that inheritance descend, with every mark of an honorable conveyance. The little it will cost, compared with the worth of the states, the greatness of the object, and the value of the national character, will be a profitable exchange.

But that which must more forcibly strike a thoughtful, penetrating mind, and which includes and renders easy all inferior concerns, is the UNION OF THE STATES. On this our great national character depends. It is this which must give us importance abroad and security at home. It is through this only that we are, or can be, nationally known in the world; it is the flag of the United States which renders our ships and commerce safe on the seas, or in a foreign port. Our Mediterranean passes must be obtained under the same style. All our treaties, whether of alliance, peace, or commerce, are formed under the sovereignty of the United States, and Europe knows us by no other name or title.

Had the states severally been less able than they were when the war began, their united strength would not have been equal to the undertaking, and they must in all human probability have failed. – And, on the other hand, had they severally been more able, they might not have seen, or, what is more, might not have felt, the necessity of uniting: and, either by attempting to stand alone or in small confederacies would have been separately conquered.

Now, as we cannot see a time (and many years must pass away before it can arrive) when the strength of any one state, or several united, can be equal to the whole of the present United States, and as we have seen the extreme difficulty of collectively prosecuting the war to a successful issue, and preserving our national importance in the world, therefore, from the experience we have had, and the knowledge we have gained, we must, unless we make a waste of wisdom, be strongly impressed with the advantage, as well as the necessity of strengthening that happy union which had been our salvation, and without which we should have been a ruined people.

The division of the empire into states is for our own convenience, but abroad this distinction ceases. The affairs of each state are local. They can go no further than to itself. And were the whole worth of even the richest of them expended in revenue, it would not be sufficient to support sovereignty against a foreign attack. In short, we have no other national sovereignty than as United States. It would even be fatal for us if we had – too expensive to be maintained, and impossible to be supported. Individuals, or individual states, may call themselves what they please; but the world, and especially the world of enemies, is not to be held in awe by the whistling of a name. Sovereignty must have power to protect all the parts that compose and constitute it: and as UNITED STATES we are equal to the importance of the title, but otherwise we are not. Our union, well and wisely regulated and cemented, is the cheapest way of being great – the easiest way of being powerful, and the happiest invention in government which the circumstances of America can admit of. – Because it collects from each state, that which, by being inadequate, can be of no use to it, and forms an aggregate that serves for all.

The states of Holland are an unfortunate instance of the effects of individual sovereignty. Their disjointed condition exposes them to numerous intrigues, losses, calamities, and enemies; and the almost impossibility of bringing their measures to a decision, and that decision into execution, is to them, and would be to us, a source of endless misfortune.

It is with confederated states as with individuals in society; something must be yielded up to make the whole secure. In this view of things we gain by what we give, and draw an annual interest greater than the capital. – I ever feel myself hurt when I hear the union, that great palladium of our liberty and safety, the least irreverently spoken of. It is the most sacred thing in the constitution of America, and that which every man should be most proud and tender of. Our citizenship in the United States is our national character. Our citizenship in any particular state is only our local distinction. By the latter we are known at home, by the former to the world. Our great title is AMERICANS – our inferior one varies with the place.

It was the cause of America that made me an author. The force with which it struck my mind, and the dangerous condition the country appeared to me in, by courting an impossible and an unnatural reconciliation with those who were determined to reduce her, instead of striking out into the only line that could cement and save her, A DECLARATION OF INDEPENDENCE, made it impossible for me, feeling as I did, to be silent: and if, in the course of more than seven years, I have rendered her any service, I have likewise added something to the reputation of literature, by freely and disinterestedly employing it in the great cause of mankind, and showing that there may be genius without prostitution.

But as the scenes of war are closed, and every man preparing for home and happier times, I therefore take my leave of the subject. I have most sincerely followed it from beginning to end, and through all its turns and windings: and whatever country I may hereafter be in, I shall always feel an honest pride at the part I have taken and acted, and a gratitude to nature and providence for putting it in my power to be of some use to mankind.

COMMON SENSE
PHILADELPHIA, April 19, 1783

[ETP]

The United States and Great Britain, Treaty of Peace

1783

Cornwallis surrendered Oct. 19, 1781, and Feb. 27, 1782, Parliament voted against continuing the American War. Lord North's ministry went out and the new administration dispatched Richard Oswald to negotiate peace with Benjamin Franklin at Paris. The negotiations extended from April till Nov. 30, 1782, when the provisional or preliminary articles of peace were signed. These articles were "to be inserted in and constitute the treaty of peace" which should be concluded when Great Britain and France should have arranged terms of peace. The definitive treaty was signed as below, Sept. 3, 1783.

— Note by Howard W. Preston

DEFINITIVE TREATY OF PEACE BETWEEN THE UNITED STATES OF AMERICA AND HIS BRITANNIC MAJESTY. CONCLUDED SEPTEMBER 3, 1783.

IN THE NAME of the Most Holy and Undivided Trinity.

It having pleased the Divine Providence to dispose the heart of the most serene and most potent Prince George the Third, by the Grace of God King of Great Britain, France and Ireland, Defender of the Faith, Duke of Brunswick and Luneburg, Arch-Treasurer and Prince Elector of the Holy Roman Empire, &ca., and of the United States of America, to forget all past misunderstandings and differences that have unhappily interrupted the good correspondence and friendship which they mutually wish to re-store; and to establish such a beneficial and satisfactory intercourse between the two countries, upon the ground of reciprocal advantages and mutual convenience, as may promote and secure to both perpetual peace and harmony: And having for this desirable end already laid the foundation of peace and reconciliation, by the provisional articles, signed at Paris on the 30th of Nov'r, 1782, by the commissioners empowered on each part, which articles were agreed to be inserted in and to constitute the treaty of peace proposed to be concluded between the Crown of Great Britain and the said United States, but which treaty was not to be concluded until terms of peace should be agreed upon between Great Britain and France, and His Britannic Majesty should be ready to conclude such treaty accordingly; and the treaty between Great Britain and France having since been concluded, His Britannic Majesty and the United States of America, in order to carry into full effect the provisional articles above mentioned, according to the tenor thereof, have constituted and appointed, that is to say, His Britannic Majesty on his part, David Hartley, esqr., member of the Parliament of Great Britain; and the said United States on their part, John Adams, esqr., late a commissioner of the United States of America at the Court of Versailles, late Delegate in Congress from the State of Massachusets, and chief justice of the said State, and Minister Plenipotentiary of the said United States to their High Mightinesses the States General of the United Netherlands; Benjamin Franklin, esq're, late Delegate in Congress, from the State of Pennsylvania, president of the convention of the said State, and Minister Plenipotentiary from the United States of America at the Court of Versailles; John Jay, esq're, late president of Congress, and chief justice of the State of New York, and Minister Plenipotentiary from the said United States at the Court of Madrid, to be the Plenipotentiaries for the concluding and signing the present definitive treaty; who, after having reciprocally communicated their respective full powers, have agreed upon and confirmed the following articles:

ARTICLE I.

HIS Britannic Majesty acknowledges the said United States, viz. New Hampshire, Massachusetts Bay, Rhode Island, and Providence Plantations, Connecticut, New York, New Jersey, Pennsylvania, Delaware, Maryland, Virginia, North Carolina, South Carolina, and Georgia, to be free, sovereign and independent States; that he treats with them as such, and for himself, his heirs and successors, relinquishes all claims to the Government, propriety and territorial rights of the same, and every part thereof.

ARTICLE II.

AND that all disputes which might arise in future, on the subject of the boundaries of the United States may be prevented, it is hereby agreed and declared, that the following are, and shall be their boundaries, viz : From the north-west angle of Nova Scotia, viz. that angle which is formed by a line drawn due north from the source of Saint Croix River to the Highlands; along the said Highlands which divide those rivers that empty themselves into the river St. Lawrence, from those which fall into the Atlantic Ocean, to the northwesternmost head of Connecticut River; thence down along the middle of that river, to the forty-fifth degree of north latitude; from thence, by a line due west on the said latitude, until it strikes the river Iroquois or Cataraquy; thence along the middle of said river into Lake Ontario, through the middle of said lake until it strikes the communication by water between that lake and Lake Erie; thence along the middle of said communication into Lake Erie, through the middle of said lake until it arrives at the water communication between that lake and Lake Huron; thence along the middle of said water communication into the Lake Huron; thence through the middle of said lake to the water communication between that lake and Lake Superior; thence through Lake Superior northward of the Isles Royal and Philipeaux, to the Long Lake; thence through the middle of said Long Lake, and the water communication between it and the Lake of the Woods, to the said Lake of the Woods; thence through the said lake to the most northwestern point thereof, and from thence on a due west course to the river Mississippi; thence by a line to be drawn along the middle of the said river Mississippi until it shall intersect the northernmost part of the thirty-first degree of north latitude. South, by a line to be drawn due east from the determination of the line last mentioned, in the latitude of thirty-one degrees north of the Equator, to the middle of the river Apalachicola or Catahouche; thence along the middle thereof to its junction with the Flint River; thence strait to the head of St. Mary's River; and thence down along the middle of St. Mary's River to the Atlantic Ocean. East, by a line to be drawn along the middle of the river St. Croix, from its mouth in the Bay of Fundy to its source, and from its source directly north to the aforesaid Highlands, which divide the rivers that fall into the Atlantic Ocean from those which fall into the river St. Lawrence; comprehending all islands within twenty leagues of any part of the shores of the United States, and lying between lines to be drawn due east from the points where the aforesaid boundaries between Nova Scotia on the one part, and East Florida on the other, shall respectively touch the Bay of Fundy and the Atlantic Ocean; excepting such islands as now are, or heretofore have been, within the limits of the said province of Nova Scotia.

ARTICLE III.

IT is agreed that the people of the United States shall continue to enjoy unmolested the right to take fish of every kind on the Grand Bank, and on all the other banks of Newfoundland; also in the Gulph of Saint Lawrence, and at all other places in the sea where the inhabitants of both countries used at any time heretofore to fish. And also that the inhabitants of the United States shall have liberty to take fish of every kind on such part of the coast of Newfoundland as British fishermen shall use (but not to dry or cure the same on that island) and also on the coasts, bays, and creeks of all other of His Britannic Majesty's dominions in America; and that the American fishermen shall have liberty to dry and cure fish in any of the unsettled bays, harbours, and creeks of Nova Scotia, Magdalen Islands, and Labrador, so long as the same shall remain unsettled; but so soon as the same or either of them shall be settled, it shall not be lawful for the said fishermen to dry or cure fish at such settlement, without a previous agreement for that purpose with the inhabitants, proprietors, or possessors of the ground.

ARTICLE IV.

IT is agreed that creditors on either side shall meet with no lawful impediment to the recovery of the full value in sterling money, of all bona fide debts heretofore contracted.

ARTICLE V.

IT is agreed that the Congress shall earnestly recommend it to the legislatures of the respective States, to provide for the restitution of all estates, rights, and properties which have been confiscated, belonging to real British subjects, and also of the estates, rights, and properties of persons resident in districts in the possession of His Majesty's arms, and who have not borne arms against the said United States. And that persons of any other description shall have free liberty to go to any part or parts of any of the thirteen United States, and therein to remain twelve months, unmolested in their endeavors to obtain the restitution of such of their estates, rights, and properties as may have been confiscated; and that Congress shall also earnestly recommend to the several States a reconsideration and revision of all acts or laws regarding the premises, so as to render the said laws or acts perfectly consistent, not only with justice and equity but with that spirit of conciliation which, on the return of the blessings of peace, should universally prevail. And that Congress shall also earnestly recommend to the several States, that the estates, rights, and properties of such last mentioned persons, shall be restored to them, they refunding to any persons who may be now in possession, the bona fide price (where any has been given) which such persons may have paid on purchasing any of the said lands, rights, or properties, since the confiscation. And it is agreed, that all persons who have any interest in confiscated lands, either by debts, marriage settlements, or otherwise, shall meet with no lawful impediment in the prosecution of their just rights.

ARTICLE VI.

THAT there shall be no future confiscations made, nor any prosecutions commenc'd, against any person or persons for, or by reason of the part which he or they may have taken in the present war; and that no person shall, on that account, suffer any future loss or damage, either in his person, liberty or property; and that those who may be in confinement on such charges, at the time of the ratification of the treaty in America, shall be immediately set at liberty, and the prosecutions so commenced be discontinued.

ARTICLE VII.

THERE shall be a firm and perpetual peace between His Britannic Majesty and the said States, and between the subjects of the one and the citizens of the other, wherefore all hostilities, both by sea and land, shall from henceforth cease: All prisoners on both sides shall be set at liberty, and His Britannic Majesty shall, with all convenient speed, and without causing any destruction, or carrying away any negroes or other property of the American inhabitants, withdraw all his armies, garrisons, and fleets from the said United States, and from every port, place, and harbour within the same; leaving in all fortifications the American artillery that may be therein: And shall also order and cause all archives, records, deeds, and papers, belonging to any of the said States, or their citizens, which in the course of the war, may have fallen into the hands of his officers, to be forthwith restored and delivered to the proper States and persons to whom they belong.

ARTICLE VIII.

THE navigation of the river Mississippi, from its source to the ocean, shall forever remain free and open to the subjects of Great Britain, and the citizens of the United States.

ARTICLE IX.

IN case it should so happen that any place or territory belonging to Great Britain or to the United States, should have been conquer'd by the arms of either from the other, before the arrival of the said provisional articles in America, it is agreed, that the same shall be restored without difficulty, and without requiring any compensation.

ARTICLE X.

THE solemn ratifications of the present treaty, expedited in good and due form, shall be exchanged between the contracting parties, in the space of six months, or sooner if possible, to be computed from the day of the signature of the present treaty. In witness whereof, we the undersigned, their Ministers Plenipotentiary, have in their name and in virtue of our full powers, signed with our hands the present definitive treaty, and caused the seals of our arms to be affix'd thereto.

Done at Paris, this third day of September, in the year of our Lord one thousand seven hundred and eighty-three.

D. HARTLEY. [L. S.]
JOHN ADAMS. [L. S.]
B. FRANKLIN. [L. S.]
JOHN JAY. [L. S.]

The Early Republic
and the Constitution

James Madison, Memoranda on "Vices of the Political System of the United States"

April 1787

On account of his penetrating analysis here and elsewhere of the defects of the Articles of Confederation, his drafting of the Virginia Plan, his theories of political science and shrewd compromises at the Federal Convention, his authorship of many of the Federalist Papers, *and finally his agile defense of the Constitution at Virginia's Ratifying Convention in June 1788, James Madison (1751–1836) is justifiably regarded as "The Father of the Constitution." He became the fourth President of the United States in 1809.*

1. FAILURE OF THE States to comply with the Constitutional requisitions.

   This evil has been so fully experienced both during the war and since the peace, results so naturally from the number and independent authority of the States and has been so uniformly exemplified in every similar Confederacy, that it may be considered as not less radically and permanently inherent in, than it is fatal to the object of, the present system.

2. Encroachments by the States on the federal authority.

   Examples of this are numerous and repetitions may be foreseen in almost every case where any favorite object of a State shall present a temptation. Among these examples are the wars and Treaties of Georgia with the Indians—the unlicensed compacts between Virginia and Maryland, and between

Pennsylvania and New Jersey—the troops raised and to be kept up by Massachusetts.

3. Violations of the law of nations and of treaties.

From the number of legislatures, the sphere of life from which most of their members are taken, and the circumstances under which their legislative business is carried on, irregularities of this kind must frequently happen. Accordingly not a year has passed without instances of them in some one or other of the States. The treaty of peace—the treaty with France—the treaty with Holland have each been violated. The causes of these irregularities must necessarily produce frequent violations of the law of nations in other respects.

As yet foreign powers have not been rigorous in animadverting on us. This moderation however cannot be mistaken for a permanent partiality to our faults, or a permanent security against those disputes with other nations, which being among the greatest of public calamities, it ought to be least in the power of any part of the community to bring on the whole.

4. Trespasses of the States on the rights of each other.

These are alarming symptoms, and may be daily apprehended as we are admonished by daily experience. See the law of Virginia restricting foreign vessels to certain ports—of Maryland in favor of vessels belonging to her own citizens—of New York in favor of the same.

Paper money, installments of debts, occlusion of courts, making property a legal tender, may likewise be deemed aggressions on the rights of other States. As the citizens of every State aggregately taken stand more or less in the relation of creditors or debtors, to the citizens of every other States, acts of the debtor State in favor of debtors, affect the creditor State, in the same manner, as they do its own citizens who are relatively creditors towards other citizens. This remark may be extended to foreign nations. If the exclusive regulation of the value and alloy of coin was properly delegated to the federal authority, the policy of it equally requires a control on the States in the cases above mentioned. It must have been meant

1. to preserve uniformity in the circulating medium throughout the nation.

2. to prevent those frauds on the citizens of other States, and the subjects of foreign powers, which might disturb the tranquility at home, or involve the Union in foreign contests.

The practice of many States in restricting the commercial intercourse with other States, and putting their productions and manufactures on the same footing with those of foreign nations, though not contrary to the federal articles, is certainly adverse to the spirit of the Union, and tends to beget retaliating regulations, not less expensive and vexatious in themselves, than they are destructive of the general harmony.

5. Want of concert in matters where common interest requires it.

This defect is strongly illustrated in the state of our commercial affairs. How much has the national dignity, interest, and revenue suffered from this cause? Instances of inferior moment are the want of uniformity in the laws concerning naturalization and literary property; of provision for national seminaries, for grants of incorporation for national purposes, for canals and other works of general utility, which may at present be defeated by the perverseness of particular States whose concurrence is necessary.

6. Want of guaranty to the States of their Constitutions and laws against internal violence.

The confederation is silent on this point and therefore by the second article the hands of the federal authority are tied. According to republican theory, right and power being both vested in the majority, are held to be synonymous. According to fact and experience a minority may in an appeal to force, be an overmatch for the majority.

1. If the minority happen to include all such as possess the skill and habits of military life, and such as possess the great pecuniary resources, one third only may conquer the remaining two thirds.

2. One third of those who participate in the choice of the rulers may be rendered a majority by the accession of those whose poverty excludes them from a right of suffrage, and who for obvious reasons will be more likely to join the standard of sedition than that of the established government.

3. Where slavery exists the republican theory becomes still more fallacious.

7. Want of sanction to the laws, and of coercion in the Government of the Confederacy.

A sanction is essential to the idea of law, as coercion is to that of government. The federal system being destitute of both, wants the great vital principles of a political constitution. Under the form of such a constitution, it is in fact nothing more than a treaty of amity of commerce and of alliance between so many independent and sovereign States. From what cause could so fatal an omission have happened in the Articles of Confederation? From a mistaken confidence that the justice, the good faith, the honor, the sound policy, of the several legislative assemblies would render superfluous any appeal to the ordinary motives by which the laws secure the obedience of individuals: a confidence which does honor to the enthusiastic virtue of the compilers, as much as the inexperience of the crisis apologizes for their errors. The time which has since elapsed has had the double effect, of increasing the light, and tempering the warmth, with which the arduous work may be revised. It is no longer doubted that a unanimous and punctual obedience of 13 independent bodies, to the acts of the federal government, ought not be calculated on. Even during the war, when external danger supplied in some degree the defect of legal and coercive sanctions, how imperfectly did the States fulfill their obligations to the Union? In time of peace, we see already what is to be expected. How indeed could it be otherwise?

In the first place, every general act of the Union must necessarily bear unequally hard on some particular member or members of it.

Secondly, the partiality of the members to their own interests and rights, a partiality which will be fostered by the courtiers of popularity, will naturally exaggerate the inequality where it exists, and even suspect it where it has no existence.

Thirdly, a distrust of the voluntary compliance of each other may prevent the compliance of any, although it should be the latent disposition of all. Here are causes and pretexts which will never fail to render federal measures abortive. If the laws of the States were merely recommendatory to their citizens, or if they were to be rejudged by county authorities, what security, what probability would exist, that they would be carried into execution? Is the security or probability greater in favor of the acts of Congress which depending for their execution on the will of the state legislatures, which are though nominally authoritative, in fact recommendatory only.

8. Want of ratification by the people of the Articles of Confederation.

In some of the States the Confederation is recognized by, and forms a part of, the Constitution. In others however it has received no other sanction than that of the legislative authority. From this defect two evils result:

1. Whenever a law of a State happens to be repugnant to an act of Congress, particularly when the latter is of posterior date to the former, it will be at least questionable whether the latter must not prevail; and as the question must be decided if by the Tribunals of the State, they will be most likely to lean on the side of the State.

2. As far as the Union of the States is to be regarded as a league of sovereign powers, and not as a political constitution by virtue of which they are become one sovereign power, so far it seems to follow from the doctrine of compacts, that a breach of any of the articles of the confederation by any of the parties to it, absolves the other parties from their respective obligations, and gives them a right if they choose to exert it, of dissolving the Union altogether.

9. Multiplicity of laws in the several States.

In developing the evils which vitiate the political system of the U.S., it is proper to include those which are found within the States individually, as well as those which directly affect the States collectively, since the former class have an indirect influence on the general malady and must not be overlooked in forming a complete remedy. Among the evils then of our situation may well be ranked the multiplicity of laws from which no State is exempt. As far as laws are necessary, to mark with precision the duties of those who are to obey them, and to take from those who are to administer them a discretion, which might be abused, their number is the price of liberty. As far as the laws exceed this limit, they are a nuisance: a nuisance of the most pestilent kind. Try the codes of the several States by this test, and what a luxuriance of legislation do they present. The short period of independency has filled as many pages as the century which preceded it. Every year, almost every session, adds a new volume. This may be the effect in part, but it can only be in part, of the situation in which the revolution has placed us. A review of the several codes will show that every necessary and useful part of the least voluminous of them might be compressed into one tenth of the compass, and at the same time be rendered tenfold as perspicuous.

10. Mutability of the laws of the States.

This evil is intimately connected with the former yet deserves a distinct notice as it emphatically denotes a vicious legislation. We daily see laws repealed or superseded, before any trial can have been made of their merits: and even before knowledge of them can have reached the remoter districts within which they were to operate. In the regulations of trade this instability becomes a snare not only to our citizens but to foreigners also.

11. Injustice of the laws of States.

If the multiplicity and mutability of laws prove a want of wisdom, their injustice betrays a defect still more alarming: more alarming not merely because it is a greater evil in itself, but because it brings more into question the fundamental principle of republican government, that the majority who rule in such governments, are the safest guardians both of public good and of private rights. To what causes is this evil to be ascribed?
These causes lie:
1. In the representative bodies.
2. In the people themselves.
   1. Representative appointments are sought from three motives.
      1. ambition
      2. personal interest.
      3. public good.
         Unhappily the two first are proved by experience to be most prevalent. Hence the candidates who feel them, particularly, the second, are most industrious, and most successful in pursuing their object: and forming often a majority in the legislative councils, with interested views, contrary to the interest, and views, of their constituents, join in a perfidious sacrifice of the latter to the former. A succeeding election it might be supposed, would displace the offenders, and repair the mischief. But how easily are base and selfish measures, masked by pretexts of

public good and apparent expediency? How frequently will a repetition of the same arts and industry which succeeded in the first instance, again prevail on the unwary to misplace their confidence?

How frequently too will the honest but unenlightened representative be the dupe of a favorite leader, veiling his selfish views under the professions of public good, and varnishing his sophistical arguments with the glowing colors of popular eloquence?

2. A still more fatal if not more frequent cause lies among the people themselves. All civilized societies are divided into different interests and factions, as they happen to be creditors or debtors——Rich or poor——husbandmen, merchants or manufacturers——members of different religious sects——followers of different political leaders——inhabitants of different districts——owners of different kinds of property etc., etc. In republican government the majority, however composed, ultimately give the law. Whenever therefore an apparent interest or common passion unites a majority what is to restrain them from unjust violations of the rights and interests of the minority, or of individuals? Three motives only:

1. A prudent regard to their own good as involved in the general and permanent good of the community. This consideration although of decisive weight in itself, is found by experience to be too often unheeded. It is too often forgotten, by nations as well as by individuals that honesty is the best policy.

2. Respect for character. However strong this motive may be in individuals, it is considered as very insufficient to restrain them from injustice. In a multitude its efficacy is diminished in proportion to the number which is to share the praise or the blame. Besides, as it has reference to public opinion, which within a particular society is the opinion of the majority, the standard is fixed by those whose conduct is to be measured by it. The public opinion without the society will be little respected by the people at large of any country. Individuals of extended views, and of national pride, may bring the public proceedings to this standard, but the example will never be followed by the multitude. Is it to be imagined

that an ordinary citizen or even an assemblyman of Rhode Island in estimating the policy of paper money, ever considered or cared in what light the measure would be viewed in France or Holland; or even in Massachusetts or Connecticut? It was a sufficient temptation to both that it was for their interest: it was a sufficient sanction to the latter that it was popular in the state; to the former that it was so in the neighborhood.

3. Will religion, the only remaining motive, be a sufficient restraint? It is not pretended to be such on men individually considered. Will its effect be greater on them considered in an aggregate view? Quite the reverse. The conduct of every popular assembly acting on oath, the strongest of religious ties, proves that individuals join without remorse in acts, against which their consciences would revolt if proposed to them under the like sanction, separately in their closets. When indeed religion is kindled into enthusiasm, its force like that of other passions is increased by the sympathy of a multitude. But enthusiasm is only a temporary state of religion, and while it lasts will hardly be seen with pleasure at the helm of government. Besides as religion in its coolest state is not infallible, it may become a motive to oppression as well as a restraint from injustice. Place three individuals in a situation wherein the interest of each depends on the voice of the others, and give to two of them an interest opposed to the rights of the third? Will the latter be secure? The prudence of every man would shun the danger. The rules and forms of justice suppose and guard against it. Will two thousand in a like situation be less likely to encroach on the rights of one thousand? The contrary is witnessed by the notorious factions and oppressions which take place in corporate towns limited as the opportunities are, and in little republics when uncontrolled by apprehensions of external danger. If an enlargement of the sphere is found to lessen the insecurity of private rights, it is not because the impulse of a common interest or passion is less predominant in this case with the majority; but because a common interest or passion is less apt to be

felt and the requisite combinations less easy to be formed by a great than by a small number. The society becomes broken into a greater variety of interests, of pursuits, of passions, which check each other, whilst those who may feel a common sentiment have less opportunity of communication and concert. It may be inferred that the inconveniences of popular states contrary to the prevailing theory are in proportion not to the extent, but to the narrowness of their limits.

The great desideratum in government is such a modification of the sovereignty as will render it sufficiently neutral between the different interests and factions, to control one part of the society from invading the rights of another and at the same time sufficiently controlled itself, from setting up an interest adverse to that of the whole society. In absolute monarchies, the prince is sufficiently neutral towards his subjects, but frequently sacrifices their happiness to his ambition or his avarice. In small republics, the sovereign will is sufficiently controlled from such a sacrifice of the entire society, but is not sufficiently neutral towards the parts composing it. As a limited monarchy tempers the evils of an absolute one, so an extensive republic meliorates the administration of a small republic.

An auxiliary desideratum for the melioration of the republican form is such a process of elections as will most certainly extract from the mass of the society the purest and noblest characters which it contains; such as will at once feel most strongly the proper motives to pursue the end of their appointment, and be most capable to devise the proper means of attaining it.

12. Impotence of the laws of the States.

[USC]

Edmund Randolph, The "Virginia Plan" Offered to the Federal Convention

May 29, 1787

James Madison prepared this plan, essentially a first draft of the Constitution, but Edmund Randolph, the governor of Virginia, presented it. In its course over the next few months, the Virginia Plan would be challenged, revised, and modified in many details, but its primary direction remained.

FEDERAL CONVENTION, PHILADELPHIA

1. *RESOLVED, THAT THE* Articles of the Confederation ought to be so corrected and enlarged as to accomplish the objects proposed by their institution; namely, common defence, security of liberty, and general welfare.

2. *Resolved,* therefore, That the right of suffrage, in the national legislature, ought to be proportioned to the quotas of contribution, or to the number of free inhabitants, as the one or the other may seem best, in different cases.

3. *Resolved,* That the national legislature ought to consist of two branches.

4. *Resolved,* That the members of the first branch of national legislature ought to be elected by the people of the several states, every ____, for the term of ____, to be of the age of ____ years, at least; to receive liberal stipends, by which they may be compensated for the devotion of their time to the public service; to be ineligible to any office established by a particular state, or under the authority of the United States (except those peculiarly belonging to

the functions of the first branch) during the term of service and for the space of _____ after its expiration; to be incapable of reelection for the space of _____ after the expiration of their term of service; and to be subject to recall.

5. *Resolved,* That the members of the second branch of the national legislature ought to be elected by those of the first, out of a proper number of persons nominated by the individual legislatures, to be of the age of _____ years, at least; to hold their offices for a term sufficient to insure their independency; to receive liberal stipends, by which they may be compensated for the devotion of their time to the public service; and to be ineligible to any office established by a particular state, or under the authority of the United States (except those particularly belonging to the functions of the second branch) during the term of service; and for the space of _____ after the expiration thereof.

6. *Resolved,* That each branch ought to possess the right of originating acts; that the national legislature ought to be empowered to enjoy the legislative right vested in Congress by the Confederation; and, moreover, to legislate in all cases to which the separate states are incompetent, or in which the harmony of the United States may be interrupted by the exercise of individual legislation; to negative all laws passed by the several states, contravening, in the opinion of the national legislature, the articles of union, or any treaty subsisting under the authority of the Union; and to call forth the force of the Union against any member of the Union failing to fulfill its duty under the articles thereof.

7. *Resolved,* That a national executive be instituted, to be chosen by the national legislature for the term of _____ years, to receive punctually, at stated times, a fixed compensation for the services rendered, in which no increase or diminution shall be made, so as to affect the magistracy existing at the time of the increase or diminution; to be ineligible a second time; and that, besides a general authority to execute the national laws, it ought to enjoy the executive rights vested in Congress by the Confederation.

8. *Resolved,* That the executive, and a convenient number of the national judiciary, ought to compose a council of revision, with authority to examine every act of the national legislature, before it shall operate, and every act of a particular legislature, before a negative thereon shall be final; and that the dissent of the said council shall amount to a rejection, unless the act of the national legislature

be again passed, or that of a particular legislature be again negative by ____ of the members of each branch.

9. *Resolved,* That a national judiciary be established to hold their office during good behavior, and to receive punctually, at stated times, a fixed compensation for their services, in which no increase or diminution shall be made, so as to affect the persons actually in office at the time of such increase or diminution. That the jurisdiction of the inferior tribunals shall be to hear and determine in the first instance, and of the supreme tribunal to hear and determine in the *dernier resort,* all piracies and felonies on the seas; captures from an enemy; cases in which foreigners, or citizens of other states, applying to such jurisdictions, may be interested, or which respect the collection of the national revenue; impeachments of any national officer; and questions which involve the national peace or harmony.

10. *Resolved,* That provision ought to be made for the admission of states, lawfully arising within the limits of the United States, whether from a voluntary junction of government or territory, or otherwise, with the consent of a number of voices in the national legislature less than the whole.

11. *Resolved,* That a republican government and the territory of each state (except in the instance of a voluntary junction of government and territory) ought to be guarantied by the United States to each state.

12. *Resolved,* That provision ought to be made for the continuance of Congress, and their authorities and privileges, until a given day, after the reform of the articles of union shall be adopted, and for the completion of all their engagements.

13. *Resolved,* That provision ought to be made for the amendment of the articles of union, whenever it shall seem necessary; and that the assent of the national legislature ought not to be required thereto.

14. *Resolved,* That the legislative, executive, and judiciary powers within the several states ought to be bound by oath to support the articles of union.

15. *Resolved,* That the amendments, which shall be offered to the Confederation by the Convention, ought, at a proper time or times, after the approbation of Congress, to be submitted to an assembly or assemblies of representatives, recommended by the several legislatures, to be expressly chosen by the people to consider and decide thereon.

[USC]

Gunning Bedford of Delaware, Speech in Debate in the Constitutional Convention on Small States Versus the Large States

June 30, 1787

The "Great Compromise" (or Connecticut Compromise) that would come on July 16 involved apportioning equal representation in the Senate and proportional representation in the House of Representatives. Gunning Bedford, Jr., was a lawyer with a hot-tempered manner that riled some of his colleagues at the Convention. In this impassioned speech, he gave voice, in any case, to the concerns of the smaller states and eventually helped Delaware become the first state to ratify the Constitution.

FEDERAL CONVENTION, PHILADELPHIA

THAT ALL THE states at present are equally sovereign and independent has been asserted from every quarter of this house. Our deliberations here are a confirmation of the position; and I may add to it, that each of them acts from interested and many from ambitious motives. Look at the votes which have been given on the floor of this house, and it will be found that their numbers, wealth, and local views have actuated their determinations, and that the larger states proceed as if our eyes were already perfectly blinded. Impartiality, with them, is already out of the question; the reported plan is their political creed, and they support it, right or wrong. Even the diminutive state of Georgia has an eye to her future wealth and greatness. South Carolina, puffed up with the possession of her wealth and negroes, and North Carolina are all, from different views, united with the great states. And these latter, although it is said they can never from interested views form a coalition, we find closely united in one scheme of interest and ambition (notwithstanding they endeavor to amuse us with the purity of their principle and the rectitude of their intentions) in asserting that the general government must be drawn from an equal representation of the people.

Pretenses to support ambition are never wanting. Their cry is, "Where is the danger?" And they insist that although the powers of the general government will be increased, yet it will be for the good of the whole; and although the three great states form nearly a majority of the people of America, they never will hurt or injure the lesser states. I do not, gentlemen, trust you. If you possess the power, the abuse of it could not be checked; and what then would prevent you from exercising it to our destruction? You gravely allege that there is no danger of combination, and triumphantly ask, "How could combinations be effected? The large states," you say, "all differ in productions and commerce; and experience shows that, instead of combinations, they would be rivals, and counteract the views of one another." This, I repeat, is language calculated only to amuse us. Yes, sir, the larger states will be rivals, but not against each other—they will be rivals against the rest of the states. But it is urged that such a government would suit the people, and that its principles are equitable and just. How often has this argument been refuted, when applied to a federal government! The small states never can agree to the Virginia plan; and why, then, is it still urged? But it is said that it is not expected that the state governments will approve the proposed system, and that this house must directly carry it to the people for their approbation! Is it come to this, then, that the sword must decide this controversy, and that the horrors of war must be added to the rest of our misfortunes? But what have the people already said? "We find the Confederation defective. Go, and give additional powers to the Confederation—give to it the imposts, regulation of trade, power to collect the taxes, and the means to discharge our foreign and domestic debts."

Can we not, then, as their delegates, agree upon these points? As their ambassadors, can we not clearly grant those powers? Why, then, when we are met, must entire distinct and new grounds be taken, and a government of which the people had no idea be instituted? And are we to be told, if we won't agree to it, it is the last moment of our deliberations? I say, it is indeed the last moment, if we do not agree to this assumption of power. The states will never again be entrapped into a measure like this. The people will say, The small states would confederate, and grant further powers to Congress; but you, the large states, would not. Then the fault would be yours, and all the nations of the earth will justify us. But what is to become of our public debts, if we dissolve the Union? Where is your plighted faith? Will you crush the smaller states, or must they be left unmolested? Sooner than be ruined, there are foreign powers who will take us by the hand.

I say not this to threaten or intimidate, but that we should reflect seriously before we act. If we once leave this floor, and solemnly renounce your new project, what will be the consequence? You will annihilate your federal government, and ruin must stare you in the face. Let us, then, do what is in our power—amend and enlarge the Confederation, but not alter the federal system. The people expect this, and no more. We all agree in the necessity of a more efficient government—and cannot this be done? Although my state is small, I know and respect its rights as much, at least, as those who have the honor to represent any of the larger states.

[USC]

Northwest Ordinance

July 13, 1787

On the same day (March 1, 1784) that Virginia ceded her western territory to Congress, Thomas Jefferson reported in Congress a plan for the temporary government of this newly acquired territory. Among its provisions was the prohibition of slavery after 1800, but this clause was cancelled. The measure passed April 23, 1784. From this time many plans were reported by various committees, but no definite action was taken till 1787, when, on July 13, the "Ordinance for the Government of the Territory of the United States north-west of the river Ohio" was passed. This ordinance, even when ordered to a third reading, did not contain, [wrote Peter Force], "those great principles for which it has since been distinguished as one of the greatest monuments of civil jurisprudence," above all the prohibition of slavery, which Mr. Dane, of Massachusetts, offered as an amendment, July 12.

"The ordinance of 1787, in particular, deserves to rank among immortal parchments both for what it accomplished and what it inspired. Nor would it be wild hyperbole to opine that save for the adoption and unflinching execution of that ordinance by Congress in early times, the American Union would ere to-day have found a grave," [wrote James Schouler].

In 1790 this ordinance, excepting certain clauses, was extended to the territory south of the river Ohio.

— Note by Howard W. Preston

THE NORTHWEST TERRITORIAL GOVERNMENT

[THE CONFEDERATE CONGRESS]

AN ORDINANCE FOR the government of the territory of the United States northwest of the river Ohio.

SECTION 1. *Be it ordained by the United States in Congress assembled,* That the said Territory, for the purpose of temporary government, be one district, subject, however, to be divided into two districts, as future circumstances may, in the opinion of Congress, make it expedient.

SEC. 2. *Be it ordained by the authority aforesaid,* That the estates both of resident and non-resident proprietors in the said territory, dying intestate, shall descend to, and be distributed among, their children and the descendants of a deceased child in equal parts, the descendants of a deceased child or grandchild to take the share of their deceased parent in equal parts among them; and where there shall be no children or descendants, then in equal parts to the next of kin, in equal degree; and among collaterals, the children of a deceased brother or sister of the intestate shall have, in equal parts among them, their deceased parent's share; and there shall, in no case, be a distinction between kindred of the whole and half blood; saving in all cases to the widow of the intestate, her third part of the real estate for life, and one-third part of the personal estate; and this law relative to descents and dower, shall remain in full force until altered by the legislature of the district. And until the governor and judges shall adopt laws as hereinafter mentioned, estates in the said territory may be devised or bequeathed by wills in writing, signed and sealed by him or her in whom the estate may be, (being of full age,) and attested by three witnesses; and real estates may be conveyed by lease and release, or bargain and sale, signed, sealed, and delivered by the person, being of full age, in whom the estate may be, and attested by two witnesses, provided such wills be duly proved, and such conveyances be acknowledged, or the execution thereof duly proved, and be recorded within one year after proper magistrates, courts, and registers, shall be appointed for that purpose; and personal property may be transferred by delivery, saving, however, to the French and Canadian inhabitants, and other settlers of the Kaskaskies, Saint Vincents, and the neighboring villages, who have heretofore professed themselves citizens of Virginia, their laws and customs now in force among them, relative to the descent and conveyance of property.

SEC. 3. *Be it ordained by the authority aforesaid,* That there shall be appointed, from time to time, by Congress, a governor, whose commission shall continue in force for the term of three years, unless sooner revoked by Congress; he shall reside in the district, and have a freehold estate therein, in one thousand acres of land, while in the exercise of his office.

SEC. 4. There shall be appointed from time to time, by Congress, a secretary, whose commission shall continue in force for four years, unless sooner revoked; he shall reside in the district, and have a freehold estate therein, in five hundred acres of land, while in the exercise of his office. It shall be his duty to keep and preserve the acts and laws passed by the legislature, and the public records of the district, and the proceedings of the governor in his executive department, and transmit authentic copies of such acts and proceedings every six months to the Secretary of Congress. There shall also be appointed a court, to consist of three judges, any two of whom to form a court, who shall have a common-law jurisdiction and reside in the district, and have each therein a freehold estate, in five hundred acres of land, while in the exercise of their offices; and their commissions shall continue in force during good behavior.

SEC. 5. The governor and judges, or a majority of them, shall adopt and publish in the district such laws of the original States, criminal and civil, as may be necessary, and best suited to the circumstances of the district, and report them to Congress from time to time, which laws shall be in force in the district until the organization of the general assembly therein, unless disapproved of by Congress; but afterwards the legislature shall have authority to alter them as they shall think fit.

SEC. 6. The governor, for the time being, shall be commander-in-chief of the militia, appoint and commission all officers in the same below the rank of general officers; all general officers shall be appointed and commissioned by Congress.

SEC. 7. Previous to the organization of the general assembly the governor shall appoint such magistrates, and other civil officers, in each county or township, as he shall find necessary for the preservation of the peace and good order in the same. After the general assembly shall be organized the powers and duties of magistrates and other civil officers shall be regulated and defined by the said assembly; but all magistrates and other civil officers, not herein otherwise directed, shall, during the continuance of this temporary government, be appointed by the governor.

SEC. 8. For the prevention of crimes, and injuries, the laws to be adopted or made shall have force in all parts of the district, and for the execution of process, criminal and civil, the governor shall make proper divisions thereof; and he shall proceed, from time to time, as circumstances may require, to lay out the parts of the district in which the Indian titles shall have been extinguished, into counties and townships, subject, however, to such alterations as may thereafter be made by the legislature.

SEC. 9. So soon as there shall be five thousand free male inhabitants, of full age, in the district, upon giving proof thereof to the governor, they shall receive authority, with time and place, to elect representatives from their counties or townships, to represent them in the general assembly: *Provided,* That for every five hundred free male inhabitants there shall be one representative, and so on, progressively, with the number of free male inhabitants, shall the right of representation increase, until the number of representatives shall amount to twenty-five; after which the number and proportion of representatives shall be regulated by the legislature; *Provided,* That no person be eligible or qualified to act as a representative, unless he shall have been a citizen of one of the United States three years, and be a resident in the district, or unless he shall have resided in the district three years; and, in either case, shall likewise hold in his own right, in fee-simple, two hundred acres of land within the same: *Provided also,* That a freehold in fifty acres of land in the district, having been a citizen of one of the States, and being resident in the district, or the like freehold and two years' residence in the district, shall be necessary to qualify a man as an elector of a representative.

SEC. 10. The representatives thus elected shall serve for the term of two years; and in case of the death of a representative, or removal from office, the governor shall issue a writ to the county or township, for which he was a member, to elect another in his stead, to serve for the residue of the term.

SEC. 11. The general assembly, or legislature, shall consist of the governor, legislative council, and a house of representatives. The legislative council shall consist of five members, to continue in office five years, unless sooner removed by Congress; any three of whom to be a quorum; and the members of the council shall be nominated and appointed in the following manner, to wit:

As soon as representatives shall be elected the governor shall appoint a time and place for them to meet together, and when met they shall nominate ten persons, resident in the district, and each possessed of a freehold in five hundred acres of land, and return their names to Congress, five of whom Congress shall appoint and commission to serve as aforesaid; and whenever a vacancy shall happen in the council, by death or removal from office, the house of representatives shall nominate two persons, qualified as aforesaid, for each vacancy, and return their names to Congress, one of whom Congress shall appoint and commission for the residue of the term; and every five years, four months at least before the expiration of the time of service of the members of the council, the said house shall nominate ten persons, qualified as aforesaid, and return their names to Congress, five of whom Congress shall appoint and commission to serve as members of the council five years, unless sooner removed. And the governor, legislative council, and house of representatives shall have authority to make laws in all cases for the good government of the district, not repugnant to the principles and articles in this ordinance established and declared. And all bills, having passed by a majority in the house, and by a majority in the council, shall be referred to the governor for his assent; but no bill, or legislative act whatever, shall be of any force without his assent. The governor shall have power to convene, prorogue, and dissolve the general assembly when, in his opinion, it shall be expedient.

SEC. 12. The governor, judges, legislative council, secretary, and such other officers as Congress shall appoint in the district, shall take an oath or affirmation of fidelity, and of office; the governor before the President of Congress, and all other officers before the governor. As soon as a legislature shall be formed in the district, the council and house assembled, in one room, shall have authority, by joint ballot, to elect a delegate to Congress, who shall have a seat in Congress, with a right of debating, but not of voting, during this temporary government.

SEC. 13. And for extending the fundamental principles of civil and religious liberty, which form the basis whereon these republics, their laws and constitutions, are erected; to fix and establish those principles as the basis of all laws, constitutions, and governments, which forever hereafter shall be formed in the said territory; to provide, also, for the establishment of States, and permanent government therein, and for their admission to a share in the Federal councils on an equal footing with the original States, at as early periods as may be consistent with the general interest:

SEC. 14. It is hereby ordained and declared, by the authority aforesaid, that the following articles shall be considered as articles of compact, between the original States and the people and States in the said territory, and forever remain unalterable, unless by common consent, to wit:

ARTICLE I.

No person, demeaning himself in a peaceable and orderly manner, shall ever be molested on account of his mode of worship, or religious sentiments, in the said territory.

ARTICLE II.

The inhabitants of the said territory shall always be entitled to the benefits of the writs of *habeas corpus,* and of the trial by jury; of a proportionate representation of the people in the legislature, and of judicial proceedings according to the course of the common law. All persons shall be bailable, unless for capital offences, where the proof shall be evident, or the presumption great. All fines shall be moderate; and no cruel or unusual punishments shall be inflicted. No man shall be deprived of his liberty or property, but by the judgment of his peers, or the law of the land, and should the public exigencies make it necessary, for the common preservation, to take any person's property, or to demand his particular services, full compensation shall be made for the same. And, in the just preservation of rights and property, it is understood and declared, that no law ought ever to be made or have force in the said territory, that shall, in any manner whatever, interfere with or affect private contracts, or engagements, *bona fide,* and without fraud previously formed.

ARTICLE III.

Religion, morality, and knowledge being necessary to good government and the happiness of mankind, schools and the means of education shall forever be encouraged. The utmost good faith shall always be observed towards the Indians; their lands and property shall never be taken from them without their consent; and in their property, rights, and liberty they never shall be invaded or disturbed, unless in just and lawful wars authorized by Congress; but laws founded in justice and humanity shall, from time to time, be made, for preventing wrongs being done to them, and for preserving peace and friendship with them.

ARTICLE IV.

The said territory, and the States which may be formed therein, shall forever remain a part of this confederacy of the United States of America, subject to the articles of Confederation, and to such alterations therein as shall be constitutionally made; and to all the acts and ordinances of the United States in Congress assembled, conformable thereto. The inhabitants and settlers in the said territory shall be subject to pay a part of the Federal debts, contracted, or to be contracted, and a proportional part of the expenses of government to be apportioned on them by Congress, according to the same common rule and measure by which apportionments thereof shall be made on the other States; and the taxes for paying their proportion shall be laid and levied by the authority and direction of the legislatures of the district, or districts, or new States, as in the original States, within the time agreed upon by the United States in Congress assembled. The legislatures of those districts, or new States, shall never interfere with the primary disposal of the soil by the United States in Congress assembled, nor with any regulations Congress may find necessary for securing the title in such soil to the *bona-fide* purchasers. No tax shall be imposed on lands the property of the United States; and in no case shall non-resident proprietors be taxed higher than residents. The navigable waters leading into the Mississippi and Saint Lawrence, and the carrying places between the same, shall be common highways, and forever free, as well to the inhabitants of the said territory as to the citizens of the United States, and those of any other States that may be admitted into the confederacy, without any tax, impost, or duty therefor.

ARTICLE V.

There shall be formed in the said territory not less than three nor more than five States; and the boundaries of the States, as soon as

Virginia shall alter her act of cession and consent to the same, shall become fixed and established as follows, to wit: The western State, in the said territory, shall be bounded by the Mississippi, the Ohio, and the Wabash Rivers; a direct line drawn from the Wabash and Post Vincents, due north, to the territorial line between the United States and Canada; and by the said territorial line to the Lake of the Woods and Mississippi. The middle State shall be bounded by the said direct line, the Wabash from Post Vincents to the Ohio, by the Ohio, by a direct line drawn due north from the mouth of the Great Miami to the said territorial line, and by the said territorial line. The eastern State shall be bounded by the last-mentioned direct line, the Ohio, Pennsylvania, and the said territorial line: *Provided, however,* And it is further understood and declared, that the boundaries of these three States shall be subject so far to be altered, that, if Congress shall hereafter find it expedient, they shall have authority to form one or two States in that part of the said territory which lies north of an east and west line drawn through the southerly bend or extreme of Lake Michigan. And whenever any of the said States shall have sixty thousand free inhabitants therein, such State shall be admitted by its delegates, into the Congress of the United States, on an equal footing with the original States, in all respects whatever; and shall be at liberty to form a permanent constitution and State government: *Provided,* The constitution and government, so to be formed, shall be republican, and in conformity to the principles contained in these articles, and, so far as it can be consistent with the general interest of the confederacy, such admission shall be allowed at an earlier period, and when there may be a less number of free inhabitants in the State than sixty thousand.

ARTICLE VI.

There shall be neither slavery nor involuntary servitude in the said territory, otherwise than in the punishment of crimes, whereof the party shall have been duly convicted: *Provided always,* That any person escaping into the same, from whom labor or service is lawfully claimed in any one of the original States, such fugitive may be lawfully reclaimed, and conveyed to the person claiming his or her labor or service as aforesaid.

Be it ordained by the authority aforesaid, That the resolutions of the 23d of April, 1784, relative to the subject of this ordinance, be, and the same are hereby, repealed, and declared null and void.

Done by the United States, in Congress assembled, the 13th day of July, in the year of our Lord 1787, and of their sovereignty and independence the twelfth.

[DIH]

Luther Martin, John Rutledge, George Mason, Charles Pinckney, and Others, Debate in the Constitutional Convention on the Slave Trade

August 21–22, 1787

FEDERAL CONVENTION, PHILADELPHIA

Article I, Section 9, of the Constitution ("The Migration or Importation of such Persons as any of the States now existing shall think proper to admit, shall not be prohibited by the Congress prior to the Year one thousand eight hundred and eight, but a Tax or duty may be imposed on such Importation, not exceeding ten dollars for each Person") does not contain the words "slavery" or "slave," in part because slavery was even then a shameful practice, highlighting all by itself the hypocrisy of the enlightened Christian men of the Constitutional Convention, many of whom prided themselves on having fought for independence and individual liberty. Representatives from South Carolina, notably Charles Pinckney, threatened that attempts to outlaw or limit slavery would dissolve South Carolina's, North Carolina's, and Georgia's agreement to the new document. Several delegates advocated ducking this topic as a moral issue, preferring to proceed as if slavery were an entrenched, untouchable business and that the people enslaved could be considered when divvying political power (the infamous "three-fifths" rule) but not as individual souls.

Tuesday, August 21

ON THE QUESTION on Article 7, Section 4, as far as to "no tax shall be laid on exports," it passed in the affirmative,—

Massachusetts, Connecticut, Maryland, Virginia (General Washington and Mr. Madison, *no*), North Carolina, South Carolina, Georgia, *aye*—seven; New Hampshire, New Jersey, Pennsylvania, Delaware, *no*—four.

MR. L. MARTIN proposed to vary Article 7, Section 4, so as to allow a prohibition or tax on the importation of slaves. In the first place, as five slaves are to be counted as three freemen, in the apportionment of Representatives, such a clause would leave an encouragement to this traffic. In the second place, slaves weakened one part of the Union, which the other parts were bound to protect; the privilege of importing them was therefore unreasonable. And in the third place, it was inconsistent with the principles of the revolution, and dishonorable to the American character, to have such a feature in the Constitution.

MR. RUTLEDGE did not see how the importation of slaves could be encouraged by this section. He was not apprehensive of insurrections, and would readily exempt the other states from the obligation to protect the Southern against them. Religion and humanity had nothing to do with this question. Interest alone is the governing principle with nations. The true question at present is, whether the Southern states shall or shall not be parties to the Union. If the Northern states consult their interest, they will not oppose the increase of slaves, which will increase the commodities of which they will become the carriers.

MR. ELLSWORTH was for leaving the clause as it stands. Let every state import what it pleases. The morality or wisdom of slavery are considerations belonging to the states themselves. What enriches a part enriches the whole, and the states are the best judges of their particular interest. The old Confederation had not meddled with this point; and he did not see any greater necessity for bringing it within the policy of the new one.

MR. PINCKNEY. South Carolina can never receive the plan if it prohibits the slave-trade. In every proposed extension of the powers of Congress, that state has expressly and watchfully excepted that of meddling with the importation of negroes. If the states be all left at liberty on this subject, South Carolina may perhaps, by degrees, do of herself what is wished, as Virginia and Maryland already have done. Adjourned.

Wednesday, August 22

In Convention.—Article 7, Section 4, was resumed.

MR. SHERMAN was for leaving the clause as it stands. He disapproved of the slave trade; yet as the states were now possessed of the right to import slaves, as the public good did not require it to be taken from them, and as it was expedient to have as few objections as possible to the proposed scheme of government, he thought it best to leave the matter as we find it. He observed that the abolition of slavery seemed to be going on in the United States, and that the good sense of the several states would probably by degrees complete it. He urged on the Convention the necessity of dispatching its business.

MR. MASON. This infernal traffic originated in the avarice of British Merchants. The British government constantly checked the attempts of Virginia to put a stop to it. The present question concerns not the importing states alone but the whole Union. The evil of having slaves was experienced during the late war. Had slaves been treated as they might have been by the enemy, they would have proved dangerous instruments in their hands. But their folly dealt by the slaves, as it did by the Tories. He mentioned the dangerous insurrections of the slaves in Greece and Sicily; and the instructions given by Cromwell to the commissioners sent to Virginia to arm the servants and slaves, in case other means of obtaining its submission should fail. Maryland and Virginia, he said, had already prohibited the importation of slaves expressly. North Carolina had done the same in substance. All this would be in vain if South Carolina and Georgia be at liberty to import. The Western people are already calling out for slaves for their new lands, and will fill that country with slaves if they can be got through South Carolina and Georgia. Slavery discourages arts and manufactures. The poor despise labor when performed by slaves. They prevent the immigration of Whites, who really enrich and strengthen a country. They produce the most pernicious effect on manners. Every master of slaves is born a petty tyrant. They bring the judgment of heaven on a country. As nations can not be rewarded or punished in the next world they must be in this. By an inevitable chain of causes and effects providence punishes national sins by national calamities. He lamented that some of our Eastern brethren had from a lust of gain embarked in this nefarious traffic. As to the states being in possession of the right to import, this was the case with many other rights, now to be properly given up. He held it essential in every point of view that the general government should have power to prevent the increase of slavery.

MR. ELLSWORTH, as he had never owned a slave, could not judge of the effects of slavery on character. He said, however, that if it was to be considered in a moral light, we ought to go further and free those already in the country. As slaves also multiply so fast in Virginia and Maryland that it is cheaper to raise than import them, whilst in the sickly rice-swamps foreign supplies are necessary; if we go no further than is urged, we shall be unjust towards South Carolina and Georgia. Let us not intermeddle. As population increases, poor laborers will be so plenty as to render slaves useless. *Slavery, in time, will not be a speck in our country.* Provision is already made in Connecticut for abolishing it; and the abolition has already taken place in Massachusetts. As to the danger of insurrections from foreign influence, that will become a motive to kind treatment of the slaves.

MR. [CHARLES] PINCKNEY. If slavery be wrong, it is justified by the example of the entire world. He cited the case of Greece, Rome, and other ancient states, the sanction given by France, England, Holland and other modern states. In all ages one half of mankind have been slaves. If the Southern states were let alone, they will probably of themselves stop importations. He would himself, as a citizen of South Carolina, vote for it. An attempt to take away the right, as proposed, will produce serious objections to the Constitution, which he wished to see adopted.

GEN. [CHARLES COTESWORTH] PINCKNEY declared it to be his firm opinion that if himself and all his colleagues were to sign the Constitution, and use their personal influence, it would be of no avail towards obtaining the assent of their constituents. South Carolina and Georgia cannot do without slaves. As to Virginia, she will gain by stopping the importations. Her slaves will rise in value, and she has more than she wants. It would be unequal to require South Carolina and Georgia to confederate on such unequal terms. He said, the royal assent, before the Revolution, had never been refused to South Carolina as to Virginia. He contended that the importation of slaves would be for the interest of the whole Union. The more slaves, the more produce to employ the carrying-trade; the more consumption also: and, the more of this, the more revenue for the common treasury. He admitted it to be reasonable that slaves should be dutied like other imports; but should consider a rejection of the clause as an exclusion of South Carolina from the Union.

MR. BALDWIN had conceived national objects alone to be before the Convention; not such as, like the present, were of a local nature. Georgia was decided on this point. That state has always hitherto supposed a general government to be the pursuit of the central states, who wished to have a vortex for everything; that her distance would preclude her, from equal advantage; and that she could not prudently purchase it by yielding national powers. From this it might be understood in what light she would view an attempt to abridge one of her favorite prerogatives. If left to herself, she may probably put a stop to the evil. As one ground for this conjecture, he took notice of the sect of _____, which he said was a respectable class of people, who carried their ethics beyond the mere *equality of men,* extending their humanity to the claims of the whole animal creation.

MR. WILSON observed that if South Carolina and Georgia were themselves disposed to get rid of the importation of slaves in a short time, as had been suggested, they would never refuse to unite because the importation might be prohibited. As the section now stands, all articles imported are to be taxed. Slaves alone are exempt. This is in fact a bounty on that article.

MR. GERRY thought we had nothing to do with the conduct of the states as to slaves, but ought to be careful not to give any sanction to it.

MR. DICKINSON considered it as inadmissible, on every principle of honor and safety, that the importation of slaves should be authorized to the states by the Constitution. The true question was, whether the national happiness would be promoted or impeded by the importation; and this question ought to be left to the national government, not to the states particularly interested. If England and France permit slavery, slaves are, at the same time, excluded from both those kingdoms. Greece and Rome were made unhappy by their slaves. He could not believe that the Southern states would refuse to confederate on the account apprehended; especially as the power was not likely to be immediately exercised by the general government.

MR. WILLIAMSON stated the law of North Carolina on the subject, to wit, that it did not directly prohibit the importation of slaves. It imposed a duty of £5 on each slave imported from Africa; £10 on each from elsewhere; and £50 on each from a state licensing manumission. He thought the Southern states could not be members of the Union, if the clause should be rejected; and that it was wrong to force anything down not absolutely necessary, and which any state must disagree to.

MR. KING thought the subject should be considered in a political light only. If two states will not agree to the Constitution, as stated on one side, he could affirm with equal belief, on the other, that great and equal opposition would be experienced from the other states. He remarked on the exemption of slaves from duty, whilst every other import was subjected to it, as an inequality that could not fail to strike the commercial sagacity of the Northern and Middle states.

MR. LANGDON was strenuous for giving the power to the general government. He could not, with a good conscience, leave it with the states, who could then go on with the traffic, without being restrained by the opinions here given, that they will themselves cease to import slaves.

GENERAL PINCKNEY thought himself bound to declare candidly that he did not think South Carolina would stop her importations of slaves, in any short time; but only stop them occasionally as she now does. He moved to commit the clause that slaves might be made liable to an equal tax with other imports, which he thought right, and which would remove one difficulty that had been started.

MR. RUTLEDGE. If the Convention thinks that North Carolina, South Carolina, and Georgia, will ever agree to the plan, unless their right to import slaves be untouched, the expectation is vain. The people of those states will never be such fools as to give up so important an interest. He was strenuous against striking out the section, and seconded the motion of General Pinckney for a commitment.

MR. GOUVERNEUR MORRIS wished the whole subject to be committed, including the clauses relating to taxes on exports and to a navigation act. These things may form a bargain among the Northern and Southern states.

MR. BUTLER declared that he never would agree to the power taxing exports.

MR. SHERMAN said it was better to let the Southern states import slaves than to part with them, if they made that a *sine qua non*. He was opposed to a tax on slaves imported, as making the matter worse, because it implied they were *property*. He acknowledged that if the power of prohibiting the importation should be given to the general government, that it would be exercised. He thought it would be its duty to exercise the power.

MR. READ was for the commitment, provided the clause concerning taxes on exports should also be committed.

MR. SHERMAN observed that that clause had been agreed to, and therefore could not be committed.

MR. RANDOLPH was for committing, in order that some middle ground might, if possible, be found. He could never agree to the clause as it stands. He would sooner risk the Constitution. He dwelt on the dilemma to which the convention was exposed. By agreeing to the clause, it would revolt the Quakers, the Methodists, and many others in states having no slaves. On the other hand, two states might be lost to the union. Let us then, he said, try the chance of a commitment.

On the question for committing the remaining part of Sections 4 and 5, of Article 7,—Connecticut, New Jersey, Maryland, Virginia, North Carolina, South Carolina, Georgia, *aye*—seven; New Hampshire, Pennsylvania, Delaware, *no*—eight; Massachusetts absent.

[USC]

Benjamin Franklin, Address to the Constitutional Convention

September 17, 1787

Benjamin Franklin (1706–1790) and George Washington (1732–1799) were the two most famous men in America recognized for their wisdom and leadership. On this, the final day of the Federal Convention, Franklin, apparently in ill health, asked his fellow Pennsylvania delegate James Wilson to read aloud these words for him to the Convention. Three delegates, in spite of Franklin's plea for unanimity, refused to sign.

FEDERAL CONVENTION, PHILADELPHIA

MR. PRESIDENT,

I confess that there are several parts of this constitution which I do not at present approve, but I am not sure I shall never approve them: For having lived long, I have experienced many instances of being obliged by better information, or fuller consideration, to change opinions even on important subjects, which I once thought right, but found to be otherwise. It is therefore that the older I grow, the more apt I am to doubt my own judgment, and to pay more respect to the judgment of others. Most men indeed, as well as most sects in religion, think themselves in possession of all truth, and that wherever others differ from them it is so far error. Steele, a Protestant, in a dedication tells the Pope that the only difference between our churches in their opinions of the certainty of their doctrines is, the Church of Rome is infallible and the Church of England is never in the wrong. But though many private persons think almost as highly of their own infallibility as of that of their sect, few express it so naturally as a certain French lady, who in a dispute with her sister, said, "I don't know how it happens, sister, but I meet with nobody but myself that's always in the right.—*Il n'y a que moi qui a toujours raison.*"

In these sentiments, sir, I agree to this Constitution with all its faults, if they are such; because I think a general government necessary for us, and there is no form of government but what may be a blessing to the people if well administered, and believe farther that this is likely to be well administered for a course of years, and can only end in despotism, as other forms have done before it, when the people shall become so corrupted as to need despotic government, being incapable of any other. I doubt too whether any other convention we can obtain may be able to make a better Constitution. For when you assemble a number of men to have the advantage of their joint wisdom, you inevitably assemble with those men all their prejudices, their passions, their errors of opinion, their local interests, and their selfish views. From such an assembly, can a perfect production be expected? It therefore astonishes me, sir, to find this system approaching so near to perfection as it does; and I think it will astonish our enemies, who are waiting with confidence to hear that our councils are confounded like those of the builders of Babel; and that our states are on the point of separation, only to meet hereafter for the purpose of cutting one another's throats. Thus I consent, sir, to this Constitution because I expect no better, and because I am not sure that it is not the best. The opinions I have had of its errors, I sacrifice to the public good. I have never whispered a syllable of them abroad. Within these walls they were born, and here they shall die. If every one of us in returning to our constituents were to report the objections he has had to it, and endeavor to gain partisans in support of them, we might prevent its being generally received, and thereby lose all the salutary effects and great advantages resulting naturally in our favor among foreign nations as well as among ourselves from our real or apparent unanimity. Much of the strength and efficiency of any government in procuring and securing happiness to the people, depends on opinion, on the general opinion of the goodness of the government, as well as of the wisdom and integrity of its governors. I hope therefore that for our own sakes as a part of the people, and for the sake of posterity, we shall act heartily and unanimously in recommending this Constitution (if approved by Congress and confirmed by the conventions) wherever our influence may extend, and turn our future thoughts and endeavors to the means of having it well administered.

On the whole, sir, I can not help expressing a wish that every member of the convention who may still have objections to it, would with me, on this occasion, doubt a little of his own infallibility, and to make manifest our unanimity, put his name to this instrument.

[USC]

The Constitution of the United States of America

September 17, 1787

The making of the Constitution is one of the most satisfying of American stories: through a summer's worth of debates and arguments in Philadelphia at the Constitutional Convention of 1787, the delegates presented to the states—and to history—the most effective national legal document ever created. "The American Constitution has functioned and endured longer than any other written constitution of the modern era. It imbues the nation with energy to act, at the same time restraining its agents from acting out of line," writes the scholar Richard B. Morris. "Above all, the Constitution is the mortar that binds the fifty-state edifice under the concept of federalism, the unifying symbol of a nation composed of many millions of people claiming different national origins, races, and religions."[1]

WE THE PEOPLE of the United States, in Order to form a more perfect Union, establish Justice, insure domestic Tranquility, provide for the common defence, promote the general Welfare, and secure the Blessings of Liberty to ourselves and our Posterity, do ordain and establish this Constitution for the United States of America.

ARTICLE. I.

Section. 1.

All legislative Powers herein granted shall be vested in a Congress of the United States, which shall consist of a Senate and House of Representatives.

---

[1] Richard B. Morris. *Witnesses at the Creation: Hamilton, Madison, Jay and the Constitution.* New York: Henry Holt. 1985. 3.

Section. 2.

The House of Representatives shall be composed of Members chosen every second Year by the People of the several States, and the Electors in each State shall have the Qualifications requisite for Electors of the most numerous Branch of the State Legislature.

No Person shall be a Representative who shall not have attained to the Age of twenty five Years, and been seven Years a Citizen of the United States, and who shall not, when elected, be an Inhabitant of that State in which he shall be chosen.

Representatives and direct Taxes shall be apportioned among the several States which may be included within this Union, according to their respective Numbers, which shall be determined by adding to the whole Number of free Persons, including those bound to Service for a Term of Years, and excluding Indians not taxed, three fifths of all other Persons. The actual Enumeration shall be made within three Years after the first Meeting of the Congress of the United States, and within every subsequent Term of ten Years, in such Manner as they shall by Law direct. The Number of Representatives shall not exceed one for every thirty Thousand, but each State shall have at Least one Representative; and until such enumeration shall be made, the State of New Hampshire shall be entitled to chuse three, Massachusetts eight, Rhode-Island and Providence Plantations one, Connecticut five, New-York six, New Jersey four, Pennsylvania eight, Delaware one, Maryland six, Virginia ten, North Carolina five, South Carolina five, and Georgia three.

When vacancies happen in the Representation from any State, the Executive Authority thereof shall issue Writs of Election to fill such Vacancies.

The House of Representatives shall chuse their Speaker and other Officers; and shall have the sole Power of Impeachment.

Section. 3.

The Senate of the United States shall be composed of two Senators from each State, chosen by the Legislature thereof for six Years; and each Senator shall have one Vote.

Immediately after they shall be assembled in Consequence of the first Election, they shall be divided as equally as may be into three Classes. The Seats of the Senators of the first Class shall be vacated at the Expiration of the second Year, of the second Class at the Expiration of the fourth Year, and of the third Class at the Expiration of the sixth Year, so that one third may be chosen every second Year; and if Vacancies happen by Resignation, or otherwise, during the Recess of the Legislature of any State, the Executive thereof may make temporary Appointments until the next Meeting of the Legislature, which shall then fill such Vacancies.

No Person shall be a Senator who shall not have attained to the Age of thirty Years, and been nine Years a Citizen of the United States, and who shall not, when elected, be an Inhabitant of that State for which he shall be chosen.

The Vice President of the United States shall be President of the Senate, but shall have no Vote, unless they are equally divided.

The Senate shall chuse their other Officers, and also a President pro tempore, in the Absence of the Vice President, or when he shall exercise the Office of President of the United States.

The Senate shall have the sole Power to try all Impeachments. When sitting for that Purpose, they shall be on Oath or Affirmation. When the President of the United States is tried, the Chief Justice shall preside: And no Person shall be convicted without the Concurrence of two thirds of the Members present.

Judgment in Cases of Impeachment shall not extend further than to removal from Office, and disqualification to hold and enjoy any Office of honor, Trust or Profit under the United States: but the Party convicted shall nevertheless be liable and subject to Indictment, Trial, Judgment and Punishment, according to Law.

Section. 4.

The Times, Places and Manner of holding Elections for Senators and Representatives, shall be prescribed in each State by the Legislature thereof; but the Congress may at any time by Law make or alter such Regulations, except as to the Places of chusing Senators.

The Congress shall assemble at least once in every Year, and such Meeting shall be on the first Monday in December, unless they shall by Law appoint a different Day.

Section. 5.

Each House shall be the Judge of the Elections, Returns and Qualifications of its own Members, and a Majority of each shall constitute a Quorum to do Business; but a smaller Number may adjourn from day to day, and may be authorized to compel the Attendance of absent Members, in such Manner, and under such Penalties as each House may provide.

Each House may determine the Rules of its Proceedings, punish its Members for disorderly Behaviour, and, with the Concurrence of two thirds, expel a Member.

Each House shall keep a Journal of its Proceedings, and from time to time publish the same, excepting such Parts as may in their Judgment require Secrecy; and the Yeas and Nays of the Members of either House on any question shall, at the Desire of one fifth of those Present, be entered on the Journal.

Neither House, during the Session of Congress, shall, without the Consent of the other, adjourn for more than three days, nor to any other Place than that in which the two Houses shall be sitting.

Section. 6.

The Senators and Representatives shall receive a Compensation for their Services, to be ascertained by Law, and paid out of the Treasury of the United States. They shall in all Cases, except Treason, Felony and Breach of the Peace, be privileged from Arrest during their Attendance at the Session of their respective Houses, and in going to and returning from the same; and for any Speech or Debate in either House, they shall not be questioned in any other Place.

No Senator or Representative shall, during the Time for which he was elected, be appointed to any civil Office under the Authority of the United States, which shall have been created, or the Emoluments whereof shall have been encreased during such time; and no Person holding any Office under the United States, shall be a Member of either House during his Continuance in Office.

Section. 7.

All Bills for raising Revenue shall originate in the House of Representatives; but the Senate may propose or concur with Amendments as on other Bills.

Every Bill which shall have passed the House of Representatives and the Senate, shall, before it become a Law, be presented to the President of the United States: If he approve he shall sign it, but if not he shall return it, with his Objections to that House in which it shall have originated, who shall enter the Objections at large on their Journal, and proceed to reconsider it. If after such Reconsideration two thirds of that House shall agree to pass the Bill, it shall be sent, together with the Objections, to the other House, by which it shall likewise be reconsidered, and if approved by two thirds of that House, it shall become a Law. But in all such Cases the Votes of both Houses shall be determined by yeas and Nays, and the Names of the Persons voting for and against the Bill shall be entered on the Journal of each House respectively. If any Bill shall not be returned by the President within ten Days (Sundays excepted) after it shall have been presented to him, the same shall be a Law, in like Manner as if he had signed it, unless the Congress by their Adjournment prevent its Return, in which Case it shall not be a Law.

Every Order, Resolution, or Vote to which the Concurrence of the Senate and House of Representatives may be necessary (except on a question of Adjournment) shall be presented to the President of the United States; and before the Same shall take Effect, shall be approved by him, or being disapproved by him, shall be repassed by two thirds of the Senate and House of Representatives, according to the Rules and Limitations prescribed in the Case of a Bill.

Section. 8.

The Congress shall have Power To lay and collect Taxes, Duties, Imposts and Excises, to pay the Debts and provide for the common Defence and general Welfare of the United States; but all Duties, Imposts and Excises shall be uniform throughout the United States;

To borrow Money on the credit of the United States;

To regulate Commerce with foreign Nations, and among the several States, and with the Indian Tribes;

To establish an uniform Rule of Naturalization, and uniform Laws on the subject of Bankruptcies throughout the United States;

To coin Money, regulate the Value thereof, and of foreign Coin, and fix the Standard of Weights and Measures;

To provide for the Punishment of counterfeiting the Securities and current Coin of the United States;

To establish Post Offices and post Roads;

To promote the Progress of Science and useful Arts, by securing for limited Times to Authors and Inventors the exclusive Right to their respective Writings and Discoveries;

To constitute Tribunals inferior to the Supreme Court;

To define and punish Piracies and Felonies committed on the high Seas, and Offences against the Law of Nations;

To declare War, grant Letters of Marque and Reprisal, and make Rules concerning Captures on Land and Water;

To raise and support Armies, but no Appropriation of Money to that Use shall be for a longer Term than two Years;

To provide and maintain a Navy;

To make Rules for the Government and Regulation of the land and naval Forces;

To provide for calling forth the Militia to execute the Laws of the Union, suppress Insurrections and repel Invasions;

To provide for organizing, arming, and disciplining, the Militia, and for governing such Part of them as may be employed in the Service of the United States, reserving to the States respectively, the Appointment of the Officers, and the Authority of training the Militia according to the discipline prescribed by Congress;

To exercise exclusive Legislation in all Cases whatsoever, over such District (not exceeding ten Miles square) as may, by Cession of particular States, and the Acceptance of Congress, become the Seat of the Government of the United States, and to exercise like Authority over all Places purchased by the Consent of the Legislature of the State in which the Same shall be, for the Erection of Forts, Magazines, Arsenals, dock-Yards, and other needful Buildings;—And

To make all Laws which shall be necessary and proper for carrying into Execution the foregoing Powers, and all other Powers vested by this Constitution in the Government of the United States, or in any Department or Officer thereof.

Section. 9.

The Migration or Importation of such Persons as any of the States now existing shall think proper to admit, shall not be prohibited by the Congress prior to the Year one thousand eight hundred and eight, but a Tax or duty may be imposed on such Importation, not exceeding ten dollars for each Person.

The Privilege of the Writ of Habeas Corpus shall not be suspended, unless when in Cases of Rebellion or Invasion the public Safety may require it.

No Bill of Attainder or ex post facto Law shall be passed.

No Capitation or other direct, Tax shall be laid, unless in Proportion to the Census or enumeration herein before directed to be taken.

No Tax or Duty shall be laid on Articles exported from any State.

No Preference shall be given by any Regulation of Commerce or Revenue to the Ports of one State over those of another; nor shall Vessels bound to, or from, one State, be obliged to enter, clear, or pay Duties in another.

No Money shall be drawn from the Treasury, but in Consequence of Appropriations made by Law; and a regular Statement and Account of the Receipts and Expenditures of all public Money shall be published from time to time.

No Title of Nobility shall be granted by the United States: And no Person holding any Office of Profit or Trust under them, shall, without the Consent of the Congress, accept of any present, Emolument, Office, or Title, of any kind whatever, from any King, Prince, or foreign State.

Section. 10.

No State shall enter into any Treaty, Alliance, or Confederation; grant Letters of Marque and Reprisal; coin Money; emit Bills of Credit; make any Thing but gold and silver Coin a Tender in Payment of Debts; pass any Bill of Attainder, ex post facto Law, or Law impairing the Obligation of Contracts, or grant any Title of Nobility.

No State shall, without the Consent of the Congress, lay any Imposts or Duties on Imports or Exports, except what may be absolutely necessary for executing it's inspection Laws: and the net Produce of all Duties and Imposts, laid by any State on Imports or Exports, shall be for the Use of the Treasury of the United States; and all such Laws shall be subject to the Revision and Control of the Congress.

No State shall, without the Consent of Congress, lay any Duty of Tonnage, keep Troops, or Ships of War in time of Peace, enter into any Agreement or Compact with another State, or with a foreign Power, or engage in War, unless actually invaded, or in such imminent Danger as will not admit of delay.

ARTICLE. II.

Section. 1.

The executive Power shall be vested in a President of the United States of America. He shall hold his Office during the Term of four Years, and, together with the Vice President, chosen for the same Term, be elected, as follows:

Each State shall appoint, in such Manner as the Legislature thereof may direct, a Number of Electors, equal to the whole Number of Senators and Representatives to which the State may be entitled in the Congress: but no Senator or Representative, or Person holding an Office of Trust or Profit under the United States, shall be appointed an Elector.

The Electors shall meet in their respective States, and vote by Ballot for two Persons, of whom one at least shall not be an Inhabitant of the same State with them. And they shall make a List of all the Persons voted for, and of the Number of Votes for each; which List they shall sign and certify, and transmit sealed to the Seat of the Government of the United States, directed to the President of the Senate. The President of the Senate shall, in the Presence of the Senate and House of Representatives, open all the Certificates, and the Votes shall then be counted. The Person having the greatest Number of Votes shall be the President, if such Number be a Majority of the whole Number of Electors appointed; and if there be more than one who have such Majority, and have an equal Number of Votes, then the House of Representatives shall immediately chuse by Ballot one of them for President; and if no Person have a Majority, then from the five highest on the List the said House shall in like Manner chuse the President. But in chusing the President, the Votes shall be taken by States, the Representation from each State having one Vote; a quorum for this purpose shall consist of a Member or Members from two thirds of the States, and a Majority of all the States shall be necessary to a Choice. In every Case, after the Choice of the President, the Person having the greatest Number of Votes of the Electors shall be the Vice President. But if there should remain two or more who have equal Votes, the Senate shall chuse from them by Ballot the Vice President.

The Congress may determine the Time of chusing the Electors, and the Day on which they shall give their Votes; which Day shall be the same throughout the United States.

No Person except a natural born Citizen, or a Citizen of the United States, at the time of the Adoption of this Constitution, shall be eligible to the Office of President; neither shall any Person be eligible to that Office who shall not have attained to the Age of thirty five Years, and been fourteen Years a Resident within the United States.

In Case of the Removal of the President from Office, or of his Death, Resignation, or Inability to discharge the Powers and Duties of the said Office, the Same shall devolve on the Vice President, and the Congress may by Law provide for the Case of Removal, Death, Resignation or Inability, both of the President and Vice President, declaring what Officer shall then act as President, and such Officer shall act accordingly, until the Disability be removed, or a President shall be elected.

The President shall, at stated Times, receive for his Services, a Compensation, which shall neither be increased nor diminished during the Period for which he shall have been elected, and he shall not receive within that Period any other Emolument from the United States, or any of them.

Before he enter on the Execution of his Office, he shall take the following Oath or Affirmation:—"I do solemnly swear (or affirm) that I will faithfully execute the Office of President of the United States, and will to the best of my Ability, preserve, protect and defend the Constitution of the United States."

Section. 2.

The President shall be Commander in Chief of the Army and Navy of the United States, and of the Militia of the several States, when called into the actual Service of the United States; he may require the Opinion, in writing, of the principal Officer in each of the executive Departments, upon any Subject relating to the Duties of their respective Offices, and he shall have Power to grant Reprieves and Pardons for Offences against the United States, except in Cases of Impeachment.

He shall have Power, by and with the Advice and Consent of the Senate, to make Treaties, provided two thirds of the Senators present concur; and he shall nominate, and by and with the Advice and Consent of the Senate, shall appoint Ambassadors, other public Ministers and Consuls, Judges of the supreme Court, and all other Officers of the United States, whose Appointments are not herein otherwise provided for, and which shall be established by Law: but the Congress may by Law vest the Appointment of such inferior Officers, as they think proper, in the President alone, in the Courts of Law, or in the Heads of Departments.

The President shall have Power to fill up all vacancies that may happen during the Recess of the Senate, by granting Commissions which shall expire at the End of their next Session.

Section. 3.

He shall from time to time give to the Congress Information of the State of the Union, and recommend to their Consideration such Measures as he shall judge necessary and expedient; he may, on extraordinary Occasions, convene both Houses, or either of them, and in Case of Disagreement between them, with Respect to the Time of Adjournment, he may adjourn them to such Time as he shall think proper; he shall receive Ambassadors and other public Ministers; he shall take Care that the Laws be faithfully executed, and shall Commission all the Officers of the United States.

Section. 4.

The President, Vice President and all civil Officers of the United States, shall be removed from Office on Impeachment for, and Conviction of, Treason, Bribery, or other high Crimes and Misdemeanors.

ARTICLE. III.

Section. 1.

The judicial Power of the United States shall be vested in one supreme Court, and in such inferior Courts as the Congress may from time to time ordain and establish. The Judges, both of the supreme and inferior Courts, shall hold their Offices during good Behaviour, and shall, at stated Times, receive for their Services a Compensation, which shall not be diminished during their Continuance in Office.

Section. 2.

The judicial Power shall extend to all Cases, in Law and Equity, arising under this Constitution, the Laws of the United States, and Treaties made, or which shall be made, under their Authority;—to all Cases affecting Ambassadors, other public Ministers and Consuls;—to all Cases of admiralty and maritime Jurisdiction;—to Controversies to which the United States shall be a Party;—to Controversies between two or more States;—between a State and

Citizens of another State;—between Citizens of different States;—between Citizens of the same State claiming Lands under Grants of different States, and between a State, or the Citizens thereof, and foreign States, Citizens or Subjects.

In all Cases affecting Ambassadors, other public Ministers and Consuls, and those in which a State shall be Party, the Supreme Court shall have original Jurisdiction. In all the other Cases before mentioned, the supreme Court shall have appellate Jurisdiction, both as to Law and Fact, with such Exceptions, and under such Regulations as the Congress shall make.

The Trial of all Crimes, except in Cases of Impeachment, shall be by Jury; and such Trial shall be held in the State where the said Crimes shall have been committed; but when not committed within any State, the Trial shall be at such Place or Places as the Congress may by Law have directed.

Section. 3.

Treason against the United States, shall consist only in levying War against them, or in adhering to their Enemies, giving them Aid and Comfort. No Person shall be convicted of Treason unless on the Testimony of two Witnesses to the same overt Act, or on Confession in open Court.

The Congress shall have Power to declare the Punishment of Treason, but no Attainder of Treason shall work Corruption of Blood, or Forfeiture except during the Life of the Person attainted.

ARTICLE. IV.

Section. 1.

Full Faith and Credit shall be given in each State to the public Acts, Records, and judicial Proceedings of every other State. And the Congress may by general Laws prescribe the Manner in which such Acts, Records and Proceedings shall be proved, and the Effect thereof.

Section. 2.

The Citizens of each State shall be entitled to all Privileges and Immunities of Citizens in the several States.

A Person charged in any State with Treason, Felony, or other Crime, who shall flee from Justice, and be found in another State, shall on Demand of the executive Authority of the State from which he fled, be delivered up, to be removed to the State having Jurisdiction of the Crime.

No Person held to Service or Labour in one State, under the Laws thereof, escaping into another, shall, in Consequence of any Law or Regulation therein, be discharged from such Service or Labour, but shall be delivered up on Claim of the Party to whom such Service or Labour may be due.

Section. 3.

New States may be admitted by the Congress into this Union; but no new State shall be formed or erected within the Jurisdiction of any other State; nor any State be formed by the Junction of two or more States, or Parts of States, without the Consent of the Legislatures of the States concerned as well as of the Congress.

The Congress shall have Power to dispose of and make all needful Rules and Regulations respecting the Territory or other Property belonging to the United States; and nothing in this Constitution shall be so construed as to Prejudice any Claims of the United States, or of any particular State.

Section. 4.

The United States shall guarantee to every State in this Union a Republican Form of Government, and shall protect each of them against Invasion; and on Application of the Legislature, or of the Executive (when the Legislature cannot be convened), against domestic Violence.

ARTICLE. V.

The Congress, whenever two thirds of both Houses shall deem it necessary, shall propose Amendments to this Constitution, or, on the Application of the Legislatures of two thirds of the several States, shall call a Convention for proposing Amendments, which, in either Case, shall be valid to all Intents and Purposes, as Part of this Constitution, when ratified by the Legislatures of three fourths of the several States, or by Conventions in three fourths thereof, as the one or the other Mode of Ratification may be proposed by the Congress; Provided that no Amendment which may be made prior to the Year One thousand eight hundred and eight shall in any

Manner affect the first and fourth Clauses in the Ninth Section of the first Article; and that no State, without its Consent, shall be deprived of its equal Suffrage in the Senate.

ARTICLE. VI.

All Debts contracted and Engagements entered into, before the Adoption of this Constitution, shall be as valid against the United States under this Constitution, as under the Confederation.

This Constitution, and the Laws of the United States which shall be made in Pursuance thereof; and all Treaties made, or which shall be made, under the Authority of the United States, shall be the supreme Law of the Land; and the Judges in every State shall be bound thereby, any Thing in the Constitution or Laws of any State to the Contrary notwithstanding.

The Senators and Representatives before mentioned, and the Members of the several State Legislatures, and all executive and judicial Officers, both of the United States and of the several States, shall be bound by Oath or Affirmation, to support this Constitution; but no religious Test shall ever be required as a Qualification to any Office or public Trust under the United States.

ARTICLE. VII.

The Ratification of the Conventions of nine States shall be sufficient for the Establishment of this Constitution between the States so ratifying the same.

The Word, "the," being interlined between the seventh and eighth Lines of the first Page, the Word "Thirty" being partly written on an Erazure in the fifteenth Line of the first Page, The Words "is tried" being interlined between the thirty second and thirty third Lines of the first Page and the Word "the" being interlined between the forty third and forty fourth Lines of the second Page.
Attest William Jackson Secretary

Done in Convention by the Unanimous Consent of the States present the Seventeenth Day of September in the Year of our Lord one thousand seven hundred and Eighty seven and of the Independence of the United States of America the Twelfth[.] In witness whereof We have hereunto subscribed our Names,

G°. *Washington Presidt and deputy from Virginia*

Delaware *Geo: Read Gunning Bedford jun John Dickinson Richard Bassett Jaco: Broom*
Maryland *James McHenry Dan of St Thos. Jenifer Danl. Carroll*
Virginia *John Blair James Madison Jr.*
North Carolina *Wm. Blount Richd. Dobbs Spaight Hu Williamson*
South Carolina *J. Rutledge Charles Cotesworth Pinckney Charles Pinckney Pierce Butler*
Georgia *William Few Abr Baldwin*
New Hampshire *John Langdon Nicholas Gilman*
Massachusetts *Nathaniel Gorham Rufus King*
Connecticut *Wm. Saml. Johnson Roger Sherman*
New York *Alexander Hamilton*
New Jersey *Wil: Livingston David Brearley Wm. Paterson Jona: Dayton*
Pennsylvania *B Franklin Thomas Mifflin Robt. Morris Geo. Clymer Thos. FitzSimons Jared Ingersoll James Wilson Gouv Morris*

[USC]

George Mason, Notes, Objections to the Constitution

October 1787

Virginia's George Mason (1725–1792), one of the most important and active delegates at the Convention, refused to sign the Constitution. As the author of Virginia's Declaration of Rights he had many fears about the absence of a bill of rights in this Constitution, and though he continued to oppose its ratification in Virginia, his objections helped prepare the way for the Bill of Rights in 1791. Mason wrote these notes on a rough draft of the Constitution.

THERE IS NO Declaration of Rights, and the laws of the general government being paramount to the laws and constitutions of the several states, the Declarations of Rights in the separate states are no security. Nor are the people secured even in the enjoyment of the benefits of the common law.

In the House of Representatives, there is not the substance, but the shadow only of representation; which can never produce proper information in the legislature, or inspire confidence in the people; the laws will therefore be generally made by men little concerned in, and unacquainted with their effects and consequences.

The Senate have the power of altering all money bills, and of originating appropriations of money, and the salaries of the officers of their own appointment, in conjunction with the president of the United States; although they are not the representatives of the people, or amenable to them.

These, with their other great powers (viz: their power in the appointment of ambassadors and all public officers, in making treaties, and in trying all impeachments), their influence upon and connection with the supreme executive from these causes, their duration of office, and their being a constant existing body, almost continually sitting, joined with their being one complete branch of the legislature will destroy any balance in the government, and enable them to accomplish what usurpations they please upon the rights and liberty of the people.

The judiciary of the United States is so constructed and extended, as to absorb and destroy the judiciaries of the several states; thereby rendering law as tedious, intricate and expensive, and justice as unattainable, by a great part of the community, as in England, and enabling the rich to oppress and ruin the poor.

The President of the United States has no constitutional council (a thing unknown in any safe and regular government); he will therefore be unsupported by proper information and advice; and will generally be directed by minions and favorites. Or he will become a tool to the Senate — or a council of state will grow out of the principal officers of the great departments; the worst and most dangerous of all ingredients for such a council, in a free country.

From this fatal defect has arisen the improper power of the Senate in the appointment of public officers, and the alarming dependence and connection between that branch of the legislature and the supreme executive.

Hence also sprung that unnecessary officer, the Vice-President; who for want of other employment is made President of the Senate; thereby dangerously blending the executive and legislative powers; besides always giving to some one of the states an unnecessary and unjust preeminence over the others.

The President of the United States has the unrestrained power of granting pardons for treason; which may be sometimes exercised to screen from punishment those whom he had secretly instigated to commit the crime, and thereby prevent a discovery of his own guilt.

By declaring all treaties supreme laws of the land, the executive and the Senate have in many cases an exclusive power of legislation; which might have been avoided by proper distinctions with respect to treaties, and requiring the assent of the House of Representatives, where it could be done, with safety.

By requiring a majority to make all commercial and navigation laws, the five Southern states (whose produce and circumstances are totally different from that of the eight Northern and Eastern states) may be ruined; for such rigid and premature regulations may be made, as will enable the merchants of the Northern and Eastern states not only to demand an exorbitant freight, but to monopolize the purchase of the commodities at their own price, for many years; to the great Injury of the landed interest, and impoverishment of the people; and the danger is the greater, as the gain on one side will be in proportion to the loss on the other. Whereas requiring two thirds of the members present in both Houses would have produced mutual moderation, promoted the general interest, and removed an insuperable objection to the adoption of this government.

Under their own construction of the general clause, at the end of the enumerated powers, the Congress may grant monopolies in trade and commerce, constitute new crimes, inflict unusual and severe punishments, and extend their powers as far as they shall think proper; so that the state legislatures have no security for their powers now presumed to remain to them, or the people for their rights.

There is no declaration of any kind, for preserving the liberty of the press, or the trial by jury in civil causes; nor against the danger of standing armies in time of peace.

The state legislatures are restrained from laying import duties on their own produce.

Both the general legislature★ and the state legislatures are expressly prohibited making ex post facto laws: though there never was, nor can be a legislature but must and will make such laws, when necessity and the public safety require them; which will hereafter be a breach of all the Constitutions in the Union, and afford precedents for other innovations.

This government will set out a moderate aristocracy: it is at present impossible to foresee whether it will, in its operation, produce a monarchy, or a corrupt tyrannical aristocracy; it will most probably vibrate some years between the two, and then terminate in the one or the other.

[USC]

★ *Mason's note:* The general Legislature is restrained from prohibiting the further Importation of Slaves for twenty odd years; tho' such Importations render the United States weaker, more vulnerable, and less capable of Defence.

James Madison, *The Federalist,* No. 10, "The Union as a Safeguard Against Domestic Faction and Insurrection"

November 22, 1787

The eighty-five essays that make up the Federalist Papers *were composed by John Jay, Alexander Hamilton, and James Madison to convince the voters of New York to ratify the Constitution. Though written for newspapers at the rate of two or three a week from the fall of 1787 into the late spring of 1788, their haste did not deter their power in fending off anti-Federalist attacks and illuminating every major point of the Constitution. Thomas Jefferson declared the collection "the best commentary on the principles of government which was ever written." This essay embodies some of Madison's boldest, most important ideas. (The originally untitled articles were all signed "Publius," as the team of authors sought to persuade voters without calling attention to each man's own, well-known, occasionally contradictory personal views.)*

To the People of the State of New York:

AMONG THE NUMEROUS advantages promised by a well-constructed Union, none deserves to be more accurately developed than its tendency to break and control the violence of faction. The friend of popular governments never finds himself so much alarmed for their character and fate, as when he contemplates their propensity to this dangerous vice. He will not fail, therefore, to set a due value on any plan which, without violating the principles to which he is attached, provides a proper cure for it. The instability, injustice, and confusion introduced into the public councils, have, in truth, been the mortal diseases under which popular governments have everywhere perished; as they continue to be the favorite and fruitful topics from which the adversaries to liberty derive their most specious declamations. The valuable improvements made by the American constitutions on the popular models, both ancient and modern, cannot certainly be too much admired; but it would be an unwarrantable partiality, to contend that they have as effectually obviated the danger on this side, as was wished and expected. Complaints are everywhere heard from our most considerate and virtuous citizens, equally the friends of public and private faith, and of public and personal liberty, that our governments are too unstable, that the public good is disregarded in the conflicts of rival parties, and that measures are too often decided, not according to the rules of justice and the rights of the minor party, but by the superior force of an interested and overbearing majority. However anxiously we may wish that these complaints had no foundation, the evidence, of known facts will not permit us to deny that they are in some degree true. It will be found, indeed, on a candid review of our situation, that some of the distresses under which we labor have been erroneously charged on the operation of our governments; but it will be found, at the same time, that other causes will not alone account for many of our heaviest misfortunes; and, particularly, for that prevailing and increasing distrust of public engagements, and alarm for private rights, which are echoed from one end of the continent to the other. These must be chiefly, if not wholly, effects of the unsteadiness and injustice with which a factious spirit has tainted our public administrations.

By a faction, I understand a number of citizens, whether amounting to a majority or a minority of the whole, who are united and actuated by some common impulse of passion, or of interest, adversed to the rights of other citizens, or to the permanent and aggregate interests of the community.

There are two methods of curing the mischiefs of faction: the one, by removing its causes; the other, by controlling its effects.

There are again two methods of removing the causes of faction: the one, by destroying the liberty which is essential to its existence; the other, by giving to every citizen the same opinions, the same passions, and the same interests.

It could never be more truly said than of the first remedy, that it was worse than the disease. Liberty is to faction what air is to fire, an aliment without which it instantly expires. But it could not be less folly to abolish liberty, which is essential to political life, because it nourishes faction, than it would be to wish the annihilation of air, which is essential to animal life, because it imparts to fire its destructive agency.

The second expedient is as impracticable as the first would be unwise. As long as the reason of man continues fallible, and he is at liberty to exercise it, different opinions will be formed. As long as the connection subsists between his reason and his self-love, his opinions and his passions will have a reciprocal influence on each other; and the former will be objects to which the latter will attach them. The diversity in the faculties of men, from which the rights of property originate, is not less an insuperable obstacle to a uniformity of interests. The protection of these faculties is the first object of government. From the protection of different and unequal faculties of acquiring property, the possession of different degrees and kinds of property immediately results; and from the influence of these on the sentiments and views of the respective proprietors, ensues a division of the society into different interests and parties.

The latent causes of faction are thus sown in the nature of man; and we see them everywhere brought into different degrees of activity, according to the different circumstances of civil society. A zeal for different opinions concerning religion, concerning government, and many other points, as well of speculation as of practice; an attachment to different leaders ambitiously contending for pre-eminence and power; or to persons of other descriptions whose fortunes have been interesting to the human passions, have, in turn, divided mankind into parties, inflamed them with mutual animosity, and rendered them much more disposed to vex and oppress each other than to co-operate for their common good. So strong is this propensity of mankind to fall into mutual animosities, that where no substantial occasion presents itself, the most frivolous and fanciful distinctions have been sufficient to kindle their unfriendly passions and excite their most violent conflicts. But the most common and durable source of factions has been the various and unequal distribution of property. Those who hold and those who are without property have ever formed distinct interests in society. Those who are creditors, and those who are debtors, fall under a like discrimination. A landed interest, a manufacturing interest, a mercantile interest, a moneyed interest, with many lesser interests, grow up of necessity in civilized nations, and divide them into different classes, actuated by different sentiments and views. The regulation of these various and interfering interests forms the principal task of modern legislation, and involves the spirit of party and faction in the necessary and ordinary operations of the government.

No man is allowed to be a judge in his own cause, because his interest would certainly bias his judgment, and, not improbably, corrupt his integrity. With equal, nay with greater reason, a body of men are unfit to be both judges and parties at the same time; yet what are many of the most important acts of legislation, but so many judicial determinations, not indeed concerning the rights of single persons, but concerning the rights of large bodies of citizens? And what are the different classes of legislators but advocates and parties to the causes which they determine? Is a law proposed concerning private debts? It is a question to which the creditors are parties on one side and the debtors on the other. Justice ought to hold the balance between them. Yet the parties are, and must be, themselves the judges; and the most numerous party, or, in other words, the most powerful faction must be expected to prevail. Shall domestic manufactures be encouraged, and in what degree, by restrictions on foreign manufactures? Are questions which would be differently decided by the landed and the manufacturing classes, and probably by neither with a sole regard to justice and the public good. The apportionment of taxes on the various descriptions of property is an act which seems to require the most exact impartiality; yet there is, perhaps, no legislative act in which greater opportunity and temptation are given to a predominant party to trample on the rules of justice. Every shilling with which they overburden the inferior number is a shilling saved to their own pockets.

It is in vain to say that enlightened statesmen will be able to adjust these clashing interests, and render them all subservient to the public good. Enlightened statesmen will not always be at the helm. Nor, in many cases, can such an adjustment be made at all without taking into view indirect and remote considerations, which will rarely prevail over the immediate interest which one party may find in disregarding the rights of another or the good of the whole.

The inference to which we are brought is, that the CAUSES of faction cannot be removed, and that relief is only to be sought in the means of controlling its EFFECTS.

If a faction consists of less than a majority, relief is supplied by the republican principle, which enables the majority to defeat its sinister views by regular vote. It may clog the administration, it may convulse the society; but it will be unable to execute and mask its violence under the forms of the Constitution. When a majority is included in a faction, the form of popular government, on the other hand, enables it to sacrifice to its ruling passion or interest both the public good and the rights of other citizens. To secure the public good and private rights against the danger of such a faction, and at the same time to preserve the spirit and the form of popular government, is then the great object to which our inquiries are directed. Let me add that it is the great desideratum by which this form of government can be rescued from the opprobrium under which it has so long labored, and be recommended to the esteem and adoption of mankind.

By what means is this object attainable? Evidently by one of two only. Either the existence of the same passion or interest in a majority at the same time must be prevented, or the majority, having such coexistent passion or interest, must be rendered, by their number and local situation, unable to concert and carry into effect schemes of oppression. If the impulse and the opportunity be suffered to coincide, we well know that neither moral nor religious motives can be relied on as an adequate control. They are not found to be such on the injustice and violence of individuals, and lose their efficacy in proportion to the number combined together, that is, in proportion as their efficacy becomes needful.

From this view of the subject it may be concluded that a pure democracy, by which I mean a society consisting of a small number of citizens, who assemble and administer the government in person, can admit of no cure for the mischiefs of faction. A common passion or interest will, in almost every case, be felt by a majority of the whole; a communication and concert result from the form of government itself; and there is nothing to check the inducements to sacrifice the weaker party or an obnoxious individual. Hence it is that such democracies have ever been spectacles of turbulence and contention; have ever been found incompatible with personal security or the rights of property; and have in general been as short in their lives as they have been violent in their deaths. Theoretic politicians, who have patronized this species of government, have erroneously supposed that by reducing mankind to a perfect equality in their political rights, they would, at the same time, be perfectly equalized and assimilated in their possessions, their opinions, and their passions.

A republic, by which I mean a government in which the scheme of representation takes place, opens a different prospect, and promises the cure for which we are seeking. Let us examine the points in which it varies from pure democracy, and we shall comprehend both the nature of the cure and the efficacy which it must derive from the Union.

The two great points of difference between a democracy and a republic are: first, the delegation of the government, in the latter, to a small number of citizens elected by the rest; secondly, the greater number of citizens, and greater sphere of country, over which the latter may be extended.

The effect of the first difference is, on the one hand, to refine and enlarge the public views, by passing them through the medium of a chosen body of citizens, whose wisdom may best discern the true interest of their country, and whose patriotism and love of justice will be least likely to sacrifice it to temporary or partial considerations. Under such a regulation, it may well happen that the public voice, pronounced by the representatives of the people, will be more consonant to the public good than if pronounced by the people themselves, convened for the purpose. On the other hand, the effect may be inverted. Men of factious tempers, of local prejudices, or of sinister designs, may, by intrigue, by corruption, or by other means, first obtain the suffrages, and then betray the interests, of the people. The question resulting is, whether small or extensive republics are more favorable to the election of proper guardians of the public weal; and it is clearly decided in favor of the latter by two obvious considerations:

In the first place, it is to be remarked that, however small the republic may be, the representatives must be raised to a certain number, in order to guard against the cabals of a few; and that, however large it may be, they must be limited to a certain number, in order to guard against the confusion of a multitude. Hence, the number of representatives in the two cases not being in proportion to that of the two constituents, and being proportionally greater in the small republic, it follows that, if the proportion of fit characters be not less in the large than in the small republic, the former will present a greater option, and consequently a greater probability of a fit choice.

In the next place, as each representative will be chosen by a greater number of citizens in the large than in the small republic, it will be more difficult for unworthy candidates to practice with success the vicious arts by which elections are too often carried; and the suffrages of the people being more free, will be more likely to centre in men who possess the most attractive merit and the most diffusive and established characters. It must be confessed that in this, as in most other cases, there is a mean, on both sides of which inconveniences will be found to lie. By enlarging too much the number of electors, you render the representatives too little acquainted with all their local circumstances and lesser interests; as by reducing it too much, you render him unduly attached to these, and too little fit to comprehend and pursue great and national objects. The federal Constitution forms a happy combination in this respect; the great and aggregate interests being referred to the national, the local and particular to the state legislatures.

The other point of difference is, the greater number of citizens and extent of territory which may be brought within the compass of republican than of democratic government; and it is this circumstance principally which renders factious combinations less to be dreaded in the former than in the latter. The smaller the society, the fewer probably will be the distinct parties and interests composing it; the fewer the distinct parties and interests, the more frequently will a majority be found of the same party; and the smaller the number of individuals composing a majority, and the smaller the compass within which they are placed, the more easily will they concert and execute their plans of oppression. Extend the sphere, and you take in a greater variety of parties and interests; you make it less probable that a majority of the whole will have a common motive to invade the rights of other citizens; or if such a common motive exists, it will be more difficult for all who feel it to discover their own strength, and to act in unison with each other. Besides other impediments, it may be remarked that, where there is a consciousness of unjust or dishonorable purposes, communication is always checked by distrust in proportion to the number whose concurrence is necessary.

Hence, it clearly appears, that the same advantage which a republic has over a democracy, in controlling the effects of faction, is enjoyed by a large over a small republic,—is enjoyed by the Union over the states composing it. Does the advantage consist in the substitution of representatives whose enlightened views and virtuous sentiments render them superior to local prejudices and schemes of injustice? It will not be denied that the representation of the Union will be most likely to possess these requisite endowments. Does it consist in the greater security afforded by a greater variety of parties, against the event of any one party being able to outnumber and oppress the rest? In an equal degree does the increased variety of parties comprised within the Union, increase this security. Does it, in fine, consist in the greater obstacles opposed to the concert and accomplishment of the secret wishes of an unjust and interested majority? Here, again, the extent of the Union gives it the most palpable advantage.

The influence of factious leaders may kindle a flame within their particular states, but will be unable to spread a general conflagration through the other states. A religious sect may degenerate into a political faction in a part of the Confederacy; but the variety of sects dispersed over the entire face of it must secure the national councils against any danger from that source. A rage for paper money, for an abolition of debts, for an equal division of property, or for any other improper or wicked project, will be less apt to pervade the whole body of the Union than a particular member of it; in the same proportion as such a malady is more likely to taint a particular county or district, than an entire state. In the extent and proper structure of the Union, therefore, we behold a republican remedy for the diseases most incident to republican government. And according to the degree of pleasure and pride we feel in being republicans, ought to be our zeal in cherishing the spirit and supporting the character of Federalists.

PUBLIUS.

[USC]

James Madison, *The Federalist*, No. 51, "Checks and Balances"

February 6, 1788

No one believed as deeply in the ultimate and practical benefits of the Constitution as James Madison. His knowledge of its strengths and weaknesses allowed him to maintain continuous explications of and arguments for it.

To the People of the State of New York:

To WHAT EXPEDIENT, then, shall we finally resort, for maintaining in practice the necessary partition of power among the several departments, as laid down in the Constitution? The only answer that can be given is, that as all these exterior provisions are found to be inadequate, the defect must be supplied, by so contriving the interior structure of the government as that its several constituent parts may, by their mutual relations, be the means of keeping each other in their proper places. Without presuming to undertake a full development of this important idea, I will hazard a few general observations, which may perhaps place it in a clearer light, and enable us to form a more correct judgment of the principles and structure of the government planned by the convention.

In order to lay a due foundation for that separate and distinct exercise of the different powers of government, which to a certain extent is admitted on all hands to be essential to the preservation of liberty, it is evident that each department should have a will of its own; and consequently should be so constituted that the members of each should have as little agency as possible in the appointment of the members of the others. Were this principle rigorously adhered to, it would require that all the appointments for the supreme executive, legislative, and judiciary magistracies should be drawn from the same fountain of authority, the people, through channels having no communication whatever with one another. Perhaps such a plan of constructing the several departments would be less difficult in practice than it may in contemplation appear. Some difficulties, however, and some additional expense would attend the execution of it. Some deviations, therefore, from the principle must be admitted. In the constitution of the judiciary department in particular, it might be inexpedient to insist rigorously on the principle: first, because peculiar qualifications being essential in the members, the primary consideration ought to be to select that mode of choice which best secures these qualifications; secondly, because the permanent tenure by which the appointments are held in that department, must soon destroy all sense of dependence on the authority conferring them.

It is equally evident, that the members of each department should be as little dependent as possible on those of the others, for the emoluments annexed to their offices. Were the executive magistrate, or the judges, not independent of the legislature in this particular, their independence in every other would be merely nominal.

But the great security against a gradual concentration of the several powers in the same department, consists in giving to those who administer each department the necessary constitutional means and personal motives to resist encroachments of the others. The provision for defense must in this, as in all other cases, be made commensurate to the danger of attack. Ambition must be made to counteract ambition. The interest of the man must be connected with the constitutional rights of the place. It may be a reflection on human nature, that such devices should be necessary to control the abuses of government. But what is government itself, but the greatest of all reflections on human nature? If men were angels, no government would be necessary. If angels were to govern men, neither external nor internal controls on government would be necessary. In framing a government which is to be administered by men over men, the great difficulty lies in this: you must first enable the government to control the governed; and in the next place oblige it to control itself. A dependence on the people is, no doubt, the primary control on the government; but experience has taught mankind the necessity of auxiliary precautions.

This policy of supplying, by opposite and rival interests, the defect of better motives, might be traced through the whole system of human affairs, private as well as public. We see it particularly displayed in all the subordinate distributions of power, where the constant aim is to divide and arrange the several offices in such a manner as that each may be a check on the other that the private interest of every individual may be a sentinel over the public rights. These inventions of prudence cannot be less requisite in the distribution of the supreme powers of the state.

But it is not possible to give to each department an equal power of self-defense. In republican government, the legislative authority necessarily predominates. The remedy for this inconveniency is to divide the legislature into different branches; and to render them, by different modes of election and different principles of action, as little connected with each other as the nature of their common functions and their common dependence on the society will admit. It may even be necessary to guard against dangerous encroachments by still further precautions. As the weight of the legislative authority requires that it should be thus divided, the weakness of the executive may require, on the other hand, and that it should be fortified. An absolute negative on the legislature appears, at first view, to be the natural defense with which the executive magistrate should be armed. But perhaps it would be neither altogether safe nor alone sufficient. On ordinary occasions it might not be exerted with the requisite firmness, and on extraordinary occasions it might be perfidiously abused. May not this defect of an absolute negative be supplied by some qualified connection between this weaker department and the weaker branch of the stronger department, by which the latter may be led to support the constitutional rights of the former, without being too much detached from the rights of its own department?

If the principles on which these observations are founded be just, as I persuade myself they are, and they be applied as a criterion to the several state constitutions, and to the federal Constitution it will be found that if the latter does not perfectly correspond with them, the former are infinitely less able to bear such a test.

There are, moreover, two considerations particularly applicable to the federal system of America, which place that system in a very interesting point of view.

First. In a single republic, all the power surrendered by the people is submitted to the administration of a single government; and the usurpations are guarded against by a division of the government into distinct and separate departments. In the compound republic of America, the power surrendered by the people is first divided between two distinct governments, and then the portion allotted to each subdivided among distinct and separate departments. Hence a double security arises to the rights of the people. The different governments will control each other; at the same time that each will be controlled by itself.

Second. It is of great importance in a republic not only to guard the society against the oppression of its rulers, but to guard one part of the society against the injustice of the other part. Different interests necessarily exist in different classes of citizens. If a majority be united by a common interest, the rights of the minority will be insecure. There are but two methods of providing against this evil: the one by creating a will in the community independent of the majority that is, of the society itself; the other, by comprehending in the society so many separate descriptions of citizens as will render an unjust combination of a majority of the whole very improbable, if not impracticable. The first method prevails in all governments possessing an hereditary or self-appointed authority. This, at best, is but a precarious security; because a power independent of the society may as well espouse the unjust views of the major, as the rightful interests of the minor party, and may possibly be turned against both parties. The second method will be exemplified in the federal republic of the United States. Whilst all authority in it will be derived from and dependent on the society, the society itself will be broken into so many parts, interests, and classes of citizens, that the rights of individuals, or of the minority, will be in little danger from interested combinations of the majority. In a free government the security for civil rights must be the same as that for religious rights. It consists in the one case in the multiplicity of interests, and in the other in the multiplicity of sects. The degree of security in both cases will depend on the number of interests and sects; and this may be presumed to depend on the extent of country and number of people comprehended under the same government. This view of the subject must particularly recommend a proper federal system to all the sincere and considerate friends of republican government, since it shows that in exact proportion as the territory of the Union may be formed into more circumscribed Confederacies, or states oppressive combinations of a majority will be facilitated: the best security, under the republican forms, for the rights of every class of citizens, will be diminished: and consequently the stability and independence of some member of the government, the only other security, must be proportionately increased. Justice is the end of government. It is the end of civil society. It ever has been and ever will be pursued until it be obtained, or until liberty be lost in the pursuit. In a society under the forms of which the stronger faction can readily unite and oppress the weaker, anarchy may as truly be said to reign as in a state of nature, where the weaker individual is not secured against the violence of the stronger; and as, in the latter state, even the stronger individuals are prompted, by the uncertainty of their condition, to submit to a government which may protect the weak as well as themselves; so, in the former state, will the more powerful factions or parties be gradually induced, by a like motive, to wish for a government which will protect all parties, the weaker as well as the more powerful. It can be little doubted that if the state of Rhode Island was separated from the Confederacy and left to itself, the insecurity of rights under the popular form of government within such narrow limits would be displayed by such reiterated oppressions of factious majorities that some power altogether independent of the people would soon be called for by the voice of the very factions whose misrule had proved the necessity of it. In the extended republic of the United States, and among the great variety of interests, parties, and sects which it embraces, a coalition of a majority of the whole society could seldom take place on any other principles than those of justice and the general good; whilst there being thus less danger to a minor from the will of a major party, there must be less pretext, also, to provide for the security of the former, by introducing into the government a will not dependent on the latter, or, in other words, a will independent of the society itself. It is no less certain than it is important, notwithstanding the contrary opinions which have been entertained, that the larger the society, provided it lie within a practical sphere, the more duly capable it will be of self-government. And happily for the *republican cause,* the practicable sphere may be carried to a very great extent, by a judicious modification and mixture of the *federal principle.*

PUBLIUS.

[USC]

John Jay, Address to the People of the State of New York by "A Citizen of New York"

March–April, 1788

John Adams (1735–1826), reflecting on the battle for ratification, believed that John Jay (1745–1829) "had as much influence in the preparatory measures in digesting the Constitution, and obtaining its adoption, as any man in the nation." This essay, published as a pamphlet, takes in more topics more comprehensively than any of the five articles Jay wrote for The Federalist *Papers. At the time, Jay was Secretary for Foreign Affairs for the United States. He would become the first Chief Justice of the Supreme Court in 1789.*

FRIENDS AND FELLOW-CITIZENS: The Convention concurred in opinion with the people, that a national government, competent to every national object, was indispensably necessary; and it was as plain to them, as it now is to all America, that the present Confederation does not provide for such a government. These points being agreed, they proceeded to consider how and in what manner such a government could be formed, as, on the one hand, should be sufficiently energetic to raise us from our prostrate and distressed situation, and, on the other, be perfectly consistent with the liberties of the people of every state. Like men to whom the experience of other ages and countries had taught wisdom, they not only determined that it should be erected by, and depend on, the people, but, remembering the many instances in which governments vested solely in one man, or one body of men, had degenerated into tyrannies, they judged it most prudent that the three great branches of power should be committed to different hands, and therefore that the executive should be separated from the legislative, and the judicial from both. Thus far the propriety of their work is easily seen and understood, and therefore is thus far almost universally approved; for no one man or thing under the sun ever yet pleased every body.

The next question was, what particular powers should be given to these three branches. Here the different views and interests of the different states, as well as the different abstract opinions of their members on such points, interposed many difficulties. Here the business became complicated, and presented a wide field for investigation—too wide for every eye to take a quick and comprehensive view of it.

It is said that "in a multitude of counselors there is safety," because, in the first place, there is greater security for probity; and in the next, if every member cast in only his mite of information and argument, their joint stock of both will thereby become greater than the stock possessed by any one single man out of doors. Gentlemen out of doors, therefore, should not be hasty in condemning a system which probably rests on more good reasons than they are aware of, especially when formed under such advantages, and recommended by so many men of distinguished worth and abilities.

The difficulties before mentioned occupied the Convention a long time; and it was not without mutual concessions that they were at last surmounted. These concessions serve to explain to us the reason why some parts of the system please in some states which displease in others, and why many of the objections which have been made to it are so contradictory and inconsistent with one another. It does great credit to the temper and talents of the Convention, that they were able so to reconcile the different views and interests of the different states, and the clashing opinions of their members, as to unite with such singular and almost perfect unanimity in any plan whatever, on a subject so intricate and perplexed. It shows that it must have been thoroughly discussed and understood; and probably, if the community at large had the same lights and reasons before them, they would, if equally candid and uninfluenced, be equally unanimous.

It would be arduous, and indeed impossible, to comprise within the limits of this address a full discussion of every part of the plan. Such a task would require a volume; and few men have leisure or inclination to read volumes on any subject. The objections made to it are almost without number, and many of them without reason. Some of them are real and honest, and others merely ostensible. There are friends to union and a national government who have serious doubts, who wish to be informed, and to be convinced; and there are others, who, neither wishing for union nor any national government at all will oppose and object to any plan that can be contrived.

We are told, among other strange things, that the liberty of the press is left insecure by the proposed Constitution; and yet that Constitution says neither more nor less about it than the Constitution of the state of New York does. We are told that it deprives us of trial by jury; whereas the fact is, that it expressly secures it in certain cases, and takes it away in none. It is absurd to construe the silence of this, or of our own Constitution, relative to a great number of our rights, into a total extinction of them. Silence and blank paper neither grant nor take away any thing. Complaints are also made that the proposed Constitution is not accompanied by a bill of rights; and yet they who make these complaints know, and are content, that no bill of rights accompanied the Constitution of this state. In days and countries where monarchs and their subjects were frequently disputing about prerogative and privileges, the latter then found it necessary, as it were, to run out the line between them, and oblige the former to admit, by solemn acts, called bills of rights, that certain enumerated rights belonged to the people, and were not comprehended in the royal prerogative. But, thank God, we have no such disputes; we have no monarchs to contend with, or demand admissions from. The proposed government is to be the government of the people: all its officers are to be their officers, and to exercise no rights but such as the people commit to them. The Constitution only serves to point out that part of the people's business, which they think proper by it to refer to the management of the persons therein designated: those persons are to receive that business to manage, not for themselves, and as their own, but as agents and overseers for the people, to whom they are constantly responsible, and by whom only they are to be appointed.

But the design of this address is not to investigate the merits of the plan, nor of the objections made to it. They, who seriously contemplate the present state of our affairs, will be convinced that other considerations, of at least equal importance, demand their attention. Let it be admitted that this plan, like every thing else devised by man, has its imperfections. That it does not please every body is certain; and there is little reason to expect one that will. It is a question of great moment to you, whether the probability of our being able seasonably to obtain a better, is such as to render it prudent and advisable to reject this, and run the risk. Candidly to consider this question, is the design of this address.

As the importance of this question must be obvious to every man, whatever his private opinions respecting it may be, it becomes us all to treat it in that calm and temperate manner which a subject so deeply interesting to the future welfare of our country, and prosperity, requires. Let us, therefore, as much as possible, repress and compose that irritation in our minds which too warm disputes about it may have excited. Let us endeavor to forget that this or that man is on this or that side; and that we ourselves, perhaps without sufficient reflection, have classed ourselves with one or the other party. Let us remember that this is not to be regarded as a matter that only touches our local parties, but as one so great, so general, and so extensive, in its future consequence to America, that, for our deciding upon it according to the best of our unbiased judgment, we must be highly responsible both here and hereafter.

The question now before us naturally leads to three inquiries:—

1. Whether it is probable that a better plan can be obtained.

2. Whether, if attainable, it is likely to be in season.

3. What would be our situation if, after rejecting this, all our efforts to obtain a better should prove fruitless.

The men who formed this plan are Americans, who had long deserved and enjoyed our confidence, and who are as much interested in having a good government as any of us are or can be. They were appointed to that business at a time when the states had become very sensible of the derangement of our national affairs, and of the impossibility of retrieving them under the existing Confederation. Although well persuaded that nothing but a good national government could oppose and divert the tide of evils that was flowing in upon us, yet those gentlemen met in Convention with minds perfectly unprejudiced in favor of any particular plan. The minds of their constituents were at that time equally cool and dispassionate. All agreed in the necessity of doing something; but no one ventured to say decidedly what precisely ought to be done. Opinions were then fluctuating and unfixed; and whatever might have been the wishes of a few individuals, yet while the Convention deliberated, the people remained in silent suspense. Neither wedded to favorite systems of their own, nor influenced by popular ones abroad, the members were more desirous to receive light from, than to impress their private sentiments on, one another.

These circumstances naturally opened the door to that spirit of candor, of calm inquiry, of mutual accommodation, and mutual respect, which entered into the Convention with them, and regulated their debates and proceedings.

The impossibility of agreeing upon any plan, that would exactly quadrate with the local policy and objects of every state, soon became evident; and they wisely thought it better mutually to coincide and accommodate, and in that way to fashion their system as much as possible by the circumstances and wishes of the different states, than, by pertinaciously adhering each to his own ideas, oblige the Convention to rise without doing any thing. They were sensible that obstacles, arising from local circumstances, would not cease while those circumstances continued to exist; and, so far as those circumstances depended on differences of climate, productions, and commerce, that no change was to be expected. They were likewise sensible that, on a subject so comprehensive, and involving such a variety of points and questions, the most able, the most candid, and the most honest men will differ in opinion. The same proposition seldom strikes many minds exactly in the same point of light. Different habits of thinking, different degrees and modes of education, different prejudices and opinions, early formed and long entertained, conspire, with a multitude of other circumstances, to produce among men a diversity and contrariety of opinions on questions of difficulty. Liberality, therefore, as well as prudence, induced them to treat each other's opinions with tenderness; to argue without asperity; and to endeavor to convince the judgment, without hurting the feelings, of each other. Although many weeks were passed in these discussions, some points remained on which a unison of opinions could not be affected. Here, again, that same happy disposition to unite and conciliate induced them to meet each other; and enabled them, by mutual concessions, finally to complete and agree to the plan they have recommended, and that, too, with a degree of unanimity which, considering the variety of discordant views and ideas they had to reconcile, is really astonishing.

They tell us, very honestly, that this plan is the result of accommodation. They do not hold it up as the best of all possible ones, but only as the best which they could unite in and agree to. If such men, appointed and meeting under such auspicious circumstances, and so sincerely disposed to conciliation, could go no farther in their endeavors to please every state and every body, what reason have we, at present, to expect any system that would give more general satisfaction?

Suppose this plan to be rejected; what measures would you propose for obtaining a better? Some will answer, "Let us appoint another convention; and, as every thing has been said and written that can well be said and written on the subject, they will be better informed than the former one was, and consequently be better able to make and agree upon a more eligible one."

This reasoning is fair, and, as far as it goes, has weight; but it nevertheless takes one thing for granted which appears very doubtful; for, although the new convention might have more information, and perhaps equal abilities, yet it does not from thence follow that they would be equally disposed to agree. The contrary of this position is most probable. You must have observed that the same temper and equanimity which prevailed among the people on former occasions, no longer exist. We have unhappily become divided into parties; and this important subject has been handled with such indiscreet and offensive acrimony, and with so many little, unhandsome artifices and misrepresentations, that pernicious heats and animosities have been kindled, and spread their flames far and wide among us. When, therefore, it becomes a question who shall be deputed to the new convention, we cannot flatter ourselves that the talents and integrity of the candidates will determine who shall be elected. Federal electors will vote for federal deputies and anti-federal electors for anti-federal ones. Nor will either party prefer the most moderate of their adherents; for, as the most stanch and active partisans will be the most popular, so the men most willing and able to carry points, to oppose and divide, and embarrass their opponents, will be chosen. A convention formed at such a season, and of such men, would be but too exact an epitome of the great body that named them. The same party views, the same propensity to opposition, the same distrusts and jealousies, and the same unaccommodating spirit, which prevail without, would be concentrated and ferment with still greater violence within. Each deputy would recollect who sent him, and why he was sent, and be too apt to consider himself bound in honor to contend and act vigorously under the standard of his party, and not hazard their displeasure by preferring compromise to victory. As vice does not sow the seed of virtue, so neither does passion cultivate the fruits of reason. Suspicions and resentments create no disposition to conciliate; nor do they infuse a desire of making partial and personal objects bend to general union and the common good. The utmost efforts of that excellent disposition were necessary to enable the late Convention to perform their task; and although contrary causes sometimes operate similar effects, yet to expect that discord and animosity should produce the fruits of confidence and agreement, is to expect "grapes from thorns, and figs from thistles."

The states of Georgia, Delaware, Jersey, and Connecticut, have adopted the present plan with unexampled unanimity. They are content with it as it is; and consequently their deputies, being apprised of the sentiments of their constituents, will be little inclined to make alterations, and cannot be otherwise than averse to changes, which they have no reason to think would be agreeable to their people. Some other states, though less unanimous, have nevertheless adopted it by very respectable majorities—and for reasons so evidently cogent, that even the minority in one of them have nobly pledged themselves for its promotion and support. From these circumstances, the new convention would derive and experience difficulties unknown to the former. Nor are these the only additional difficulties they would have to encounter. Few are ignorant that there has lately sprung up a sect of politicians who teach, and profess to believe, that the extent of our nation is too great for the superintendence of one national government, and on that principle argue that it ought to be divided into two or three. This doctrine, however mischievous in its tendency and consequences, has its advocates; and, should any of them be sent to the convention, it will naturally be their policy rather to cherish than to prevent divisions; for, well knowing that the institution of any national government would blast their favorite system, no measures that lead to it can meet with their aid or approbation.

Nor can we be certain whether or not any, and what, foreign influence would, on such an occasion, be indirectly exerted, nor for what purposes. Delicacy forbids an ample discussion of this question. Thus much may be said without error or offence, viz.: that such foreign nations as desire the prosperity of America, and would rejoice to see her become great and powerful, under the auspices of a government wisely calculated to extend her commerce, to encourage her navigation and marine, and to direct the whole weight of her power and resources as her interest and honor may require, will doubtless be friendly to the union of states, and to the establishment of a government able to perpetuate, protect, and dignify it. Such other foreign nations, if any such there be, who, jealous of our growing importance, and fearful that our commerce and navigation should impair their own, behold our rapid population with regret, and apprehend that the enterprising spirit of our people, when seconded by power and probability of success, may be directed to objects not consistent with their policy or interests, cannot fail to wish that we may continue a weak and a divided people.

These considerations merit much attention; and candid men will judge how far they render it probable that a new convention would be able either to agree in a better plan, or, with tolerable unanimity, in any plan at all. Any plan, forcibly carried, by a slender majority, must expect numerous opponents among the people, who, especially in their present temper, would be more inclined to reject than adopt any system so made and carried. We should, in such a case, again see the press teeming with publications for and against it; for, as the minority would take pains to justify their dissent, so would the majority be industrious to display the wisdom of their proceedings. Hence new divisions, new parties, and new distractions, would ensue; and no one can foresee or conjecture when or how they would terminate.

Let those who are sanguine in their expectations of a better plan from a new convention, also reflect on the delays and risks to which it would expose us. Let them consider whether we ought, by continuing much longer in our present humiliating condition, to give other nations further time to perfect their restrictive systems of commerce, reconcile their own people to them, and to fence, and guard, and strengthen them by all those regulations and contrivances in which a jealous policy is ever fruitful. Let them consider whether we ought to give further opportunities to discord to alienate the hearts of our citizens from one another, and thereby encourage new Cromwells to bold exploits. Are we certain that our foreign creditors will continue patient, and ready to proportion their forbearance to our delays? Are we sure that our distresses, dissensions, and weakness, will neither invite hostility nor insult? If they should, how ill prepared shall we be for defence, without union, without government, without money, and without credit!

It seems necessary to remind you that some time must yet elapse before all the states will have decided on the present plan. If they reject it, some time must also pass before the measure of a new convention can be brought about and generally agreed to. A further space of time will then be requisite to elect their deputies, and send them on to convention. What time they may expend, when met, cannot be divined; and it is equally uncertain how much time the several states may take to deliberate and decide on any plan they may recommend. If adopted, still a further space of time will be necessary to organize and set it in motion. In the mean time, our affairs are daily going on from bad to worse; and it is not rash to say that our distresses are accumulating like compound interest.

But if, for the reasons already mentioned, and others that we cannot now perceive, the new convention, instead of producing a better plan, should give us only a history of their disputes, or should offer us one still less pleasing than the present, where should we be then? The old Confederation has done its best, and cannot help us; and is now so relaxed and feeble, that, in all probability, it would not survive so violent a shock. Then, "To your tents, O Israel!" would be the word. Then, every band of union would be severed. Then, every state would be a little nation, jealous of its neighbors, and anxious to strengthen itself, by foreign alliances, against its former friends. Then farewell to fraternal affection, unsuspecting intercourse, and mutual participation in commerce, navigation, and citizenship. Then would arise mutual restrictions and fears, mutual garrisons and standing armies, and all those dreadful evils which for so many ages plagued England, Scotland, Wales, and Ireland, while they continued disunited, and were played off against each other.

Consider, my fellow citizens, what you are about, before it is too late—consider what in such an event would be your particular case.—You know the geography of your state, and the consequences of your local position. Jersey and Connecticut, to whom you imposed laws have been unkind—Jersey and Connecticut, who have adopted the present plan, and expect much good from it, will impute its miscarriage and all the consequent evils to you.

They now consider your opposition as dictated more by your fondness for your impost than for those rights to which they have never been behind you in attachment. They cannot, they will not love you—they border upon you, and are your neighbors, but you will soon cease to regard their neighborhood as a blessing. You have but one port and outlet to your commerce, and how you are to keep that outlet free and uninterrupted merits consideration. What advantages Vermont, in combination with others, might take of you, may easily be conjectured; nor will you be at a loss to perceive how much reason the people of Long Island, whom you cannot protect, have to deprecate being constantly exposed to the depredations of every invader.

There are short hints—they ought not to be more developed—you can easily in your own minds dilate and trace them through all their relative circumstances and connections. Pause then for a moment and reflect whether the matters you are disputing about are of sufficient moment to justify your running such extravagant risks. Reflect that the present plan comes recommended to you by men and fellow-citizens, who have given you the highest proofs that men can give of their justice, their love for liberty and their country, of their prudence, of their application, and of their talents. They tell you it is the best that they could form, and that, in their opinion, it is necessary to redeem you from those calamities which already begin to be heavy upon us all. You find that not only those men, but others of similar characters, and of whom you have also had very ample experience, advise you to adopt it. You find that whole states concur in the sentiment, and among them are your neighbors; both of whom have shed much blood in the cause of liberty, and have manifested as strong and constant a predilection for a free republication government as any states in the Union, and perhaps in the world. They perceive not those latent mischiefs in it with which some double-sighted politicians endeavor to alarm you. You cannot but be sensible that this plan or Constitution will always be in the hands and power of the people, and that if on experiment it should be found defective or incompetent, they may either remedy its defects or substitute another in its room. The objectionable parts of it are certainly very questionable, for otherwise there would not be such a contrariety of opinions about them. Experience will better determine such questions than theoretical arguments, and so far as the danger of abuses is urged against the institution of a government, remember that a power to do good always involves a power to do harm. We must in the business of government as well as in all other business have some degree of confidence as well as a great degree of caution. Who on a sick bed would refuse medicines from a physician merely because it is as much in his power to administer deadly poison as salutary remedies?

You cannot be certain, that by rejecting the proposed plan you would not place yourselves in a very awkward situation. Suppose nine states should nevertheless adopt it, would you not in that case be obliged either to separate from the Union or rescind your dissent? The first would not be eligible, nor could the latter be pleasant—a mere hint is sufficient on this topic. You cannot but be aware of the consequences.

Consider, then, how weighty and how many considerations advise and persuade the people of America to remain in the safe and easy path of union; to continue to move and act, as they hitherto have done, as a band of brothers; and to have confidence in themselves and in one another; and, since all cannot see with the same eyes, at least to give the proposed Constitution a fair trial, and to mend it as time, occasion, and experience, may dictate. It would little become us to verify the predictions of those who ventured to prophesy that peace, instead of blessing us with happiness and tranquility, would serve only as the signal for factions, discord, and civil contentions, to rage in our land, and overwhelm it with misery and distress.

Let us also be mindful that the cause of freedom greatly depends on the use we make of the singular opportunities we enjoy of governing ourselves wisely; for, if the event should prove that the people of this country either cannot or will not govern themselves, who will hereafter be advocates for systems which, however charming in theory and prospect, are not reducible to practice? If the people of our nation, instead of consenting to be governed by laws of their own making, and rulers of their own choosing, should let licentiousness, disorder, and confusion, reign over them, the minds of men every where will insensibly become alienated from republican forms, and prepared to prefer and acquiesce in governments which, though less friendly to liberty, afford more peace and security.

Receive this address with the same candor with which it is written; and may the spirit of wisdom and patriotism direct and distinguish your councils and your conduct.

[USC]

Alexander Hamilton, *The Federalist,* No. 85, "Concluding Remarks"

May 28, 1788

The brilliant and difficult Alexander Hamilton (1755–1804), who had served as George Washington's aide in the Revolutionary War, was the spearhead of The Federalist, *writing fifty-nine of them, with this being the last. He would become the first Secretary of the Treasury, and was the creator of the controversial national bank. He died in a duel with Aaron Burr.*

To the People of the State of New York:
ACCORDING TO THE formal division of the subject of these papers, announced in my first number, there would appear still to remain for discussion two points: "the analogy of the proposed government to your own state constitution," and "the additional security which its adoption will afford to republican government, to liberty, and to property." But these heads have been so fully anticipated and exhausted in the progress of the work, that it would now scarcely be possible to do any thing more than repeat, in a more dilated form, what has been heretofore said, which the advanced stage of the question, and the time already spent upon it, conspire to forbid.

It is remarkable, that the resemblance of the plan of the convention to the act which organizes the government of this state holds, not less with regard to many of the supposed defects, than to the real excellences of the former. Among the pretended defects are the re-eligibility of the Executive, the want of a council, the omission of a formal bill of rights, the omission of a provision respecting the liberty of the press. These and several others which have been noted in the course of our inquiries are as much chargeable on the existing constitution of this state, as on the one proposed for the Union; and a man must have slender pretensions to consistency, who can rail at the latter for imperfections which he finds no difficulty in excusing in the former. Nor indeed can there be a better proof of the insincerity and affectation of some of the zealous adversaries of the plan of the convention among us, who profess to be the devoted admirers of the government under which they live, than the fury with which they have attacked that plan, for matters in regard to which our own constitution is equally or perhaps more vulnerable.

The additional securities to republican government, to liberty and to property, to be derived from the adoption of the plan under consideration, consist chiefly in the restraints which the preservation of the Union will impose on local factions and insurrections, and on the ambition of powerful individuals in single states, who may acquire credit and influence enough, from leaders and favorites, to become the despots of the people; in the diminution of the opportunities to foreign intrigue, which the dissolution of the Confederacy would invite and facilitate; in the prevention of extensive military establishments, which could not fail to grow out of wars between the states in a disunited situation; in the express guaranty of a republican form of government to each; in the absolute and universal exclusion of titles of nobility; and in the precautions against the repetition of those practices on the part of the state governments which have undermined the foundations of property and credit, have planted mutual distrust in the breasts of all classes of citizens, and have occasioned an almost universal prostration of morals.

Thus have I, fellow-citizens, executed the task I had assigned to myself; with what success, your conduct must determine. I trust at least you will admit that I have not failed in the assurance I gave you respecting the spirit with which my endeavors should be conducted. I have addressed myself purely to your judgments, and have studiously avoided those asperities which are too apt to disgrace political disputants of all parties, and which have been not a little provoked by the language and conduct of the opponents of the Constitution. The charge of a conspiracy against the liberties of the people, which has been indiscriminately brought against the advocates of the plan, has something in it too wanton and too malignant, not to excite the indignation of every man who feels in his own bosom a refutation of the calumny. The perpetual changes which have been rung upon the wealthy, the well-born, and the great, have been such as to inspire the disgust of all sensible men. And the unwarrantable concealments and misrepresentations which have been in various ways practiced to keep the truth from the public eye, have been of a nature to demand the reprobation of all honest men. It is not impossible that these circumstances may have occasionally betrayed me into intemperances of expression which I did not intend; it is certain that I have frequently felt a struggle between sensibility and moderation; and if the former has in some instances prevailed, it must be my excuse that it has been neither often nor much.

Let us now pause and ask ourselves whether, in the course of these papers, the proposed Constitution has not been satisfactorily vindicated from the aspersions thrown upon it; and whether it has not been shown to be worthy of the public approbation, and necessary to the public safety and prosperity. Every man is bound to answer these questions to himself, according to the best of his conscience and understanding, and to act agreeably to the genuine and sober dictates of his judgment. This is a duty from which nothing can give him a dispensation. 'Tis one that he is called upon, nay, constrained by all the obligations that form the bands of society, to discharge sincerely and honestly. No partial motive, no particular interest, no pride of opinion, no temporary passion or prejudice, will justify to himself, to his country, or to his posterity, an improper election of the part he is to act. Let him beware of an obstinate adherence to party; let him reflect that the object upon which he is to decide is not a particular interest of the community, but the very existence of the nation; and let him remember that a majority of America has already given its sanction to the plan which he is to approve or reject.

I shall not dissemble that I feel an entire confidence in the arguments which recommend the proposed system to your adoption, and that I am unable to discern any real force in those by which it has been opposed. I am persuaded that it is the best which our political situation, habits, and opinions will admit, and superior to any the revolution has produced.

Concessions on the part of the friends of the plan, that it has not a claim to absolute perfection, have afforded matter of no small triumph to its enemies. "Why," say they, "should we adopt an imperfect thing? Why not amend it and make it perfect before it is irrevocably established?" This may be plausible enough, but it is only plausible. In the first place I remark, that the extent of these concessions has been greatly exaggerated. They have been stated as amounting to an admission that the plan is radically defective, and that without material alterations the rights and the interests of the community cannot be safely confided to it. This, as far as I have understood the meaning of those who make the concessions, is an entire perversion of their sense. No advocate of the measure can be found, who will not declare as his sentiment, that the system, though it may not be perfect in every part, is, upon the whole, a good one; is the best that the present views and circumstances of the country will permit; and is such an one as promises every species of security which a reasonable people can desire.

I answer in the next place, that I should esteem it the extreme of imprudence to prolong the precarious state of our national affairs, and to expose the Union to the jeopardy of successive experiments, in the chimerical pursuit of a perfect plan. I never expect to see a perfect work from imperfect man. The result of the deliberations of all collective bodies must necessarily be a compound, as well of the errors and prejudices, as of the good sense and wisdom, of the individuals of whom they are composed. The compacts which are to embrace thirteen distinct states in a common bond of amity and union, must as necessarily be a compromise of as many dissimilar interests and inclinations. How can perfection spring from such materials?

The reasons assigned in an excellent little pamphlet lately published in this city,[1] are unanswerable to show the utter improbability of assembling a new convention, under circumstances in any degree so favorable to a happy issue, as those in which the late convention met, deliberated, and concluded. I will not repeat the arguments there used, as I presume the production itself has had an extensive circulation. It is certainly well worthy the perusal of every friend to his country. There is, however, one point of light in which the subject of amendments still remains to be considered, and in which it has not yet been exhibited to public view. I cannot resolve to conclude without first taking a survey of it in this aspect.

---

[1] Entitled "An Address to the People of the State of New York." — *Publius*. [That is, John Jay's pamphlet, which precedes Hamilton in this volume. – ED.]

It appears to me susceptible of absolute demonstration, that it will be far more easy to obtain subsequent than previous amendments to the Constitution. The moment an alteration is made in the present plan, it becomes, to the purpose of adoption, a new one, and must undergo a new decision of each state. To its complete establishment throughout the Union, it will therefore require the concurrence of thirteen states. If, on the contrary, the Constitution proposed should once be ratified by all the states as it stands, alterations in it may at any time be effected by nine states. Here, then, the chances are as thirteen to nine[2] in favor of subsequent amendment, rather than of the original adoption of an entire system.

This is not all. Every Constitution for the United States must inevitably consist of a great variety of particulars, in which thirteen independent states are to be accommodated in their interests or opinions of interest. We may of course expect to see, in any body of men charged with its original formation, very different combinations of the parts upon different points. Many of those who form a majority on one question, may become the minority on a second, and an association dissimilar to either may constitute the majority on a third. Hence the necessity of moulding and arranging all the particulars which are to compose the whole, in such a manner as to satisfy all the parties to the compact; and hence, also, an immense multiplication of difficulties and casualties in obtaining the collective assent to a final act. The degree of that multiplication must evidently be in a ratio to the number of particulars and the number of parties.

But every amendment to the Constitution, if once established, would be a single proposition, and might be brought forward singly. There would then be no necessity for management or compromise, in relation to any other point; no giving nor taking. The will of the requisite number would at once bring the matter to a decisive issue. And consequently, whenever nine, or rather ten states, were united in the desire of a particular amendment, that amendment must infallibly take place. There can, therefore, be no comparison between the facility of affecting an amendment, and that of establishing in the first instance a complete Constitution.

---

[2] It may rather be said *ten,* for though two thirds may set on foot the measure, three fourths must ratify. — *Publius*

In opposition to the probability of subsequent amendments, it has been urged that the persons delegated to the administration of the national government will always be disinclined to yield up any portion of the authority of which they were once possessed. For my own part I acknowledge a thorough conviction that any amendments which may, upon mature consideration, be thought useful, will be applicable to the organization of the government, not to the mass of its powers; and on this account alone, I think there is no weight in the observation just stated. I also think there is little weight in it on another account. The intrinsic difficulty of governing thirteen states at any rate, independent of calculations upon an ordinary degree of public spirit and integrity, will, in my opinion constantly impose on the national rulers the necessity of a spirit of accommodation to the reasonable expectations of their constituents. But there is yet a further consideration, which proves beyond the possibility of a doubt, that the observation is futile. It is this that the national rulers, whenever nine states concur, will have no option upon the subject. By the fifth article of the plan, the Congress will be obliged "on the application of the legislatures of two thirds of the states, which at present amount to nine, to call a convention for proposing amendments, which shall be valid, to all intents and purposes, as part of the Constitution, when ratified by the legislatures of three fourths of the states, or by conventions in three fourths thereof." The words of this article are peremptory. The Congress "shall call a convention." Nothing in this particular is left to the discretion of that body. And of consequence, all the declamation about the disinclination to a change vanishes in air. Nor however difficult it may be supposed to unite two thirds or three fourths of the state legislatures, in amendments which may affect local interests, can there be any room to apprehend any such difficulty in a union on points which are merely relative to the general liberty or security of the people. We may safely rely on the disposition of the state legislatures to erect barriers against the encroachments of the national authority.

If the foregoing argument is a fallacy, certain it is that I am myself deceived by it, for it is, in my conception, one of those rare instances in which a political truth can be brought to the test of a mathematical demonstration. Those who see the matter in the same light with me, however zealous they may be for amendments, must agree in the propriety of a previous adoption, as the most direct road to their own object.

The zeal for attempts to amend, prior to the establishment of the Constitution, must abate in every man who is ready to accede to the truth of the following observations of a writer equally solid and ingenious: "To balance a large state or society (says he), whether monarchical or republican, on general laws, is a work of so great difficulty, that no human genius, however comprehensive, is able, by the mere dint of reason and reflection, to effect it. The judgments of many must unite in the work; experience must guide their labor; time must bring it to perfection, and the feeling of inconveniences must correct the mistakes which they *inevitably* fall into in their first trials and experiments."[3] These judicious reflections contain a lesson of moderation to all the sincere lovers of the Union, and ought to put them upon their guard against hazarding anarchy, civil war, a perpetual alienation of the states from each other, and perhaps the military despotism of a victorious demagogue, in the pursuit of what they are not likely to obtain, but from time and experience. It may be in me a defect of political fortitude, but I acknowledge that I cannot entertain an equal tranquility with those who affect to treat the dangers of a longer continuance in our present situation as imaginary. A nation, without a national government, is, in my view, an awful spectacle. The establishment of a Constitution, in time of profound peace, by the voluntary consent of a whole people, is a prodigy, to the completion of which I look forward with trembling anxiety. I can reconcile it to no rules of prudence to let go the hold we now have, in so arduous an enterprise, upon seven out of the thirteen states, and after having passed over so considerable a part of the ground, to recommence the course. I dread the more the consequences of new attempts, because I know that powerful individuals, in this and in other states, are enemies to a general national government in every possible shape.

Publius.

[USC]

---

[3] David Hume's *Essays,* Vol. I, page 128: "The Rise of Arts and Sciences."
— *Publius.*

Patrick Henry, Speech at the Virginia Ratifying Convention on "Altering Our Government"

June 4, 1788

Patrick Henry (1736–1799), a Revolutionary War hero and former governor of Virginia, was opposed to a centralized government from the start. He was the most eloquent of any of the speakers pro or con in Virginia, and overcoming his persuasiveness with voters took a concerted effort by Madison and others. On June 26, Virginia became the tenth state to ratify the Constitution, in a vote of 88–79.

MR. CHAIRMAN, THE public mind, as well as my own, is extremely uneasy at the proposed change of government. Give me leave to form one of the number of those who wish to be thoroughly acquainted with the reasons of this perilous and uneasy situation, and why we are brought hither to decide on this great national question. I consider myself as the servant of the people of this commonwealth, as a sentinel over their rights, liberty, and happiness. I represent their feelings when I say that they are exceedingly uneasy at being brought from that state of full security, which they enjoyed, to the present delusive appearance of things. A year ago, the minds of our citizens were at perfect repose. Before the meeting of the late Federal Convention at Philadelphia, a general peace and a universal tranquility prevailed in this country; but, since that period, they are exceedingly uneasy and disquieted. When I wished for an appointment to this Convention, my mind was extremely agitated for the situation of public affairs. I conceived the republic to be in extreme danger. If our situation be thus uneasy, whence has arisen this fearful jeopardy? It arises from this fatal system; it arises from a proposal to change our government—a proposal that goes to the utter annihilation of the most solemn engagements of the states—a proposal of establishing nine states into a confederacy, to the eventual exclusion of four states. It goes to the annihilation of those solemn treaties we have formed with foreign nations.

The present circumstances of France—the good offices rendered us by that kingdom—require our most faithful and most punctual adherence to our treaty with her. We are in alliance with the Spaniards, the Dutch, the Prussians; those treaties bound us as thirteen states confederated together. Yet here is a proposal to sever that confederacy. Is it possible that we shall abandon all our treaties and national engagements? And for what? I expected to hear the reasons for an event so unexpected to my mind and many others. Was our civil polity, or public justice, endangered or sapped? Was the real existence of the country threatened, or was this preceded by a mournful progression of events? This proposal of altering our federal government is of a most alarming nature! Make the best of this new government—say it is composed by anything but inspiration—you ought to be extremely cautious, watchful, jealous of your liberty; for, instead of securing your rights, you may lose them forever. If a wrong step be now made, the republic may be lost forever. If this new government will not come up to the expectation of the people, and they shall be disappointed, their liberty will be lost, and tyranny must and will arise. I repeat it again, and I beg gentlemen to consider, that a wrong step, made now, will plunge us into misery and our republic will be lost.

It will be necessary for this Convention to have a faithful historical detail of the facts that preceded the session of the Federal Convention, and the reasons that actuated its members in proposing an entire alteration of government, and to demonstrate the dangers that awaited us. If they were of such awful magnitude as to warrant a proposal so extremely perilous as this, I must assert, that this Convention has an absolute right to a thorough discovery of every circumstance relative to this great event. And here I would make this inquiry of those worthy characters who composed a part of the late Federal Convention. I am sure they were fully impressed with the necessity of forming a great consolidated government, instead of a confederation. That this is a consolidated government is demonstrably clear; and the danger of such a government is, to my mind, very striking.

I have the highest veneration for those gentlemen; but, sir, give me leave to demand, What right had they to say, "We, the people"? My political curiosity, exclusive of my anxious solicitude for the public welfare, leads me to ask, Who authorized them to speak the language of "We, the people," instead of "We, the states"? States are the characteristics and the soul of a confederation. If the states be not the agents of this compact, it must be one great, consolidated, national government, of the people of all the states. I have the highest respect for those gentlemen who formed the Convention, and, were some of them not here, I would express some testimonial of esteem for them. America had, on a former occasion, put the utmost confidence in them—a confidence which was well placed; and I am sure, sir, I would give up any thing to them; I would cheerfully confide in them as my representatives. But, sir, on this great occasion, I would demand the cause of their conduct. Even from that illustrious man who saved us by his valor [*George Washington*], I would have a reason for his conduct: that liberty which he has given us by his valor, tells me to ask this reason; and sure I am, were he here, he would give us that reason. But there are other gentlemen here, who can give us this information.

The people gave them no power to use their name. That they exceeded their power is perfectly clear. It is not mere curiosity that actuates me: I wish to hear the real, actual, existing danger, which should lead us to take those steps, so dangerous in my conception. Disorders have arisen in other parts of America; but here, sir, no dangers, no insurrection or tumult have happened; everything has been calm and tranquil. But, notwithstanding this, we are wandering on the great ocean of human affairs. I see no landmark to guide us. We are running we know not whither. Difference of opinion has gone to a degree of inflammatory resentment in different parts of the country, which has been occasioned by this perilous innovation. The Federal Convention ought to have amended the old system; for this purpose they were solely delegated; the object of their mission extended to no other consideration. You must, therefore, forgive the solicitation of one unworthy member to know what danger could have arisen under the present Confederation, and what are the causes of this proposal to change our government.

[USC]

The New Nation

President George Washington, First Inaugural Address

April 30, 1789

Under the framework of the new Constitution, the first Congress was scheduled to convene in New York on March 4, 1789, but it wasn't until April 5th that enough members were present to comprise a quorum in both the House and Senate. The following day the electoral votes for president were counted. There were no candidates for the office other than George Washington, and no other name received a single vote; at the same time, John Adams was designated the first vice president. Charles Thomson, secretary of Congress, was dispatched to Mount Vernon to notify Washington officially of his election, arriving there on April 14th. Washington left two days later for New York, reaching the city on April 23rd. His progress north from Virginia to take office was marked by continuous fanfare and ceremony; but nothing could match the final leg of the journey, when he was rowed on a barge from Elizabethtown, New Jersey, to Murray's Wharf at the foot of New York's Wall Street by a contingent of thirteen sailors—one for each state—and saluted as they passed scores of other boats and ships in the harbor. Arriving in New York, the president-elect was greeted by New York's governor George Clinton and other dignitaries, and proceeded to the Franklin House on Cherry Street, which would be his official residence during his first administration.

On April 30, 1789, Washington took the oath of office as prescribed by the Constitution. It was administered by New York State chancellor Robert Livingston, Chief Justice of the New York Judiciary, on the balcony of Federal Hall, not far from where the Ward statue of Washington still stands. The first president then entered the building, and in a low and nervous voice read the new Congress his brief inaugural address. One of those present later commented, "The great man was agitated and embarrassed more than ever he was by the loaded cannon or pointed musket."

— *Note by John Grafton*

FELLOW-CITIZENS OF the Senate and of the House of Representatives:

Among the vicissitudes incident to life no event could have filled me with greater anxieties than that of which the notification was transmitted by your order, and received on the 14th day of the present month. On the one hand, I was summoned by my country, whose voice I can never hear but with veneration and love, from a retreat which I had chosen with the fondest predilection, and, in my flattering hopes, with an immutable decision, as the asylum of my declining years—a retreat which was rendered every day more necessary as well as more dear to me by the addition of habit to inclination, and of frequent interruptions in my health to the gradual waste committed on it by time. On the other hand, the magnitude and difficulty of the trust to which the voice of my country called me, being sufficient to awaken in the wisest and most experienced of her citizens a distrustful scrutiny into his qualifications, could not but overwhelm with despondence one who (inheriting inferior endowments from nature and unpracticed in the duties of civil administration) ought to be peculiarly conscious of his own deficiencies. In this conflict of emotions all I dare aver is that it has been my faithful study to collect my duty from a just appreciation of every circumstance by which it might be affected. All I dare hope is that if, in executing this task, I have been too much swayed by a grateful remembrance of former instances, or by an affectionate sensibility to this transcendent proof of the confidence of my fellow-citizens, and have thence too little consulted my incapacity as well as disinclination for the weighty and untried cares before me, my error will be palliated by the motives which mislead me, and its consequences be judged by my country with some share of the partiality in which they originated.

Such being the impressions under which I have, in obedience to the public summons, repaired to the present station, it would be peculiarly improper to omit in this first official act my fervent supplications to that Almighty Being who rules over the universe, who presides in the councils of nations, and whose providential aids can supply every human defect, that His benediction may consecrate to the liberties and happiness of the people of the United States a Government instituted by themselves for these essential purposes, and may enable every instrument employed in its administration to execute with success the functions allotted to his charge. . . . No people can be bound to acknowledge and adore the Invisible Hand which conducts the affairs of men more than those of the United States. Every step by which they have advanced to the character of an independent nation seems to have been distinguished by some token of providential agency; and in the important revolution just accomplished in the system of their united government the tranquil deliberations and voluntary consent of so many distinct communities from which the event has resulted can not be compared with the means by which most governments have been established without some return of pious gratitude, along with an humble anticipation of the future blessings which the past seem to presage. . . .

By the article establishing the executive department it is made the duty of the President "to recommend to your consideration such measures as he shall judge necessary and expedient." The circumstances under which I now meet you will acquit me from entering into that subject further than to refer to the great constitutional charter under which you are assembled, and which, in defining your powers, designates the objects to which your attention is to be given. It will be more consistent with those circumstances, and far more congenial with the feelings which actuate me, to substitute, in place of a recommendation of particular measures, the tribute that is due to the talents, the rectitude, and the patriotism which adorn the characters selected to devise and adopt them. In these honorable qualifications I behold the surest pledges that as on one side no local prejudices or attachments, no separate views nor party animosities, will misdirect the comprehensive and equal eye which ought to watch over this great assemblage of communities and interests, so, on another, that the foundation of our national policy will be laid in the pure and immutable principles of private morality, and the preeminence of free government be exemplified by all the attributes which can win the affections of its citizens and command the respect of the world. I dwell on this prospect with every satisfaction which an ardent love for my country can inspire, since there is no truth more thoroughly established than that there exists in the economy and course of nature an indissoluble union between virtue and happiness; between duty and advantage; between the genuine maxims of an honest and magnanimous policy and the solid rewards of public prosperity and felicity; since we ought to be no less persuaded that the propitious smiles of Heaven can never be expected on a nation that disregards the eternal rules of order and right which Heaven itself has ordained; and since the preservation of the sacred fire of liberty and the destiny of the republican model of government are justly considered, perhaps, as *deeply,* as *finally,* staked on the experiment entrusted to the hands of the American people.

Besides the ordinary objects submitted to your care, it will remain with your judgment to decide how far an exercise of the occasional power delegated by the fifth article of the Constitution is rendered expedient at the present juncture by the nature of objections which have been urged against the system, or by the degree of inquietude which has given birth to them. . . .

To the foregoing observations I have one to add, which will be most properly addressed to the House of Representatives. It concerns myself, and will therefore be as brief as possible. When I was first honored with a call into the service of my country, then on the eve of an arduous struggle for its liberties, the light in which I contemplated my duty required that I should renounce every pecuniary compensation. From this resolution I have in no instance departed; and being still under the impressions which produced it, I must decline as inapplicable to myself any share in the personal emoluments which may be indispensably included in a permanent provision for the executive department, and must accordingly pray that the pecuniary estimates for the station in which I am placed may during my continuance in it be limited to such actual expenditures as the public good may be thought to require.

Having thus imparted to you my sentiments as they have been awakened by the occasion which brings us together, I shall take my present leave; but not without resorting once more to the benign Parent of the Human Race in humble supplication that, since He has been pleased to favor the American people with opportunities for deliberating in perfect tranquility, and dispositions for deciding with unparalleled unanimity on a form of government for the security of their union and the advancement of their happiness, so His divine blessing may be equally *conspicuous* in the enlarged views, the temperate consultations, and the wise measures on which the success of this Government must depend.

[DI]

Secretary of the Treasury Alexander Hamilton, Report on the Subject of a National Bank

December 13, 1790

Hamilton's state papers are the measure by which the value of all subsequent efforts on the same subject is estimated. The law establishing the bank did not differ from Hamilton's plan in any essentials, except that the life of the bank was limited to twenty years.

— Note by Albert Bushnell Hart

[…] THE ESTABLISHMENT OF banks in this country seems to be recommended by reasons of a peculiar nature. Previously to the revolution, circulation was in a great measure carried on by paper emitted by the several local governments. […] This auxiliary may be said to be now at an end. And it is generally supposed, that there has been for some time past, a deficiency of circulating medium. . . .

If the supposition of such a deficiency be in any degree founded, and some aid to circulation be desirable, it remains to inquire what ought to be the nature of that aid.

The emitting of paper money by the authority of government, is wisely prohibited to the individual states, by the national constitution; and the spirit of that prohibition ought not be disregarded by the government of the United States. [….]

Among other material differences between a paper currency, issued by the mere authority of government, and one issued by a bank, payable in coin, is this: that in the first case, there is no standard to which an appeal can be made, as to the quantity which will only satisfy, or which will surcharge the circulation; in the last, that standard results from the demand. If more should be issued than is necessary, it will return upon the bank. Its emissions [...] must always be in a compound ratio to the fund and the demand:—Whence it is evident, that there is a limitation in the nature of the thing; while the discretion of the government is the only measure of the extent of the emissions, by its own authority. [...]

The payment of the interest of the public debt, at thirteen different places, is a weighty reason, peculiar to our immediate situation, for desiring a bank circulation. Without a paper, in general currency, equivalent to gold and silver, a considerable proportion of the specie of the country must always be suspended from circulation, and left to accumulate, preparatory to each day of payment; and as often as one approaches, there must in several cases be an actual transportation of the metals at both expense and risk, from their natural and proper reservoirs, to distant places. [...]

Assuming it then as a consequence, from what has been said, that a national bank is a desirable institution, two inquiries emerge—is there no such institution, already in being, which has a claim to that character, and which supersedes the propriety or necessity of another? If there be none, what are the principles upon which one ought to be established?

There are at present three banks in the United States: that of North-America, established in the city of Philadelphia; that of New-York, established in the city of New-York; that of Massachusetts, established in the town of Boston. Of these three, the first is the only one which has at any time had a direct relation to the government of the United States. [...]

The directors of this bank, on behalf of their constituents, have since *accepted* and *acted* under a new charter from the state of Pennsylvania, materially variant from their original one; and which so narrows the foundation of the institution, as to render it an incompetent basis for the extensive purposes of a national bank. [...]

The order of the subject, leads next to the inquiry into the principles upon which a national bank ought to be organized.

The situation of the United States naturally inspires a wish that the form of the institution could admit of a plurality of branches. But various considerations discourage from pursuing this idea. [. . .]

Another wish, dictated by the particular situation of the country, is, that the bank could be so constituted as to be made an immediate instrument of loans to the proprietors of land; but this wish also yields to the difficulty of accomplishing it. Land is alone an unfit fund for a bank circulation. If the notes issued upon it were not to be payable in coin, on demand, or at a short date, this would amount to nothing more than a repetition of the paper emissions, which are now exploded by the general voice. If the notes are to be payable in coin, the land must first be converted into it, by sale or mortgage. The difficulty of effecting the latter, is the very thing which begets the desire of finding another resource; and the former would not be practicable on a sudden emergency, but with sacrifices which would make the cure worse than the disease. Neither is the idea of constituting the fund partly of coin and partly of land, free from impediments. These two species of property do not, for the most part, unite in the same hands. [...]

Considerations of public advantage suggest a further wish, which is, that the bank could be established upon principles that would cause the profits of it to redound to the immediate benefit of the state. This is contemplated by many who speak of a national bank, but the idea seems liable to insuperable objections. To attach full confidence to an institution of this nature, it appears to be an essential ingredient in its structure, that it shall be under a *private,* not a *public* direction, under the guidance of *individual interest,* not of *public policy;* which would be supposed to be, and in certain emergencies, under a feeble or too sanguine administration, would really be, liable to being too much influenced by *public necessity.* The suspicion of this would most probably be a canker that would continually corrode the vitals of the credit of the bank, and would be most likely to prove fatal in those situations in which the public good would require that they should be most sound and vigorous. It would, indeed, be little less than a miracle, should the credit of the bank be at the disposal of the government, if in a long series of time, there was not experienced a calamitous abuse of it. [...]

As far as may concern the aid of the bank, within the proper limits, a good government has nothing more to wish for, than it will always possess; though the management be in the hands of private individuals. As the institution, if rightly constituted, must depend for its renovation from time to time on the pleasure of the government, it will not be likely to feel a disposition to render itself by its conduct unworthy of public patronage. The government, too, in the administration of its finances, has it in its power to reciprocate benefits to the bank, of not less importance than those which the bank affords to the government, and which, besides, are never unattended with an immediate and adequate compensation. [...]

It will not follow, from what has been said, that the state may not be the holder of a part of the stock of a bank, and consequently a sharer in the profits of it. It will only follow, that it ought not to desire any participation in the direction of it, and therefore, ought not to own the whole or a principal part of the stock [...]

There is one thing, however, which the government owes to itself and to the community; at least to all that part of it, who are not stockholders; which is to reserve to itself a right of ascertaining, as often as may be necessary, the state of the bank, excluding, however, all pretension to control. . . .

Abandoning, therefore, ideas which, however agreeable or desirable, are neither practicable nor safe; the following plan for the constitution of a National Bank, is respectfully submitted to the consideration of the house.

I. The capital stock of the bank shall not exceed ten millions of dollars, divided into twenty-five thousand shares, each share being four hundred dollars. [...] Bodies politic, as well as individuals, may subscribe.

II. The amount of each share shall be payable, one fourth in gold and silver coin, and three fourths in that part of the public debt, which [...] shall bear an accruing interest at the time of payment of six per centum per annum. [...]

IV. The subscribers to the bank and their successors shall be incorporated, and shall so continue, until the final redemption of that part of its stock which shall consist of the public debt.

V. The capacity of the corporation to hold real and personal estate, shall be limited to fifteen millions of dollars, including the amount of its capital or original stock. [...]

VI. The totality of the debts of the company, whether by bond, bill, note, or other contract, (credits for deposits excepted,) shall never exceed the amount of its capital stock. In case of excess, the directors, under whose administration it shall happen, shall be liable for it in their private or separate capacities. Those who may have dissented may excuse themselves from this responsibility, by immediately giving notice of the fact and their dissent, to the President of the United States, and to the stockholders, at a general meeting to be called by the president of the bank, at their request.

VII. The company may sell or demise its lands and tenements, or may sell the whole or any part of the public debt, whereof its stock shall consist; but shall *trade* in nothing, except bills of exchange, gold and silver bullion, or in the sale of goods pledged for money lent: nor shall take more than at the rate of six per centum per annum, upon its loans or discounts.

VIII. No loan shall be made by the bank, for the use or on account of the government of the United States, or of either of them, to an amount exceeding fifty thousand dollars, or of any foreign prince or state; unless previously authorized by a law of the United States. . . .

X. The affairs of the bank shall be under the management of twenty-five directors, one of whom shall be the president. [...]

XIII. None but a stockholder, being a citizen of the United States, shall be eligible as a director. [...]

XX. The bills and notes of the bank originally made payable, or which shall have become payable on demand, in gold and silver coin, shall be receivable in all payments to the United States.

XXI. The officer at the head of the treasury department of the United States, shall be furnished from time to time, as often as he may require, not exceeding once a week, with statements of the amount of the capital stock of the bank, and of the debts due to the same, of the monies deposited therein, of the notes in circulation, and of the cash in hand; and shall have a right to inspect such general accounts in the books of the bank, as shall relate to the said statements; provided that this shall not be construed to imply a right of inspecting the account of any private individual or individuals, with the bank.

XXII. No similar institution shall be established by any future act of the United States, during the continuance of the one hereby proposed to be established.

XXIII. It shall be lawful for the directors of the bank to establish offices, wheresoever they shall think fit, within the United States, for the purposes of discount and deposit only, and upon the same terms, and in the same manner, as shall be practised at the bank . . .

XXIV. And lastly. The President of the United States shall be authorized to cause a subscription to be made to the stock of the said company, on behalf of the United States, to an amount not exceeding two millions of dollars . . . borrowing of the bank an equal sum, to be applied to the purposes for which the said monies shall have been procured, reimbursable in ten years by equal annual instalments; or at any time sooner, or in any greater proportions, that the government may think fit. [...]

The combination of a portion of the public debt, in the formation of the capital, is the principal thing of which an explanation is requisite. The chief object of this is, to enable the creation of a capital sufficiently large to be the basis of an extensive circulation, and an adequate security for it. [...] But to collect such a sum in this country in gold and silver, into one depository, may, without hesitation, be pronounced impracticable. Hence the necessity of an auxiliary, which the public debt at once presents.

This part of the fund will be always ready to come in aid of the specie. It will more and more command a ready sale; and can therefore expeditiously be turned into coin if an exigency of the bank should at any time require it. This quality of prompt convertibility into coin renders it an equivalent for that necessary agent of bank circulation; and distinguishes it from a fund in land, of which the sale would generally be far less compendious, and at great disadvantage. . . .

The interdiction of loans on account of the United States, or of any particular state, beyond the moderate sum specified, or of any foreign power, will serve as a barrier to executive encroachments and to combinations inauspicious to the safety, or contrary to the policy of the Union.

The limitation of the rate of interest is dictated by the consideration, that different rates prevail in different parts of the Union; and as the operations of the bank may extend through the whole, some rule seems to be necessary. [...]

The last thing which requires any explanatory remark, is, the authority proposed to be given to the President to subscribe to the amount of two millions of dollars, on account of the public. The main design of this is, to enlarge the specie fund of the bank, and to enable it to give a more early extension to its operations. Though it is proposed to borrow with one hand what is lent with the other; yet the disbursement of what is borrowed, will be progressive, and bank notes may be thrown into circulation, instead of the gold and silver. Besides, there is to be an annual reimbursement of a part of the sum borrowed, which will finally operate as an actual investment of so much specie. In addition to the inducements to this measure, which result from the general interest of the government to enlarge the sphere of the utility of the bank, there is this more particular consideration, to wit, that as far as the dividend on the stock shall exceed the interest paid on the loan, there is a positive profit.

[AHC]

Seneca chiefs Cornplanter, Half Town and Big Tree, Address to President Washington, "The land we live on our fathers received from God"

December 1790

In this dictated speech, three Seneca chiefs address President George Washington about the Iroquois' role in the Revolutionary War and the Senecas' rights to their land.

FATHER, THE VOICE of the Seneca Nations speaks to you, the great counsellor, in whose heart the wise men of all the Thirteen Fires have placed their wisdom; it may be very small in your ears, and we therefore entreat you to hearken with attention, for we are about to speak of things which are to us very great.

When your army entered the country of the Six Nations, we called you the town-destroyer; and to this day, when your name is heard, our women look behind them and turn pale, and our children cling close to the necks of their mothers. Our counsellors and warriors are men, and cannot be afraid; but their hearts are grieved with the fears of our women and children, and desire that it may be buried so deep as to be heard no more.

When you gave us peace we called you father, because you promised to secure us in the possession of our lands. Do this, and so long as the land shall remain, that beloved name shall be in the heart of every Seneca.

Father, we mean to open our hearts before you, and we earnestly desire that you will let us clearly understand what you resolve to do.

When our chiefs returned from the treaty at Fort Stanwix, and laid before our council what had been done there, our nation was surprised to hear how great a country you had compelled them to give up to you without your paying to us anything for it. Everyone said that your hearts were yet swelled with resentment against us for what had happened during the war, but that one day you would consider it with more kindness. We asked each other, what have we done to deserve such severe chastisement?

Father, when you kindled your Thirteen Fires separately [before the union of the States:—*Buchanan's note**], the wise men assembled at them told us that you were all brothers, the children of one great father, who regarded the red people as his children. They called us brothers, and invited us to his protection. They told us that he resided beyond the great water where the sun first rises; that he was a king whose power no people could resist, and that his goodness was as bright as the sun: what they said went to our hearts. We accepted the invitation, and promised to obey him. What the Seneca Nation promises they faithfully perform; and when you refused obedience to that king, he commanded us to assist his beloved men in making you sober. In obeying him, we did no more than you had led us to promise. The men who claimed this promise told us that you were children and had no guns; that when they had shaken you, you would submit. We hearkened unto them, and were deceived until your army approached our towns. We were deceived, but your people teaching us to confide in that king had helped to deceive us, and we now appeal to your heart, is all the blame ours?

Father, when we saw that we had been deceived, and heard the invitation which you gave us to draw near to the fire you had kindled and talk with you concerning peace, we made haste toward it. You then told us you could crush us to nothing, and you demanded from us a great country as the price of that peace which you had offered to us; as if our want of strength had destroyed our rights. Our chiefs had felt your power and were unable to contend against you, and they therefore gave up that country. What they agreed to has bound our nation; but your anger against us must by this time be cooled, and although our strength is not increased, nor

---

*James Buchanan. *Sketches of the History, Manners, and Customs of the North American Indians with a Plan for Their Amelioration.* New York: William Borradaile, 1824. 108–116.

your power becomes less, we ask you to consider calmly: Were the terms dictated to us by your commissioners reasonable and just?

Father, your commissioners, when they drew the line which separated the land then given up to you from that which you agreed should remain to be ours, did most solemnly promise that we should be secured in the peaceable possession of the land which we inhabited, east and north of that line. —Does this promise bind you?

Hear, now, we entreat you, what has since happened concerning that land. On the day we finished the treaty at Fort Stanwix, commissioners from Pennsylvania told our chiefs that they had come there to purchase from lines of their state; and they told us that all the lands belonging to us within the line would strike the river Susquehanna below Tioga branch. They then left us to consider of the bargain until next day. The next day we let them know that we were unwilling to sell all the land within their state, and proposed to let them have a part of it, which we pointed out to them in their map. They told us that they must have the whole, that it was already ceded to them by the great king at the time of making peace with you, and was then their own; but they said that they would not take advantage of that, and were willing to pay us for it, after the manner of their ancestors. Our chiefs were unable to contend at that time, and therefore they sold the lands up to the line, which was then shown them as the line of that state. What the commissioners had said about the land having been ceded to them at the peace, they considered as intended only to lessen the price, and they passed it by with very little notice; but since that time we have heard so much from others about the right to our lands which the king gave when you made peace with him, that it is our earnest desire that you will tell us what it means.

Our nation empowered J. L. to let out a part of our lands; he told us that he was sent by Congress to do this for us, and we fear he has deceived us in the writing he obtained from us; for since the time of our giving that power, a man named P— has come and claimed our whole country northward of the line of Pennsylvania, under a purchase from that L. to whom he said he had paid twenty thousand dollars for it; he also said, that he had bought it from the council of the Thirteen Fires, and paid them twenty thousand more for the same; and he also said that it did not belong to us, for that the great king had ceded the whole of it, when you made peace with him. Thus he claimed the whole country north of Pennsylvania, and west of the lands belonging to the Cayugas. He demanded it; he insisted on his demand, and declared to us that he would have it all. It was impossible for us to grant him this, and we immediately refused it. After some days he proposed to run a line a small distance eastward of our western boundary, which we also refused to agree to. He then threatened us with immediate war if we did not comply.

Upon this threat our chiefs held a council, and they agreed that no event of war could be worse than to be driven, with our wives and children, from the only country which we had any right to; and therefore, weak as our nation was, they determined to take the chance of war rather than submit to such unjust demands, which seemed to have no bounds. Mr. Street, the great trader at Niagara, was then with us, having come at the request of P—; and as he had always professed to be our great friend, we consulted him on this subject. He also told us that our lands had been ceded by the king, and that we must give them up. Astonished at what we heard from every quarter, with hearts aching with compassion for our women and children, we were thus compelled to give up all our country north of the line of Pennsylvania, and east of the Chenesee river up to the great forks, and east of a south-line drawn up from that fork to the line of Pennsylvania. For this land P— agreed to pay us ten thousand dollars in hand, and one thousand dollars a year for ever. He paid us two thousand five hundred dollars, and he sent for us to come last spring and receive our money; but instead of paying us the residue (or remainder) of the ten thousand dollars, and the one thousand dollars due for the first year, he offered only five hundred dollars, and insisted that he had agreed with us for that sum to be paid yearly.

We debated with him for six days, during all which time he persisted in refusing to pay us our just demand; and he insisted that we should receive the five hundred dollars; and Street from Niagara also insisted on our receiving the money as it was offered us. The last reason which he assigned for continuing to refuse paying us was—that the king had ceded the land to the Thirteen Fires, and that he had bought them from you and paid you for them.

Father, we could bear this confusion no longer and determined to press through every difficulty, and lift up our voice so that you might hear us, and to claim that security in the possession of our lands, which your commissioners so solemnly promised us; and we now entreat you to inquire into our complaints, and to redress our wrongs.

Father, our writings were lodged in the hands of Street of Niagara, as we supposed him to be our friend; but when we saw P— consulting Street on every occasion, we doubted of his honesty towards us; and we have since heard that he was to receive for his endeavors to deceive us a piece of land ten miles in width west of the Chenesee river; and near forty miles in length extending to Lake Ontario; and the lines of this tract have been run accordingly, although no part of it is within the bounds which limit this purchase.

Father, you have said that we were in your hand, and that by closing it you could crush us to nothing. Are you then determined to crush us? If you are, tell us so, that those of our nation who have become your children, and have determined to die so, may know what to do. In this case one chief has said he would ask you to put him out of his pain. Another, who will not think of dying by the hand of his father, or of his brother, has said he will retire to the Chataughque, eat of the fatal root, and sleep with his fathers in peace.

Before you determine a measure so unjust, look up to God, who made us as well as you; we hope he will not permit you to destroy the whole of our nation.

Father, hear our case: Many nations inhabited this country, but they had no wisdom, therefore they warred together; the Six Nations were powerful and compelled them to peace. The land for a great extent was given up to them, but the nations which were not destroyed all continued on those lands: and claimed the protection of the Six Nations, as brothers of their fathers. They were men, and when at peace had a right to live upon the earth.

The French came among us, and built Niagara; they became our fathers, and took care of us. Sir William Johnson came, and took that fort from the French; he became our father, and promised to take care of us, and he did so until you were too strong for his king. To him we gave four miles round Niagara, as a place of trade. We have already said how we came to join against you; we saw that we were wrong, we wished for peace, you demanded a great country to be given up to you, it was surrendered to you as the price of peace, and we ought to have peace and possession of the little land which you then left us.

Father, when that great country was given up to you there were but few chiefs present, and they were compelled to give it up. And it is not the Six Nations only that reproach those chiefs with having given up that country. The Chippewas, and all the nations who lived on these lands westward, call to us, and ask us, "Brothers of our fathers, where is the place which you have reserved for us to lie down upon?"

Father, you have compelled us to do that which makes us ashamed. We have nothing to answer to the children of the brothers of our fathers. When last spring they called upon us to go to war to secure them a bed to lie down upon, the Senecas entreated them to be quiet until we had spoken to you; but on our way down, we heard that your army had gone towards the country which those nations inhabited; and if they meet together, the best blood on both sides will stain the ground.

Father, we will not conceal from you that the great God, and not men, has preserved Cornplanter from the hands of his own nation. For they ask continually, "Where is the land on which our children, and their children after them, are to lie down upon? You told us," say they, "that the line drawn from Pennsylvania to Lake Ontario would mark it forever on the east, and the line running from Beaver Creek to Pennsylvania would mark it on the west, and we see that it is not so; for first one, and then another, come and take it away by order of that people which you tell us promised to secure it to us." He is silent, for he has nothing to answer. When the sun goes down he opens his heart before God; and earlier than the sun appears again upon the hills he gives thanks for his protection during the night; for he feels that among men, become desperate by the injuries they sustain, it is God only that can preserve him. He loves peace, and all he had in store he has given to those who have been robbed by your people, lest they should plunder the innocent to repay themselves. The whole season, which others have employed in providing for their families, he has spent in endeavors to preserve peace; and this moment his wife and children are lying on the ground, and in want of food: his heart is in pain for them, but he perceives that the Great Spirit will try his firmness in doing what is right.

Father, the game which the Great Spirit sent into our country for us to eat is going from among us. We thought he intended we should till the ground with the plough as the white people do, and we talked to one another about it. But before we speak to you concerning this, we must know from you whether you mean to leave us and our children any land to till. Speak plainly to us concerning this great business.

All the land we have been speaking of belonged to the Six Nations: no part of it ever belonged to the King of England, and he could not give it up to you. The land we live on our fathers received from God, and they transmitted it to us for our children, and we cannot part with it.

Father, we told you that we would open our hearts to you: hear us once more. At Fort Stanwix we agreed to deliver up those of our people who should do you any wrong, and that you might try them and punish them according to your law. We delivered up two men accordingly; but instead of trying them according to your law, the lowest of your people took them from your magistrate, and put them immediately to death. It is just to punish the murderer with death, but the Senecas will not deliver up their people to men who disregard the treaties of their own nation.

Father, innocent men of our nation are killed, one after another, and of our best families; but none of your people who have committed those murders have been punished. We recollect that you did promise to punish those who killed our people; and we ask, was it intended that your people should kill the Senecas, and not only remain unpunished, but be protected from the next of kin?

Father, these are to us very great things; we know that you are very strong, and we have heard that you are wise, and we shall wait to hear your answer that we may know that you are just.

[GSNA]

The Bill of Rights, Amendments I–X to the Constitution

December 15, 1791

What was and continues to be known as the "Bill of Rights" are the first ten amendments to the Constitution. The pervasive call for their inclusion during the state conventions on the Constitution's ratification made these amendments an essential supplement to that document.

Preamble

CONGRESS OF THE United States begun and held at the City of New-York, on Wednesday the fourth of March, one thousand seven hundred and eighty nine.

The Conventions of a number of the States, having at the time of their adopting the Constitution, expressed a desire, in order to prevent misconstruction or abuse of its powers, that further declaratory and restrictive clauses should be added: And as extending the ground of public confidence in the Government, will best ensure the beneficent ends of its institution.

Resolved by the Senate and House of Representatives of the United States of America, in Congress assembled, two thirds of both Houses concurring, that the following Articles be proposed to the Legislatures of the several States, as amendments to the Constitution of the United States, all, or any of which Articles, when ratified by three fourths of the said Legislatures, to be valid to all intents and purposes, as part of the said Constitution; viz.

ARTICLES in addition to, and Amendment of the Constitution of the United States of America, proposed by Congress, and ratified by the Legislatures of the several States, pursuant to the fifth Article of the original Constitution.

Amendment I

Congress shall make no law respecting an establishment of religion, or prohibiting the free exercise thereof; or abridging the freedom of speech, or of the press; or the right of the people peaceably to assemble, and to petition the Government for a redress of grievances.

Amendment II

A well regulated Militia, being necessary to the security of a free State, the right of the people to keep and bear Arms, shall not be infringed.

Amendment III

No Soldier shall, in time of peace be quartered in any house, without the consent of the Owner, nor in time of war, but in a manner to be prescribed by law.

Amendment IV

The right of the people to be secure in their persons, houses, papers, and effects, against unreasonable searches and seizures, shall not be violated, and no Warrants shall issue, but upon probable cause, supported by Oath or affirmation, and particularly describing the place to be searched, and the persons or things to be seized.

Amendment V

No person shall be held to answer for a capital, or otherwise infamous crime, unless on a presentment or indictment of a Grand Jury, except in cases arising in the land or naval forces, or in the Militia, when in actual service in time of War or public danger; nor shall any person be subject for the same offence to be twice put in jeopardy of life or limb; nor shall be compelled in any criminal case to be a witness against himself, nor be deprived of life, liberty, or property, without due process of law; nor shall private property be taken for public use, without just compensation.

Amendment VI

In all criminal prosecutions, the accused shall enjoy the right to a speedy and public trial, by an impartial jury of the State and district wherein the crime shall have been committed, which district shall have been previously ascertained by law, and to be informed of the nature and cause of the accusation; to be confronted with the witnesses against him; to have compulsory process for obtaining witnesses in his favor, and to have the Assistance of Counsel for his defence.

Amendment VII

In Suits at common law, where the value in controversy shall exceed twenty dollars, the right of trial by jury shall be preserved, and no fact tried by a jury, shall be otherwise re-examined in any Court of the United States, than according to the rules of the common law.

Amendment VIII

Excessive bail shall not be required, nor excessive fines imposed, nor cruel and unusual punishments inflicted.

Amendment IX

The enumeration in the Constitution, of certain rights, shall not be construed to deny or disparage others retained by the people.

Amendment X

The powers not delegated to the United States by the Constitution, nor prohibited by it to the States, are reserved to the States respectively, or to the people.

[USC]

The United States and the Six Nations, Treaty

November 11, 1794

The confederation of Indian tribes known as the Iroquois, or Six Nations, included the Mohawks, the Oneidas, the Onondagas, the Cayugas, the Senecas, and the Tuscaroras. This treaty, concluded November 11, 1794, fixed the limits of the territory to be left in the possession of these tribes, who had fought against the colonies in the War of Independence.

— Note by Charles W. Eliot

THE PRESIDENT OF the United States having determined to hold a conference with the Six Nations of Indians, for the purpose of removing from their minds all causes of complaint, and establishing a firm and permanent friendship with them; and Timothy Pickering being appointed sole agent for that purpose; and the agent having met and conferred with the Sachems, Chiefs and Warriors of the Six Nations, in a general council: Now in order to accomplish the good design of this conference, the parties have agreed on the following articles, which, when ratified by the President, with the advice and consent of the Senate of the United States, shall be binding on them and the Six Nations.

ARTICLE I

Peace and friendship are hereby firmly established, and shall be perpetual, between the United States and the Six Nations.

ARTICLE II

The United States acknowledge the lands reserved to the Oneida, Onondaga and Cayuga Nations, in their respective treaties with the state of New York, and called their reservations, to be their property; and the United States will never claim the same, nor disturb them or either of the Six Nations, nor their Indian friends residing thereon and united with them, in the free use and enjoyment thereof: but the said reservations shall remain theirs, until they choose to sell the same to the people of the United States who have right to purchase.

ARTICLE III

The land of the Seneka nation is bounded as follows: Beginning on Lake Ontario, at the north-west corner of the land they sold to Oliver Phelps, the line run westerly along the lake, as far as O-yōng-wong-yeh Creek at Johnson's Landing-place, about four miles eastward from the fort of Niagara; then southerly up that creek to its main fork, then straight to the main fork of Stedman's Creek, which empties into the river Niagara, above Fort Schlosser, and then onward, from that fork, continuing the same straight course, to that river; (this line, from the mouth of O-yōng-wong-yeh Creek to the river Niagara, above Fort Schlosser, being the eastern boundary of a strip of land, extending from the same line to Niagara River, which the Seneka nation ceded to the King of Great Britain, at a treaty held about thirty years ago, with Sir William Johnson;) then the line runs along the river Niagara to Lake Erie; then along Lake Erie to the north-east corner of a triangular piece of land which the United States conveyed to the state of Pennsylvania, as by the President's patent, dated the third day of March, 1792; then due south to the northern boundary of that state; then due east to the south-west corner of the land sold by the Seneka nation to Oliver Phelps; and then north and northerly, along Phelps's line, to the place beginning on Lake Ontario. Now, the United States acknowledge all the land within the aforementioned boundaries, to be the property of the Seneka nation; and the United States will never claim the same, nor disturb the Seneka nation, nor any of the Six Nations, or their Indian friends residing thereon and united with them, in the free use and enjoyment thereof: but it shall remain theirs, until they choose to sell the same to the people of the United States, who have the right to purchase.

ARTICLE IV

The United States having thus described and acknowledged what lands belong to the Oneidas, Onondagas, Cayugas, and Senekas, and engaged never to claim the same, nor to disturb them, or any of the Six Nations, or their Indian friends residing thereon and united with them, in the free use and enjoyment thereof: Now the Six Nations, and each of them, hereby engage that they will never claim any other lands within the boundaries of the United States; nor ever disturb the people of the United States in the free use and enjoyment thereof.

ARTICLE V

The Seneka nation, all others of the Six Nations concurring, cede to the United States the right of making a wagon road from Fort Schlosser to Lake Erie, as far south as Buffaloe Creek; and the people of the United States shall have the free and undisturbed use of this road, for the purposes of travelling and transportation. And the Six Nations, and each of them, will forever allow to the people of the United States, a free passage through their lands, and the free use of their harbors and rivers adjoining and within their respective tracts of land, for the passing and securing of vessels and boats, and liberty to land their cargoes when necessary for their safety.

ARTICLE VI

In consideration of the peace and friendship hereby established, and of the engagements entered into by the Six Nations; and because the United States desire, with humanity and kindness, to contribute to their comfortable support; and to render the peace and friendship hereby established strong and perpetual; the United States now deliver to the Six Nations, and the Indians of the other nations residing among and united with them, a quantity of goods of the value of ten thousand dollars. And for the same consider-ations, and with a view to promote the future welfare of the Six Nations, and of their Indian friends aforesaid, the United States will add the sum of three thousand dollars to the one thousand five hundred dollars, heretofore allowed them by an article ratified by the President, on the twenty-third day of April 1792; making in the whole, four thousand five hundred dollars; which shall be expended yearly forever, in purchasing clothing, domestic animals, implements of husbandry and other utensils suited to their circumstances, and in compensating useful artificers, who shall reside with them or near them, and be employed for their benefit. The immediate application of the whole annual allowance now stipulated, to be made by the superintendent appointed by the President for the affairs of the Six Nations, and their Indian friends aforesaid.

ARTICLE VII

Lest the firm peace and friendship now established should be interrupted by the misconduct of individuals, the United States and Six Nations agree, that for injuries done by individuals on either side, no private revenge or retaliation shall take place; but, instead thereof, complaint shall be made by the party injured, to the other: By the Six Nations or any of them, to the President of the United States, or the Superintendent by him appointed: and by the Superintendent, or other person appointed by the President, to the principal chiefs of the Six Nations, or of the nation to which the offender belongs: and such prudent measures shall then be pursued as shall be necessary to preserve our peace and friendship unbroken; until the legislature (or great council) of the United States shall make the equitable provision for the purpose.

NOTE: It is clearly understood by the parties to this treaty, that the annuity stipulated in the sixth article, is to be applied to the benefit of such of the Six Nations and of their Indian friends united with them as aforesaid, as do or shall reside within the boundaries of the United States: for the United States do not interfere with nations, tribes or families, of Indians elsewhere resident.

[AHD]

President George Washington, Farewell Address

September 19, 1796

George Washington contemplated retirement in 1792 when his first term in office was nearing its end, and with awareness that he would be establishing a precedent, decided to prepare a valedictory message to the American people. Acting on this impulse in May of 1792, he wrote James Madison a letter outlining the points he wished to cover, and Madison prepared a draft for him incorporating these ideas. When the idea of retirement in 1792 was abandoned and he agreed to accept a second term, Madison's draft of the planned farewell message was put aside. In 1796, however, Washington had no doubt that the time to leave office was at hand, and it is reported by many that he believed the Farewell Address would at least have the effect of leaving no doubt that he was not available as a candidate for a third term.

In May of 1796, Washington revised the draft which Madison had prepared four years earlier, and sent it to Alexander Hamilton for comments and improvements. For the next several months, Hamilton and Washington corresponded frequently about the proposed address, sending drafts back and forth. Finally, at Washington's request, Hamilton discussed their efforts at length with John Jay, and then delivered a final version to the president. Washington made some final revisions and delivered the final draft of his Farewell Address in handwritten form to his cabinet in September 1796. On September 19, 1796, the document was printed by Philadelphia printer David C. Claypoole in his newspaper, the American Daily Advertiser. *A week later, it appeared in a leading Boston paper, the* Independent Chronicle, *and subsequently in other newspapers throughout the country. It was never delivered as a speech.*

The ideas expressed in the Farewell Address, however much others contributed to its final written form, were distinctly Washington's. It contains

*no surprises, just a reasoned expression of the accumulated wisdom of a long
and eventful life. He outlined the benefits of the American system of government, echoing the lengthy debate over the new Constitution a decade earlier.
He stressed the dangers of parties, warned against foreign entanglements,
cautioned the country about the evils of a too powerful military establishment,
and pointed out the advantages to maintaining the public credit in good order
and avoiding the accumulation of debt. As a personal statement of great force,
clarity, and power, it brought down the curtain on his era more effectively than
anything else could possibly have done.*

– Note by John Grafton

United States 19th September 1796
Friends, & Fellow-Citizens.

THE PERIOD FOR a new election of a Citizen, to Administer the
Executive government of the United States, being not far distant,
and the time actually arrived, when your thoughts must be employed in designating the person, who is to be cloathed with that
important trust, it appears to me proper, especially as it may con-
duce to a more distinct expression of the public voice, that I should
now apprise you of the resolution I have formed, to decline being
considered among the number of those, out of whom a choice is
to be made.

I beg you, at the same time, to do me the justice to be assured,
that this resolution has not been taken, without a strict regard to all
the considerations appertaining to the relation, which binds a dutiful Citizen to his country—and that, in withdrawing the tender of
service which silence in my Situation might imply, I am influenced
by no diminution of zeal for your future interest, no deficiency of
grateful respect for your past kindness; but am supported by a full
conviction that the step is compatible with both.

The acceptance of, & continuance hitherto in, the Office to
which your Suffrages have twice called me, have been a uniform
sacrifice of inclination to the opinion of duty, and to a deference
for what appeared to be your desire. I constantly hoped, that it
would have been much earlier in my power, consistently with motives, which I was not at liberty to disregard, to return to that retirement, from which I had been reluctantly drawn. The strength of
my inclination to do this, previous to the last Election, had even led
to the preparation of an address to declare it to you; but mature

reflection on the then perplexed & critical posture of our Affairs with foreign nations, and the unanimous advice of persons entitled to my confidence, impelled me to abandon the idea.

I rejoice, that the state of your concerns, external as well as internal, no longer renders the pursuit of inclination incompatible with the sentiment of duty, or propriety; & am persuaded whatever partiality may be retained for my services, that in the present circumstances of our country, you will not disapprove my determination to retire.

The impressions, with which, I first undertook the arduous trust, were explained on the proper occasion. In the discharge of this trust, I will only say, that I have, with good intentions, contributed towards the Organization and Administration of the government, the best exertions of which a very fallible judgment was capable. Not unconscious, in the outset, of the inferiority of my qualifications, experience in my own eyes, perhaps still more in the eyes of others, has strengthened the motives to diffidence of myself; and every day the increasing weight of years admonishes me more and more, that the shade of retirement is as necessary to me as it will be welcome. Satisfied that if any circumstances have given peculiar value to my services, they were temporary, I have the consolation to believe, that while choice and prudence invite me to quit the political scene, patriotism does not forbid it.

In looking forward to the moment, which is intended to terminate the career of my public life, my feelings do not permit me to suspend the deep acknowledgment of that debt of gratitude which I owe to my beloved country, for the many honors it has conferred upon me; still more for the steadfast confidence with which it has supported me; and for the opportunities I have thence enjoyed of manifesting my inviolable attachment, by services faithful & persevering, though in usefulness unequal to my zeal. If benefits have resulted to our country from these services, let it always be remembered to your praise, and as an instructive example in our annals, that, under circumstances in which the Passions agitated in every direction were liable to mislead, amidst appearances sometimes dubious, vicissitudes of fortune often discouraging, in situations in which not unfrequently want of Success has countenanced the spirit of criticism, the constancy of your support was the essential prop of the efforts, and a guarantee of the plans by which they were effected. Profoundly penetrated with this idea, I shall carry it with me to my grave, as a strong incitement to unceasing vows that Heaven may continue to you the choicest tokens of its beneficence—that your Union & brotherly affection may be perpetual—that the free constitution, which is the work of your hands, may be sacredly maintained—that its Administration in every department may be stamped with wisdom and Virtue—that, in fine, the happiness of the people of these States, under the auspices of liberty, may be made complete, by so careful a preservation and so prudent a use of this blessing as will acquire to them the glory of recommending it to the applause, the affection—and adoption of every nation which is yet a stranger to it.

Here, perhaps, I ought to stop. But solicitude for your welfare, which cannot end but with my life, and the apprehension of danger, natural to that solicitude, urge me on an occasion like the present, to offer to your solemn contemplation, and to recommend to your frequent review, some sentiments; which are the result of much reflection, of no inconsiderable observation, and which appear to me all important to the permanency of your felicity as a People. These will be offered to you with the more freedom as you can only see in them the disinterested warnings of a parting friend, who can possibly have no personal motive to bias his counsel. Nor can I forget, as an encouragement to it, your indulgent reception of my sentiments on a former and not dissimilar occasion.

Interwoven as is the love of liberty with every ligament of your hearts, no recommendation of mine is necessary to fortify or confirm the Attachment.

The Unity of Government which constitutes you one people is also now dear to you. It is justly so; for it is a main Pillar in the Edifice of your real independence, the support of your tranquility at home; your peace abroad; of your safety; of your prosperity; of that very Liberty which you so highly prize. But as it is easy to foresee, that from different causes & from different quarters, much pains will be taken, many artifices employed, to weaken in your minds the conviction of this truth; as this is the point in your political fortress against which the batteries of internal & external enemies will be most constantly and actively (though often covertly & insidiously) directed, it is of infinite moment, that you should properly estimate the immense value of your national Union to your collective & individual happiness; that you should cherish a cordial, habitual & immoveable attachment to it; accustoming yourselves to think and speak of it as of the Palladium of your political safety and prosperity; watching for its preservation with jealous anxiety; discountenancing whatever may suggest even a suspicion that it can in any event be abandoned, and indignantly frowning upon the first dawning of every attempt to alienate any portion of our Country from the rest, or to enfeeble the sacred ties which now link together the various parts.

For this you have every inducement of sympathy and interest. Citizens by birth or choice, of a common country, that country has a right to concentrate your affections. The name of American, which belongs to you, in your national capacity, must always exalt the just pride of Patriotism, more than any appellation derived from local discriminations. With slight shades of difference, you have the same Religion, Manners, Habits & political Principles. You have in a common cause fought & triumphed together—the independence & liberty you possess are the work of joint councils, and joint efforts—of common dangers, sufferings and successes.

But these considerations, however powerfully they address themselves to your sensibility are greatly outweighed by those which apply more immediately to your Interest. Here every portion of our country finds the most commanding motives for carefully guarding & preserving the Union of the whole.

The North, in an unrestrained intercourse with the South, protected by the equal Laws of a common government, finds in the productions of the latter, great additional resources of Maratime & commercial enterprise and—precious materials of manufacturing industry. The South in the same Intercourse, benefitting by the Agency of the North, sees its agriculture grow & its commerce expand. Turning partly into its own channels the seamen of the North, it finds its particular navigation invigorated; and while it contributes, in different ways, to nourish & increase the general mass of the National navigation, it looks forward to the protection of a Maratime strength, to which itself is unequally adapted. The East, in a like intercourse with the West, already finds, and in the progressive improvement of interior communications, by land & water, will more & more find a valuable vent for the commodities which it brings from abroad, or manufactures at home. The West derives from the East supplies requisite to its growth & comfort—and what is perhaps of still greater consequence, it must of necessity owe the Secure enjoyment of indispensable outlets for its own productions to the weight, influence, and the future maritime strength of the Atlantic side of the Union, directed by an indissoluble community of Interest as one Nation. Any other tenure, by which the West can hold this essential advantage, whether derived from its own separate strength, or from an apostate & unnatural connection with any foreign Power, must be intrinsically precarious.

While then every part of our country thus feels an immediate & particular Interest in Union, all the parts combined cannot fail to find in the united mass of means & efforts greater strength, greater resource, proportionally greater security from external danger, a less frequent interruption of their Peace by foreign Nations; and, what is of inestimable value! they must derive from Union an exemption from those broils and Wars between themselves, which so frequently afflict neighboring countries, not tied together by the same government; which their own rivalships alone would be sufficient to produce, but which opposite foreign alliances, attachments & intrigues would stimulate & embitter. Hence likewise they will avoid the necessity of those overgrown Military establishments, which under any form of Government are inauspicious to liberty, and which are to be regarded as particularly hostile to Republican Liberty: In this sense it is, that your union ought to be considered as a main prop of your liberty, and that the love of the one ought to endear to you the preservation of the other.

These considerations speak a persuasive language to every reflecting & virtuous mind, and exhibit the continuance of the Union as a primary object of Patriotic desire. Is there a doubt, whether a common government can embrace so large a sphere? Let experience solve it. To listen to mere speculation in such a case were criminal. We are authorized to hope that a proper organization of the whole, with the auxiliary agency of governments for the respective Subdivisions, will afford a happy issue to the experiment. 'Tis well worth a fair and full experiment. With such powerful and obvious motives to Union, affecting all parts of our country, while experience shall not have demonstrated its impracticability, there will always be reason, to distrust the patriotism of those, who in any quarter may endeavor to weaken its bands.

In contemplating the causes which may disturb our Union, it occurs as matter of serious concern, that any ground should have been furnished for characterizing parties by Geographical discriminations—Northern and Southern—Atlantic and Western;

whence designing men may endeavor to excite a belief that there is a real difference of local interests and views. One of the expedients of Party to acquire influence, within particular districts, is to misrepresent the opinions & aims of other Districts. You cannot shield yourselves too much against the jealousies & heart burnings which spring from these misrepresentations. They tend to render Alien to each other that who ought to be bound together by fraternal Affection. The Inhabitants of our Western country have lately had a useful lesson on this head. They have Seen, in the Negotiation by the Executive, and in the unanimous ratification by the Senate, of the Treaty with Spain, and in the universal satisfaction at that event, throughout the United States, a decisive proof how unfounded were the suspicions propagated among them of a policy in the General Government and in the Atlantic States unfriendly to their Interests in regard to the Mississippi. They have been witnesses to the formation of two Treaties, that with G: Britain and that with Spain, which secure to them every thing they could desire, in respect to our foreign relations, towards confirming their prosperity. Will it not be their wisdom to rely for the preservation of these advantages on the Union by whom they were procured? Will they not henceforth be deaf to those Advisers, if such there are, who would sever them from their Brethren and connect them with Aliens?

To the efficacy and permanency of Your Union, a Government for the whole is indispensable. No Alliances however strict between the parts can be an adequate substitute. They must inevitably experience the infractions & interruptions which all Alliances in all times have experienced. Sensible of this momentous truth, you have improved upon your first essay, by the adoption of a Constitution of Government, better calculated than your former for an intimate Union, and for the efficacious management of your common concerns. This government, the offspring of our own choice uninfluenced and unawed, adopted upon full investigation & mature deliberation, completely free in its principles, in the distribution of its powers, uniting security with energy, and containing within itself a provision for its own amendment, has a just claim to your confidence and your support. Respect for its authority, compliance with its Laws, acquiescence in its measures, are duties enjoined by the fundamental maxims of true Liberty. The basis of our political Systems is the right of the people to make and to alter their

Constitutions of Government. But the Constitution which at any time exists, 'till changed by an explicit and authentic act of the whole People, is sacredly obligatory upon all. The very idea of the power and the right of the People to establish Government presupposes the duty of every Individual to obey the established Government.

All obstructions to the execution of the Laws, all combinations and Associations, under whatever plausible character, with the real design to direct, control, counteract, or awe the regular deliberation and action of the Constituted authorities are destructive of this fundamental principle and of fatal tendency. They serve to Organize faction, to give it an artificial and extraordinary force—to put in the place of the delegated will of the Nation, the will of a party; often a small but artful and enterprising minority of the Community; and, according to the alternate triumphs of different parties, to make the public Administration the Mirror of the ill concerted and incongruous projects of faction, rather than the Organ of consistent and wholesome plans digested by common councils and modified by mutual interests. However combinations or Associations of the above description may now & then answer popular ends, they are likely, in the course of time and things, to become potent engines, by which cunning, ambitious and unprincipled men will be enabled to subvert the Power of the People, & to usurp for themselves the reins of Government; destroying afterwards the very engines which have lifted them to unjust dominion.

Towards the preservation of your Government and the permanency of your present happy state, it is requisite, not only that you steadily discountenance irregular oppositions to its acknowledged authority, but also that you resist with care the spirit of innovation upon its principles however specious the pretexts. One method of assault may be to effect, in the forms of the Constitution, alterations which will impair the energy of the system, and thus to undermine what cannot be directly overthrown. In all the changes to which you may be invited, remember that time and habit are at least as necessary to fix the true character of Governments, as of other human institutions—that experience is the surest standard, by which to test the real tendency of the existing Constitution of a Country—that facility in changes upon the credit of mere hypotheses & opinion exposes to perpetual change, from the endless variety of hypotheses and opinion: and remember, especially, that for the efficient management of your common interests, in a country so extensive as ours, a Government of as much vigor as is consistent with the perfect security of Liberty is indispensable—Liberty itself will find in such a Government, with powers properly distributed and adjusted, its surest Guardian. It is indeed little else than a name, where the Government is too feeble to withstand the enterprises of faction, to confine each member of the Society within the limits prescribed by the laws & to maintain all in the secure & tranquil enjoyment of the rights of person & property.

I have already intimated to you the danger of Parties in the State, with particular reference to the founding of them on Geographical discriminations. Let me now take a more comprehensive view, & warn you in the most solemn manner against the baneful effects of the Spirit of Party, generally.

This Spirit, unfortunately, is inseparable from our nature, having its root in the strongest passions of the human Mind. It exists under different shapes in all Governments, more or less stifled, controlled, or repressed; but in those of the popular form it is seen in its greatest rankness and is truly their worst enemy.

The alternate domination of one faction over another, sharpened by the spirit of revenge natural to party dissention, which in different ages & countries has perpetrated the most horrid enormities, is itself a frightful despotism. But this leads at length to a more formal and permanent despotism. The disorders & miseries, which result, gradually incline the minds of men to seek security & repose in the absolute power of an Individual: and sooner or later the chief of some prevailing faction more able or more fortunate than his competitors turns this disposition to the purposes of his own elevation, on the ruins of Public Liberty.

Without looking forward to an extremity of this kind (which nevertheless ought not to be entirely out of sight) the common & continual mischiefs of the spirit of Party are sufficient to make it the interest and the duty of a wise People to discourage and restrain it.

It serves always to distract the Public Councils and enfeeble the Public Administration. It agitates the Community with ill founded Jealousies and false alarms, kindles the animosity of one part against another, foments occasionally riot & insurrection. It opens the door to foreign influence & corruption, which find a facilitated access to the government itself through the channels of party passions. Thus the policy and the will of one country, are subjected to the policy and will of another.

There is an opinion that parties in free countries are useful checks upon the Administration of the Government and serve to keep alive the spirit of Liberty. This within certain limits is probably true and in Governments of a Monarchical cast Patriotism may look with indulgence, if not with favour, upon the spirit of party. But in those of the popular character, in Governments purely elective, it is a spirit not to be encouraged. From their natural tendency, it is certain there will always be enough of that spirit for every salutary purpose. And there being constant danger of excess, the effort ought to be, by force of public opinion, to mitigate & assuage it. A fire not to be quenched; it demands a uniform vigilance to prevent its bursting into a flame, lest instead of warming it should consume.

It is important, likewise, that the habits of thinking in a free Country should inspire caution in those entrusted with its Administration, to confine themselves within their respective Constitutional Spheres; avoiding in the exercise of the Powers of one department to encroach upon another. The spirit of encroachment tends to consolidate the powers of all the departments in one, and thus to create whatever the form of government, a real despotism. A just estimate of that love of power, and proneness to abuse it, which predominates in the human heart, is sufficient to satisfy us of the truth of this position. The necessity of reciprocal checks in the exercise of political power; by dividing and distributing it into different depositories, & constituting each the Guardian of the Public Weal against invasions by the others, has been evinced by experiments ancient & modern; some of them in our country & under our own eyes. To preserve them must be as necessary as to institute them. If in the opinion of the People, the distribution or modification of the Constitutional powers be in any particular wrong, let it be corrected by an amendment in the way which the Constitution designates. But let there be no change by usurpation; for though this, in one instance, may be the instrument of good, it is the customary weapon by which free governments are destroyed. The precedent must always greatly overbalance in permanent evil any partial or transient benefit which the use can at any time yield.

Of all the dispositions and habits which lead to political prosperity, Religion and morality are indispensable supports. In vain would that man claim the tribute of Patriotism, who should labour to subvert these great Pillars of human happiness, these firmest props of the duties of Men & citizens. The mere Politican, equally with the pious man ought to respect & to cherish them. A volume could not trace all their connections with private & public felicity. Let it simply be asked where the security for property, for reputation, for life, is if the sense of religious obligation desert the Oaths, which are the instruments of investigation in Courts of Justice? And let us with caution indulge the supposition, that morality can be maintained without religion. Whatever may be conceded to the influence of refined education on minds of peculiar structure—reason & experience both forbid us to expect that National morality can prevail in exclusion of religious principle.

'Tis substantially true, that virtue or morality is a necessary spring of popular government. The rule indeed extends with more or less force to every species of Free Government. Who that is a sincere friend to it, can look with indifference upon attempts to shake the foundation of the fabric.

Promote then as an object of primary importance, Institutions for the general diffusion of knowledge. In proportion as the structure of a government gives force to public opinion, it is essential that public opinion should be enlightened.

As a very important source of strength & security, cherish public credit. One method of preserving it is to use it as sparingly as possible: avoiding occasions of expense by cultivating peace, but remembering also that timely disbursements to prepare for danger frequently prevent much greater disbursements to repel it—avoiding likewise the accumulation of debt, not only by shunning occasions of expense, but by vigorous exertions in time of Peace to discharge the Debts which unavoidable wars may have occasioned, not ungenerously throwing upon posterity the burthen which we ourselves ought to bear. The execution of these maxims belongs to your Representatives, but it is necessary that public opinion should cooperate. To facilitate to them the performance of their duty, it is essential that you should practically bear in mind, that towards the payment of debts there must be Revenue—that to have Revenue there must be taxes—that no taxes can be devised which are not more or less inconvenient & unpleasant—that the intrinsic embarrassment inseparable from the Selection of the proper objects (which is always a choice of difficulties) ought to be a decisive motive for a candid construction of the Conduct of the Government in making it, and for a spirit of acquiescence in the measures for obtaining Revenue which the public exigencies may at any time dictate.

Observe good faith & justice towards all Nations. Cultivate peace & harmony with all—Religion & morality enjoin this conduct; and can it be that good policy does not equally enjoin it? It will be worthy of a free, enlightened, and, at no distant period, a great Nation, to give to mankind the magnanimous and too novel example of a People always guided by an exalted justice & benevolence. Who can doubt that in the course of time and things the fruits of such a plan would richly repay any temporary advantages which might be lost by a steady adherence to it? Can it be, that Providence has not connected the permanent felicity of a Nation with its virtue? The experiment, at least, is recommended by every sentiment which ennobles human Nature. Alas! is it rendered impossible by its vices?

In the execution of such a plan nothing is more essential than that permanent inveterate antipathies against particular Nations and passionate attachments for others should be excluded; and that in place of them just & amicable feelings towards all should be cultivated. The Nation, which indulges towards another an habitual hatred, or an habitual fondness, is in some degree a slave. It is a slave to its animosity or to its affection, either of which is sufficient to lead it astray from its duty and its interest. Antipathy in one Nation against another—disposes each more readily to offer insult and injury, to lay hold of slight causes of umbrage, and to be haughty and intractable, when accidental or trifling occasions of dispute occur. Hence frequent collisions, obstinate envenomed and bloody contests. The Nation, prompted by ill will & resentment sometimes impels to War the Government, contrary to the best calculations of policy. The Government sometimes participates in the national propensity, and adopts through passion what reason would reject; at other times, it makes the animosity of the Nation subservient to projects of hostility Instigated by pride, ambition and other sinister & pernicious motives. The peace often, sometimes perhaps the Liberty, of Nations has been the victim.

So likewise, a passionate attachment of one Nation for another produces a variety of evils. Sympathy for the favourite nation, facilitating the illusion of an imaginary common interest, in cases where no real common interest exists, and infusing into one the enmities of the other, betrays the former into a participation in the quarrels & Wars of the latter, without adequate inducement or justification: It leads also to concessions to the favourite Nation of privileges denied to others, which is apt doubly to injure the Nation making the concessions—by unnecessarily parting with what ought to have been retained—& by exciting jealousy, ill will, and a disposition to retaliate, in the parties from whom equal privileges are withheld: And it gives to ambitious, corrupted, or deluded citizens (who devote themselves to the favourite Nation) facility to betray, or sacrifice the interests of their own country, without odium, sometimes even with popularity; gilding with the appearances of a virtuous sense of obligation, a commendable deference for public opinion, or a laudable zeal for public good, the base or foolish compliances of ambition, corruption or infatuation.

As avenues to foreign influence in innumerable ways, such attachments are particularly alarming to the truly enlightened and independent Patriot. How many opportunities do they afford to tamper with domestic factions, to practice the arts of seduction, to mislead public opinion, to influence or awe the public Councils! Such an attachment of a small or weak, towards a great & powerful Nation, dooms the former to be the satellite of the latter.

Against the insidious wiles of foreign influence, (I conjure you to believe me fellow citizens), the jealousy of a free people ought to be constantly awake; since history and experience prove that foreign influence is one of the most baneful foes of Republican Government. But that jealousy to be useful must be impartial; else it becomes the instrument of the very influence to be avoided, instead of a defence against it. Excessive partiality for one foreign nation and excessive dislike of another, cause those whom they actuate to see danger only on one side, and serve to veil and even second the arts of influence on the other. Real Patriots, who may resist the intrigues of the favourite, are liable to become suspected and odious; while its tools and dupes usurp the applause & confidence of the people, to surrender their interests.

The Great rule of conduct for us, in regard to foreign Nations is in extending our commercial relations to have with them as little political connection as possible. So far as we have already formed engagements let them be fulfilled, with perfect good faith. Here let us stop.

Europe has a set of primary interests, which to us have none, or a very remote relation. Hence she must be engaged in frequent controversies, the causes of which are essentially foreign to our concerns. Hence therefore it must be unwise in us to implicate ourselves, by artificial ties, in the ordinary vicissitudes of her politics, or the ordinary combinations & collisions of her friendships, or enmities.

Our detached & distant situation invites and enables us to pursue a different course. If we remain one People, under an efficient government, the period is not far off, when we may defy material injury from external annoyance; when we may take such an attitude as will cause the neutrality we may at any time resolve upon to be scrupulously respected; when belligerent nations, under the impossibility of making acquisitions upon us, will not lightly hazard the giving us provocation; when we may choose peace or War, as our interest guided by justice shall Counsel.

Why forego the advantages of so peculiar a situation? Why quit our own to stand upon foreign ground? Why, by interweaving our destiny with that of any part of Europe, entangle our peace and prosperity in the toils of European Ambition, Rivalship, Interest, Humor or Caprice?

'Tis our true policy to steer clear of permanent Alliances, [note] with any portion of the foreign World—So far, I mean, as we are now at liberty to do it—for let me not be understood as capable of patronizing infidelity to existing engagements, (I hold the maxim no less applicable to public than to private affairs, that honesty is always the best policy)—I repeat it therefore, Let those engagements be observed in their genuine sense. But in my opinion, it is unnecessary and would be unwise to extend them.

Taking care always to keep ourselves, by suitable establishments, on a respectably defensive posture, we may safely trust to temporary alliances for extraordinary emergencies.

Harmony, liberal intercourse with all Nations, are recommended by policy, humanity and interest. But even our Commercial policy should hold an equal and impartial hand: neither seeking nor granting exclusive favours or preferences; consulting the natural course of things; diffusing & diversifying by gentle means the streams of Commerce, but forcing nothing; establishing with Powers so disposed—in order to give to trade a stable course, to define the rights of our Merchants, and to enable the Government to support them—conventional rules of intercourse; the best that present circumstances and mutual opinion will permit, but temporary, & liable to be from time to time abandoned or varied, as experience and circumstances shall dictate; constantly keeping in view, that 'tis folly in one Nation to look for disinterested favors from another—that it must pay with a portion of its Independence for whatever it may accept under that character—that by such acceptance, it may place itself in the condition of having given equivalents for nominal favours and yet of being reproached with ingratitude for not giving more. There can be no greater error than to expect, or calculate upon real favours from Nation to Nation. 'Tis an illusion which experience must cure, which a just pride ought to discard.

In offering to you, my Countrymen, these counsels of an old and affectionate friend, I dare not hope they will make the strong and lasting impression, I could wish—that they will control the usual current of the passions, or prevent our Nation from running the course which has hitherto marked the Destiny of Nations: But if I may even flatter myself, that they may be productive of some partial benefit, some occasional good; that they may now & then recur to moderate the fury of party spirit, to warn against the mischiefs of foreign Intrigue, to guard against the Impostures of pretended patriotism—this hope will be a full recompense for the solicitude for your welfare, by which they have been dictated.

How far in the discharge of my Official duties, I have been guided by the principles which have been delineated, the public Records and other evidences of my conduct must witness to you and to the world. To me, the assurance of my own conscience is, that I have at least believed myself to be guided by them.

In relation to the still subsisting War in Europe, my Proclamation of the 22d of April 1793 is the index to my Plan. Sanctioned by your approving voice and by that of Your Representatives in both Houses of Congress, the spirit of that measure has continually governed me; uninfluenced by any attempts to deter or divert me from it.

After deliberate examination with the aid of the best lights I could obtain I was well satisfied that our Country, under all the circumstances of the case, had a right to take, and was bound in duty and interest, to take a Neutral position. Having taken it, I determined, as far as should depend upon me, to maintain it, with moderation, perseverance & firmness.

The considerations, which respect the right to hold this conduct, it is not necessary on this occasion to detail. I will only observe, that according to my understanding of the matter, that right, so far from being denied by any of the Belligerent Powers has been virtually admitted by all.

The duty of holding a neutral conduct may be inferred, without any thing more, from the obligation which justice and humanity impose on every Nation, in cases in which it is free to act, to maintain inviolate the relations of Peace and amity towards other Nations.

The inducements of interest for observing that conduct will best be referred to your own reflections & experience. With me, a predominant motive has been to endeavor to gain time to our country to settle & mature its yet recent institutions, and to progress without interruption, to that degree of strength & consistency, which is necessary to give it, humanly speaking, the command of its own fortunes.

Though in reviewing the incidents of my Administration, I am unconscious of intentional error—I am nevertheless too sensible of my defects not to think it probable that I may have committed many errors. Whatever they may be I fervently beseech the Almighty to avert or mitigate the evils to which they may tend. I shall also carry with me the hope that my Country will never cease to view them with indulgence; and that after forty five years of my life dedicated to its Service, with an upright zeal, the faults of incompetent abilities will be consigned to oblivion, as myself must soon be to the Mansions of rest.

Relying on its kindness in this as in other things, and actuated by that fervent love towards it, which is so natural to a Man, who views in it the native soil of himself and his progenitors for several Generations; I anticipate with pleasing expectation that retreat, in which I promise myself to realize, without alloy, the sweet enjoyment of partaking, in the midst of my fellow Citizens, the benign influence of good Laws under a free Government—the ever favourite object of my heart, and the happy reward, as I trust, of our mutual cares, labours and dangers.

Go: Washington

[DI]

Alien and Sedition Laws

June 25 and July 14, 1798

*During the French [Revolution] excitement the Federalists pushed through
Congress two acts which proved the ruin of their party. The Alien Act of
June 25, 1795, "which stands without a parallel in American legislation," was
followed, July 6, by a second act directed against "Alien Enemies." The Alien
Act passed the house by a close vote of 46 to 40. The Sedition Act of July 14,
1798, passed the house by a still closer vote of 44 to 41. Five years before
(1792) England had passed an alien act followed by other acts of similar tenor.*

*The first prosecution under the Sedition Act was peculiar. Matthew
Lyon, M.C., from Vermont, was tried, convicted and sentenced to four
months' imprisonment and $1000 fine. In 1840, long after Lyon's death,
Congress restored to his heirs the fine paid, with the accrued interest.*

*The opposition to these acts formulated itself in numerous petitions from
all sections, north as well as south, and finally in the Virginia and Kentucky
Revolutions.*

– Note by Howard W. Preston

AN ACT CONCERNING ALIENS.

SECTION I. BE IT ENACTED *by the Senate and House of Representatives
of the United States of America in Congress assembled,* That it shall be
lawful for the President of the United States at any time during the
continuance of this act to *order* all such *aliens* as he shall judge dangerous to the peace and safety of the United States, or shall have
reasonable grounds to suspect are concerned in any treasonable or
secret machinations against the government thereof, to depart out
of the territory of the United States, within such time as shall be
expressed in such order, which order shall be served on such alien

by delivering him a copy thereof, or leaving the same at his usual abode, and returned to the office of the Secretary of State, by the marshal or other person to whom the same shall be directed. And in case any alien, so ordered to depart, shall be found at large within the United States after the time limited in such order for his departure, and not having obtained a *licence* from the President to reside therein, or having obtained such *licence* shall not have conformed thereto, every such alien shall, on conviction thereof, be imprisoned for a term not exceeding three years, and shall never after be admitted to become a citizen of the United States. *Provided always, and be it further enacted,* that if any alien so ordered to depart shall prove to the satisfaction of the President, by evidence to be taken before such person or persons as the President shall direct, who are for that purpose hereby authorized to administer oaths, that no injury or danger to the United States will arise from suffering such alien to reside therein, the President of the United States may grant a *licence* to such alien to remain within the United States for such time as he shall judge proper, and at such place as he may designate. And the President may also require of such alien to enter into a bond to the United States, in such penal sum as he may direct, with one or more sufficient sureties to the satisfaction of the person authorized by the President to take the same, conditioned for the good behavior of such alien during his residence in the United States, and not violating his licence, which licence the President may revoke whenever he shall think proper.

SEC. 2. *And be it further enacted,* That it shall be lawful for the President of the United States, whenever he may deem it necessary for the public safety, to order to be removed out of the territory thereof, any alien, who may or shall be in prison in pursuance of this act; and to cause to be arrested and sent out of the United States such of those aliens as shall have been ordered to depart therefrom and shall not have obtained a licence as aforesaid, in all cases where, in the opinion of the President, the public safety requires a speedy removal. And if any alien so removed or sent out of the United States by the President, shall voluntarily return thereto, unless by permission of the President of the United States, such alien on conviction thereof shall be imprisoned so long as, in the opinion of the President, the public safety may require.

SEC. 3. *And be it further enacted,* That every master or commander of any ship or vessel which shall come into any port of the United

States after the first day of July next, shall immediately on his arrival make report in writing to the collector or other chief officer of the customs of such port, of all aliens, if any, on board his vessel, specifying their names, age, the place of nativity, the country from which they shall have come, the nation to which they belong and owe allegiance, their occupation and a description of their persons, as far as he shall be informed thereof, and on failure, every such master and commander shall forfeit and pay three hundred dollars, for the payment whereof on default of such master or commander, such vessel shall also be holden, and may by such collector or other officer of the customs be detained. And it shall be the duty of such collector or other officer of the customs, forthwith to transmit to the office of the department of State true copies of all such returns.

SEC. 4. *And be it further enacted,* That the circuit and district courts of the United States shall respectively have cognizance of all crimes and offences against this act. And all marshals and other officers of the United States are required to execute all precepts and orders of the President of the United States issued in pursuance or by virtue of this act.

SEC. 5. *And be it further enacted,* That it shall be lawful for any alien who may be ordered to be removed from the United States, by virtue of this act, to take with him such part of his goods, chattels, or other property as he may find convenient; and all property left in the United States by any alien, who may be removed, as aforesaid, shall be, and remain subject to his order and disposal, in the same manner as if this act had not been passed.

SEC. 6. *And be it further enacted,* That this act shall continue and be in force for and during the term of two years from the passing thereof. Approved June 25, 1798

AN ACT IN ADDITION TO THE ACT ENTITLED "AN ACT FOR THE PUNISHMENT OF CERTAIN CRIMES AGAINST THE UNITED STATES.

SECTION 1. *Be it enacted by the Senate and House of Representatives of the United States of America assembled,* That if any persons shall unlawfully combine or conspire together, with intent to oppose any measure or measures of the government of the United States, which are or shall be directed by proper authority, or to impede the operation of any law of the United States, or to intimidate or prevent any person holding a place or office in or under the government of the United States, from undertaking, performing or executing his trust or duty; and if any person or persons, with intent as aforesaid, shall counsel, advise or attempt to procure any insurrection, riot, unlawful assembly, or combination, whether such conspiracy, threatening, counsel, advice, or attempt shall have the proposed effect or not, he or they shall be deemed guilty of a high misdemeanor, and on conviction, before any court of the United States having jurisdiction thereof, shall be punished by a fine not exceeding five thousand dollars and by imprisonment during a term not less than six months nor exceeding five years; and further at the discretion of the court may be holden to find sureties for his good behavior in such sum, and for such time, as the said court may direct.

SEC. 2. *And be it further enacted,* That if any person shall write, print, utter or publish, or shall cause or procure to be written, printed, uttered or published or shall knowingly and willingly assist or aid in writing, printing, uttering or publishing any false, scandalous and malicious writing or writings against the government of the United States, or either house of the Congress of the United States, or the President of the United States, with intent to defame the said government, or either house of the said Congress, or the said President, or to bring them or either of them, into contempt or disrepute; or to excite against them, or either, or any of them, the hatred of the good people of the United States, or to stir up sedition within the United States, or to excite any unlawful combinations therein, for opposing or resisting any law of the United States, or any act of the President of the United States, and one in pursuance of any such law, or of the powers in him vested by the constitution of the United States, or to resist, oppose, or defeat any such law or act, or to aid, encourage or abet any hostile designs of any foreign nation against the United States, their people or government, then such person, being thereof convicted before any court of the United States having jurisdiction thereof, shall be punished by a fine not exceeding two thousand dollars, and by imprisonment not exceeding two years.

SEC. 3. *And be it further enacted, and declared,* That if any person shall be prosecuted under this act, for the writing or publishing any libel aforesaid, it shall be lawful for the defendant, upon the trial of the cause, to give in evidence in his defence, the truth of the matter contained in the publication charged as a libel. And the jury who shall try the cause, shall have a right to determine the law and the fact, under the direction of the court, as in other cases.

SEC. 4. *And be it further enacted,* That this act shall continue and be in force until the third day of March, one thousand eight hundred and one, and no longer: *Provided,* that the expiration of the act shall not prevent or defeat a prosecution and punishment of any offence against the law, during the time it shall be in force.

Approved, July 14, 1798.

[DIH]

President Thomas Jefferson, First Inaugural Address

March 4, 1801

Thomas Jefferson served as secretary of state under George Washington and as vice president under John Adams, after losing the 1796 election as the Republican candidate to the Federalist Adams. In the election of 1800, the Federalists lost, and the two Republican candidates—Thomas Jefferson and Aaron Burr—received equal electoral votes. It then became the responsibility of the House of Representatives to choose one of them to be president, with the other to be designated vice president. Jefferson gained the support of many prominent Federalists who considered him more reliable than Burr, and he won the election in the House to become the nation's third president.

Jefferson's inaugural address, the first delivered in the new capital city of Washington, D.C., was at once a classic statement of basic democratic philosophy—displaying all the literary talent which was uniquely his—and an intentionally conciliatory statement of basic democratic principles. The intent was to bring the nation past the divisiveness of the past four years by appealing to Federalists and Republicans to come together. This approach largely worked since Jefferson easily won re-election in 1804, garnering 162 of the 176 electoral votes cast, including that of his old and now retired adversary, John Adams.

— Note by John Grafton

Friends and Fellow-Citizens:

CALLED UPON TO undertake the duties of the first executive office of our country, I avail myself of the presence of that portion of my fellow-citizens which is here assembled to express my grateful thanks for the favor with which they have been pleased to look toward me, to declare a sincere consciousness that the task is above my talents, and that I approach it with those anxious and awful presentiments which the greatness of the charge and the weakness of my powers so justly inspire. A rising nation, spread over a wide and fruitful land, traversing all the seas with the rich productions of their industry, engaged in commerce with nations who feel power and forget right, advancing rapidly to destinies beyond the reach of mortal eye—when I contemplate these transcendent objects, and see the honor, the happiness, and the hopes of this beloved country committed to the issue and the auspices of this day, I shrink from the contemplation, and humble myself before the magnitude of the undertaking. Utterly, indeed, should I despair did not the presence of many whom I here see remind me that in the other high authorities provided by our Constitution I shall find resources of wisdom, of virtue, and of zeal on which to rely under all difficulties. To you, then; gentlemen, who are charged with the sovereign functions of legislation, and to those associated with you, I look with encouragement for that guidance and support which may enable us to steer with safety the vessel in which we are all embarked amidst the conflicting elements of a troubled world.

During the contest of opinion through which we have passed the animation of discussions and of exertions has sometimes worn an aspect which might impose on strangers unused to think freely and to speak and to write what they think; but this being now decided by the voice of the nation, announced according to the rules of the Constitution, all will, of course, arrange themselves under the will of the law, and unite in common efforts for the common good. All, too, will bear in mind this sacred principle, that though the will of the majority is in all cases to prevail, that will to be rightful must be reasonable; that the minority possess their equal rights, which equal law must protect, and to violate would be oppression. Let us, then, fellow-citizens, unite with one heart and one mind. Let us restore to social intercourse that harmony and affection without which liberty and even life itself are but dreary things. And let us reflect that, having banished from our land that religious intolerance under which mankind so long bled and suffered, we have yet gained little if we countenance a political intolerance as despotic, as wicked, and capable of as bitter and bloody persecutions. During the throes and convulsions of the ancient world, during the agonizing spasms of infuriated man, seeking through blood and slaughter his long-lost liberty, it was not wonderful that the agitation of the billows should reach even this distant and peaceful shore; that this should be more felt and feared by some and less by others, and should divide opinions as to measures of safety. But every difference of opinion is not a difference of principle. We have called by different names brethren of the same principle. We are all Republicans, we are all Federalists. If there be any among us who would wish to dissolve this Union or to change its republican form, let them stand undisturbed as monuments of the safety with which error of opinion may be tolerated where reason is left free to combat it. I know, indeed, that some honest men fear that a republican government can not be strong, that this Government is not strong enough; but would the honest patriot, in the full tide of successful experiment, abandon a government which has so far kept us free and firm on the theoretic and visionary fear that this Government, the world's best hope, may by possibility want energy to preserve itself? I trust not. I believe this, on the contrary, the strongest Government on earth. I believe it the only one where every man, at the call of the law, would fly to the standard of the law, and would meet invasions of the public order as his own personal concern. Sometimes it is said that man can not be trusted with the government of himself. Can he, then, be trusted with the government of others? Or have we found angels in the forms of kings to govern him? Let history answer this question.

Let us, then, with courage and confidence pursue our own Federal and Republican principles, our attachment to union and representative government. Kindly separated by nature and a wide ocean from the exterminating havoc of one quarter of the globe; too high-minded to endure the degradations of the others; possessing a chosen country, with room enough for our descendants to the thousandth and thousandth generation; entertaining a due sense of our equal right to the use of our own faculties, to the acquisitions of our own industry, to honor and confidence from our fellow-citizens, resulting not from birth, but from our actions and their sense of them; enlightened by a benign religion, professed, indeed, and practiced in various forms, yet all of them inculcating honesty, truth, temperance, gratitude, and the love of man; acknowledging and adoring an overruling Providence, which by all its dispensations proves that it delights in the happiness of man here and his greater happiness hereafter—with all these blessings, what more is necessary to make us a happy and a prosperous people? Still one thing more, fellow-citizens—a wise and frugal Government, which shall restrain men from injuring one another, shall leave them otherwise free to regulate their own pursuits of industry and improvement, and shall not take from the mouth of labor the bread it has earned. This is the sum of good government, and this is necessary to close the circle of our felicities.

About to enter, fellow-citizens, on the exercise of duties which comprehend everything dear and valuable to you, it is proper you should understand what I deem the essential principles of our Government, and consequently those which ought to shape its Administration. I will compress them within the narrowest compass they will bear, stating the general principle, but not all its limitations. Equal and exact justice to all men, of whatever state or persuasion, religious or political; peace, commerce, and honest friendship with all nations, entangling alliances with none; the support of the State governments in all their rights, as the most competent administrations for our domestic concerns and the surest bulwarks against antirepublican tendencies; the preservation of the General Government in its whole constitutional vigor, as the sheet anchor of our peace at home and safety abroad; a jealous care of the right of election by the people—a mild and safe corrective of abuses which are lopped by the sword of revolution where peaceable remedies are unprovided; absolute acquiescence in the decisions of the majority, the vital principle of republics, from which is no appeal but to force, the vital principle and immediate parent of despotism; a well-disciplined militia, our best reliance in peace and for the first moments of war, till regulars may relieve them; the supremacy of the civil over the military authority; economy in the public expense, that labor may be lightly burthened; the honest payment of our debts and sacred preservation of the public faith; encouragement of agriculture, and of commerce as its handmaid; the diffusion of information and arraignment of all abuses at the bar of the public reason; freedom of religion; freedom of the press, and freedom of person under the protection of the habeas corpus, and trial by juries impartially selected. These principles form the bright constellation which has gone before us and guided our steps through an age of revolution and reformation. The wisdom of our sages and blood of our heroes have been devoted to their attainment. They should be the creed of our political faith, the text of civic instruction, the touchstone by which to try the services of those we trust; and should we wander from them in moments of error or of alarm, let us hasten to retrace our steps and to regain the road which alone leads to peace, liberty, and safety.

I repair, then, fellow-citizens, to the post you have assigned me. With experience enough in subordinate offices to have seen the difficulties of this the greatest of all, I have learnt to expect that it will rarely fall to the lot of imperfect man to retire from this station with the reputation and the favor which bring him into it. Without pretensions to that high confidence you reposed in our first and greatest revolutionary character, whose preeminent services had entitled him to the first place in his country's love and destined for him the fairest page in the volume of faithful history, I ask so much confidence only as may give firmness and effect to the legal administration of your affairs. I shall often go wrong through defect of judgment. When right, I shall often be thought wrong by those whose positions will not command a view of the whole ground. I ask your indulgence for my own errors, which will never be intentional, and your support against the errors of others, who may condemn what they would not if seen in all its parts. The approbation implied by your suffrage is a great consolation to me for the past, and my future solicitude will be to retain the good opinion of those who have bestowed it in advance, to conciliate that of others by doing them all the good in my power, and to be instrumental to the happiness and freedom of all.

Relying, then, on the patronage of your good will, I advance with obedience to the work, ready to retire from it whenever you become sensible how much better choice it is in your power to make. And may that Infinite Power which rules the destinies of the universe lead our councils to what is best, and give them a favorable issue for your peace and prosperity.

[DI]

President Thomas Jefferson, Instructions to Meriwether Lewis

June 20, 1803

Captain Meriwether Lewis (1774–1809) headed the expedition President Thomas Jefferson set up through the War Department. The President desired Lewis and his chosen men to investigate the Missouri River to its source and cross the Rocky Mountains to find the best means of crossing to the Pacific Ocean. The expedition was aided greatly in its crossing of the Rocky Mountains by a Shoshone woman, Sacagawea, and reached the Oregon coast in November of 1805. The final draft of Jefferson's "Instructions to Lewis" is reproduced here from Reuben Gold Twaites's superb 1904 edition of the extraordinarily interesting journals kept by Lewis and Captain William Clark (1770–1838). Jefferson had sent Lewis a rough draft of these instructions in early May.

[From original MS. in Bureau of Rolls—Jefferson Papers, series I, vol. 9, doc. 269.]

TO MERIWETHER LEWIS, *esquire, Captain of the 1st regiment of infantry of the United States of America:* Your situation as Secretary of the President of the United States has made you acquainted with the objects of my confidential message of Jan. 18, 1803, to the legislature. you have seen the act they passed, which, tho' expressed in general terms, was meant to sanction those objects, and you are appointed to carry them into execution.

Instruments for ascertaining by celestial observations the geography of the country thro' which you will pass, have already been provided. light articles for barter, & presents among the Indians, arms for your attendants, say for from 10 to 12 men, boats, tents, & other travelling apparatus, with ammunition, medicine, surgical instruments & provisions you will have prepared with such aids as the Secretary at War can yield in his department; & from him also you will receive authority to engage among our troops, by voluntary agreement, the number of attendants above mentioned, over whom you, as their commanding officer are invested with all the powers the laws give in such a case.

As your movements while within the limits of the U. S. will be better directed by occasional communications, adapted to circumstances as they arise, they will not be noticed here. what follows will respect your proceedings after your departure from the U. S.

Your mission has been communicated to the Ministers here from France, Spain & Great Britain, and through them to their governments: and such assurances given them as to it's objects as we trust will satisfy them. the country of Louisiana having been ceded by Spain to France, the passport you have from the Minister of France, the representative of the present sovereign of the country, will be a protection with all it's subjects: And that from the Minister of England will entitle you to the friendly aid of any traders of that allegiance with whom you may happen to meet.

The object of your mission is to explore the Missouri river, & such principal stream of it, as, by it's course & communication with the waters of the Pacific Ocean, may offer the most direct & practicable water communication across this continent, for the purposes of commerce.

Beginning at the mouth of the Missouri, you will take observations of latitude & longitude, at all remarkable points on the river, & especially at the mouths of rivers, at rapids, at islands & other places & objects distinguished by such natural marks & characters of a durable kind, as that they may with certainty be recognized hereafter. the courses of the river between these points of observation may be supplied by the compass, the log-line & by time, corrected by the observations themselves. the variations of the compass too, in different places, should be noticed.

The interesting points of the portage between the heads of the Missouri & the water offering the best communication with the Pacific Ocean should also be fixed by observation, & the course of that water to the ocean, in the same manner as that of the Missouri.

Your observations are to be taken with great pains & accuracy, to be entered distinctly, & intelligibly for others as well as yourself, to comprehend all the elements necessary, with the aid of the usual tables, to fix the latitude and longitude of the places at which they were taken, & are to be rendered to the war office, for the purpose of having the calculations made concurrently by proper persons within the U. S. several copies of these, as well as your other notes, should be made at leisure times & put into the care of the most trustworthy of your attendants, to guard by multiplying them, against the accidental losses to which they will be exposed. a further guard would be that one of these copies be written on the paper of the birch, as less liable to injury from damp than common paper.

The commerce which may be carried on with the people inhabiting the line you will pursue, renders a knoledge of these people important. you will therefore endeavor to make yourself acquainted, as far as a diligent pursuit of your journey shall admit,

with the names of the nations & their numbers;
the extent & limits of their possessions;
their relations with other tribes or nations;
their language, traditions, monuments;
their ordinary occupations in agriculture, fishing, hunting, war, arts, & the implements for these;
their food, clothing, & domestic accommodations;
the diseases prevalent among them, & the remedies they use;
moral & physical circumstances which distinguish them from the tribes we know;
peculiarities in their laws, customs & dispositions;
and articles of commerce they may need or furnish, & to what extent.

And considering the interest which every nation has in extending & strengthening the authority of reason & justice among the people around them, it will be useful to acquire what knoledge you can of the state of morality, religion & information among them, as it may better enable those who endeavor to civilize & instruct them, to adapt their measures to the existing notions & practices of those on whom they are to operate.

Other object worthy of notice will be
the soil & face of the country, it's growth & vegetable productions; especially those not of the U. S.

the animals of the country generally, & especially those not known in the U. S.

the remains and accounts of any which may deemed rare or extinct;

the mineral productions of every kind; but more particularly metals, limestone, pit coal & saltpetre; salines & mineral waters, noting the temperature of the last, & such circumstances as may indicate their character.

Volcanic appearances.

climate as characterized by the thermometer, by the proportion of rainy, cloudy & clear days, by lightening, hail, snow, ice, by the access & recess of frost, by the winds prevailing at different seasons, the dates at which particular plants put forth or lose their flowers, or leaf, times of appearance of particular birds, reptiles or insects.

Altho' your route will be along the channel of the Missouri, yet you will endeavor to inform yourself, by inquiry, of the character & extent of the country watered by it's branches, & especially on it's Southern side. the North river or Rio Bravo which runs into the gulph of Mexico, and the North river, or Rio colorado, which runs into the gulph of California, are understood to be the principal streams heading opposite to the waters of the Missouri, and running Southwardly. whether the dividing grounds between the Missouri & them are mountains or flatlands, what are their distance from the Missouri, the character of the intermediate country, & the people inhabiting it, are worthy of particular enquiry. The Northern waters of the Missouri are less to be enquired after, because they have been ascertained to a considerable degree, and are still in a course of ascertainment by English traders & travelers. but if you can learn anything certain of the most Northern source of the Missisippi, & of it's position relative to the lake of the woods, it will be interesting to us. some account too of the path of the Canadian traders from the Missisippi at the mouth of the Ouisconsin river, to where it strikes the Missouri and of the soil & rivers in it's course, is desireable.

In all your intercourse with the natives treat them in the most friendly & conciliatory manner which their own conduct will admit; allay all jealousies as to the object of your journey, satisfy them of it's innocence, make them acquainted with the position, extent, character, peaceable & commercial dispositions of the U. S.

of our wish to be neighborly, friendly & useful to them, & of our dispositions to a commercial intercourse with them; confer with them on the points most convenient as mutual emporiums, & the articles of most desireable interchange for them & us. if a few of their influential chiefs, within practicable distance, wish to visit us, arrange such a visit with them, and furnish them with authority to call on our officers, on their entering the U. S. to have them conveyed to this place at public expense. if any of them should wish to have some of their young people brought up with us, & taught such arts as may be useful to them, we will receive, instruct & take care of them. such a mission, whether of influential chiefs, or of young people, would give some security to your own party. carry with you some matter of the kine-pox, inform those of them with whom you may be of it' efficacy as a preservative from the small-pox; and instruct & incourage them in the use of it. this may be especially done wherever you winter.

As it is impossible for us to foresee in what manner you will be received by those people, whether with hospitality or hostility, so is it impossible to prescribe the exact degree of perseverance with which you are to pursue your journey. we value too much the lives of citizens to offer them to probably destruction. your numbers will be sufficient to secure you against the unauthorised opposition of individuals, or of small parties: but if a superior force, authorised or not authorised, by a nation, should be arrayed against your further passage, & inflexibly determined to arrest it, you must decline it's further pursuit, and return. in the loss of yourselves, we should lose also the information you will have acquired. by returning safely with that, you may enable us to renew the essay with better calculated means. to your own discretion therefore must be left the degree of danger you may risk, & the point at which you should decline, only saying we wish you to err on the side of your safety, & bring back your party safe, even if it be with less information.

As far up the Missouri as the white settlements extend, an intercourse will probably be found to exist between them and the Spanish posts at S^t. Louis, opposite Cahokia, or S^{te}. Genevieve opposite Kaskaskia. from still farther up the river, the traders may furnish a conveyance for letters. beyond that you may perhaps be able to engage Indians to bring letters for the government to Cahokia or Kaskaskia, on promising that they shall there receive such special compensation as you shall have stipulated with them. avail yourself of these means to communicate to us, at seasonable intervals, a copy of your journal, notes & observations of every kind, putting into cypher whatever might do injury if betrayed.

Should you reach the Pacific ocean inform yourself of the circumstances which may decide whether the furs of those parts may not be collected as advantageously at the head of the Missouri (convenient as is supposed to the waters of the Colorado & Oregon or Columbia) as at Nootka sound or any other point of that coast; & that trade be consequently conducted through the Missouri & U. S. more beneficially than by the circumnavigation now practised.

On your arrival on that coast endeavor to learn if there be any port within your reach frequented by the sea-vessels of any nation, and to send two of your trusty people back by sea, in such way as shall appear practicable, with a copy of your notes. and should you be of opinion that the return of your party by the way they went will be eminently dangerous, then ship the whole, & return by sea by way of Cape Horn or the Cape of good Hope, as you shall be able. as you will be without money, clothes or provisions, you must endeavor to use the credit of the U. S. to obtain them; for which purpose open letters of credit shall be furnished you authorising you to draw on the Executive of the U. S. or any of its officers in any part of the world, on which drafts can be disposed of, and to apply with our recommendations to the Consuls, agents, merchants or citizens of any nation with which we have intercourse, assuring them in our name that any aids they may furnish you, shall honorably repaid, and on demand. Our consuls Thomas Howes at Batavia in Java, William Buchanan of the isles of France and Bourbon, & John Elmslie at the Cape of good hope will be able to supply your necessities by draughts on us.

Should you find it safe to return by the way you go, after sending two of your party round by sea, or with your whole party, if no conveyance by sea can be found, do so; making such observations on your return as may serve to supply, correct or confirm those made on your outward journey.

In re-entering the U. S. and reaching a place of safety, discharge any of your attendants who may desire & deserve it, procuring for them immediate payment of all arrears of pay & clothing which may have incurred since their departure; & assure them that they shall be recommended to the liberality of the legislature for the grant of a soldier's portion of land each, as proposed in my message to Congress & repair yourself with your papers to the seat of government.

To provide, on the accident of your death, against anarchy, dispersion & the consequent danger to your party, and total failure of the enterprise, you are hereby authorised, by any instrument signed & written in your hand, to name the person among them who shall succeed to the command on your decease, & by like instruments to change the nomination from time to time, as further experience of the characters accompanying you shall point out superior fitness: and all the powers & authorities given to yourself are, in the event of your death, transferred to & vested in the successor so named, with further power to him, & his successors in like manner to name each his successor, who, on the death of his predecessor, shall be invested with all the powers & authorities given to yourself.

Given under my hand at the city of Washington, this 20th. day of June 1803

TH. JEFFERSON
Pr. U S. of America

[OJLC]

The Louisiana Purchase, Treaty with France

October 21, 1803

By a treaty concluded in 1795, Spain had agreed to allow to the United States the use of New Orleans or an equivalent port on the Mississippi; but in 1802 she violated this agreement by closing the Mississippi, and ceding all Louisiana to France. President Thomas Jefferson, realizing the danger of having such a power as France holding the natural outlet for a large proportion of the produce of the country, persuaded Congress to appropriate $2,000,000 to purchase New Orleans. Minister to France Robert R. Livingston and Minister to the United Kingdom James Monroe concluded with Napoleon the purchase of the whole Louisiana territory for $15,000,000; their action was ratified; and the United States took possession on Dec. 20, 1805.

— Note by Charles W. Eliot

TREATY WITH FRANCE FOR THE CESSION OF LOUISIANA, CONCLUDED AT PARIS, APRIL 30, 1803; RATIFICATION ADVISED BY SENATE, OCTOBER 20, 1803; RATIFIED BY PRESIDENT OCTOBER 21, 1803; RATIFICATIONS EXCHANGED AT WASHINGTON OCTOBER 21, 1803; PROCLAIMED OCTOBER 21, 1803.

THE PRESIDENT OF the United States of America, and the First Consul of the French Republic, in the name of the French people, desiring to remove all source of misunderstanding relative to objects of discussion mentioned in the second and fifth articles of the convention of the 8th Vendémiaire, an 9 (30th September, 1800) relative to the rights claimed by the United States, in virtue of the treaty concluded at Madrid, the 27th of October, 1795, between

His Catholic Majesty and the said United States, and willing to strengthen the union and friendship which at the time of the said convention was happily re-established between the two nations, have respectively named their Plenipotentiaries, to wit: the President of the United States, [of America,] by and with the advice and consent of the Senate of the said States, Robert R. Livingston, Minister Plenipotentiary of the United States, and James Monroe, Minister Plenipotentiary and Envoy Extraordinary of the said States, near the Government of the French Republic; and the First Consul, in the name of the French people, Citizen Francis Barbé Marbois, Minister of the Public Treasury; who, after having respectively exchanged their full powers, have agreed to the following articles:

ARTICLE I

Whereas by the article of the third of the treaty concluded at St. Idelfonso, the 9th Vendémiaire, an 9 (1st October, 1800,) between the First Consul of the French Republic and His Catholic Majesty, it was agreed as follows: "His Catholic Majesty promises and engages on his part, to cede to the French Republic, six months after the full and entire execution of the conditions and stipulations herein relative to His Royal Highness the Duke of Parma, the colony or province of Louisiana, with the same extent that it now has in the hands of Spain, and that it had when France possessed it, and such as it should be after the treaties subsequently entered into between Spain and other States." And whereas, in pursuance of the treaty, and particularly of the third article, the French Republic has an incontestable title to the domain and to the possession of the said territory: The First Consul of the French Republic desiring to give to the United States a strong proof of his friendship, doth hereby cede to the said United States, in the name of the French Republic, forever and in full sovereignty, the said territory, with all its rights and appurtenances, as fully and in the same manner as they have been acquired by the French Republic, in virtue of the above-mentioned treaty, concluded with His Catholic Majesty.

ARTICLE II

In the cession made by the preceding article are included the adjacent islands belonging to Louisiana, all public lots and squares, vacant lands, and all public buildings, fortifications, barracks and other edifices which are not private property. The archives, papers, and documents, relative to the domain and sovereignty of Louisiana and its dependences, will be left in the possession of the commissaries of the United States, and copies will be afterwards given in due form to the magistrates and municipal officers of such of the said papers and documents as may be necessary to them.

ARTICLE III

The inhabitants of the ceded territory shall be incorporated in the Union of the United States, and admitted as soon as possible, according to the principles of the Federal constitution, to the enjoyment of all the rights, advantages, and immunities of citizens of the United States; and in the mean time they shall be maintained and protected in the free enjoyment of their liberty, property, and the religion which they profess.

ARTICLE IV

There shall be sent by the Government of France a commissary to Louisiana, to the end that he do every act necessary, as well to receive from the officers of His Catholic Majesty the said country and its dependences, in the name of the French Republic, if it has not been already done, as to transmit it in the name of the French Republic to the commissary or agent of the United States.

ARTICLE V

Immediately after the ratification of the present treaty by the President of the United States, and in case that of the First Consul shall have been previously obtained, the commissary of the French Republic shall remit all military posts of New Orleans, and other parts of the ceded territory, to the commissary or commissaries named by the President to take possession; the troops, whether of France or Spain, who may be there shall cease to occupy any military post from the time of taking possession, and shall be embarked as soon as possible, in the course of three months after the ratification of this treaty.

ARTICLE VI

The United States promise to execute such treaties and articles as may have been agreed between Spain and the tribes and nations of Indians, until, by mutual consent of the United States and the said tribes or nations, other suitable articles shall have been agreed upon.

ARTICLE VII

As it is reciprocally advantageous to the commerce of France and the United States to encourage the communication of both nations for a limited time in the country ceded by the present treaty, until general arrangements relative to the commerce of both nations may be agreed on; it has been agreed between the contracting parties, that the French ships coming directly from France or any of her colonies, loaded only with the produce and manufactures of France or her said colonies; and the ships of Spain coming directly from Spain or any of her colonies, loaded only with the produce or manufactures of Spain or her colonies, shall be admitted during the space of twelve years in the port of New Orleans, and in all other legal ports of entry within the ceded territory, in the same manner as the ships of the United States coming directly from France or Spain, or any of their colonies, without being subject to any other or greater duty on merchandize, or other or greater tonnage than that paid by the citizens of the United States.

During the space of time above mentioned, no other nation shall have a right to the same privileges in the ports of the ceded territory; the twelve years shall commence three months after the exchange of ratifications, if it shall take place in France, or three months after it shall have been notified at Paris to the French Government, if it shall take place in the United States; it is however well understood that the object of the above article is to favor the manufactures, commerce, freight, and navigation of France and of Spain, so far as relates to the importations that the French and Spanish shall make into the said ports of the United States, without in any sort affecting the regulations that the United States may make concerning the exportation of the produce and merchandize of the United States, or any right they may have to make such regulations.

ARTICLE VIII

In future and forever after the expiration of the twelve years, the ships of France shall be treated upon the footing of the most favored nations in the ports above mentioned.

ARTICLE IX

The particular convention signed this day by the respective ministers, having for its object to provide for the payment of debts due to the citizens of the United States by the French Republic prior to the 30th Sept., 1800, (8th Vendémiaire, an 9,) is approved, and to have its execution in the same manner as if it had been inserted in this present treaty; and it shall be ratified in the same form and in the same time, so that the one shall not be ratified distinct from the other.

Another particular convention signed at the same date as the present treaty relative to a definitive rule between the contracting parties is in the like manner approved, and will be ratified in the same form, and in the same time, and jointly.

ARTICLE X

The present treaty shall be ratified in good and due form, and the ratifications shall be exchanged in the space of six months after the date of the signature by the Ministers Plenipotentiary, or sooner if possible.

In faith whereof, the respective Plenipotentiaries have signed these articles in the French and English languages; declaring nevertheless that the present treaty was originally agreed to in the French language; and have thereunto affixed their seals.

Done at Paris the tenth day of Floréal, in the eleventh year of the French Republic, and the 30th of April, 1803.

ROBT. R. LIVINGSTON [L. S.]
JAS. MONROE [L. S.]
F. BARBÉ MARBOIS [L. S.]

[AHD]

Red Jacket, Sagoyewatha, Speech, "The Great Spirit"

1805

The foremost embodiment of the tradition of Iroquois oratory and probably the greatest of orators in Native American history, the Seneca Red Jacket (c. 1751–1830)—unlike, for instance, Pontiac, Tecumseh, Black Hawk, or Sitting Bull—was no warrior. His fiery, incisive eloquence, however, inspired cultural pride and resistance, and sometimes even affected the behavior of his non-Indian auditors. He understood English, but determinedly refused to speak it in public. His name—Sagoyewatha—means "He is prepared." In the following speech, he answered a young missionary named Cram who had come to convert the Senecas to Christianity.

FRIEND AND BROTHER: It was the will of the Great Spirit that we should meet together this day. He orders all things, and has given us a fine day for our council. He has taken his garment from before the sun and caused it to shine with brightness upon us. For all these things we thank the Great Ruler, and Him *only!*

Brother, this council-fire was kindled by you. It was at your request that we came together at this time. We have listened with joy to what you have said. You requested us to speak our minds freely. This gives us great joy, for we now consider that we stand upright before you and can speak what we think. All have heard your voice and can speak to you as one man. Our minds are agreed.

Brother, listen to what we say. There was a time when our forefathers owned this great island. Their seats extended from the rising to the setting sun. The Great Spirit had made it for the use of Indians. He had created the buffalo, the deer and other animals for food. He had made the bear and the beaver. Their skins served us for clothing. He had scattered them over the country and taught us how to take them. He had caused the earth to produce corn for bread. All this he had done for his red children because he loved them. If we had some disputes about our hunting-ground, they were generally settled without the shedding of much blood. But an evil day came upon us. Your forefathers crossed the great water and landed upon this island. Their numbers were small. They found us friends and not enemies. They told us they had fled from their own country on account of wicked men, and had come here to enjoy their religion. They asked for a small seat. We took pity on them and granted their request, and they sat down amongst us. We gave them corn and meat; they gave us poison [rum] in return.

The white people, brother, had now found our country. Tidings were carried back, and more came amongst us. Yet we did not fear them. We took them to be friends. They called us brothers; we believed them, and gave them a larger seat. At length their numbers had greatly increased. They wanted more land; they wanted our country. Our eyes were opened, and our minds became uneasy. Wars took place. Indians were hired to fight against Indians, and many of our people were destroyed. They also brought strong liquor amongst us. It was strong and powerful and has slain thousands.

Brother, our seats were once large, and yours were small. You have now become a great people, and we have scarcely a place left to spread our blankets. You have got our country, but are not satisfied; you want to force your religion upon us.

Brother, continue to listen. You say that you are sent to instruct us how to worship the Great Spirit agreeable to his mind; and if we do not take hold of the religion which you white people teach, we shall be unhappy hereafter. You say that you are right, and we are lost. How do we know this to be true? We understand that your religion is written in a book. If it was intended for us as well as you, why has not the Great Spirit given to us—and not only to us, but to our forefathers—the knowledge of that book, with the means of understanding it rightly? We only know what you tell us about it. How shall we know when to believe, being so often deceived by the white people?

Brother, you say there is but one way to worship and serve the Great Spirit. If there is but one religion, why do you white people differ so much about it? Why not all agree, as you can all read the book?

Brother, we do not understand these things. We are told that your religion was given to your forefathers, and has been handed down from father to son. We, also, have a religion which was given to our forefathers, and has been handed down to us, their children. We worship in that way. It teaches us to be thankful for all the favors we receive; to love each other, and be united. We never quarrel about religion, because it is a matter which concerns each man and the Great Spirit.

Brother, we do not wish to destroy your religion or take it from you; we only want to enjoy our own.

Brother, we have been told that you have been preaching to the white people in this place. These people are our neighbors. We are acquainted with them. We will wait a little while and see what effect your preaching has upon them. If we find it does them good, makes them honest and less disposed to cheat Indians, we will consider again of what you have said.

Brother, you have now heard our talk, and this is all we have to say at present. As we are going to part, we will come and take you by the hand, and hope the Great Spirit will protect you on your journey, and return you safely to your friends.

[GSNA]

Act to Prohibit the Importation of Slaves

March 2, 1807

The Constitution had famously barred for twenty years any prohibition of "the importation" of slaves. In 1807, both the House of Representatives and the Senate introduced bills to begin this prohibition in 1808. The domestic slave trade continued untouched.

AN ACT TO prohibit the importation of slaves into any port or place within the jurisdiction of the United States, from and after the first day of January, in the year of our Lord one thousand eight hundred and eight.

Be it enacted by the Senate and House of Representatives of the United States of America in Congress assembled, That from and after the first day of January, one thousand eight hundred and eight, it shall not be lawful to import or bring into the United States or the territories thereof from any foreign kingdom, place, or country, any negro, mulatto, or person of colour, with intent to hold, sell, or dispose of such negro, mulatto, or person of colour, as a slave, or to be held to service or labour.

SEC. 2. *And be it further enacted,* That no citizen or citizens of the United States, or any other person, shall, from and after the first day of January, in the year of our Lord one thousand eight hundred and eight, for himself, or themselves, or any other person whatsoever, either as master, factor, or owner, build, fit, equip, load or otherwise prepare any ship or vessel, in any port or place within the jurisdiction of the United States, nor shall cause any ship or vessel to sail from any port or place within the same, for the purpose of procuring any negro, mulatto, or person of colour, from any foreign kingdom, place, or country, to be transported to any port or place whatsoever, within the jurisdiction of the United States, to be held, sold, or disposed of as slaves, or to be held to service or labor; and if any ship or vessel shall be so fitted out for the purpose aforesaid, or shall be caused to sail so as aforesaid, every such ship or vessel, her tackle, apparel, and furniture, shall be forfeited to the United States, and shall be liable to be seized, prosecuted, and condemned in any of the circuit courts or district courts, for the district where the said ship or vessel may be found or seized.

SEC. 3. *And be it further enacted,* That all and every person so building, fitting out, equipping, loading, or otherwise preparing or sending away, any ship or vessel, knowing or intending that the same shall be employed in such trade or business, from and after the first day of January, one thousand eight hundred and eight, contrary to the true intent and meaning of this act, or any ways aiding or abetting therein, shall severally forfeit and pay twenty thousand dollars, one moiety thereof to the use of the United States, and the other moiety to the use of any person or persons who shall sue for and prosecute the same to effect.

SEC. 4. *And be it further enacted,* If any citizen or citizens of the United States, or any person resident within the jurisdiction of the same, shall, from and after the first day of January, one thousand eight hundred and eight, take on board, receive or transport from any of the coasts or kingdoms of Africa, or from any other foreign kingdom, place, or country, any negro, mulatto, or person of colour, in any ship or vessel, for the purpose of selling them in any port or place within the jurisdiction of the United States as slaves, or to be held to service or labour, or shall be in any ways aiding or abetting therein, such citizen or citizens, or person, shall severally forfeit and pay five thousand dollars, one moiety thereof to the use of any person or persons who shall sue for and prosecute the same to effect; and every such ship or vessel in which, such negro, mulatto, or person of colour, shall have been taken on board, received, or transported as aforesaid, her tackle, apparel, and furniture, and the goods and effects which shall be found on board the same, shall be forfeited to the United States, and shall be liable to be seized, prosecuted, and condemned in any of the circuit courts or district courts in the district where the said ship or vessel may be found or seized. And neither the importer, nor any person or persons claiming from or under him, shall hold any right or title whatsoever to any negro, mulatto, or person of colour, nor to the service or labour thereof, who may be imported or brought within the United States, or territories thereof, in violation of this law, but the same shall remain subject to any regulations not contravening the provisions of this act, which the legislatures of the several states or territories at any time hereafter may make, for disposing of any such negro, mulatto, or person of colour.

SEC. 5. *And be it further enacted,* That if any citizen or citizens of the United States, or any other person resident within the jurisdiction of the same, shall, from and after the first day of January, one thousand eight hundred and eight, contrary to the true intent and meaning of this act, take on board any ship or vessel from any of the coasts or kingdoms of Africa, or from any other foreign kingdom, place, or country, any negro, mulatto, or person of colour, with intent to sell him, her, or them, for a slave, or slaves, or to be held to service or labour, and shall transport the same to any port or place within the jurisdiction of the United States, and there sell such negro, mulatto, or person of colour, so transported as aforesaid, for a slave, or to be held to service or labour, every such offender shall be deemed guilty of a high misdemeanor, and being thereof convicted before any court having competent jurisdiction, shall suffer imprisonment for not more than ten years nor less than five years, and be fined not exceeding ten thousand dollars, nor less than one thousand dollars.

SEC. 6. *And be it further enacted,* That if any person or persons whatsoever, shall, from and after the first day of January, one thousand eight hundred and eight, purchase or sell any negro, mulatto, or person of colour, for a slave, or to be held to service or labour, who shall have been imported, or brought from any foreign kingdom, place, or country, or from the dominions of any foreign state, immediately adjoining to the United States, into any port or place within the jurisdiction of the United States, after the last day of December, one thousand eight hundred and seven, knowing at the time of such purchase or sale, such negro, mulatto, or person of colour, was sought within the jurisdiction of the United States, as aforesaid, such purchaser and seller shall severally for fee and pay for every negro, mulatto, or person of colour, so purchased or sold as aforesaid, eight hundred dollars; one moiety thereof to the United States, and the other moiety to the use of any person or persons who shall sue for and prosecute the same to effect: Provided, that the aforesaid forfeiture shall not extend to the seller or purchaser of any negro, mulatto, or person of colour, who may be sold or disposed of in virtue of any regulation which may hereafter be made by any of the legislatures of the several states in that respect, in pursuance of act, and the constitution of the United States.

SEC. 7. *And be it further enacted,* That if any ship or vessel shall be found, from and after the first day of January, one thousand eight hundred and eight, in any river, port, bay, or harbor, or on the high seas within the jurisdictional limits of the United States, or hovering on the coast thereof, having on board any negro, mulatto, or person of colour for the purpose of selling them as slaves, or with intent to land the same, in any port or place within the jurisdiction of the United States, contrary to the prohibition of this act, every such ship or vessel, together with her tackle, apparel, and furniture, and the goods or effects which shall be found on board the same, shall be forfeited to the use of the United States, and may be seized, prosecuted, and condemned, in any court of the United States, having jurisdiction thereof. And it shall be lawful for the President of the United States, and he is hereby authorized, should he deem it expedient, to cause any of the armed vessels of the United States to be manned and employed to cruise on any part the coast of the United States, or territories thereof, where he may judge attempts will be made to violate the provisions of this act, and to instruct and direct the commanders of armed vessels of the United States, to seize, take, and bring into any port of the United States all such ships or vessels, and moreover to seize, take, and bring into any port of the United States all ships or vessels of the United States, where so ever found on the high seas, contravening the provisions of this act, to be proceeded against, according to law, and the captain, master, or commander of every such ship or vessel, so found and seized as aforesaid, shall be deemed guilty of a high misdemeanor, and shall be liable to be prosecuted before any court of the United States, having jurisdiction thereof; and being thereof convicted, shall be fined not exceeding ten thousand dollars, and be imprisoned not less than two years, and not exceeding four years. And the proceeds of all ships and vessels, their tackle, apparel, and furniture, and the goods and effects on board of them, which shall be so seized, prosecuted and condemned, shall be divided equally between the United States and the officers and men who shall make such seizure, take, or bring the same into port for condemnation, whether such seizure be made by an armed vessel of the United States, or revenue cutters thereof, and the same shall be distributed in like manner, as is provided by law for the distribution of prizes taken from an enemy: *Provided,* that the officers and men, to be entitled to one half of the proceeds aforesaid, shall safe keep every negro, mulatto, or person of colour, found on board of any ship or vessel so by them seized, taken, or brought into port for condemnation, and shall deliver every such negro, mulatto, or person of colour, to such person or persons as shall be appointed by the respective states, to receive the same; and if no such person or persons shall be appointed by the respective states, they shall deliver every such negro, mulatto, or person of colour, to the overseers of the poor of the port or place where such ship or vessel may be brought or found, and shall immediately transmit to the governor or chief magistrate of the state an account of their proceedings, together with the number of such negroes, mulattoes, or persons of colour, and a descriptive list of the same, that he may give directions respecting such negroes mulattoes, or persons of colour.

SEC. 8. *And be it further enacted,* That no captain, master or commander of any ship or vessel, of less burthen than forty tons, shall, from and after the first day of January, one thousand eight hundred and eight, take on board and transport any negro, mulatto, or person of colour, to any port or place whatsoever, for the purpose of selling or disposing of the same as a slave, or with intent that the same may be sold or disposed of to be held to service or labour, on penalty of forfeiting for every such negro, mulatto, or person of colour, so taken on board and transported, as aforesaid, the sum of eight hundred dollars; one moiety thereof to the use of the United States, and the other moiety to any person or persons who shall sue for, and prosecute the same to effect: Provided however, That nothing in this section shall extend to prohibit the taking on board or transporting on any river, or inland bay of the sea, within the jurisdiction of the United States, any negro, mulatto, or person of colour, (not imported contrary to the provisions of this act) in any vessel or species of craft whatever.

SEC. 9. *And be it further enacted,* That the captain, master, or commander of any ship or vessel of the burthen of forty tons or more, from and after the first day of January, one thousand eight hundred and eight, sailing coastwise, from any port in the United States, to any port or place within the jurisdiction of the same, having on board any negro, mulatto, or person of colour, for the purpose of transporting them to be used or disposed of as slaves, or to be held to service or labour, shall, previous to the departure of such ship or vessel, make out and subscribe duplicate manifests of every such negro, mulatto, or person of colour, on board such ship or vessel, therein specifying the name and sex of each person, their age and stature, as near as may be, and the class to which they respectively belong, whether negro, mulatto, or person of colour, with the name and place of residence of every owner or shipper of the same, and shall deliver such manifests to the collector of the port, if there be one, otherwise to the surveyor, before whom the captain, master, or commander, together with the owner or shipper, shall severally swear or affirm to the best of their knowledge and belief, that the persons therein specified were not imported or brought into the United States, from and after the first day of January, one thousand eight hundred and eight, and that under the laws of the state, they are held to service or labour; whereupon the said collector or surveyor shall certify the same on the said manifests, one of which he shall return to the said captain, master, or commander, with a permit, specifying thereon the number, names, and general description of such persons, and authorizing him to proceed to the port of his destination. And if any ship or vessel, being laden and destined as aforesaid, shall depart from the port where she may then be, without the captain, master, or commander being first made out and subscribed duplicate manifests, of every negro, mulatto, and person of colour, on board such ship or vessel, as aforesaid, and without having previously delivered the same to the said collector or surveyor, and obtained a permit, in manner as herein required, or shall, previous to her arrival at the port of her destination, take on board any negro, mulatto, or person of colour, other than those specified in the manifests, as aforesaid, every such ship or vessel, together with her tackle, apparel and furniture, shall be forfeited to the use of the United States, and may be seized, prosecuted and condemned in any court of the United States, having jurisdiction thereof; and the captain, master, or commander of every such ship or vessel, shall moreover forfeit, for every such negro, mulatto, or person of colour, so transported or taken on board, contrary to the provisions of this act, the sum of one thousand dollars, one moiety thereof to the United States, and the other moiety to the use of any person or persons who shall sue for and prosecute the same to effect.

SEC. 10. *And be it further enacted,* That the captain, master, or commander of every ship or vessel, of the burthen of forty tons or more, from and after the first day of January, one thousand eight hundred and eight, sailing coastwise, and having on board any negro, mulatto, or person of colour, to sell or dispose of as slaves, or to be held to service or labour, and arriving in any port within the jurisdiction of the United States, from any other port within the same, shall, previous to the unloading or putting on shore any of the persons aforesaid, or suffering them to go on shore, deliver to the collector, if there be one, or if not, to the surveyor residing at the port of her arrival, the manifest certified by the collector or surveyor of the port from whence she sailed, as is herein before directed, to the truth of which, before such officer, he shall swear or affirm, and if the collector or surveyor shall be satisfied therewith, he shall thereupon grant a permit for unlading or suffering such negro, mulatto, or person of colour, to be put on shore, and if the captain, master, or commander of any such ship or vessel being laden as aforesaid, shall neglect or refuse to deliver the manifest at the time and in the manner herein directed, or shall land or put on shore any negro, mulatto, or person of colour, for the purpose aforesaid, before he shall have delivered his manifest as aforesaid, and obtained a permit for that purpose, every such captain, master, or commander, shall forfeit and pay ten thousand dollars, one moiety thereof to the United States, the other moiety to the use of any person or persons who shall sue for and prosecute the same to effect.

APPROVED, March 2, 1807.

[AST]

Tecumseh, Speech to the Choctaws and Chickasaws

September 1811

Tecumseh (c. 1768–1813), a farseeing and brave leader of the Shawnee, a dynamo of war and oratory, respected and feared by whites and Native Americans alike, was indefatigable in trying to organize a confederacy of resistance to American encroachment on Native American lands. He traveled from his lands in Indiana to Florida, to Missouri, to the Plains, and into Canada in his efforts to galvanize a union of tribes. In spite of his charisma, he was not successful in persuading the Choctaw leader Pushmataha.

IN VIEW OF questions of vast importance, have we met together in solemn council to-night. Nor should we here debate whether we have been wronged and injured, but by what measures we should avenge ourselves; for our merciless oppressors, having long since planned out their proceedings, are not about to make, but have and are still making attacks upon those of our race who have as yet come to no resolution. Nor are we ignorant by what steps, and by what gradual advances, the whites break in upon our neighbors. Imagining themselves to be still undiscovered, they show themselves the less audacious because you are insensible. The whites are already nearly a match for us all united, and too strong for any one tribe alone to resist; so that unless we support one another with our collective and united forces; unless every tribe unanimously combines to give a check to the ambition and avarice of the whites, they will soon conquer us apart and disunited, and we will be driven away from our native country and scattered as autumnal leaves before the wind.

But have we not courage enough remaining to defend our country and maintain our ancient independence? Will we calmly suffer the white intruders and tyrants to enslave us? Shall it be said of our race that we knew not how to extricate ourselves from the three most to be dreaded calamities—folly, inactivity and cowardice? But what need is there to speak of the past? It speaks for itself and asks, "Where today is the Pequot? Where the Narragansetts, the Mohawks, Pocanokets, and many other once powerful tribes of our race?" They have vanished before the avarice and oppression of the white men, as snow before a summer sun. In the vain hope of alone defending their ancient possessions, they have fallen in the wars with the white men. Look abroad over their once beautiful country, and what see you now? Naught but the ravages of the pale-face destroyers meet your eyes. So it will be with you Choctaws and Chickasaws! Soon your mighty forest trees, under the shade of whose wide spreading branches you have played in infancy, sported in boyhood, and now rest your wearied limbs after the fatigue of the chase, will be cut down to fence in the land which the white intruders dare to call their own. Soon their broad roads will pass over the graves of your fathers, and the place of their rest will be blotted out forever. The annihilation of our race is at hand unless we unite in one common cause against the common foe. Think not, brave Choctaws and Chickasaws that you can remain passive and indifferent to the common danger, and thus escape the common fate. Your people too will soon be as falling leaves and scattering clouds before their blighting breath. You too will be driven away from your native land and ancient domains as leaves are driven before the wintry storms.

Sleep not longer, O Choctaws and Chickasaws, in false security and delusive hopes. Our broad domains are fast escaping from our grasp. Every year our white intruders become more greedy, exacting, oppressive and overbearing. Every year contentions spring up between them and our people and when blood is shed we have to make atonement whether right or wrong, at the cost of the lives of our greatest chiefs, and the yielding up of large tracts of our lands. Before the pale-faces came among us, we enjoyed the happiness of unbounded freedom, and were acquainted with neither riches, wants, nor oppression. How is it now? Wants and oppressions are our lot; for are we not controlled in everything, and dare we move without asking, by your leave? Are we not being stripped day by day of the little that remains of our ancient liberty? Do they not even now kick and strike us as they do their black-faces? How long will it be before they will tie us to a post and whip us, and make us work for them in their com fields as they do them? Shall we wait for that moment or shall we die fighting before submitting to such ignominy?

Have we not for years had before our eyes a sample of their designs, and are they not sufficient harbingers of their future determinatioris? Will we not soon be driven from our respective countries and the graves of our ancestors? Will not the bones of our dead be plowed up, and their graves be turned into fields? Shall we calmly wait until they become so numerous that we will no longer be able to resist oppression? Will we wait to be destroyed in our turn, without making an effort worthy our race? Shall we give up our homes, our country, bequeathed to us by the Great Spirit, the graves of our dead, and everything that is dear and sacred to us, without a struggle? I know you will cry with me. Never! Never! Then let us by unity of action destroy them all, which we now can do, or drive them back whence they came. War or extermination is now our only choice. Which do you choose? I know your answer. Therefore, I now call on you, brave Choctaws and Chickasaws, to assist in the just cause of liberating our race from the grasp of our faithless invaders and heartless oppressors. The white usurpation in our common country must be stopped, or we, its rightful owners, be forever destroyed and wiped out as a race of people. I am now at the head of many warriors backed by the strong arm of English soldiers. Choctaws and Chickasaws, you have too long borne with grievous usurpation inflicted by the arrogant Americans. Be no longer their dupes. If there be one here tonight who believes that his rights will not sooner or later be taken from him by the avaricious American pale-faces, his ignorance ought to excite pity, for he knows little of the character of our common foe. And if there be one among you mad enough to undervalue the growing power of the white race among us, let him tremble in considering the fearful woes he will bring down upon our entire race, if by his criminal indifference he assists the designs of our common enemy against our common country. Then listen to the voice of duty, of honor, of nature and of your endangered country. Let us form one body, one heart, and defend to the last warrior our country, our homes, our liberty, and the graves of our fathers.

Choctaws and Chickasaws, you are among the few of our race who sit indolently at ease. You have indeed enjoyed the reputation of being brave, but will you be indebted for it more from report than fact? Will you let the whites encroach upon your domains even to your very door before you will assert your rights in resistance? Let no one in this council imagine that I speak more from malice against the pale-face Americans than just grounds of complaint. Complaint is just toward friends who have failed in their duty; accusation is against enemies guilty of injustice. And surely, if any people ever had, we have good and just reasons to believe we have ample grounds to accuse the Americans of injustice; especially when such great acts of injustice have been committed by them upon our race, of which they seem to have no manner of regard, or even to reflect. They are a people fond of innovations, quick to contrive and quick to put their schemes into effectual execution, no matter how great the wrong and injury to us; while we are content to preserve what we already have. Their design [is] to enlarge their possessions by taking yours in turn; and will you, can you longer dally, O Choctaws and Chickasaws? Do you imagine that that people will not continue longest in the enjoyment of peace who timely prepare to vindicate themselves, and manifest a determined resolution to do themselves right whenever they are wronged? Far otherwise. Then haste to the relief of our common cause, as by consanguinity of blood you are bound; lest the day be not far distant when you will be left single-handed and alone to the cruel mercy of our most inveterate foe.

[GSNA]

House Speaker Henry Clay, Debate on the Continuance of the War of 1812

December 29, 1812–January 14, 1813

Clay (1777–1852) was for forty years a supreme leader in national affairs. He served his country as representative, senator, envoy, and cabinet officer, and remained to the last the most popular of the second generation of states-men. He was primarily a partisan, but his ardor for the Union led him to propose many compromises that seemed necessary to the preservation of the unity of the nation, and to defend them with his surpassing oratory. He was at the head of the party in Congress that overcame President James Madison's reluctance to the declaration of war. "This debate," wrote Senator Thomas Hart Benton, "although arising on a subject which implied a lim-ited discussion, soon passed beyond its apparent bounds, and, instead of being confined to the simple military question of raising additional troops, expanded into a discussion of the whole policy, objects, and causes of the war, and became the principal debate of the session. All the leading members of the House took part in it; and many new members, then young, and whose names have since become famous, then took their start."[1]

— Note by Albert Bushnell Hart

THE WAR WAS declared because Great Britain arrogated to herself the pretension of regulating foreign trade, under the delusive name of retaliatory Orders in Council—a pretension by which she

---

[1] *Great Debates in American History. Volume Two. Foreign Relations: Part 1.* Edited by Marion Mills Miller. New York: Current Literature Publishing Co. 1913.

undertook to proclaim to American enterprise, "Thus far shalt thou go, and no farther." Orders which she refused to revoke after the alleged cause of their enactment had ceased; because she persisted in the act of impressing American seamen; because she had instigated the Indians to commit hostilities against us; and because she refused indemnity for her past injuries upon our commerce. . . .

. . . But it is said, that the Orders in Council are done away, no matter from what cause; and, that having been the sole motive for declaring the war, the relations of peace ought to be restored. . . .

. . . I have no hesitation then in saying, that I have always considered the impressment of American seamen as much the most serious aggression. But, sir, how have those orders at last been repealed? Great Britain, it is true, has intimated a willingness to suspend their practical operation, but she still arrogates to herself the right to revive them upon certain contingencies, of which she constitutes herself the sole judge. She waives the temporary use of the rod, but she suspends it *in terrorem* over our heads. Supposing it was conceded to gentlemen that such a repeal of the Orders in Council, as took place on the 23d of June last, exceptionable as it is, being known before the war, would have prevented the war, does it follow that it ought to induce us to lay down our arms without the redress of any other injury? Does it follow, in all cases, that that which would have prevented the war in the first instance should terminate the war? By no means. It requires a great struggle for a nation, prone to peace as this is, to burst through its habits and encounter the difficulties of war. Such a nation ought but seldom to go to war. When it does, it should be for clear and essential rights alone, and it should firmly resolve to extort, at all hazards, their recognition. . . . And who is prepared to say that American seamen shall be surrendered the victims to the British principle of impressment? . . . It is in vain to assert the inviolability of the obligation of allegiance. It is in vain to set up the plea of necessity, and to allege that she cannot exist without the impressment of her seamen. The truth is, she comes, by her press gangs, on board of our vessels, seizes our native seamen, as well as naturalized, and drags them into her service. It is the case, then, of the assertion of an erroneous principle, and a practice not conformable to the principle — a principle which, if it were theoretically right, must be forever practically wrong. [. . .] If Great Britain desires a mark by which she can know her own subjects, let her give them an ear mark. The colors that float from the mast-head should be the credentials of our seamen. There is no safety to us, and the gentlemen have shown it, but in the rule that all who sail under the flag (not being enemies) are protected by the flag. It is impossible that this country should ever abandon the gallant tars who have won for us such splendid trophies. . . .

The gentleman from Delaware sees in Canada no object worthy of conquest. . . . Other gentlemen consider the invasion of that country as wicked and unjustifiable. Its inhabitants are represented as unoffending, connected with those of the bordering States by a thousand tender ties, interchanging acts of kindness, and all the offices of good neighborhood. Canada innocent! Canada unoffending! Is it not in Canada that the tomahawk of the savage has been moulded into its deathlike form? From Canadian magazines, Malden, and others, that those supplies have been issued which nourish and sustain the Indian hostilities? . . . What does a state of war present? The united energies of one people arrayed against the combined energies of another; a conflict in which each party aims to inflict all the injury it can, by sea and land, upon the territories, property, and citizens of the other, subject only to the rules of mitigated war practised by civilized nations. The gentlemen would not touch the continental provinces of the enemy, nor I presume, for the same reason, her possessions in the West Indies. The same humane spirit would spare the seamen and soldiers of the enemy. The sacred person of His Majesty must not be attacked, for the learned gentlemen on the other side are quite familiar with the maxim, that the King can do no wrong. Indeed, sir, I know of no person on whom we may make war, upon the principles of the honorable gentlemen, except Mr. Stephen, the celebrated author of the Orders in Council, or the Board of Admiralty, who authorize and regulate the practice of impressment.

The disasters of the war admonish us, we are told, of the necessity of terminating the contest. If our achievements upon the land have been less splendid than those of our intrepid seamen, it is not because the American soldier is less brave. On the one element, organization, discipline, and a thorough knowledge of their duties, exist on the part of the officers and their men. On the other, almost everything is yet to be acquired. We have, however, the consolation that our country abounds with the richest materials, and that, in no instance, when engaged in an action, have our arms been tarnished. . . . It is true, that the disgrace of Detroit remains to be wiped off. . . . With the exception of that event, the war, even upon the land, had been attended by a series of the most brilliant exploits, which, whatever interest they may inspire on this side of the mountains, have given the greatest pleasure on the other. . . .

What cause, Mr. Chairman, which existed for declaring the war has been removed? We sought indemnity for the past and security for the future. The Orders in Council are suspended, not revoked; no compensation for spoliations; Indian hostilities, which were before secretly instigated, now openly encouraged; and the practice of impressment unremittingly persevered in and insisted upon. Yet Administration has given the strongest demonstrations of its love of peace. On the 29th June, less than ten days after the declaration of war, the Secretary of State writes to Mr. Russell, authorizing him to agree to an armistice, upon two conditions only; and what are they? That the Orders in Council should be repealed, and the practice of impressing American seamen cease, those already impressed being released. . . . When Mr. Russell renews the overture, in what was intended as a more agreeable form to the British Government, Lord Castlereagh is not content with a simple rejection, but clothes it in the language of insult. . . . The honorable gentleman from North Carolina (Mr. PEARSON) supposes that if Congress would pass a law, prohibiting the employment of British seamen in our service, upon condition of a like prohibition on their part, and repeal the act of non-importation, peace would immediately follow. Sir, I have no doubt if such a law were passed, with all the requisite solemnities, and the repeal to take place, Lord Castlereagh would laugh at our simplicity. No, sir, Administration has erred in the steps which it has taken to restore peace, but its error has been not in doing too little but in betraying too great a solicitude for that event. An honorable peace is attainable only by an efficient war. My plan would be to call out the ample resources of the country, give them a judicious direction, prosecute the war with the utmost vigor, strike wherever we can reach the enemy, at sea or on land, and negotiate the terms of a peace at Quebec or Halifax. We are told that England is a proud and lofty nation that disdaining to wait for danger, meets it half-way. Haughty as she is, we once triumphed over her, and if we do not listen to the councils of timidity and despair we shall again prevail. In such a cause, with the aid of

Providence, we must come out crowned with success; but if we fail, let us fail like men—lash ourselves to our gallant tars, and expire together in one common struggle, fighting for "seamen's rights and free trade."

[AHC]

The Missouri Compromise

March 6, 1820

Missouri Territory came into the possession of the United States with the Louisiana Purchase of 1803. In 1818, the citizens of Missouri Territory put forward their petition to become a state. When the question arose whether slavery would be allowed or not, the most heated political controversy of the time began. The "compromise," which was admired for its cleverness then but which can only be regarded today as a deal with the devil, was brokered by Representative Henry Clay; Congress would allow Missouri to have slavery while Maine, formerly part of Massachusetts, would be admitted at the same time as a state but without slavery.

AN ACT TO *authorize the people of the Missouri territory to form a constitution and state government, and for the admission of such state into the Union on an equal footing with the original states, and to prohibit slavery in certain territories.*

Be it enacted by the Senate and House of Representatives of the United States of America, in Congress assembled, That the inhabitants of that portion of the Missouri territory included within the boundaries herein after designated, be, and they are hereby, authorized to form for themselves a constitution and state government, and to assume such name as they shall deem proper; and the said state, when formed, shall be admitted into the Union, upon an equal footing with the original states, in all respects whatsoever.

SEC. 2. And be it further enacted, That the said state shall consist of all the territory included within the following boundaries, to wit: Beginning in the middle of the Mississippi river, on the parallel of thirty-six degrees of north latitude; thence west, along that parallel of latitude, to the St. Francois river; thence up, and following the course of that river, in the middle of the main channel thereof, to the parallel of latitude of thirty-six degrees and thirty minutes; thence west, along the same, to a point where the said parallel is intersected by a meridian line passing through the middle of the mouth of the Kansas river, where the same empties into the Missouri river, thence, from the point aforesaid north, along the said meridian line, to the intersection of the parallel of latitude which passes through the rapids of the river Des Moines, making the said line to correspond with the Indian boundary line; thence east, from the point of intersection last aforesaid, along the said parallel of latitude, to the middle of the channel of the main fork of the said river Des Moines; thence down and along the middle of the main channel of the said river Des Moines, to the mouth of the same, where it empties into the Mississippi river; thence, due east, to the middle of the main channel of the Mississippi river; thence down, and following the course of the Mississippi river, in the middle of the main channel thereof, to the place of beginning: Provided, The said state shall ratify the boundaries aforesaid. And provided also, That the said state shall have concurrent jurisdiction on the river Mississippi, and every other river bordering on the said state so far as the said rivers shall form a common boundary to the said state; and any other state or states, now or hereafter to be formed and bounded by the same, such rivers to be common to both; and that the river Mississippi, and the navigable rivers and waters leading into the same, shall be common highways, and for ever free, as well to the inhabitants of the said state as to other citizens of the United States, without any tax, duty impost, or toll, therefor, imposed by the said state.

SEC. 3. And be it further enacted, That all free white male citizens of the United States, who shall have arrived at the age of twenty-one years, and have resided in said territory: three months previous to the day of election, and all other persons qualified to vote for representatives to the general assembly of the said territory, shall be qualified to be elected and they are hereby qualified and authorized to vote, and choose representatives to form a convention, who shall be apportioned amongst the several counties as follows: From the county of Howard, five representatives. From the county of Cooper, three representatives. From the county of Montgomery, two representatives. From the county of Pike, one representative. From the county of Lincoln, one representative. From the county of St. Charles, three representatives. From the county of Franklin, one representative. From the county of St. Louis, eight representatives. From the county of Jefferson, one representative. From the county of Washington, three representatives. From the county of St. Genevieve, four representatives. From the county of Madison, one representative. From the county of Cape Girardeau, five representatives. From the county of New Madrid, two representatives. From the county of Wayne, and that portion of the county of Lawrence which falls within the boundaries herein designated, one representative.

And the election for the representatives aforesaid shall be holden on the first Monday, and two succeeding days of May next, throughout the several counties aforesaid in the said territory, and shall be, in every respect, held and conducted in the same manner, and under the same regulations as is prescribed by the laws of the said territory regulating elections therein for members of the general assembly, except that the returns of the election in that portion of Lawrence county included in the boundaries aforesaid, shall be made to the county of Wayne, as is provided in other cases under the laws of said territory.

SEC. 4. And be it further enacted, That the members of the convention thus duly elected, shall be, and they are hereby authorized to meet at the seat of government of said territory on the second Monday of the month of June next; and the said convention, when so assembled, shall have power and authority to adjourn to any other place in the said territory, which to them shall seem best for the convenient transaction of their business; and which convention, when so met, shall first determine by a majority of the whole number elected, whether it be, or be not, expedient at that time to form a constitution and state government for the people within the said territory, as included within the boundaries above designated; and if it be deemed expedient, the convention shall be, and hereby is, authorized to form a constitution and state government; or, if it be deemed more expedient, the said convention shall provide by ordinance for electing representatives to form a constitution or frame of government; which said representatives shall be chosen in such manner, and in such proportion as they shall designate; and shall meet at such time and place as shall be prescribed by the said ordinance; and shall then form for the people of said territory, within the boundaries aforesaid, a constitution and state government: Provided, That the same, whenever formed, shall be republican, and not repugnant to the constitution of the United States; and that the legislature of said state shall never interfere with the primary disposal of the soil by the United States, nor with any regulations Congress may find necessary for securing the title in such soil to the bona fide purchasers; and that no tax shall be imposed on lands the property of the United States and in no case shall non-resident proprietors be taxed higher than residents.

SEC. 5. And be it further enacted, That until the next general census shall be taken, the said state shall be entitled to one representative in the House of Representatives of the United States.

SEC. 6. And be it further enacted, That the following propositions be, and the same are hereby, offered to the convention of the said territory of Missouri, when formed, for their free acceptance or rejection, which, if accepted by the convention, shall be obligatory upon the United States:

First. That section numbered sixteen in every township, and when such section has been sold, or otherwise disposed of, other lands equivalent thereto, and as contiguous as may be, shall be granted to the state for the use of the inhabitants of such township, for the use of schools.

Second. That all salt springs, not exceeding twelve in number, with six sections of land adjoining to each, shall be granted to the said state for the use of said state, the same to be selected by the legislature of the said state, on or before the first day of January, in the year one thousand eight hundred and twenty-five; and the same, when so selected, to be used under such terms, conditions, and regulations, as the legislature of said state shall direct: Provided, That no salt spring, the right whereof now is, or hereafter shall be, confirmed or adjudged to any individual or individuals, shall, by this section, be granted to the said state: And provided also, That the legislature shall never sell or lease the same, at any one time, for a longer period than ten years, without the consent of Congress.

Third. That five per cent, of the net proceeds of the sale of lands lying within the said territory or state, and which shall be sold by Congress, from and after the first day of January next, after deducting all expenses incident to the same, shall be reserved for making public roads and canals, of which three fifths shall be applied to those objects within the state, under the direction of the legislature thereof; and the other two fifths in defraying, under the direction of Congress, the expenses to be incurred in making of a road or roads, canal or canals, leading to the said state.

Fourth. That four entire sections of land be, and the same are hereby, granted to the said state, for the purpose of fixing their seat of government thereon; which said sections shall, under the direction of the legislature of said state, be located, as near as may be, in one body, at any time, in such townships and ranges as the legislature aforesaid may select, on any of the public lands of the United States: Provided, That such locations shall be made prior to the public sale of the lands of the United States surrounding such location.

Fifth. That thirty-six sections, or one entire township, which shall be designated by the President of the United States, together with the other lands heretofore reserved for that purpose, shall be reserved for the use of a seminary of learning, and vested in the legislature of said state, to be appropriated solely to the use of such seminary by the said legislature: Provided, That the five foregoing propositions herein offered, are on the condition that the convention of the said state shall provide, by an ordinance, irrevocable without the consent or the United States, that every and each tract of land sold by the United States, from and after the first day of January next, shall remain exempt from any tax laid by order or under the authority of the state, whether for state, county, or township, or any other purpose whatever, for the term of five years from and after the day of sale; And further, That the bounty lands granted, or hereafter to be granted, for military services during the late war, shall, while they continue to be held by the patentees, or their heirs remain exempt as aforesaid from taxation for the term of three year; from and after the date of the patents respectively.

SEC. 7. And be it further enacted, That in case a constitution and state government shall be formed for the people of the said territory of Missouri, the said convention or representatives, as soon thereafter as may be, shall cause a true and attested copy of such constitution or frame of state government, as shall be formed or provided, to be transmitted to Congress.

SEC. 8. And be it further enacted. That in all that territory ceded by France to the United States, under the name of Louisiana, which lies north of thirty-six degrees and thirty minutes north latitude, not included within the limits of the state, contemplated by this act, slavery and involuntary servitude, otherwise than in the punishment of crimes, whereof the parties shall have been duly convicted, shall be, and is hereby, forever prohibited: Provided always, That any person escaping into the same, from whom labour or service is lawfully claimed, in any state or territory of the United States, such fugitive may be lawfully reclaimed and conveyed to the person claiming his or her labour or service as aforesaid.

APPROVED, March 6, 1820.

[NARA]

President James Monroe,
The Monroe Doctrine

December 2, 1823

The notion that Europe and America were separate spheres of political action, and that it would be in America's best interest to keep them that way, can be found in many early documents, including George Washington's Farewell Address and the first inaugural address of Thomas Jefferson. Despite the established and enduring currency of this idea, two new diplomatic challenges brought it to the point where the concept found its most permanent exposition in a statement to Congress delivered by the fifth president of the United States, James Monroe, on December 2, 1823. Because of these circumstances it is forever associated with his name.

The first challenge came from Russia in the form of a decree forbidding ships—including American ones—from entering the presumed territorial waters of its settlements in what is now Alaska. This was perceived by many as approximating an incursion on American prerogatives, and the ban was aggressively disputed by the secretary of state, John Quincy Adams. Around the same time, the fear arose in Washington that various European nations might be persuaded to assist Spain in restoring its sovereignty over several of its former Latin American colonies that had undergone revolutions, achieved autonomy, and—in some cases—been recognized by the United States government as independent nations.

When James Monroe delivered his message to Congress, the relevant portions of which are reprinted in full here, he argued that foreign intervention in the politics of Western hemisphere nations would not be tolerated by the United States; that "the American continents . . . are henceforth not to be considered as subjects for future colonization by any European powers"; and that America would as a matter of principle stand aloof from purely

European conflicts. This formulation of American foreign policy became known as the Monroe Doctrine about thirty years after Monroe himself had departed the political scene; and while not always strictly observed and practiced by succeeding American administrations, it was nonetheless a cornerstone of American policy not only in the Western hemisphere, but also in the world at large ever since its first expression.

— *Note by John Grafton*

[...] AT THE PROPOSAL of the Russian Imperial Government, made through the minister of the Emperor residing here, a full power and instructions have been transmitted to the minister of the United States at St. Petersburg to arrange by amicable negotiation the respective rights and interests of the two nations on the northwest coast of this continent. A similar proposal had been made by His Imperial Majesty to the Government of Great Britain, which has likewise been acceded to. The Government of the United States has been desirous by this friendly proceeding of manifesting the great value which they have invariably attached to the friendship of the Emperor and their solicitude to cultivate the best understanding with his Government. In the discussions to which this interest has given rise and in the arrangements by which they may terminate the occasion has been judged proper for asserting, as a principle in which the rights and interests of the United States are involved, that the American continents, by the free and independent condition which they have assumed and maintain, are henceforth not to be considered as subjects for future colonization by any European powers. [...]

It was stated at the commencement of the last session that a great effort was then making in Spain and Portugal to improve the condition of the people of those countries, and that it appeared to be conducted with extraordinary moderation. It need scarcely be remarked that the result has been so far very different from what was then anticipated. Of events in that quarter of the globe, with which we have so much intercourse and from which we derive our origin, we have always been anxious and interested spectators. The citizens of the United States cherish sentiments the most friendly in favor of the liberty and happiness of their fellow-men on that side of the Atlantic. In the wars of the European powers in matters relating to themselves we have never taken any part, nor does it comport with our policy so to do. It is only when our rights are invaded or seriously menaced that we resent injuries or make preparation for our defense. With the movements in this hemisphere we are of necessity more immediately connected, and by causes which must be obvious to all enlightened and impartial observers. The political system of the allied powers is essentially different in this respect from that of America. This difference proceeds from that which exists in their respective Governments; and to the defense of our own, which has been achieved by the loss of so much blood and treasure, and matured by the wisdom of their most enlightened citizens, and under which we have enjoyed unexampled felicity, this whole nation is devoted. We owe it, therefore, to candor and to the amicable relations existing between the United States and those powers to declare that we should consider any attempt on their part to extend their system to any portion of this hemisphere as dangerous to our peace and safety. With the existing colonies or dependencies of any European power we have not interfered and shall not interfere. But with the Governments who have declared their independence and maintained it, and whose independence we have, on great consideration and on just principles, acknowledged, we could not view any interposition for the purpose of oppressing them, or controlling in any other manner their destiny, by any European power in any other light than as the manifestation of an unfriendly disposition toward the United States. In the war between those new Governments and Spain we declared our neutrality at the time of their recognition, and to this we have adhered, and shall continue to adhere, provided no change shall occur which, in the judgment of the competent authorities of this Government, shall make a corresponding change on the part of the United States indispensable to their security.

The late events in Spain and Portugal show that Europe is still unsettled. Of this important fact no stronger proof can be adduced than that the allied powers should have thought it proper, on any principle satisfactory to them, to have interposed by force in the internal concerns of Spain. To what extent such interposition may be carried, on the same principle, is a question in which all independent powers whose governments differ from theirs are interested, even those most remote, and surely none more so than the United States. Our policy in regard to Europe, which was adopted at an early stage of the wars which have so long agitated that quarter of the globe, nevertheless remains the same, which is, not to interfere in the internal concerns of any of its powers; to consider the government *de facto* as the legitimate government for us; to cultivate friendly relations with it, and to preserve those relations by a frank, firm, and manly policy, meeting in all instances the just claims of every power, submitting to injuries from none. But in regard to those continents circumstances are eminently and conspicuously different. It is impossible that the allied powers should extend their political system to any portion of either continent without endangering our peace and happiness; nor can anyone believe that our southern brethren, if left to them, would adopt it of their own accord. It is equally impossible, therefore, that we should behold such interposition in any form with indifference. If we look to the comparative strength and resources of Spain and those new Governments, and their distance from each other, it must be obvious that she can never subdue them. It is still the true policy of the United States to leave the parties to themselves, in the hope that other powers will pursue the same course. . . .

[DI]

Senator Daniel Webster, Speech in Reply to Senator Robert Hayne, "The United States a Nation"

January 26, 1830

Daniel Webster [1782–1852], United States Senator from Massachusetts, is ranked among the world's great orators. His historic reply to Senator Robert Young Hayne, of South Carolina, dealing with issues that were then beginning to divide the North and the South, is generally considered a masterpiece of debate and eloquence. Parts of this speech, delivered in the Senate on January 26, 1830, follow.

— Note by Lewis Copeland

MR. PRESIDENT: WHEN the mariner has been tossed for many days, in thick weather, and on an unknown sea, he naturally avails himself of the first pause in the storm, the earliest glance of the sun, to take his latitude, and ascertain how far the elements have driven him from his true course. Let us imitate this prudence, and, before we float farther on the waves of this debate, refer to the point from which we departed, that we may at least be able to conjecture where we now are. I ask for the reading of the resolution.

[The secretary read the resolution.]

We have thus heard, sir, what the resolution is, which is actually before us for consideration; and it will readily occur to everyone that it is almost the only subject, about which something has not been said in the speech, running through two days, by which the Senate has been now entertained by the gentleman from South Carolina. Every topic in the wide range of our public affairs, whether past or present—everything, general or local, whether belonging to national politics, or party politics, seems to have attracted more or less of the honorable member's attention, save only the resolution before the Senate. He has spoken of everything but the public lands. They have escaped his notice. To that subject, in all his excursions, he has not paid even the cold respect of a passing glance.

When this debate, sir, was to be resumed on Thursday morning, it so happened that it would have been convenient for me to be elsewhere. The honorable member, however, did not incline to put off the discussion to another day. He had a shot, he said, to return, and he wished to discharge it. That shot, sir, which it was kind thus to inform us was coming, that we might stand out of the way, or prepare ourselves to fall before it, and die with decency, has now been received. Under all advantages, and with expectation awakened by the tone which preceded it, it has been discharged, and has spent its force. It may become me to say no more of its effect, than that, if nobody is found, after all, either killed or wounded by it, it is not the first time, in the history of human affairs, that the vigor and success of the war have not quite come up to the lofty and sounding phrase of the manifesto.

The people, sir, erected this government. They gave it a constitution, and in that constitution they have enumerated the powers which they bestow on it. They have made it a limited government. They have defined its authority. They have restrained it to the exercise of such powers as are granted; and all others, they declare, are reserved to the States, or the people. But, sir, they have not stopped here. If they had, they would have accomplished but half their work. No definition can be so clear as to avoid possibility of doubt; no limitation so precise, as to exclude all uncertainty. Who, then, shall construe this grant of the people? Who shall interpret their will, where it may be supposed they have left it doubtful? With whom do they repose this ultimate right of deciding on the powers of the government? Sir, they have settled all this in the fullest manner. They have left it, with the government itself, in its appropriate branches. Sir, the very chief end, the main design, for which the whole constitution was framed and adopted, was to establish a government that should not be obliged to act through State agency, or depend on State opinion and State discretion. The people had had quite enough of that kind of government, under the confederacy. Under that system, the legal action—the application of law to individuals—belonged exclusively to the States. Congress could only recommend—their acts were not of binding force, till the States had adopted and sanctioned them. Are we in that condition still? Are we yet at the mercy of State discretion, and State construction? Sir, if we are, then vain will be our attempt to maintain the constitution under which we sit.

But, sir, the people have wisely provided, in the constitution itself, a proper, suitable mode and tribunal for settling questions of constitutional law. There are in the constitution, grants of powers to Congress; and restrictions on these powers. There are, also, prohibitions on the States. Some authority must, therefore, necessarily exist, having the ultimate jurisdiction to fix and ascertain the interpretation of these grants, restrictions, and prohibitions. The constitution has itself pointed out, ordained, and established that authority. How has it accomplished this great and essential end? By declaring, sir, that "the constitution and the laws of the United States, made in pursuance thereof, shall be the supreme law of the land, anything in the constitution or laws of any State to the contrary notwithstanding."

This, sir, was the first great step. By this the supremacy of the constitution and laws of the United States is declared. The people so will it. No State law is to be valid which comes in conflict with the constitution, or any law of the United States passed in pursuance of it. But who shall decide this question of interference? To whom lies the last appeal? This, sir, the constitution itself decides, also, by declaring, "that the judicial power shall extend to all cases arising under the constitution and laws of the United States." These two provisions, sir, cover the whole ground. They are in truth, the keystone of the arch. With these, it is a constitution; without them, it is a confederacy. In pursuance of these clear and express provisions, Congress established, at its very first session, in the judicial act, a mode for carrying them into full effect, and for bringing all questions of constitutional power to the final decision of the supreme court. It then, sir, became a government. It then had the means of self-protection; and, but for this, it would, in all probability, have been now among things which are past. Having constituted the government, and declared its powers, the people have further said, that since somebody must decide on the extent of these powers, the government shall itself decide; subject, always, like other popular governments, to its responsibility to the people. And now, sir,

I repeat, how is it that a State legislature acquires any power to interfere? Who, or what, gives them the right to say to the people, "We, who are your agents and servants for one purpose, will undertake to decide that your other agents and servants, appointed by you for another purpose, have transcended the authority you gave them!" The reply would be, I think, not impertinent—"Who made you a judge over another's servants? To their own masters they stand or fall."

Sir, I deny this power of State legislatures altogether. It cannot stand the test of examination. Gentlemen may say that in an extreme case, a State government might protect the people from intolerable oppression. Sir, in such a case, the people might protect themselves, without the aid of the State governments. Such a case warrants revolution. It must make, when it comes, a law for itself. A nullifying act of a State legislature cannot alter the case, nor make resistance any more lawful. In maintaining these sentiments, sir, I am but asserting the rights of the people. I state what they have declared, and insist on their right to declare it. They have chosen to repose this power in the general government, and I think it my duty to support it, like other constitutional powers.

For myself, sir, I do not admit the jurisdiction of South Carolina, or any other State, to prescribe my constitutional duty; or to settle, between me and the people, the validity of laws of Congress, for which I have voted. I decline her umpirage. I have not sworn to support the constitution according to her construction of its clauses. I have not stipulated, by my oath of office, or otherwise, to come under any responsibility, except to the people, and those whom they have appointed to pass upon the question, whether laws, supported by my votes, conform to the constitution of the country. And, sir, if we look to the general nature of the case, could anything have been more preposterous, than to make a government for the whole Union, and yet leave its powers subject, not to one interpretation, but to thirteen, or twenty-four, interpretations? Instead of one tribunal, established by all, responsible to all, with power to decide for all—shall constitutional questions be left to four-and-twenty popular bodies, each at liberty to decide for it, and none bound to respect the decisions of others; and each at liberty, too, to give a new construction on every new election of its own members? Would anything, with such a principle in it, or rather with such destitution of all principle, be fit to be called a government? No, sir. It should not be denominated a constitution. It should be called, rather, a collection of topics, for everlasting controversy; heads of debate for a disputatious people. It would not be a government. It would not be adequate to any practical good, nor fit for any country to live under. To avoid all possibility of being misunderstood, allow me to repeat again, in the fullest manner, that I claim no powers for the government by forced or unfair construction. I admit that it is a government of strictly limited powers; of enumerated, specified, and particularized powers; and that whatsoever is not granted, is withheld. But notwithstanding all this, and however the grant of powers may be expressed, its limit and extent may yet, in some cases, admit of doubt; and the general government would be good for nothing, it would be incapable of long existing, if some mode had not been provided, in which those doubts, as they should arise, might be peaceably, but authoritatively, solved.

And now, Mr. President, let me run the honorable gentleman's doctrine a little into its practical application. Let us look at his probable *modus operandi*. If a thing can be done, an ingenious man can tell how it is to be done. Now, I wish to be informed, how this State interference is to be put in practice without violence, bloodshed, and rebellion. We will take the existing case of the tariff law. South Carolina is said to have made up her opinion upon it. If we do not repeal it (as we probably shall not) she will then apply to the case the remedy of her doctrine. She will, we must suppose, pass a law of her legislature, declaring the several acts of Congress, usually called the tariff laws, null and void, so far as they respect South Carolina, or the citizens thereof. So far, all is a paper transaction, and easy enough. But the collector at Charleston is collecting the duties imposed by these tariff laws—he therefore must be stopped. The collector will seize the goods if the tariff duties are not paid. The State authorities will undertake their rescue; the marshal, with his posse, will come to the collector's aid, and here the contest begins. The militia of the State will be called out to sustain the nullifying act. They will march, sir, under a very gallant leader: for I believe the honorable member himself commands the militia of that part of the State. He will raise the nullifying act on his standard, and spread it out as his banner! It will have a preamble, bearing, that the tariff laws are palpable, deliberate, and dangerous violations of the constitution! He will proceed, with this banner flying, to the custom-house in Charleston:

> "All the while,
> Sonorous metal, blowing martial sounds."

Arrived at the custom-house, he will tell the collector that he must collect no more duties under any of the tariff laws. This he will be somewhat puzzled to say, by the way, with a grave countenance, considering what hand South Carolina, herself, had in that of 1816. But, sir, the collector would, probably, not desist at his bidding. He would show him the law of Congress, the treasury instruction, and his own oath of office. He would say, he should perform his duty, come what might. Here would ensue a pause: for they say that certain stillness precedes the tempest. The trumpeter would hold his breath awhile, and before all this military array should fall on the custom-house, collector, clerks, and all, it is very probable some of those composing it, would request of their gallant commander-in-chief, to be informed a little upon the point of law; for they have, doubtless, a just respect for his opinions as a lawyer, as well as for his bravery as a soldier. They know he has read Blackstone and the constitution, as well as Turenne and Vauban. They would ask him, therefore, something concerning their rights in this matter. They would inquire whether it was not somewhat dangerous to resist a law of the United States. What would be the nature of their offence, they would wish to learn, if they, by military force and array, resisted the execution in Carolina of a law of the United States, and it should turn out, after all, that the law was constitutional? He would answer, of course, treason. No lawyer could give any other answer. John Fries, he would tell them, had learned that some years ago. How, then, they would ask, do you propose to defend us? We are not afraid of bullets, but treason has a way of taking people off, that we do not much relish. How do you propose to defend us? "Look at my floating banner," he would reply; "see there the nullifying law!" Is it your opinion, gallant commander, they would then say, that if we should be indicted for treason, that same floating banner of yours would make a good plea in bar? "South Carolina is a sovereign State," he would reply. That is true—but would the judge admit our plea? "These tariff laws," he would repeat, "are unconstitutional, palpably, deliberately, dangerously." That all may be so; but if the tribunal should not happen to be of that opinion, shall we swing for it? We are ready to die for our country, but it is rather an awkward business, this dying without touching the ground! After all, that is a sort of hemp tax, worse than any part of the tariff.

Mr. President, the honorable gentleman would be in a dilemma, like that of another great general. He would have a knot before him which he could not untie. He must cut it with his sword. He must say to his followers, defend yourselves with your bayonets; and this is war—civil war.

Direct collision, therefore, between force and force, is the unavoidable result of that remedy for the revision of unconstitutional laws which the gentleman contends for. It must happen in the very first case to which it is applied. Is not this the plain result? To resist, by force, the execution of a law, generally, is treason. Can the courts of the United States take notice of the indulgence of a State to commit treason? The common saying, that a State cannot commit treason herself, is nothing to the purpose. Can she authorize others to do it? If John Fries had produced an act of Pennsylvania, annulling the law of Congress, would it have helped his case? Talk about it as we will, these doctrines go the length of revolution. They are incompatible with any peaceable administration of the government. They lead directly to disunion and civil commotion; and, therefore, it is, that at their commencement, when they are first found to be maintained by respectable men, and in a tangible form, I enter my public protest against them all.

The honorable gentleman argues, that if this government be the sole judge of the extent of its own powers, whether that right of judging be in Congress, or the Supreme Court, it equally subverts State sovereignty. This the gentleman sees, or thinks he sees, although he cannot perceive how the right of judging, in this matter, if left to the exercise of State legislatures, has any tendency to subvert the government of the Union. The gentleman's opinion may be, that the right ought not to have been lodged with the general government; he may like better such a constitution, as we should have under the right of State interference; but I ask him to meet me on the plain matter of fact; I ask him to meet me on the constitution itself; I ask him if the power is not found there—clear and visibly found there?

But, sir, what is this danger, and what the grounds of it? Let it be remembered, that the constitution of the United States is not unalterable. It is to continue in its present form no longer than the people who established it shall choose to continue it. If they shall become convinced that they have made an injudicious or inexpedient partition and distribution of power, between the State governments and the general government, they can alter that distribution at will.

If anything be found in the national constitution, either by original provision, or subsequent interpretation, which ought not to be in it, the people know how to get rid of it. If any construction be established, unacceptable to them, so as to become, practically, a part of the constitution, they will amend it, at their own sovereign pleasure: but while the people choose to maintain it, as it is; while they are satisfied with it, and refuse to change it, who has given, or who can give, to the State legislatures a right to alter it, either by interference, construction, or otherwise? Gentlemen do not seem to recollect that the people have any power to do anything for themselves; they imagine there is no safety for them, any longer than they are under the close guardianship of the State legislatures. Sir, the people have not trusted their safety, in regard to the general constitution, to these hands. They have required other security, and taken other bonds. They have chosen to trust themselves, first, to the plain words of the instrument, and to such construction as the government itself, in doubtful cases, should put on its own powers, under their oaths of office, and subject to their responsibility to them: just as the people of a State trust their own State governments with a similar power. Secondly, they have reposed their trust in the efficacy of frequent elections, and in their own power to remove their own servants and agents, whenever they see cause. Thirdly, they have reposed trust in the judicial power, which, in order that it might be trustworthy, they have made as respectable, as disinterested, and as independent as was practicable. Fourthly, they have seen fit to rely, in case of necessity, or high expediency, on their known and admitted power, to alter or amend the constitution, peaceably and quietly, whenever experience shall point out defects or imperfections. And, finally, the people of the United States have, at no time, in no way, directly or indirectly, authorized any State legislature to construe or interpret their high instrument of government; much less to interfere, by their own power, to arrest its course and operation.

If, sir, the people in these respects, had done otherwise than they have done, their constitution could neither have been preserved, nor would it have been worth preserving. And, if its plain provisions shall now be disregarded, and these new doctrines interpolated in it, it will become as feeble and helpless a being, as its enemies, whether early or more recent, could possibly desire. It will exist in every State, but as a poor dependent on State permission. It must borrow leave to be; and will be, no longer than State pleasure, or State discretion, sees fit to grant the indulgence, and to prolong its poor existence.

But, sir, although there are fears, there are hopes also. The people have preserved this, their own chosen constitution, for forty years, and have seen their happiness, prosperity, and renown, grow with its growth, and strengthen with its strength. They are now, generally, strongly attached to it. Overthrown by direct assault, it cannot be; evaded, undermined, nullified, it will not be, if we, and those who shall succeed us here, as agents and representatives of the people, shall conscientiously and vigilantly discharge the two great branches of our public trust— faithfully to preserve, and wisely to administer it.

Mr. President, I have thus stated the reasons of my dissent to the doctrines which have been advanced and maintained. I am conscious of having detained you and the Senate much too long. I was drawn into the debate with no previous deliberation such as is suited to the discussion of so grave and important a subject. But it is a subject of which my heart is full, and I have not been willing to suppress the utterance of its spontaneous sentiments. I cannot, even now, persuade myself to relinquish it, without expressing, once more, my deep conviction, that, since it respects nothing less than the union of the States, it is of most vital and essential importance to the public happiness. I profess, sir, in my career, hitherto, to have kept steadily in view the prosperity and honor of the whole country, and the preservation of our federal Union. It is to that Union we owe our safety at home, and our consideration and dignity abroad. It is to that Union that we are chiefly indebted for whatever makes us most proud of our country. That Union we reached only by the discipline of our virtues in the severe school of adversity. It had its origin in the necessities of disordered finance, prostrate commerce, and ruined credit. Under its benign influences, these great interests immediately awoke, as from the dead, and sprang forth with newness of life. Every year of its duration has teemed with fresh proofs of its utility and its blessings; and, although our territory has stretched out wider and wider, and our population spread farther and farther, they have not outrun its protection or its benefits. It has been to us all a copious fountain of national, social, and personal happiness. I have not allowed myself, sir, to look beyond the Union, to see what might lie hidden in the dark recess behind. I have not coolly weighed the chances of preserving liberty when the bonds that unite us together shall be broken asunder. I have not accustomed myself to hang over the precipice of disunion, to see whether, with my short sight, I can fathom the depth of the abyss below; nor could I regard him as a safe counsellor in the affairs of this government, whose thoughts should be mainly bent on considering, not how the Union shall be best preserved, but how tolerable might be the condition of the people when it shall be broken up and destroyed. While the Union lasts, we have high, exciting, gratifying prospects spread out before us, for us and our children. Beyond that I seek not to penetrate the veil. God grant that, in my day, at least, that curtain may not rise. God grant that on my vision never may be opened what lies behind. When my eyes shall be turned to behold, for the last time, the sun in heaven, may I not see him shining on the broken and dishonored fragments of a once glorious Union; on States dissevered, discordant, belligerent; on a land rent with civil feuds, or drenched, it may be, in fraternal blood! Let their last feeble and lingering glance, rather behold the gorgeous ensign of the republic, now known and honored throughout the earth, still full high advanced, its arms and trophies streaming in their original lustre, not a stripe erased or polluted, nor a single star obscured—bearing for its motto, no such miserable interrogatory, as What is all this worth? Nor those other words of delusion and folly, liberty first, and union afterwards—but everywhere, spread all over in characters of living light, blazing on all its ample folds, as they float over the sea and over the land, and in every wind under the whole heavens, that other sentiment, dear to every true American heart—liberty and union, now and forever, one and inseparable.

[WGS]

William Lloyd Garrison, Prospectus for *The Liberator*

January 1, 1831

Born in 1805, from a middle-class New England family, William Lloyd Garrison became in his twenties one of the nation's dominant voices against the evils of slavery. Apprenticed to a newspaper editor at age thirteen, Garrison was a few years later publishing his own paper, hammering away at the issue of slavery. While he was working in Baltimore in the late 1820s with co-editor Benjamin Lundy on a paper called The Genius of Universal Emancipation, *the force of his convictions landed Garrison in prison for libel when he called the owner of a slave transport ship a murderer. After serving seven weeks of a six-month sentence, he was freed when supporters donated the money necessary to pay his fine. Back in Boston, Garrison launched a new paper,* The Liberator, *the editorial philosophy of which he issued in a prospectus reprinted here and first published on January 1, 1831. The spokesman for the immediate, not the gradual, end of slavery in America, Garrison campaigned tirelessly for this cause. His views were so strongly expressed that in Columbia, South Carolina, for example, the local Vigilance Committee offered a $1,500 reward for the arrest of anyone distributing* The Liberator.*

Garrison's strong and unyielding beliefs brought him into conflict with others in the anti-slavery movement, as well as with those on the other side of the issue. He disdained political action, attacked religious leaders for not being active enough in the cause of freedom, and was an early proponent of peaceful disobedience—positions not necessarily shared by everyone in the emancipation movement. Slavery was the dominant issue of his life as an activist but not the only one: the pages of The Liberator *were also used in the cause of women's rights, temperance, against cruelty to animals, and many other causes. Ratification of the thirteenth amendment to the Constitution in 1865 brought one phase of Garrison's life as a crusader to a close. "I am unspeakably happy to believe," he said with undisguised satisfaction at an occasion celebrating the end of slavery in America, "that the great mass of my countrymen are now heartily disposed to admit that I have not acted the part of a madman, fanatic, incendiary, or traitor." Garrison died in 1879.*

— Note by John Grafton.

DURING MY RECENT tour for the purpose of exciting the minds of the people by a series of discourses on the subject of slavery, every place that I visited gave fresh evidence of the fact that a greater revolution in public sentiment was to be effected in the free states—and particularly in New England—than at the South. I find contempt more bitter, opposition more active, detraction more relentless, prejudice more stubborn, and apathy more frozen, than among slaveowners themselves. Of course, there were individual exceptions to the contrary.

This state of things afflicted but did not dishearten me. I determined, at every hazard, to lift up the standard of emancipation in the eyes of the nation, within sight of Bunker Hill and in the birthplace of liberty. That standard is now unfurled; and long may it float, unhurt by the spoliations of time or the missiles of a desperate foe—yea, till every chain be broken, and every bondman set free! Let Southern oppressors tremble—let all the enemies of the persecuted black tremble. . . .

Assenting to the "self-evident truth" maintained in the American Declaration of Independence "that all men are created equal, and endowed by their Creator with certain inalienable rights—among which are life, liberty, and the pursuit of happiness," I shall strenuously contend for the immediate enfranchisement of our slave population. . . . In Park Street Church, on the Fourth of July, 1829, in an address on slavery, I unreflectingly assented to the popular but pernicious doctrine of gradual abolition. I seize this opportunity to make a full and unequivocal recantation, and thus publicly to ask pardon of my God, of my country, and of my brethren the poor slaves, for having uttered a sentiment so full of timidity, injustice, and absurdity. . . .

I am aware that many object to the severity of my language; but is there not cause for severity? I will be as harsh as truth, and as uncompromising as justice. On this subject I do not wish to think, or speak, or write, with moderation. No! No! Tell a man whose house is on fire to give a moderate alarm; tell him to moderately rescue his wife from the hands of the ravisher; tell the mother to gradually extricate her babe from the fire into which it has fallen—but urge me not to use moderation in a cause like the present. I am in earnest—I will not equivocate—I will not excuse—I will not retreat in a single inch—and I will be heard. The apathy of the people is enough to make every statue leap from its pedestal, and to hasten the resurrection of the dead.

It is pretended that I am retarding the cause of emancipation by the coarseness of my invective and the precipitancy of my measures. The charge is not true. On this question my influence—humble as it is—is felt at this moment to a considerable extent, and shall be felt in coming years —not perniciously, but beneficially—not as a curse, but as a blessing. And posterity will bear testimony that I was right.

[DI]

President Andrew Jackson, Veto of the Bank Bill

July 10, 1832

In 1832, Nicholas Biddle, president of the Bank of the United States, asked Congress to recharter his institution four years before the bank's charter was due to expire under law. The bank originated under Alexander Hamilton's leadership during the Washington administration, and with its joint private and government directorship provided needed stability and focus to the country's emerging commercial and financial infrastructure. The bill for the recharter of the bank passed the Senate on June 11th and the House on July 3rd. The House version included some revisions which were acceptable to the Senate. On July 10th, however, President Andrew Jackson [1767– 1875] vetoed the bank bill, attacking the bank as undemocratic, monopolistic, and dangerous to American principles and institutions because of undue foreign influence. Jackson's knowledge of banking and economics was primitive, but he had the frontiersman's distrust of paper money and of all banks, which he saw as tools of the rich who expected Congress to pass laws to help make them richer.

Jackson's veto statement on the bank bill, reprinted here in slightly abridged form, became one of the classic expositions of the philosophy of Jacksonian democracy, spotlighting new forces in America some five decades after the Constitution had been adopted. In a sense, it posed an older, aristocratic American politics—dominated by the heirs of venerable New England and Virginia families—in opposition to a newer American politics responsive to a more democratic population. Not tied to Europe or the Founding Fathers, and moving westward with the new country, these were the people Jackson and his supporters perceived as the foundation of their strength. An attempt to override the bank bill veto failed in the Senate, and the issue became the prime focus of the 1832 presidential campaign. Jackson may have known little about economics—and the judgment of history is that his long campaign against the Bank of the United States produced unintended consequences that impacted negatively on rich and poor alike for decades—but there was no doubt that in the immediate present he had struck a populist chord which couldn't be denied. With Martin Van Buren as his running mate, Jackson easily won reelection over Henry Clay, with a substantial majority of the popular vote and a convincing 219–49 victory in the Electoral College.

– Note by John Grafton

THE BILL "TO modify and continue" the act entitled "An act to incorporate the subscribers to the Bank of the United States" was presented to me on the 4th July instant. Having considered it with that solemn regard to the principles of the Constitution which the day was calculated to inspire, and come to the conclusion that it ought not to become a law, I herewith return it to the Senate, in which it originated, with my objections.

A bank of the United States is in many respects convenient for the Government and useful to the people. Entertaining this opinion, and deeply impressed with the belief that some of the powers and privileges possessed by the existing bank are unauthorized by the Constitution, subversive of the rights of the States, and dangerous to the liberties of the people, I felt it my duty at an early period of my Administration to call the attention of Congress to the practicability of organizing an institution combining all its advantages and obviating these objections. I sincerely regret that in the act before me I can perceive none of those modifications of the bank charter which are necessary, in my opinion, to make it compatible with justice, with sound policy, or with the Constitution of our country.

The present corporate body, denominated the president, directors, and company of the Bank of the United States, will have existed at the time this act is intended to take effect twenty years. It enjoys an exclusive privilege of banking under the authority of the General Government, a monopoly of its favor and support, and, as a necessary consequence, almost a monopoly of the foreign and domestic exchange. The powers, privileges, and favors bestowed upon it in the original charter, by increasing the value of the stock far above its par value, operated as a gratuity of many millions to the stockholders.

An apology may be found for the failure to guard against this result in the consideration that the effect of the original act of incorporation could not be certainly foreseen at the time of its passage. The act before me proposes another gratuity to the holders of the same stock, and in many cases to the same men, of at least seven millions more. This donation finds no apology in any uncertainty as to the effect of the act. On all hands it is conceded that its passage will increase at least 20 or 30 per cent more the market price of the stock, subject to the payment of the annuity of $200,000 per year secured by the act, thus adding in a moment one-fourth to its par value. It is not our own citizens only who are to receive the bounty of our Government. More than eight millions of the stock of this bank are held by foreigners. By this act the American Republic proposes virtually to make them a present of some millions of dollars. For these gratuities to foreigners, and to some of our own opulent citizens the act secures no equivalent whatever. They are the certain gains of the present stockholders under the operation of this act, after making full allowance for the payment of the bonus.

Every monopoly and all exclusive privileges are granted at the expense of the public, which ought to receive a fair equivalent. The many millions which this act proposes to bestow on the stockholders of the existing bank must come directly or indirectly out of the earnings of the American people. It is due to them, therefore, if their Government sell monopolies and exclusive privileges, that they should at least exact for them as much as they are worth in open market. The value of the monopoly in this case may be correctly ascertained. The twenty-eight millions of stock would probably be at an advance of 50 per cent, and command in market at least $42,000,000, subject to the payment of the present bonus. The present value of the monopoly, therefore, is $17,000,000, and this the act proposes to sell for three millions, payable in fifteen annual installments of $200,000 each.

It is not conceivable how the present stockholders can have any claim to the special favor of the Government. The present corporation has enjoyed its monopoly during the period stipulated in the original contract. If we must have such a corporation, why should not the Government sell out the whole stock and thus secure to the people the full market value of the privileges granted? Why should not Congress create and sell twenty-eight millions of stock, incorporating the purchases with all the powers and privileges secured in this act and putting the premium upon the sales into the Treasury?

But this act does not permit competition in the purchase of this monopoly. It seems to be predicated on the erroneous idea that the present stockholders have a prescriptive right not only to the favor but to the bounty of Government. It appears that more than a fourth part of the stock is held by foreigners and the residue is held by a few hundred of our own citizens, chiefly of the richest class. For their benefit does this act exclude the whole American people from competition in the purchase of this monopoly and dispose of it for many millions less than it is worth. This seems the less excusable because some of our citizens not now stockholders petitioned that the door of competition might be opened, and offered to take a charter on terms much more favorable to the Government and country.

But this proposition, although made by men whose aggregate wealth is believed to be equal to all the private stock in the existing bank, has been set aside, and the bounty of our Government is proposed to be again bestowed on the few who have been fortunate enough to secure the stock and at this moment wield the power of the existing institution. I can not perceive the justice or policy of this course. If our Government must sell monopolies, it would seem to be its duty to take nothing less than their full value, and if gratuities must be made once in fifteen or twenty years let them not be bestowed on the subjects of a foreign government nor upon a designated and favored class of men in our own country. It is but justice and good policy as far as the nature of the case will admit, to confine our favors to our own fellow-citizens, and let each in his turn enjoy an opportunity to profit by our bounty. In the bearings of the act before me upon these points I find ample reasons why it should not become a law.

It has been urged as an argument in favor of rechartering the present bank that the calling in its loans will produce great embarrassment and distress. The time allowed to close its concerns is ample, and if it has well managed its pressure will be light, and heavy only in case its management has been bad. If, therefore, it shall produce distress, the fault will be its own, and it would furnish a reason against renewing a power which has been so obviously abused. But will there ever be a time when this reason will be less powerful? To acknowledge its force is to admit that the bank ought to be perpetual, and as a consequence the present stockholders and those inheriting their rights as successors be established a privileged order, clothed both with great political power and enjoying immense pecuniary advantages from their connection with the Government.

The modifications of the existing charter proposed by this act are not such, in my view, as make it consistent with the rights of the States or the liberties of the people. The qualification of the right of the bank to hold real estate, the limitation of its power to establish branches, and the power reserved to Congress to forbid the circulation of small notes are restrictions comparatively of little value or importance. All the objectionable principles of the existing corporation, and most of its odious features, are retained without alleviation. . . .

In another of its bearings this provision is fraught with danger. Of the twenty-five directors of this bank five are chosen by the Government and twenty by the citizen stockholders. From all voice in these elections the foreign stockholders are excluded by the charter. In proportion, therefore, as the stock is transferred to foreign holders the extent of suffrage in the choice of directors is curtailed. Already is almost a third of the stock in foreign hands and not represented in elections. It is constantly passing out of the country, and this act will accelerate its departure. The entire control of the institution would necessarily fall into the hands of a few citizen stockholders, and the ease with which the object would be accomplished would be a temptation to designing men to secure that control in their own hands by monopolizing the remaining stock. There is danger that a president and directors would then be able to elect themselves from year to year, and without responsibility or control manage the whole concerns of the bank during the existence of its charter. It is easy to conceive that great evils to our country and its institutions might flow from such a concentration of power in the hands of a few men irresponsible to the people.

Is there no danger to our liberty and independence in a bank that in its nature has so little to bind it to our country? The president of the bank has told us that most of the State banks exist by its forbearance. Should its influence become concentered, as it may under the operation of such an act as this, in the hands of a self-elected directory whose interests are identified with those of the foreign stockholders, will there not be cause to tremble for the purity of our elections in peace and for the independence of our country in war? Their power would be great whenever they might choose to exert it; but if this monopoly were regularly renewed every fifteen or twenty years on terms proposed by themselves, they might seldom in peace put forth their strength to influence elections or control the affairs of the nation. But if any private citizen or public functionary should interpose to curtail its powers or prevent a renewal of its privileges, it can not be doubted that he would be made to feel its influence.

Should the stock of the bank principally pass into the hands of the subjects of a foreign country, and we should unfortunately become involved in a war with that country, what would be our condition? Of the course which would be pursued by a bank almost wholly owned by the subjects of a foreign power, and managed by those whose interests, if not affections, would run in the same direction there can be no doubt. All its operations within would be in aid of the hostile fleets and armies without. Controlling our currency, receiving our public moneys, and holding thousands of our citizens in dependence, it would be more formidable and dangerous than the naval and military power of the enemy.

If we must have a bank with private stockholders, every consideration of sound policy and every impulse of American feeling admonishes that it should be *purely American*. Its stockholders should be composed exclusively of our own citizens, who at least ought to be friendly to our Government and willing to support it in times of difficulty and danger. So abundant is domestic capital that competition in subscribing for the stock of local banks has recently led almost to riots. To a bank exclusively of American stockholders, possessing the powers and privileges granted by this act, subscriptions for $200,000,000 could readily be obtained. Instead of sending abroad the stock of the bank in which the Government must deposit its funds and on which it must rely to sustain its credit in times of emergency, it would rather seem to be expedient to prohibit its sale to aliens under penalty of absolute forfeiture.

It is maintained by the advocates of the bank that its constitutionality in all its features ought to be considered as settled by precedent and by the decision of the Supreme Court. To this conclusion I can not assent. Mere precedent is a dangerous source of authority, and should not be regarded as deciding questions of constitutional power except where the acquiescence of the people and the States can be considered as well settled. So far from this being the case on this subject, an argument against the bank might be based on precedent. One Congress, in 1791, decided in favor of a bank; another, in 1811, decided against it. One Congress, in 1815, decided against a bank; another, in 1816, decided in its favor. Prior to the present Congress, therefore, the precedents drawn from that source were equal. If we resort to the States, the expressions of legislative, judicial, and executive opinions against the bank have been probably to those in its favor as 4 to 1. There is nothing in precedent, therefore, which, if its authority were admitted, ought to weigh in favor of the act before me.

If the opinion of the Supreme Court covered the whole ground of this act, it ought not to control the coordinate authorities of this Government. The Congress, the Executive, and the Court must each for itself be guided by its own opinion of the Constitution. Each public officer who takes an oath to support the Constitution swears that he will support it as he understands it, and not as it is understood by others. It is as much the duty of the House of Representatives, of the Senate, and of the President to decide upon the constitutionality of any bill or resolution which may be presented to them for passage or approval as it is of the supreme judges when it may be brought before them for judicial decision. The opinion of the judges has no more authority over Congress than one opinion of Congress has over the judges, and on that point the President is independent of both. The authority of the Supreme Court must not, therefore, be permitted to control the Congress or the Executive when acting in their legislative capacities, but to have only such influence as the force of their reasoning may deserve. . . .

The bank is professedly established as an agent of the executive branch of the Government, and its constitutionality is maintained on that ground. Neither upon the propriety of present action nor upon the provisions of this act was the Executive consulted. It has had no opportunity to say that it neither needs nor wants an agent clothed with such powers and favored by such exemptions. There is nothing in its legitimate functions which makes it necessary or proper. Whatever interest or influence, whether public or private, has given birth to this act, it can not be found either in the wishes or necessities of the executive department, by which present action is deemed premature, and the powers conferred upon its agent not only unnecessary, but dangerous to the Government and country.

It is to be regretted that the rich and powerful too often bend the acts of government to their selfish purposes. Distinctions in society will always exist under every just government. Equality of talents, of education, or of wealth can not be produced by human institutions. In the full enjoyment of the gifts of Heaven and the fruits of superior industry, economy, and virtue, every man is equally entitled to protection by law; but when the laws undertake to add to these natural and just advantages artificial distinctions, to grant titles, gratuities, and exclusive privileges, to make the rich richer and the potent more powerful, the humble members of society—the farmers, mechanics, and laborers—who have neither the time nor the means of securing like favors to themselves, have a right to complain of the injustice of their Government. There are no necessary evils in government. Its evils exist only in its abuses. If it would confine itself to equal protection, and, as Heaven does its rains, shower its favors alike on the high and the low, the rich and the poor, it would be an unqualified blessing. In the act before me there seems to be a wide and unnecessary departure from these just principles.

Nor is our Government to be maintained or our Union preserved by invasions of the rights and powers of the several States. In thus attempting to make our General Government strong we make it weak. Its true strength consists in leaving individuals and States as much as possible to themselves—in making itself felt, not in its power, but in its beneficence; not in its control, but in its protection; not in binding the States more closely to the center, but leaving each more unobstructed in its proper orbit.

Experience should teach us wisdom. Most of the difficulties our Government now encounters and most of the dangers which impend over our Union have sprung from an abandonment of the legitimate objects of Government by our national legislation, and the adoption of such principles as are embodied in this act. Many of our rich men have not been content with equal protection and equal benefits, but have besought us to make them richer by act of Congress. By attempting to gratify their desires we have in the results of our legislation arrayed section against section, interest against interest, and man against man, in a fearful commotion which threatens to shake the foundations of our Union. It is time to pause in our career to review our principles, and if possible revive that devoted patriotism and spirit of compromise which distinguished the sages of the Revolution and the fathers of our Union. If we can not at once, in justice to interests vested under improvident legislation, make our Government what it ought to be, we can at least take a stand against all new grants of monopolies and exclusive privileges, against any prostitution of our Government to the advancement of the few at the expense of the many, and in favor of compromise and gradual reform in our code of laws and system of political economy.

[DI]

President Andrew Jackson, Seventh Annual Message to Congress, "Indian Removal"

December 7, 1835

President Jackson made his name as the general who defeated the British at the Battle of New Orleans in the War of 1812. Though an important and well-regarded president (he served two terms), he was known for his belligerence toward the native peoples and continually encouraged the take-over of their treaty-granted lands by white settlers. He describes in this excerpt from his presidential address the supposed generosity of the government forcing the removal of the Cherokees, who had been prospering in Georgia for many years. This betrayal was one of many in a series of treaties broken by the U.S. government. In 1837, after Jackson left office, several thousand Native Americans died on "The Trail of Tears."

THE PLAN OF removing the aboriginal people who yet remain within the settled portions of the United States to the country west of the Mississippi River approaches its consummation. It was adopted on the most mature consideration of the condition of this race, and ought to be persisted in till the object is accomplished, and prosecuted with as much vigor as a just regard to their circumstances will permit, and as fast as their consent can be obtained. All preceding experiments for the improvement of the Indians have failed. It seems now to be an established fact they cannot live in contact with a civilized community and prosper. Ages of fruitless endeavors have at length brought us to knowledge of this principle of intercommunication with them. The past we cannot recall, but the future we can provide for. Independently of the treaty stipulations into which we have entered with the various tribes for the usufructuary rights they have ceded to us, no one can doubt the moral duty of the Government of the United States to protect and if possible to preserve and perpetuate the scattered remnants of this race which are left within our borders. In the discharge of this duty an extensive region in the West has been assigned for their permanent residence. It has been divided into districts and allotted among them. Many have already removed and others are preparing to go, and with the exception of two small bands living in Ohio and Indiana, not exceeding 1,500 persons, and of the Cherokees, all the tribes on the east side of the Mississippi, and extending from Lake Michigan to Florida, have entered into engagements which will lead to their transplantation.

The plan for their removal and reestablishment is founded upon the knowledge we have gained of their character and habits, and has been dictated by a spirit of enlarged liberality. A territory exceeding in extent that relinquished has been granted to each tribe. Of its climate, fertility, and capacity to support an Indian population the representations are highly favorable. To these districts the Indians are removed at the expense of the United States, and with certain supplies of clothing, arms, ammunition, and other indispensable articles; they are also furnished gratuitously with provisions for the period of a year after their arrival at their new homes. In that time, from the nature of the country and of the products raised by them, they can subsist themselves by agricultural labor, if they choose to resort to that mode of life; if they do not they are upon the skirts of the great prairies, where countless herds of buffalo roam, and a short time suffices to adapt their own habits to the changes which a change of the animals destined for their food may require. Ample arrangements have also been made for the support of schools; in some instances council houses and churches are to be erected, dwellings constructed for the chiefs, and mills for common use. Funds have been set apart for the maintenance of the poor; the most necessary mechanical arts have been introduced, and blacksmiths, gunsmiths, wheelwrights, millwrights, etc., are supported among them. Steel and iron, and sometimes salt, are purchased for them, and plows and other farming utensils, domestic animals, looms, spinning wheels, cards, etc., are presented to them. And besides these beneficial arrangements, annuities are in all cases paid, amounting in some instances to more than $30 for each individual of the tribe, and in all cases sufficiently great, if justly divided and prudently expended, to enable them, in addition to their own exertions, to live comfortably. And as a stimulus for exertion, it is now provided by law that "in all cases of the appointment of interpreters or other persons employed for the benefit of the Indians a preference shall be given to persons of Indian descent, if such can be found who are properly qualified for the discharge of the duties."

Such are the arrangements for the physical comfort and for the moral improvement of the Indians. The necessary measures for their political advancement and for their separation from our citizens have not been neglected. The pledge of the United States has been given by Congress that the country destined for the residence of this people shall be forever "secured and guaranteed to them." A country west of Missouri and Arkansas has been assigned to them, into which the white settlements are not to be pushed. No political communities can be formed in that extensive region, except those which are established by the Indians themselves or by the Untied States for them and with their concurrence. A barrier has thus been raised for their protection against the encroachment of our citizens, and guarding the Indians as far as possible from those evils which have brought them to their present condition. Summary authority has been given by law to destroy all ardent spirits found in their country, without waiting the doubtful result and slow process of a legal seizure. I consider the absolute and unconditional interdiction of this article among these people as the first and great step in their melioration. Halfway measures will answer no purpose. These cannot successfully contend against the cupidity of the seller and the overpowering appetite of the buyer. And the destructive effects of the traffic are marked in every page of the history of our Indian intercourse.

Some general legislation seems necessary for the regulation of the relations which will exist in this new state of things between the Government and the people of the United States, and these transplanted Indian tribes; and for the establishment among the latter, and with their own consent, of some principles of intercommunication, which their juxtaposition will call for; that moral may be substituted for physical force; the authority of a few and simple laws for the tomahawk; and that an end may be put to those bloody wars, whose prosecution seems to have made part of their social system.

After the further details of this arrangement are completed, with a very general supervision over them, they ought to be left to the progress of events. These, I indulge the hope, will secure their prosperity and improvement and a large portion of the moral debt we owe them will then be paid.....

[IS]

Senator John C. Calhoun, Speech on the Reception of Abolitionist Petitions

February 6, 1837

Calhoun (1782–1850) was a fearless, conscienceless defender of the justice of slavery. He was vice president of the United States from 1825 to 1832, and then served South Carolina in the Senate as well as taking a spell as Secretary of State under President John Tyler. After his death, he became a patron devil of the Southern slaveholding interests who, having taken him at his word ("Abolition and the Union cannot co-exist") instigated secession and the Civil War. In this speech, outraged by the abolitionists' moral objections to slavery, Calhoun blusters: "... let me not be understood as admitting, even by implication, that the existing relations between the two races in the slaveholding States is an evil:—far otherwise; I hold it to be a good, as it has thus far proved itself to be to both, and will continue to prove so if not disturbed by the fell spirit of abolition."

IF THE TIME of the Senate permitted, I would feel it to be my duty to call for the reading of the mass of petitions on the table, in order that we might know what language they hold towards the slaveholding states and their institutions; but as it will not, I have selected, indiscriminately from the pile, two; one from those in manuscript, and the other from the printed, and without knowing their contents will call for the reading of them, so that we may judge, by them, of the character of the whole.

(Here the Secretary, on the call of Mr. Calhoun, read the two petitions.)

Such is the language held towards us and ours. The peculiar institution of the South—that, on the maintenance of which the very existence of the slaveholding States depends, is pronounced to be sinful and odious, in the sight of God and man; and this with a systematic design of rendering us hateful in the eyes of the world—with a view to a general crusade against us and our institutions. This, too, in the legislative halls of the Union; created by these confederated States, for the better protection of their peace, their safety, and their respective institutions;—and yet, we, the representatives of twelve of these sovereign States against whom this deadly war is waged, are expected to sit here in silence, hearing ourselves and our constituents day after day denounced, without uttering a word; for if we but open our lips, the charge of agitation is resounded on all sides, and we are held up as seeking to aggravate the evil which we resist. Every reflecting mind must see in all this a state of things deeply and dangerously diseased.

I do not belong to the school which holds that aggression is to be met by concession. Mine is the opposite creed, which teaches that encroachments must be met at the beginning, and, that those who act on the opposite principle are prepared to become slaves. In this case, in particular, I hold concession or compromise to be fatal. If we concede an inch, concession would follow concession—compromise would follow compromise, until our ranks would be so broken that effectual resistance would be impossible. We must meet the enemy on the frontier, with a fixed determination of maintaining our position at every hazard. Consent to receive these insulting petitions, and the next demand will be that they be referred to a committee in order that they may be deliberated and acted upon. At the last session we were modestly asked to receive them, simply to lay them on the table, without any view to ulterior action. I then told the Senator from Pennsylvania *(Mr. Buchanan),* who so strongly urged that course in the Senate, that it was a position that could not be maintained; as the argument in favor of acting on the petitions if we were bound to receive, could not be resisted. I then said, that the next step would be to refer the petition to a committee, and I already see indications that such is now the intention. If we yield, that will be followed by another, and we will thus proceed, step by step, to the final consummation of the object of these petitions. We are now told that the most effectual mode of arresting the progress of abolition is, to reason it down; and with this view it is urged that the petitions ought to be referred to a committee. That is the very ground which was taken at the last session in the other House, but instead of arresting its progress it has since advanced more rapidly than ever. The most unquestionable right may be rendered doubt-ful, if once admitted to be a subject of controversy, and that would be the case in the present instance. The subject is beyond the juris-diction of Congress—they have no right to touch it in any shape or form, or to make it the subject of deliberation or discussion.

In opposition to this view it is urged that Congress is bound by the constitution to receive petitions in every case and on every sub-ject, whether within its constitutional competency or not. I hold the doctrine to be absurd, and do solemnly believe, that it would be as easy to prove that it has the right to abolish slavery, as that it is bound to receive petitions for that purpose. The very existence of the rule that requires a question to be put on the reception of peti-tions is conclusive to show that there is no such obligation. It has been a standing rule from the commencement of the Government, and clearly shows the sense of those who formed the constitution on this point. The question on the reception would be absurd, if, as is contended, we are bound to receive; but I do not intend to argue the question; I discussed it fully at the last session, and the arguments then advanced neither have been nor can be answered.

As widely as this incendiary spirit has spread, it has not yet in-fected this body, or the great mass of the intelligent and business portion of the North; but unless it be speedily stopped, it will spread and work upwards till it brings the two great sections of the Union into deadly conflict. This is not a new impression with me. Several years since, in a discussion with one of the Senators from Massachu-setts (Mr. Webster), before this fell spirit had showed itself, I then predicted that the doctrine of the proclamation and the Force Bill,—that this Government had a right, in the last resort, to determine the extent of its own powers, and enforce its decision at the point of the bayonet, which was so warmly maintained by that Senator, would at no distant day arouse the dormant spirit of abolitionism. I told him that the doctrine was tantamount to the assumption of unlim-ited power on the part of the Government, and that such would be the impression on the public mind in a large portion of the Union. The consequences would be inevitable. A large portion of the Northern States believed slavery to be a sin, and would consider it as an obligation of conscience to abolish it if they should feel them-selves in any degree responsible for its continuance,—and that this doctrine would necessarily lead to the belief of such responsibility. I then predicted that it would commence as it has with this fanatical portion of society, and that they would begin their operations on the ignorant, the weak, the young, and the thoughtless,—and gradually extend upwards till they would become strong enough to obtain political control, when he and others holding the highest stations in society, would, however reluctant, be compelled to yield to their doctrines, or be driven into obscurity. But four years have since elapsed, and all this is already in a course of regular fulfilment.

Standing at the point of time at which we have now arrived, it will not be more difficult to trace the course of future events now than it was then. They who imagine that the spirit now abroad in the North, will die away of itself without a shock or convulsion, have formed a very inadequate conception of its real character; it will continue to rise and spread, unless prompt and efficient measures to stay its progress be adopted. Already it has taken possession of the pulpit, of the schools, and, to a considerable extent, of the press; those great instruments by which the mind of the rising generation will be formed.

They who imagine that the spirit now abroad in the North will die away of itself without a shock or convulsion, have formed a very inadequate conception of its real character; it will continue to rise and spread, unless prompt and efficient measures to stay its progress be adopted. Already it has taken possession of the pulpit, of the schools, and, to a considerable extent, of the press; those great instruments by which the mind of the rising generation will be formed.

However sound the great body of the non-slaveholding States are at present, in the course of a few years they will be succeeded by those who will have been taught to hate the people and institutions of nearly one-half of this Union, with hatred more deadly than one hostile nation ever entertained toward another. It is easy to see the end. By the necessary course of events, if left to them, we must become, finally, two people. It is impossible under the deadly hatred which must spring up between the two great sections, if the present causes are permitted to operate unchecked, that we should continue under the same political system. The conflicting elements would burst the Union asunder, powerful as are the links which hold it together.

Abolition and the Union cannot co-exist. As the friend of the Union, I openly proclaim it,—and the sooner it is known the better. The former may now be controlled, but in a short time it will be beyond the power of man to arrest the course of events. We of the South will not, cannot, surrender our institutions. To maintain the existing relations between the two races, inhabiting that section of the Union, is indispensable to the peace and happiness of both. It cannot be subverted without drenching the country in blood, and extirpating one or the other of the races. Be it good or bad, it has grown up with our society and institutions, and is so interwoven with them, that to destroy it would be to destroy us as a people. But let me not be understood as admitting, even by implication, that the existing relations between the two races in the slaveholding States is an evil:—far otherwise; I hold it to be a good, as it has thus far proved itself to be to both, and will continue to prove so if not disturbed by the fell spirit of abolition. I appeal to facts. Never before has the black race of Central Africa, from the dawn of history to the present day, attained a condition so civilized and so improved, not only physically, but morally and intellectually. It came among us in a low, degraded, and savage condition, and in the course of a few generations it has grown up under the fostering care of our institutions, reviled as they have been, to its present comparatively civilized condition. This, with the rapid increase of numbers, is conclusive proof of the general happiness of the race, in spite of all the exaggerated tales to the contrary. In the mean time, the white or European race has not degenerated. It has kept pace with its brethren in other sections of the Union where slavery does not exist. It is odious to make comparison; but I appeal to all sides whether the South is not equal in virtue, intelligence, patriotism, courage, disinterestedness, and all the high qualities which adorn our nature. I ask whether we have not contributed our full share of talents and political wisdom in forming and sustaining this political fabric; and whether we have not constantly inclined most strongly to the side of liberty, and been the first to see and first to resist the encroachments of power. In one thing only are we inferior—the arts of gain; we acknowledge that we are less wealthy than the Northern section of this Union, but I trace this mainly to the fiscal action of this Government, which has extracted much from and spent little among us. Had it been the reverse—if the exaction had been from the other section, and the expenditure with us—this point of superiority would not be against us now, as it was not at the formation of this Government.

But I take higher ground. I hold that in the present state of civilization, where two races of different origin, and distinguished by color, and other physical differences, as well as intellectual, are brought together, the relation now existing in the slaveholding States between the two, is, instead of an evil, a good—a positive good. I feel myself called upon to speak freely upon the subject where the honor and interests of those I represent are involved. I hold then, that there never has yet existed a wealthy and civilized society in which one portion of the community did not, in point of fact, live on the labor of the other. Broad and general as is this assertion, it is fully borne out by history. This is not the proper occasion, but if it were, it would not be difficult to trace the various devices by which the wealth of all civilized communities has been so unequally divided, and to show by what means so small a share has been allotted to those by whose labor it was produced, and so large a share given to the nonproducing classes. The devices are almost innumerable, from the brute force and gross superstition of ancient times, to the subtle and artful fiscal contrivances of modern. I might well challenge a comparison between them and the more direct, simple, and patriarchal mode by which the labor of the African race is, among us, commanded by the European.

I may say with truth, that in few countries so much is left to the share of the laborer, and so little exacted from him, or where there is more kind attention paid to him in sickness or infirmities of age. Compare his condition with the tenants of the poor houses in the more civilized portions of Europe—look at the sick, and the old and infirm slave, on one hand, in the midst of his family and friends, under the kind superintending care of his master and mistress, and compare it with the forlorn and wretched condition of the pauper in the poor house. But I will not dwell on this aspect of the question; I turn to the political; and here I fearlessly assert that the existing relation between the two races in the South, against which these blind fanatics are waging war, forms the most solid and durable foundation on which to rear free and stable political institutions. It is useless to disguise the fact. There is and always has been in an advanced stage of wealth and civilization, a conflict between labor and capital. The condition of society in the South exempts us from the disorders and dangers resulting from this conflict; and which explains why it is that the political condition of the slaveholding States has been so much more stable and quiet than that of the North. The advantages of the former, in this respect, will become more and more manifest if left undisturbed by interference from without, as the country advances in wealth and numbers.

We have, in fact, but just entered that condition of society where the strength and durability of our political institutions are to be tested; and I venture nothing in predicting that the experience of the next generation will fully test how vastly more favorable our condition of society is to that of other sections for free and stable institutions, provided we are not disturbed by the interference of others, or shall have sufficient intelligence and spirit to resist promptly and successfully such interference. It rests with us to meet and repel them.

I look not for aid to this government, or to the other states; not but there are kind feelings toward us on the part of the great body of the non-slaveholding states; but, as kind as their feelings may be, we may rest assured that no political party in those States will risk their ascendancy for our safety. If we do not defend ourselves, none will defend us; if we yield we will be more and more pressed as we recede; and if we submit we will be trampled under foot. Be assured that emancipation itself would not satisfy these fanatics: that gained, the next step would be to raise the Negroes to a social and political equality with the whites; and, that being effected, we would soon find the present condition of the two races reversed. They, and their northern allies, would be the masters, and we the slaves; the condition of the white race in the British West India Islands, bad as it is, would be happiness to ours; there the mother country is interested in sustaining the supremacy of the European race. It is true that the authority of the former master is destroyed, but the African will there still be a slave, not to individuals but to the community,—forced to labor, not by the authority of the over-seer, but by the bayonet of the soldiery and the rod of the civil magistrate.

Surrounded as the slaveholding States are with such imminent perils, I rejoice to think that our means of defence are ample, if we shall prove to have the intelligence and spirit to see and apply them before it is too late. All we want is concert, to lay aside all party differences, and unite with zeal and energy in repelling approaching dangers. Let there be concert of action, and we shall find ample means of security without resorting to secession or disunion. I speak with full knowledge and a thorough examination of the sub-ject, and for one, see my way clearly. One thing alarms me—the eager pursuit of gain which overspreads the land, and which absorbs every faculty of the mind and every feeling of the heart. Of all passions avarice is the most blind and compromising—the last to see and the first to yield to danger. I dare not hope that any thing I can say will arouse the South to a due sense of danger; I fear it is beyond the power of mortal voice to awaken it in time from the fatal security into which it has fallen.

[IS]

Horace Mann, Lecture, "The Necessity of Education in a Republican Government"

1845

The most famous and influential of American educators, Horace Mann (1796–1859), as the secretary of the Massachusetts Board of Education, wrote and lectured on "The Necessity of Education in a Republican Government." He relentlessly argued that free public education was for the moral, social and spiritual good of the people and the country. He later served in Congress.

[. . .] TO DEMONSTRATE THE necessity of education in our government, I shall not attempt to derive my proofs from the history of other Republics. Such arguments are becoming stale. Besides, there are so many points of difference between our own political institutions, and those of any other government calling itself free, which has ever existed, that the objector perpetually eludes or denies the force of our reasoning, by showing some want of analogy between the cases presented.

I propose, therefore, on this occasion, not to adduce, as proofs, what has been true only in past times; but what is true, at the present time, and must always continue to be true. I shall rely, not on precedents, but on the nature of things; and draw my arguments less from history than from humanity.

Now it is undeniable that, with the possession of certain higher faculties,—common to all mankind,—whose proper cultivation will bear us upward to hitherto undiscovered regions of prosperity and glory, we possess, also, certain lower faculties or propensities,—equally common,—whose improper indulgence leads, inevitably, to tribulation, and anguish, and ruin. The propensities to which I refer, seem indispensable to our temporal existence, and, if restricted within proper limits, they are primitive of our enjoyment; but, beyond those limits, they work dishonor and infatuation, madness and despair. As servants, they are indispensable; as masters, they torture as well as tyrannize. Now despotic and arbitrary governments have dwarfed and crippled the powers of doing evil as much as the powers of doing good; but a republican government, from the very fact of its freedom, un-reins their speed, and lets loose their strength. It is justly alleged against despotisms, that they fetter, mutilate, almost extinguish the noblest powers of the human soul; but there is a *per contra* to this, for which we have not given them credit;—they circumscribe the ability to do the greatest evil, as well as to do the greatest good.

My proposition, therefore, is simply this:—If republican institutions do wake up unexampled energies in the whole mass of a people, and give them implements of unexampled power wherewith to work out their will; then these same institutions ought also to confer upon that people unexampled wisdom and rectitude. If these institutions give greater scope and impulse to the lower order of faculties belonging to the human mind, then, they must also give more authoritative control, and more skilful guidance to the higher ones. If they multiply temptations, they must fortify against them. If they quicken the activity and enlarge the sphere of the appetites and passions, they must, at least in an equal ratio, establish the authority and extend the jurisdiction of reason and conscience. In a word, we must not add to the impulsive, without also adding to the regulating forces.

If we maintain institutions, which bring us within the action of new and unheard-of powers, without taking any corresponding measures for the government of those powers, we shall perish by the very instruments prepared for our happiness.

The truth has been so often asserted, that there is no security for a republic but in morality and intelligence, that a repetition of it seems hardly in good taste. But all permanent blessings being founded on permanent truths, a continued observance of the truth is the condition of a continued enjoyment of the blessing. I know we are often admonished that, without intelligence and virtue, as a chart and a compass, to direct us in our untried political voyage, we shall perish in the first storm; but I venture to add that, without these qualities, we shall not wait for a storm,—we cannot weather a calm. If the sea is as smooth as glass we shall founder, for we are in a stone-boat. Unless these qualities pervade the general head and the general heart, not only will republican institutions vanish from amongst us, but the words *prosperity* and *happiness* will become obsolete. And all this may be affirmed, not from historical examples merely, but from the very constitution of our nature. We are created and brought into life with a set of innate, organic dispositions or propensities, which a free government rouses and invigorates, and which, if not bridled and tamed, by our actually seeing the eternal laws of justice, as plainly as we can see the sun in the heavens,—and by our actually feeling the sovereign sentiment of duty, as plainly as we feel the earth beneath our feet,—will hurry us forward into regions populous with every form of evil. [...]

[LOE]

President James K. Polk, Annual Message to Congress, Reasons for the War in Mexico

May 11, 1846

Polk (1795–1849) as president confirmed the annexation of Texas; the war with Mexico which followed might have been averted but for the intention to conquer and annex New Mexico and California. The reasons for war given in this message to Congress do not cover the real grounds.

— Note by Albert Bushnell Hart

THE EXISTING STATE of the relations between the United States and Mexico renders it proper that I should bring the subject to the consideration of Congress. In my message at the commencement of your present session the state of these relations, the causes which led to the suspension of diplomatic intercourse between the two countries in March, 1845, and the long-continued and unrepressed wrongs and injuries committed by the Mexican Government on citizens of the United States in their persons and property were briefly set forth. [...]

Mr. Slidell arrived at Vera Cruz on the 30th of November [1845], and was courteously received by the authorities of that city. But the Government of General Herrera was then tottering to its fall. The revolutionary party had seized upon the Texas question to effect or hasten its overthrow. Its determination to restore friendly relations with the United States, and to receive our minister to negotiate for the settlement of this question, was violently assailed, and was made the great theme of denunciation against it. The

Government of General Herrera, there is good reason to believe, was sincerely desirous to receive our minister; but it yielded to the storm raised by its enemies, and on the 21st of December refused to accredit Mr. Slidell upon the most frivolous pretexts. These are so fully and ably exposed in the note of Mr. Slidell of the 24th of December last to the Mexican minister of foreign relations, herewith transmitted, that I deem it unnecessary to enter into further detail on this portion of the subject.

Five days after the date of Mr. Slidell's note General Herrera yielded the Government to General Paredes without a struggle, and on the 30th of December resigned the Presidency. This revolution was accomplished solely by the army, the people having taken little part in the contest; and thus the supreme power in Mexico passed into the hands of a military leader. [...]

Under these circumstances, Mr. Slidell, in obedience to my direction, addressed a note to the Mexican minister of foreign relations, under date of the 1st of March last, asking to be received by that Government in the diplomatic character to which he had been appointed. This minister in his reply, under date of the 12th of March, reiterated the arguments of his predecessor, and in terms that may be considered as giving just grounds of offense to the Government and people of the United States denied the application of Mr. Slidell. Nothing therefore remained for our envoy but to demand his passports and return to his own country.

Thus the Government of Mexico, though solemnly pledged by official acts in October last to receive and accredit an American envoy, violated their plighted faith and refused the offer of a peaceful adjustment of our difficulties. Not only was the offer rejected, but the indignity of its rejection was enhanced by the manifest breach of faith in refusing to admit the envoy who came because they had bound themselves to receive him. Nor can it be said that the offer was fruitless from the want of opportunity of discussing it; our envoy was present on their own soil. Nor can it be ascribed to a want of sufficient powers; our envoy had full powers to adjust every question of difference. Nor was there room for complaint that our propositions for settlement were unreasonable; permission was not even given our envoy to make any proposition whatever. Nor can it be objected that we, on our part, would not listen to any reasonable terms of their suggestion; the Mexican Government refused all negotiation, and have made no proposition of any kind.

In my message at the commencement of the present session I informed you that upon the earnest appeal both of the Congress and convention of Texas I had ordered an efficient military force to take a position "between the Nueces and the Del Norte." This had become necessary to meet a threatened invasion of Texas by the Mexican forces, for which extensive military preparations had been made. The invasion was threatened solely because Texas had determined, in accordance with a solemn resolution of the Congress of the United States, to annex herself to our Union, and under these circumstances it was plainly our duty to extend our protection over her citizens and soil.

This force was concentrated at Corpus Christi, and remained there until after I had received such information from Mexico as rendered it probable, if not certain, that the Mexican Government would refuse to receive our envoy.

Meantime Texas, by the final action of our Congress, had become an integral part of our Union. The Congress of Texas, by its act of December 19, 1836, had declared the Rio del Norte to be the boundary of that Republic. Its jurisdiction had been extended and exercised beyond the Nueces. The country between that river and the Del Norte had been represented in the Congress and in the convention of Texas, had thus taken part in the act of annexation itself, and is now included within one of our Congressional districts. Our own Congress had, moreover, with great unanimity, by the act approved December 31, 1845, recognized the country beyond the Nueces as a part of our territory by including it within our own revenue system, and a revenue officer to reside within that district has been appointed by and with the advice and consent of the Senate. It became, therefore, of urgent necessity to provide for the defense of that portion of our country. Accordingly, on the 13th of January last instructions were issued to the general in command of these troops to occupy the left bank of the Del Norte. This river, which is the southwestern boundary of the State of Texas, is an exposed frontier. . . .

The movement of the troops to the Del Norte was made by the commanding general under positive instructions to abstain from all aggressive acts toward Mexico or Mexican citizens and to regard the relations between that Republic and the United States as peaceful unless she should declare war or commit acts of hostility indicative of a state of war. He was specially directed to protect private property and respect personal rights.

The Army moved from Corpus Christi on the 11th of March, and on the 28th of that month arrived on the left bank of the Del Norte opposite to Matamoras, where it encamped on a commanding position, which has since been strengthened by the erection of field-works. A depot has also been established at Point Isabel, near the Brazos Santiago, 30 miles in rear of the encampment. The selection of his position was necessarily confided to the judgment of the general in command.

The Mexican forces at Matamoras assumed a belligerent attitude, and on the 12th of April General Ampudia, then in command, notified General Taylor to break up his camp within twenty-four hours and to retire beyond the Nueces River, and in the event of his failure to comply with these demands announced that arms, and arms alone, must decide the question. But no open act of hostility was committed until the 24th of April. On that day General Arista, who had succeeded to the command of the Mexican forces, communicated to General Taylor that "he considered hostilities commenced and should prosecute them." A party of dragoons of 63 men and officers were on the same day dispatched from the American camp up the Rio del Norte, on its left bank, to ascertain whether the Mexican troops had crossed or were preparing to cross the river, "became engaged with a large body of these troops, and after a short affair, in which some 16 were killed and wounded, appear to have been surrounded and compelled to surrender."

The grievous wrongs perpetrated by Mexico upon our citizens throughout a long period of years remain unrepressed, and solemn treaties pledging her public faith for this redress have been disregarded. A government either unable or unwilling to enforce the execution of such treaties fails to perform one of its plainest duties.

Our commerce with Mexico has been almost annihilated. It was formerly highly beneficial to both nations, but our merchants have been deterred from prosecuting it by the system of outrage and extortion which the Mexican authorities have pursued against them, whilst their appeals through their own Government for indemnity have been made in vain. Our forbearance has gone to such an extreme as to be mistaken in its character. Had we acted with vigor in repelling the insults and redressing the injuries inflicted by Mexico at the commencement, we should doubtless have escaped all the difficulties in which we are now involved.

Instead of this, however, we have been exerting our best efforts to propitiate her good will. Upon the pretext that Texas, a nation as independent as herself, thought proper to unite its destinies with our own, she has affected to believe that we have severed her rightful territory, and in official proclamations and manifestoes has repeatedly threatened to make war upon us for the purpose of reconquering Texas. In the meantime we have tried every effort at reconciliation. The cup of forbearance had been exhausted even before the recent information from the frontier of the Del Norte. But now, after reiterated menaces, Mexico has passed the boundary of the United States, has invaded our territory and shed American blood upon the American soil. She has proclaimed that hostilities have commenced, and that the two nations are now at war.

As war exists, and, notwithstanding all our efforts to avoid it, exists by the act of Mexico herself, we are called upon by every consideration of duty and patriotism to vindicate with decision the honor, the rights, and the interests of our country.

[AHC]

Declaration of Sentiments and Resolutions, Women's Rights Convention, Seneca Falls, New York

July 20, 1848

"A convention to discuss the social, civil, and religious condition and rights of woman, will be held in the Wesleyan Chapel, at Seneca Falls, N.Y., on Wednesday and Thursday, the 19th and 20th of July, current; commencing at 10 o'clock AM. During the first day the meeting will be exclusively for women, who are earnestly invited to attend. The public generally are invited to be present on the second day, when Lucretia Mott, of Philadelphia, and other ladies and gentlemen, will address the convention," announced The Seneca Courier *on July 14, 1848.*

Lucretia Mott, Martha C. Wright, Elizabeth Cady Stanton, and Mary Ann McClintock had called this meeting, because, as Stanton herself explained in History of Woman Suffrage: 1848–1861, *"They knew women had wrongs, but how to state them was the difficulty, and this was increased from the fact that they themselves were fortunately organized and conditioned; they were neither 'sour old maids,' 'childless women,' nor 'divorced wives,' as the newspapers declared them to be. While they had felt the insults incident to sex, in many ways, as every proud, thinking woman must, in the laws, religion, and literature of the world, and in the invidious and degrading sentiments and customs of all nations, yet they had not in their own experience endured the coarser forms of tyranny resulting from unjust laws, or association with immoral and unscrupulous men, but they had souls large enough to feel the wrongs of others, without being scarified in their own flesh.*

"After much delay, one of the circle took up the Declaration of 1776, and read it aloud with much spirit and emphasis, and it was at once decided to adopt the historic document, with some slight changes [...] Knowing that women must have more to complain of than men under any circumstances possibly could, and seeing the Fathers had eighteen grievances, a protracted search was made through statute books, church usages, and the customs of society to find that exact number. Several well-disposed men assisted in collecting the grievances, until, with the announcement of the eighteenth, the women felt they had enough to go before the world with a good case. [...]

"The eventful day dawned at last, and crowds in carriages and on foot, wended their way to the Wesleyan church." When those having charge of the Declaration, the resolutions, and several volumes of the Statutes of New York arrived on the scene, lo! the door was locked. However, an embryo Professor of Yale College was lifted through an open window to unbar the door; that done, the church was quickly filled. It had been decided to have no men present, but as they were already on the spot, and as the women who must take the responsibility of organizing the meeting, and leading the discussions, shrank from doing either, it was decided, in a hasty council round the altar, that this was an occasion when men might make themselves pre-eminently useful. It was agreed they should remain, and take the laboring oar through the Convention.

"James Mott, tall and dignified, in Quaker costume, was called to the chair; Mary McClintock appointed Secretary, Frederick Douglass, Samuel Tillman, Ansel Bascom, E. W. Capron, and Thomas McClintock took part throughout in the discussions. Lucretia Mott, accustomed to public speaking in the Society of Friends, stated the objects of the Convention, and in taking a survey of the degraded condition of woman the world over, showed the importance of inaugurating some movement for her education and elevation. Elizabeth and Mary McClintock, and Mrs. Stanton, each read a well-written speech; Martha Wright read some satirical articles she had published in the daily papers answering the diatribes on woman's sphere. Ansel Bascom, who had been a member of the Constitutional Convention recently held in Albany, spoke at length on the property bill for married women, just passed the Legislature, and the discussion on woman's rights in that Convention. [...]

"The Declaration having been freely discussed by many present, was re-read by Mrs. Stanton, and with some slight amendments adopted."[1]

---

[1] *History of Woman Suffrage: 1848–1861.* Volume I. Edited by Elizabeth Cady Stanton, Susan B. Anthony and Matilda Joslyn Gage. Second ed. Rochester: Charles Mann. 1889.

WHEN IN THE course of human events it becomes necessary for one portion of the family of man to assume among the people of the earth a position different from that which they have hitherto occupied, but one to which the laws of Nature and Nature's God entitles them, a decent respect to the opinions of mankind requires that they should declare the causes that impel them to such a course. We hold these truths to be self-evident; that all men and women are created equal; that they are endowed by their Creator with certain inalienable rights; that among these are life, liberty and the pursuit of happiness; that to secure these rights governments are instituted, *deriving their just powers from the* CONSENT OF THE GOVERNED. Whenever any form of government becomes destructive of these ends, it is the right of those who suffer from it to refuse allegiance to it and insist upon the institution of a new government, laying its foundation on such principles, and organizing its powers in such form as to them shall seem most likely to effect their safety and happiness. Prudence, indeed, will dictate that governments being established should not be changed for light and transient causes, and accordingly all experience hath shown that mankind are more disposed to suffer while evils are sufferable than to right themselves by abolishing the forms to which they are accustomed. But when a long train of abuses and usurpation, pursuing invariably the same object, evinces a design to reduce them under absolute despotism, it is their right, *it is their duty,* to throw off such government, and to provide new guards for their future security. Such has been the patient sufferance of the women under this government, and such is now the necessity which constrains them to demand the equal station to which they are entitled. The history of mankind is a history of repeated injuries and usurpations on the part of man toward woman, having in direct object the establishment of an absolute tyranny over her. To prove this, let facts be submitted to a candid world.

He has never permitted her to exercise her inalienable right to the elective franchise.

He has compelled her to submit to laws in the formation of which she has had no voice.

He has withheld from her rights which have been given to the most ignorant and degraded men, both native and foreigners.

He having deprived her of the first right of a citizen, the elective franchise, thereby leaving her without representation in any house of legislation, has oppressed her on all sides.

He has made her, if married, in the eye of the law civilly dead.

He has taken from her all right in property, even to the wages she earns.

He has made her morally an irresponsible being, as she can commit many crimes with impunity, provided they are done in the presence of her husband. In the covenant of marriage she is compelled to promise obedience to her husband, he becoming to all intents and purposes her master; the law giving him power to deprive her of her liberty, and to administer chastisement.

He has so formed the laws of divorce, as to what should be proper causes for divorce, and in case of separation, to whom the guardianship of the children should be given, as to be wholly unjust, and regardless of the happiness of woman; the law in all cases going upon the false supposition of the supremacy of man, and giving all power into his hands. After depriving her of all rights as a married woman—if single, and the owner of property,

He has taxed her to support a government which recognizes her only when her property can be made profitable to it.

He has monopolized nearly all the means of profitable employment, and in those which she is permitted to follow she secures but a scanty remuneration.

He closes against her all the avenues to wealth and distinction which he considers most honorable to himself.

As a teacher of theology, medicine, or law, she is not known.

He has deprived her of the facilities for a thorough education, all colleges being closed against her.

He allows her in church as well as state but a subordinate position, claiming apostolic authority for her exclusion from the ministry, and with some exceptions from any public participation in the affairs of the church.

He has created a false public sentiment, by giving to the world a different code of morals for man and woman, by which moral delinquencies which exclude women from society are not only tolerated, but deemed of little account in man.

He has usurped the prerogative of Jehovah himself, claiming it as his right to assign for her a sphere of action, when that belongs to her conscience and her God.

He has endeavored in every way that he could to destroy her confidence in her own powers, to lessen her self-respect, and to make her willing to lead a dependent and abject life.

Now in view of this entire disfranchisement of one half of the people of this country, their social and religious degradation, in view of the unjust laws above mentioned, and because women do feel themselves aggrieved, oppressed, and fraudulently deprived of their most sacred rights, therefore they do insist upon an immediate admission into all the rights and privileges which belong to them as citizens of these United States. In entering upon this great work, we anticipate no small amount of misconception, misrepresentation and ridicule, but we shall use every reasonable instrumentality within our power to effect our object. We shall employ agents to circulate tracts, petition the state and national legislatures, and endeavor to enlist the pulpit and press in our behalf.

SOURCE: *Littell's Living Age,* Volume 18 (July, August, September, 1848). Boston: E. Littell and Company. 423–424.

[LLA]

Into the Civil War

Senator John C. Calhoun, Speech on the Compromise of 1850, "The Slavery Question"

March 4, 1850

The speech from which this extract is taken was Calhoun's last statement of the principle for which he had labored constantly during the second half of his political life, viz., the principle that slavery, as the chief interest of the South, must advance.

— Note by Albert Bushnell Hart

[...] I HAVE, SENATORS, believed from the first that the agitation of the subject of slavery would, if not prevented by some timely and effective measure, end in disunion. Entertaining this opinion, I have, on all proper occasions, endeavored to call the attention of each of the two great parties which divide the country to adopt some measure to prevent so great a disaster, but without success. The agitation has been permitted to proceed, with almost no attempt to resist it, until it has reached a period when it can no longer be disguised or denied that the Union is in danger. You have thus had forced upon you the greatest and the gravest question that can ever come under your consideration: How can the Union be preserved?

[...] The first question, then, presented for consideration, in the investigation I propose to make, in order to obtain such knowledge, is: What is it that has endangered the Union? [...]

One of the causes is, undoubtedly, to be traced to the long-continued agitation of the slave question on the part of the North, and the many aggressions which they have made on the rights of the South during the time. [...]

There is another, lying back of it, with which this is intimately connected, that may be regarded as the great and primary cause. That is to be found in the fact that the equilibrium between the two sections in the Government, as it stood when the constitution was ratified and the Government put in action, has been destroyed. [...]

[...] To sum up the whole, the United States, since they declared their independence, have acquired 2,373,046 square miles of territory, from which the North will have excluded the South, if she should succeed in monopolizing the newly acquired territories, from about three-fourths of the whole, leaving to the South but about one-fourth.

Such is the first and great cause that has destroyed the equilibrium between the two sections in the Government.

The next is the system of revenue and disbursements which has been adopted by the Government. [...]

But while these measures were destroying the equilibrium between the two sections, the action of the Government was leading to a radical change in its character, by concentrating all the power of the system in itself. [...]

That the Government claims, and practically maintains, the right to decide in the last resort as to the extent of its powers, will scarcely be denied by any one conversant with the political history of the country. [...] It [...] follows that the character of the Government has been changed, in consequence, from a Federal Republic, as it originally came from the hands of its framers, and that it has been changed into a great national consolidated Democracy. It has indeed, at present, all the characteristics of the latter, and not one of the former, although it still retains its outward form.

The result of the whole of these causes combined is, that the North has acquired a decided ascendency over every department of this Government, and through it a control over all the powers of the system. . . .

As, then, the North has the absolute control over the Government, it is manifest that on all questions between it and the South, where there is a diversity of interests, the interests of the latter will be sacrificed to the former, however oppressive the effects may be, as the South possesses no means by which it can resist through the action of the Government. But if there was no question of vital importance to the South, in reference to which there was a diversity of views between the two sections, this state of things might be endured without the hazard of destruction to the South. But such is not the fact. There is a question of vital importance to the southern section, in reference to which the views and feelings of the two sections are as opposite and hostile as they can possibly be.

I refer to the relation between the two races in the southern section, which constitutes a vital portion of her social organization. Every portion of the North entertains views and feelings more or less hostile to it. [...] On the contrary, the southern section regards the relation as one which cannot be destroyed without subjecting the two races to the greatest calamity, and the section to poverty, desolation, and wretchedness; and accordingly they feel bound by every consideration of interest and safety, to defend it.

This hostile feeling on the part of the North towards the social organization of the South long lay dormant, but it only required some cause to act on those who felt most intensely that they were responsible for its continuance, to call it into action. The increasing power of this Government, and of the control of the northern section over all its departments, furnished the cause. It was this which made an impression on the minds of many that there was little or no restraint to prevent the Government from doing whatever it might choose to do. This was sufficient of itself to put the most fanatical portion of the North in action for the purpose of destroying the existing relation between the two races in the South. [...]

Such is a brief history of the agitation, as far as it has yet advanced. Now, I ask Senators, what is there to prevent its further progress, until it fulfills the ultimate end proposed, unless some decisive measure should be adopted to prevent it? Has any one of the causes, which has added to its increase from its original small and contemptible beginning until it has attained its present magnitude, diminished in force? Is the original cause of the movement, that slavery is a sin, and ought to be suppressed, weaker now than at the commencement? Or is the Abolition party less numerous or influential, or have they less influence over, or control over the two great parties of the North in elections? Or has the South greater means of influencing or controlling the movements of this Government now than it had when the agitation commenced? To all these questions but one answer can be given: no, no, no! The very reverse is true. Instead of being weaker, all the elements in favor of agitation are stronger now than they were in 1835, when it first commenced, while all the elements of influence on the part of the South are weaker. Unless something decisive is done, I again ask what is to stop this agitation, before the great and final object at which it aims—the abolition of slavery in the States—is consummated? Is it, then, not certain that if something decisive is not now done to arrest it, the South will be forced to choose between abolition and secession? [...]

[...] I return to the question with which I commenced, how can the Union be saved? There is but one way by which it can with any certainty; and that is, by a full and final settlement, on the principle of justice, of all the questions at issue between the two sections. The South asks for justice, simple justice, and less she ought not to take. She has no compromise to offer but the Constitution, and any concession or surrender to make. She has already surrendered so much that she has little left to surrender. Such a settlement would go to the root of the evil, and remove all cause of discontent, by satisfying the South she could remain honorably and safely in the Union, and thereby restore the harmony and fraternal feelings between the sections which existed anterior to the Missouri agitation. Nothing else can, with any certainty, finally and forever settle the questions at issue, terminate agitation, and save the Union.

But can this be done? Yes, easily; not by the weaker party, for it can of itself do nothing—not even protect itself—but by the stronger. The North has only to will it to accomplish it—to do justice by conceding to the South an equal right in the acquired territory, and to do her duty by causing the stipulations relative to fugitive slaves to be faithfully fulfilled—to cease the agitation of the slave question, and to provide for the insertion of a provision in the Constitution, by an amendment, which will restore to the South in substance the power she possessed of protecting herself, before the equilibrium between the sections was destroyed by the action of this Government. There will be no difficulty in devising such a provision—one that will protect the South, and which at the same time will improve and strengthen the Government, instead of impairing and weakening it.

But will the North agree to do this? It is for her to answer this question. [...]

[...] If you remain silent, you will compel us to infer by your acts what you intend. In that case, California will become the test question. If you admit her, under all the difficulties that oppose her admission, you compel us to infer that you intend to exclude us from the whole of the acquired territories.

[AHC]

Senator Daniel Webster, Speech, "Seventh of March"

March 7, 1850

Webster's "seventh-of-March speech" on the Compromise [i.e., the Fugitive Slave Act], though it brought upon him an avalanche of criticism from the anti-slavery people, is, on the whole, harmonious with his earlier utterances; for the burden of his argument was always "liberty and union," and he considered a compromise necessary to preserve the Union.

— *Note by Albert Bushnell Hart*

[...] I NOW SAY, sir, as the proposition upon which I stand this day, and upon the truth and firmness of which I intend to act until it is overthrown, that there is not, at this moment, within the United States, or any territory of the United States, a single foot of land, the character of which, in regard to its being free-soil territory or slave territory, is not fixed by some law, and some irrepealable law, beyond the power of the action of this Government. Now, is it not so with respect to Texas? Why, it is most manifestly so. [...]

But now that, under certain conditions, Texas is in, with all her territories, as a slave State, with a solemn pledge that if she is divided into many States, those States may come in as slave States south of 36° 30', how are we to deal with this subject? I know no way of honorable legislation, when the proper time comes for the enactment, but to carry into effect all that we have stipulated to do. [...]

Now, as to California and New Mexico, I hold slavery to be excluded from those territories by a law even superior to that which admits and sanctions it in Texas—I mean the law of nature—of physical geography—the law of the formation of the earth. That law settles forever, with a strength beyond all terms of human enactment, that slavery cannot exist in California or New Mexico. […] I look upon it, therefore, as a fixed fact, to use an expression current at this day, that both California and New Mexico are destined to be free, so far as they are settled at all, which I believe, especially in regard to New Mexico, will be very little for a great length of time—free by the arrangement of things by the Power above us. I have therefore to say, in this respect also, that this country is fixed for freedom, to as many persons as shall ever live there, by as irrepealable and a more irrepealable law, than the law that attaches to the right of holding slaves in Texas; and I will say further, that if a resolution, or a law, were now before us, to provide a territorial government for New Mexico, I would not vote to put any prohibition into it whatever. The use of such a prohibition would be idle, as it respects any effect it would have upon the territory; and I would not take pains to reaffirm an ordinance of nature, nor to reenact the will of God. And I would put in no Wilmot proviso, for the purpose of a taunt or a reproach. I would put into it no evidence of the votes of superior power, to wound the pride, even whether a just pride, a rational pride, or an irrational pride—to wound the pride of the gentlemen who belong to the southern States. […]

Mr. President, in the excited times in which we live, there is found to exist a state of crimination and recrimination between the North and the South. […] I will state these complaints, especially one complaint of the South, which has in my opinion just foundation; and that is, that there has been found at the North, among individuals and among the Legislatures of the North, a disinclination to perform, fully, their constitutional duties, in regard to the return of persons bound to service, who have escaped into the free States. In that respect, it is my judgment that the South is right, and the North is wrong. Every member of every northern Legislature is bound, by oath, like every other officer in the country, to support the Constitution of the United States; and this article of the Constitution, which says to these States, they shall deliver up fugitives from service, is as binding in honor and conscience as any other article. […] I put it to all the sober and sound minds at the North, as a question of morals and a question of conscience, What right have they, in all their legislative capacity, or any other, to endeavor to get round this Constitution, to embarrass the free exercise of the rights secured by the Constitution, to the persons whose slaves escape from them? None at all—none at all. Neither in the forum of conscience, nor before the face of the Constitution, are they justified, in my opinion. Of course, it is a matter for their consideration. They probably, in the turmoil of the times, have not stopped to consider of this; they have followed what seemed to be the current of thought and of motives as the occasion arose, and neglected to investigate fully the real question, and to consider their constitutional obligations, as I am sure, if they did consider, they would fulfill them with alacrity. [...]

Then, sir, there are those abolition societies, of which I am unwilling to speak, but in regard to which I have very clear notions and opinions. I do not think them useful. I think their operations for the last twenty years have produced nothing good or valuable. At the same time, I know thousands of them are honest and good men; perfectly well-meaning men. They have excited feelings; they think they must do something for the cause of liberty; and in their sphere of action, they do not see what else they can do, than to contribute to an abolition press, or an abolition society, or to pay an abolition lecturer. I do not mean to impute gross motives even to the leaders of these societies, but I am not blind to the consequences. I cannot but see what mischiefs their interference with the South has produced. [...] The bonds of the slaves were bound more firmly than before; their rivets were more strongly fastened. Public opinion, which in Virginia had begun to be exhibited against slavery, and was opening out for the discussion of the question, drew back and shut itself up in its castle. [...] We all know the fact, and we all know the cause, and everything that this agitating people have done, has been, not to enlarge, but to restrain, not to set free, but to bind faster, the slave population of the South. [...]

Now, sir, so far as any of these grievances have their foundation in matters of law, they can be redressed, and ought to be redressed; and so far as they have foundation in matters of opinion, in sentiment, in mutual crimination and recrimination, all that we can do is, to endeavor to allay the agitation, and cultivate a better feeling and more fraternal sentiments between the South and the North.

Mr. President, I should much prefer to have heard, from every member on this floor, declarations of opinion that this Union should never be dissolved, than the declaration of opinion that in any case, under the pressure of any circumstances, such dissolution was possible. I hear with pain, and anguish, and distress, the word secession, especially when it falls from the lips of those who are eminently patriotic, and known to the country, and known all over the world, for their political services. Secession! Peaceable secession! Sir, your eyes and mine are never destined to see that miracle. The dismemberment of this vast country without convulsion! The breaking up of the fountains of the great deep without ruffling the surface! Who is so foolish—I beg everybody's pardon—as to expect to see any such thing? Sir, he who sees these States, now revolving in harmony around a common centre, and expects to see them quit their places and fly off without convulsion, may look the next hour to see the heavenly bodies rush from their spheres, and jostle against each other in the realms of space, without producing the crush of the universe. There can be no such thing as a peaceable secession. Peaceable secession is an utter impossibility. Is the great Constitution under which we live here—covering this whole country—is it to be thawed and melted away by secession, as the snows on the mountain melt under the influence of a vernal sun—disappear almost unobserved, and die off? No, sir! no, sir! I will not state what might produce the disruption of the States; but, sir, I see it as plainly as I see the sun in heaven—I see that disruption must produce such a war as I will not describe, in its twofold characters.

[AHC]

The Fugitive Slave Act

September 18, 1850

The Fugitive Slave Act of 1850 was embraced by slave-owners and their sympathizers but despised by slaves, abolitionists and lovers of freedom. The act required the capture and return of escaped slaves, regardless of where in the United States they were found, and made it illegal to "aid, abet, or assist" them. This law was regularly broken by abolitionists, caused fugitive slaves to live in constant fear of recapture and led to the abduction of free Blacks, who were often sold into slavery in the South. It was repealed by Congress in 1864.
— Note by Christine Rudisel

"An Act Respecting Fugitives from Justice, and Persons Escaping from the Service of Their Masters"

SECTION 1

Be it enacted by the Senate and House of Representatives of the United States of America in Congress assembled, That the persons who have been, or may hereafter be, appointed commissioners, in virtue of any act of Congress, by the Circuit Courts of the United States, and Who, in consequence of such appointment, are authorized to exercise the powers that any justice of the peace, or other magistrate of any of the United States, may exercise in respect to offenders for any crime or offense against the United States, by arresting, imprisoning, or bailing the same under and by the virtue of the thirty-third section of the act of the twenty-fourth of September seventeen hundred and eighty-nine, entitled "An Act to establish the judicial courts of the United States" shall be, and are hereby, authorized and required to exercise and discharge all the powers and duties conferred by this act.

SECTION 2

And be it further enacted, That the Superior Court of each organized Territory of the United States shall have the same power to appoint commissioners to take acknowledgments of bail and affidavits, and to take depositions of witnesses in civil causes, which is now possessed by the Circuit Court of the United States; and all commissioners who shall hereafter be appointed for such purposes by the Superior Court of any organized Territory of the United States, shall possess all the powers, and exercise all the duties, conferred by law upon the commissioners appointed by the Circuit Courts of the United States for similar purposes, and shall moreover exercise and discharge all the powers and duties conferred by this act.

SECTION 3

And be it further enacted, That the Circuit Courts of the United States shall from time to time enlarge the number of the commissioners, with a view to afford reasonable facilities to reclaim fugitives from labor, and to the prompt discharge of the duties imposed by this act.

SECTION 4

And be it further enacted, That the commissioners above named shall have concurrent jurisdiction with the judges of the Circuit and District Courts of the United States, in their respective circuits and districts within the several States, and the judges of the Superior Courts of the Territories, severally and collectively, in term-time and vacation; shall grant certificates to such claimants, upon satisfactory proof being made, with authority to take and remove such fugitives from service or labor, under the restrictions herein contained, to the State or Territory from which such persons may have escaped or fled.

SECTION 5

And be it further enacted, That it shall be the duty of all marshals and deputy marshals to obey and execute all warrants and precepts issued under the provisions of this act, when to them directed; and should any marshal or deputy marshal refuse to receive such warrant, or other process, when tendered, or to use all proper means diligently to execute the same, he shall, on conviction thereof, be fined in the sum of one thousand dollars, to the use of such claimant, on the motion of such claimant, by the Circuit or District Court for the district of such marshal; and after arrest of such fugitive, by such marshal or his deputy, or whilst at any time in his custody under the provisions of this act, should such fugitive escape, whether with or without the assent of such marshal or his deputy, such marshal shall be liable, on his official bond, to be prosecuted for the benefit of such claimant, for the full value of the service or labor of said fugitive in the State, Territory, or District whence he escaped: and the better to enable the said commissioners, when thus appointed, to execute their duties faithfully and efficiently, in conformity with the requirements of the Constitution of the United States and of this act, they are hereby authorized and empowered, within their counties respectively, to appoint, in writing under their hands, any one or more suitable persons, from time to time, to execute all such warrants and other process as may be issued by them in the lawful performance of their respective duties; with authority to such commissioners, or the persons to be appointed by them, to execute process as aforesaid, to summon and call to their aid the bystanders, or posse comitatus of the proper county, when necessary to ensure a faithful observance of the clause of the Constitution referred to, in conformity with the provisions of this act; and all good citizens are hereby commanded to aid and assist in the prompt and efficient execution of this law, whenever their services may be required, as aforesaid, for that purpose; and said warrants shall run, and be executed by said officers, any where in the State within which they are issued.

SECTION 6

And be it further enacted, That when a person held to service or labor in any State or Territory of the United States, has heretofore or shall hereafter escape into another State or Territory of the United States, the person or persons to whom such service or labor may be due, or his, her, or their agent or attorney, duly authorized, by power of attorney, in writing, acknowledged and certified under the seal of some legal officer or court of the State or Territory in which the same may be executed, may pursue and reclaim such fugitive person, either by procuring a warrant from some one of the courts, judges, or commissioners aforesaid, of the proper circuit, district, or county, for the apprehension of such fugitive from service or labor, or by seizing and arresting such fugitive, where the same can be done without process, and by taking, or causing such person to be taken, forthwith before such court, judge, or commissioner, whose duty it shall be to hear and determine the case of such claimant in a summary manner; and upon satisfactory proof being made, by deposition or affidavit, in writing, to be taken and certified by such court, judge, or commissioner, or by other satisfactory testimony, duly taken and certified by some court, magistrate, justice of the peace, or other legal officer authorized to administer an oath and take depositions under the laws of the State or Territory from which such person owing service or labor may have escaped, with a certificate of such magistracy or other authority, as aforesaid, with the seal of the proper court or officer thereto attached, which seal shall be sufficient to establish the competency of the proof, and with proof, also by affidavit, of the identity of the person whose service or labor is claimed to be due as aforesaid, that the person so arrested does in fact owe service or labor to the person or persons claiming him or her, in the State or Territory from which such fugitive may have escaped as aforesaid, and that said person escaped, to make out and deliver to such claimant, his or her agent or attorney, a certificate setting forth the substantial facts as to the service or labor due from such fugitive to the claimant, and of his or her escape from the State or Territory in which he or she was arrested, with authority to such claimant, or his or her agent or attorney, to use such reasonable force and restraint as may be necessary, under the circumstances of the case, to take and remove such fugitive person back to the State or Territory whence he or she may have escaped as aforesaid. In no trial or hearing under this act shall the testimony of such alleged fugitive be admitted in evidence; and the certificates in this and the first [fourth] section mentioned, shall be conclusive of the right of the person or persons in whose favor granted, to remove such fugitive to the State or Territory from which he escaped, and shall prevent all molestation of such person or persons by any process issued by any court, judge, magistrate, or other person whomsoever.

SECTION 7

And be it further enacted, That any person who shall knowingly and willingly obstruct, hinder, or prevent such claimant, his agent or attorney, or any person or persons lawfully assisting him, her, or them, from arresting such a fugitive from service or labor, either with or without process as aforesaid, or shall rescue, or attempt to rescue, such fugitive from service or labor, from the custody of such claimant, his or her agent or attorney, or other person or persons lawfully assisting as aforesaid, when so arrested, pursuant to the authority herein given and declared; or shall aid, abet, or assist such person so owing service or labor as aforesaid, directly or indirectly, to escape from such claimant, his agent or attorney, or other person or persons legally authorized as aforesaid; or shall harbor or conceal such fugitive, so as to prevent the discovery and arrest of such person, after notice or knowledge of the fact that such person was a fugitive from service or labor as aforesaid, shall, for either of said offences, be subject to a fine not exceeding one thousand dollars, and imprisonment not exceeding six months, by indictment and conviction before the District Court of the United States for the district in which such offence may have been committed, or before the proper court of criminal jurisdiction, if committed within any one of the organized Territories of the United States; and shall moreover forfeit and pay, by way of civil damages to the party injured by such illegal conduct, the sum of one thousand dollars for each fugitive so lost as aforesaid, to be recovered by action of debt, in any of the District or Territorial Courts aforesaid, within whose jurisdiction the said offence may have been committed.

SECTION 8

And be it further enacted, That the marshals, their deputies, and the clerks of the said District and Territorial Courts, shall be paid, for their services, the like fees as may be allowed for similar services in other cases; and where such services are rendered exclusively in the arrest, custody, and delivery of the fugitive to the claimant, his or her agent or attorney, or where such supposed fugitive may be discharged out of custody for the want of sufficient proof as aforesaid, then such fees are to be paid in whole by such claimant, his or her agent or attorney; and in all cases where the proceedings are before a commissioner, he shall be entitled to a fee of ten dollars in full for his services in each case, upon the delivery of the said certificate to the claimant, his agent or attorney; or a fee of five dollars in cases where the proof shall not, in the opinion of such commissioner, warrant such certificate and delivery, inclusive of all services incident to such arrest and examination, to be paid, in either case, by the claimant, his or her agent or attorney. The person or persons authorized to execute the process to be issued by such commissioner for the arrest and detention of fugitives from service or labor as aforesaid, shall also be entitled to a fee of five dollars each for each person he or they may arrest, and take before any commissioner as aforesaid, at the instance and request of such claimant, with such other fees as may be deemed reasonable by such commissioner for such other additional services as may be necessarily performed by him or them; such as attending at the examination, keeping the fugitive in custody, and providing him with food and lodging during his detention, and until the final determination of such commissioners; and, in general, for performing such other duties as may be required by such claimant, his or her attorney or agent, or commissioner in the premises, such fees to be made up in conformity with the fees usually charged by the officers of the courts of justice within the proper district or county, as near as may be practicable, and paid by such claimants, their agents or attorneys, whether such supposed fugitives from service or labor be ordered to be delivered to such claimant by the final determination of such commissioner or not.

SECTION 9

And be it further enacted, That, upon affidavit made by the claimant of such fugitive, his agent or attorney, after such certificate has been issued, that he has reason to apprehend that such fugitive will he rescued by force from his or their possession before he can be taken beyond the limits of the State in which the arrest is made, it shall be the duty of the officer making the arrest to retain such fugitive in his custody, and to remove him to the State whence he fled, and there to deliver him to said claimant, his agent, or attorney. And to this end, the officer aforesaid is hereby authorized and required to employ so many persons as he may deem necessary to overcome such force, and to retain them in his service so long as circumstances may require. The said officer and his assistants, while so employed, to receive the same compensation, and to be allowed the same expenses, as are now allowed by law for transportation of criminals, to be certified by the judge of the district within which the arrest is made, and paid out of the treasury of the United States.

SECTION 10

And be it further enacted, That when any person held to service or labor in any State or Territory, or in the District of Columbia, shall escape therefrom, the party to whom such service or labor shall be due, his, her, or their agent or attorney, may apply to any court of record therein, or judge thereof in vacation, and make satisfactory proof to such court, or judge in vacation, of the escape aforesaid, and that the person escaping owed service or labor to such party. Whereupon the court shall cause a record to be made of the matters so proved, and also a general description of the person so escaping, with such convenient certainty as may be; and a transcript of such record, authenticated by the attestation of the clerk and of the seal of the said court, being produced in any other State, Territory, or district in which the person so escaping may be found, and being exhibited to any judge, commissioner, or other office, authorized by the law of the United States to cause persons escaping from service or labor to be delivered up, shall be held and taken to be full and conclusive evidence of the fact of escape, and that the service or labor of the person escaping is due to the party in such record mentioned. And upon the production by the said party of other and further evidence if necessary, either oral or by affidavit, in addition to what is contained in the said record of the identity of the person escaping, he or she shall be delivered up to the claimant. And the said court, commissioner, judge, or other person authorized by this act to grant certificates to claimants or fugitives, shall, upon the production of the record and other evidences aforesaid, grant to such claimant a certificate of his right to take any such person identified and proved to be owing service or labor as aforesaid, which certificate shall authorize such claimant to seize or arrest and transport such person to the State or Territory from which he escaped: Provided, That nothing herein contained shall be construed as requiring the production of a transcript of such record as evidence as aforesaid. But in its absence the claim shall be heard and determined upon other satisfactory proofs, competent in law.

APPROVED, SEPTEMBER 18, 1850.

[SN]

Frederick Douglass, Speech, "What to the Slave Is the Fourth of July?"

July 5, 1852

When asked to speak at the city of Rochester's annual Independence Day celebration, Douglass [1818–1895] chose not to deliver a patriotic address, but rather a scathing rebuke of the hypocrisy inherent in asking a former slave to present a speech on such an occasion. Delivered on July 5, 1852, this passionate, biting oratory would go on to become one of Douglass's most well-known and influential speeches.

— Note by James Daley

MR. PRESIDENT, FRIENDS, and Fellow Citizens.

He who could address this audience without a quailing sensation, has stronger nerves than I have. I do not remember ever to have appeared as a speaker before any assembly more shrinkingly, nor with greater distrust of my ability, than I do this day. A feeling has crept over me quite unfavorable to the exercise of my limited powers of speech. The task before me is one which requires much previous thought and study for its proper performance. I know that apologies of this sort are generally considered flat and unmeaning. I trust, however, that mine will not be so considered. Should I seem at ease, my appearance would much misrepresent me. The little experience I have had in addressing public meetings, in country schoolhouses, avails me nothing on the present occasion.

The papers and placards say that I am to deliver a Fourth of July Oration. This certainly sounds large, and out of the common way, for me. It is true that I have often had the privilege to speak in this beautiful Hall, and to address many who now honor me with their presence. But neither their familiar faces, nor the perfect gage I think I have of Corinthian Hall seems to free me from embarrassment.

The fact is, ladies and gentlemen, the distance between this platform and the slave plantation, from which I escaped, is considerable—and the difficulties to be overcome in getting from the latter to the former are by no means slight. That I am here today is, to me, a matter of astonishment as well as of gratitude. You will not, therefore, be surprised, if in what I have to say I evince no elaborate preparation, nor grace my speech with any high sounding exordium. With little experience and with less learning, I have been able to throw my thoughts hastily and imperfectly together; and trusting to your patient and generous indulgence I will proceed to lay them before you. […]

Fellow-citizens, above your national, tumultuous joy, I hear the mournful wail of millions! whose chains, heavy and grievous yesterday, are, today, rendered more intolerable by the jubilee shouts that reach them. If I do forget, if I do not faithfully remember those bleeding children of sorrow this day, "may my right hand forget her cunning, and may my tongue cleave to the roof of my mouth!" To forget them, to pass lightly over their wrongs, and to chime in with the popular theme, would be treason most scandalous and shocking, and would make me a reproach before God and the world. My subject, then, fellow-citizens, is American slavery. I shall see this day and its popular characteristics from the slave's point of view. Standing there identified with the American bondman, making his wrongs mine, I do not hesitate to declare, with all my soul, that the character and conduct of this nation never looked blacker to me than on this 4th of July! Whether we turn to the declarations of the past, or to the professions of the present, the conduct of the nation seems equally hideous and revolting. America is false to the past, false to the present, and solemnly binds herself to be false to the future. Standing with God and the crushed and bleeding slave on this occasion, I will, in the name of humanity which is outraged, in the name of liberty which is fettered, in the name of the constitution and the Bible which are disregarded and trampled upon, dare to call in question and to denounce, with all the emphasis I can command, everything that serves to perpetuate slavery—the great sin and shame of America! "I will not equivocate; I will not excuse"; I will use the severest language I can command; and yet not one word shall escape me that any man, whose judgment is not blinded by prejudice, or who is not at heart a slaveholder, shall not confess to be right and just.

But I fancy I hear some one of my audience say, "It is just in this circumstance that you and your brother abolitionists fail to make a favorable impression on the public mind. Would you argue more, and denounce less; would you persuade more, and rebuke less; your cause would be much more likely to succeed." But, I submit, where all is plain there is nothing to be argued. What point in the anti slavery creed would you have me argue? On what branch of the subject do the people of this country need light? Must I undertake to prove that the slave is a man? That point is conceded already. Nobody doubts it. The slaveholders themselves acknowledge it in the enactment of laws for their government. They acknowledge it when they punish disobedience on the part of the slave. There are seventy-two crimes in the State of Virginia which, if committed by a black man (no matter how ignorant he be), subject him to the punishment of death; while only two of the same crimes will subject a white man to the like punishment. What is this but the acknowledgment that the slave is a moral, intellectual, and responsible being? The manhood of the slave is conceded. It is admitted in the fact that Southern statute books are covered with enactments forbidding, under severe fines and penalties, the teaching of the slave to read or to write. When you can point to any such laws in reference to the beasts of the field, then I may consent to argue the manhood of the slave. When the dogs in your streets, when the fowls of the air, when the cattle on your hills, when the fish of the sea, and the reptiles that crawl, shall be unable to distinguish the slave from a brute, then will I argue with you that the slave is a man!

For the present, it is enough to affirm the equal manhood of the Negro race. Is it not astonishing that, while we are plowing, planting, and reaping, using all kinds of mechanical tools, erecting houses, constructing bridges, building ships, working in metals of brass, iron, copper, silver and gold; that, while we are reading, writing and ciphering, acting as clerks, merchants and secretaries, having among us lawyers, doctors, ministers, poets, authors, editors, orators and teachers; that, while we are engaged in all manner of enterprises common to other men, digging gold in California, capturing the whale in the Pacific, feeding sheep and cattle on the hill-side, living, moving, acting, thinking, planning, living in families as husbands, wives and children, and, above all, confessing and worshipping the Christian's God, and looking hopefully for life and immortality beyond the grave, we are called upon to prove that we are men!

Would you have me argue that man is entitled to liberty? that he is the rightful owner of his own body? You have already declared it. Must I argue the wrongfulness of slavery? Is that a question for Republicans? Is it to be settled by the rules of logic and argumentation, as a matter beset with great difficulty, involving a doubtful application of the principle of justice, hard to be understood? How should I look today, in the presence of Americans, dividing, and subdividing a discourse, to show that men have a natural right to freedom? speaking of it relatively and positively, negatively and affirmatively. To do so, would be to make myself ridiculous, and to offer an insult to your understanding.—There is not a man beneath the canopy of heaven that does not know that slavery is wrong for him.

What, am I to argue that it is wrong to make men brutes, to rob them of their liberty, to work them without wages, to keep them ignorant of their relations to their fellow men, to beat them with sticks, to flay their flesh with the lash, to load their limbs with irons, to hunt them with dogs, to sell them at auction, to sunder their families, to knock out their teeth, to burn their flesh, to starve them into obedience and submission to their masters? Must I argue that a system thus marked with blood, and stained with pollution, is wrong? No! I will not. I have better employment for my time and strength than such arguments would imply.

What, then, remains to be argued? Is it that slavery is not divine; that God did not establish it; that our doctors of divinity are mistaken? There is blasphemy in the thought. That which is inhuman, cannot be divine! Who can reason on such a proposition? They that can, may; I cannot. The time for such argument is passed.

At a time like this, scorching irony, not convincing argument, is needed. O! had I the ability, and could reach the nation's ear, I would, today, pour out a fiery stream of biting ridicule, blasting reproach, withering sarcasm, and stern rebuke. For it is not light that is needed, but fire; it is not the gentle shower, but thunder. We need the storm, the whirlwind, and the earthquake. The feeling of the nation must be quickened; the conscience of the nation must be roused; the propriety of the nation must be startled; the hypocrisy of the nation must be exposed; and its crimes against God and man must be proclaimed and denounced.

What, to the American slave, is your 4th of July? I answer; a day that reveals to him, more than all other days in the year, the gross injustice and cruelty to which he is the constant victim. To him, your celebration is a sham; your boasted liberty, an unholy license; your national greatness, swelling vanity; your sounds of rejoicing are empty and heartless; your denunciation of tyrants, brass fronted impudence; your shouts of liberty and equality, hollow mockery; your prayers and hymns, your sermons and thanksgivings, with all your religious parade and solemnity, are, to Him, mere bombast, fraud, deception, impiety, and hypocrisy—a thin veil to cover up crimes which would disgrace a nation of savages. There is not a nation on the earth guilty of practices more shocking and bloody than are the people of the United States, at this very hour. [...]

[GSFD]

Senator Charles Sumner, Speech, "The Crime Against Kansas"

May 19–20, 1856

Charles Sumner [1811–1874], Senator from Massachusetts, was probably the most militant advocate of the abolition of slavery in the United States Congress. His energy and eloquence won for him the enmity of extremists from the South. As a result of the speech, reproduced here in part, which he delivered in the Senate on May 19–20, 1856, Sumner was assaulted, in the Senate chamber, by a nephew of one of the opposing Senators. Sumner never fully recovered from this attack.

– Note by Lewis Copeland

THE WICKEDNESS WHICH I now begin to expose is immeasurably aggravated by the motive which prompted it. Not in any common lust for power did this uncommon tragedy have its origin. It is the rape of a virgin Territory, compelling it to the hateful embrace of slavery; and it may be clearly traced to a depraved longing for a new slave State, the hideous offspring of such a crime, in the hope of adding to the power of slavery in the National Government. Yes, sir; when the whole world, alike Christian and Turk, is rising up to condemn this wrong, and to make it a hissing to the nations, here in our Republic, *force*—ay, sir, FORCE—has been openly employed in compelling Kansas to this pollution, and all for the sake of political power. There is the simple fact, which you will in vain attempt to deny, but which in itself presents an essential wickedness that makes other public crimes seem like public virtues.

But this enormity, vast beyond comparison, swells to dimensions of wickedness which the imagination toils in vain to grasp, when it is understood that for this purpose are hazarded the horrors of intestine feud not only in this distant Territory, but everywhere throughout the country. Already the muster has begun. The strife is no longer local, but national. Even now, while I speak, portents hang on all the arches of the horizon threatening to darken the broad land, which already yawns with the mutterings of civil war. The fury of the propagandists of slavery, and the calm determination of their opponents, are now diffused from the distant Territory over widespread communities, and the whole country, in all its extent—marshaling hostile divisions, and foreshadowing a strife which, unless happily averted by the triumph of freedom, will become war—fratricidal, patricidal war—with an accumulated wickedness beyond the wickedness of any war in human annals; justly provoking the avenging judgment of Providence and the avenging pen of history, and constituting a strife, in the language of the ancient writer, more than *foreign,* more than *social,* more than *civil;* but something compounded of all these strifes, and in itself more than war; *sed potius commune quoddam ex omnibus, et plus quam bellum.*

Such is the crime which you are to judge. But the criminal also must be dragged into day, that you may see and measure the power by which all this wrong is sustained. From no common source could it proceed. In its perpetration was needed a spirit of vaulting ambition which would hesitate at nothing; a hardihood of purpose which was insensible to the judgment of mankind; a madness for slavery which would disregard the Constitution, the laws, and all the great examples of our history; also a consciousness of power such as comes from the habit of power; a combination of energies found only in a hundred arms directed by a hundred eyes; a control of public opinion through venal pens and a prostituted press; an ability to subsidize crowds in every vocation of life—the politician with his local importance, the lawyer with his subtle tongue, and even the authority of the judge on the bench; and a familiar use of men in places high and low, so that none, from the President to the lowest border postmaster, should decline to be its tool; all these things and more were needed, and they were found in the slave power of our Republic. There, sir, stands the criminal, all unmasked before you—heartless, grasping, and tyrannical—with an audacity beyond that of Verres, a subtlety beyond that of Machiavel, a meanness beyond that of Bacon, and an ability beyond that of Hastings. Justice to Kansas can be secured only by the prostration of this influence; for this the power behind—greater than any President—which succors and sustains the crime. Nay, the proceedings I now arraign derive their fearful consequences only from this connection.

In now opening this great matter, I am not insensible to the austere demands of the occasion; but the dependence of the crime against Kansas upon the slave power is so peculiar and important that I trust to be pardoned while I impress it with an illustration, which to some may seem trivial. It is related in Northern mythology that the god of Force, visiting an enchanted region, was challenged by his royal entertainer to what seemed a humble feat of strength—merely, sir, to lift a cat from the ground. The god smiled at the challenge, and, calmly placing his hand under the belly of the animal, with superhuman strength strove, while the back of the feline monster arched far upward, even beyond reach, and one paw actually forsook the earth, until at last the discomfited divinity desisted; but he was little surprised at his defeat when he learned that this creature, which seemed to be a cat, and nothing more, was not merely a cat, but that it belonged to and was a part of the great terrestrial serpent, which, in its innumerable folds, encircled the whole globe. Even so the creature, whose paws are now fastened upon Kansas, whatever it may seem to be, constitutes in reality a part of the slave power, which, in its loathsome folds, is now coiled about the whole land. Thus do I expose the extent of the present contest, where we encounter not merely local resistance, but also the unconquered sustaining arm behind. But out of the vastness of the crime attempted, with all its woe and shame, I derive a well-founded assurance of a commensurate vastness of effort against it by the aroused masses of the country, determined not only to vindicate right against wrong, but to redeem the Republic from the thralldom of that oligarchy which prompts, directs, and concentrates the distant wrong.

But, before entering upon the argument, I must say something of a general character, particularly in response to what has fallen from Senators who have raised themselves to eminence on this floor in championship of human wrongs. I mean the Senator from South Carolina (Mr. Butler), and the Senator from Illinois (Mr. Douglas), who, though unlike as Don Quixote and Sancho Panza, yet, like this couple, sally forth together in the same adventure. I regret much to miss the elder Senator from his seat; but the cause, against which he has run a tilt, with such activity of animosity, demands that the opportunity of exposing him should not be lost; and it is for the cause that I speak. The Senator from South Carolina has read many books of chivalry, and believes himself a chivalrous knight, with sentiments of honor and courage. Of course he has chosen a mistress to whom he has made his vows, and who, though ugly to others, is always lovely to him; though polluted in the sight of the world, is chaste in his sight—I mean the harlot, Slavery. For her, his tongue is always profuse in words. Let her be impeached in character, or any proposition made to shut her out from the extension of her wantonness, and no extravagance of manner or hardihood of assertion is then too great for this Senator. The frenzy of Don Quixote, in behalf of his wench, Dulcinea del Toboso, is all surpassed. The asserted rights of slavery, which shock equality of all kinds, are cloaked by a fantastic claim of equality. If the slave States cannot enjoy what, in mockery of the great fathers of the Republic, he misnames equality under the Constitution—in other words, the full power in the national territories to compel fellow-men to unpaid toil, to separate husband and wife, and to sell little children at the auction block—then, sir, the chivalric Senator will conduct the State of South Carolina out of the Union! Heroic knight! Exalted Senator! A second Moses come for a second exodus!

But not content with this poor menace, which we have been twice told was "measured," the Senator in the unrestrained chivalry of his nature, has undertaken to apply opprobrious words to those who differ from him on this floor. He calls them "sectional and fanatical;" and opposition to the usurpation in Kansas he denounces as "an uncalculating fanaticism." To be sure these charges lack all grace of originality and all sentiment of truth; but the adventurous Senator does not hesitate. He is the uncompromising, unblushing representative on this floor of a flagrant *sectionalism,* which now domineers over the Republic, and yet with a ludicrous ignorance of his own position—unable to see himself as others see him—or with an effrontery which even his white head ought not to protect from rebuke, he applies to those here who resist his *sectionalism* the very epithet which designates himself. The men who strive to bring back the Government to its original policy, when freedom and not slavery was sectional, he arraigns as *sectional.* This will not do. It involves too great a perversion of terms. I tell that Senator that it is to himself, and to the "organization" of which he is the "committed advocate," that this epithet belongs. I now fasten it upon them. For myself, I care little for names; but since the question has been raised here, I affirm that the Republican party of the Union is in no just sense *sectional,* but, more than any other party, *national;* and that it now goes forth to dislodge from the high places of the

Government the tyrannical sectionalism of which the Senator from South Carolina is one of the maddest zealots.

As the Senator from South Carolina is the Don Quixote, the Senator from Illinois (Mr. Douglas) is the squire of slavery, its very Sancho Panza, ready to do all its humiliating offices. This Senator, in his labored address, vindicating his labored report—piling one mass of elaborate error upon another mass—constrained himself, as you will remember, to unfamiliar decencies of speech. Of that address I have nothing to say at this moment, though before I sit down I shall show something of its fallacies. But I go back now to an earlier occasion, when, true to his native impulses, he threw into this discussion, "for a charm of powerful trouble," personalities most discreditable to this body. I will not stop to repel the imputations which he cast upon myself; but I mention them to remind you of the "sweltered venom sleeping got," which, with other poisoned ingredients, he cast into the cauldron of this debate. Of other things I speak. Standing on this floor, the Senator issued his rescript, requiring submission to the usurped power of Kansas; and this was accompanied by a manner—all his own—such as befits the tyrannical threat. Very well. Let the Senator try. I tell him now that he cannot enforce any such submission. The Senator, with the slave power at his back, is strong; but he is not strong enough for this purpose. He is bold. He shrinks from nothing. Like Danton, he may cry, *"l'audace! l'audace! toujours l'audace!"* but even his audacity cannot compass this work. The Senator copies the British officer who, with boastful swagger, said that with the hilt of his sword he would cram the "stamps" down the throats of the American people, and he will meet with a similar failure. He may convulse this country with a civil feud. Like the ancient madman, he may set fire to this temple of constitutional liberty, grander than the Ephesian dome; but he cannot enforce obedience to that tyrannical usurpation.

The Senator dreams that he can subdue the North. He disclaims the open threat, but his conduct still implies it. How little that Senator knows himself or the strength of the cause which he persecutes! He is but a mortal man; against him is an immortal principle. With finite power he wrestles with the infinite, and he must fall. Against him are stronger battalions than any marshaled by mortal arm—the inborn, ineradicable, invincible sentiments of the human heart; against him is nature in all her subtle forces; against him is God. Let him try to subdue these.

[WGS]

Supreme Court Chief Justice
Roger B. Taney et al.,
Papers and Decision on
Dred Scott v. Sandford

March 6, 1857

These papers are introduced to show the process of claiming freedom, the succession of suits, and the original question at issue in the Missouri courts. The action for trespass here described was finally decided in Dred Scott's favor, but on appeal to the Supreme Court of Missouri the decision was reversed. Meanwhile Scott [c. 1799–1858] had brought action of trespass in the United States Circuit Court, as a citizen of Missouri suing Sandford, a citizen of New York. The court gave judgment for the defendant, and Dred Scott's counsel carried the case to the United States Supreme Court on a writ of error. After the decision, which is one of the most important opinions ever handed down by the court, Scott was at once set free by his titular master.

— Note by Albert Bushnell Hart

A. DRED SCOTT'S FREEDOM SUIT

Dred Scott
vs.
Alex. Sandford,
Saml. Russel, and
Irene Emerson.

To the Honorable, the Circuit Court within and for the County of St. Louis

YOUR PETITIONER, DRED Scott, a man of color, respectfully represents that sometime in the year 1835 your petitioner was purchased as a slave by one John Emerson, since deceased, who afterwards, to-wit; about the year 1836 or 1837, conveyed your petitioner from the State of Missouri to Fort Snelling, a fort then occupied by the troops of the United States and under the jurisdiction of the United States, situated in the territory ceded by France to the United States under the name of Louisiana, lying north of 36 degrees and 30' North latitude, now included in the State of Missouri, and resided and continued to reside at Fort Snelling upwards of one year, and held your petitioner in slavery at such Fort during all that time in violation of the Act of Congress of 1806 and 1820, entitled An Act to Authorize the People of Missouri Territory to form a Constitution and State Government, and for the admission of such State into the Union on an equal footing with the original states, and to Prohibit Slavery in Certain Territories.

Your petitioner avers that said Emerson has since departed this life, leaving his widow Irene Emerson and an infant child whose name is unknown to your petitioner; and that one Alexander Sandford administered upon the estate of said Emerson and that your petitioner is now unlawfully held in slavery by said Sandford and by said administrator, and said Irene Emerson claims your petitioner as part of the estate of said Emerson and by one Samuel Russell.

Your petitioner therefore prays your Honorable Court to grant him leave to sue as a poor person, in order to establish his right to freedom, and that the necessary orders may be made in the premises.

Dred Scott.

State of Missouri
County of St. Louis } ss.

This day personally came before me, the undersigned, a Justice of the Peace, Dred Scott, the person whose name is affixed to the foregoing petition, and made oath that the facts set forth in the above petition are true to the best of his knowledge and belief, that he is entitled to his freedom. Witness my hand this 1st day of July, 1847.

his
Dred X Scott
mark.

Sworn to and subscribed before me this 1st day of July, 1847.

Peter W. Johnstone
Justice of the Peace.

Upon reading the above petition this day, it being the opinion of the Judge of the Circuit Court, that the said petition contains sufficient matter to authorize the commencement of a suit for his freedom, it is hereby ordered that the said petitioner Dred Scott be allowed to sue on giving security satisfactory to the Clerk of the Circuit Court for all costs that may be adjudged against him, and that he have reasonable liberty to attend to his counsel and the court as the occasion may require, and that he be not subject to any severity on account of this application for his freedom.

July 2d, 1847.   A. Hamilton
                        Judge of Circuit Court 8th Jud. Cir.

B. DRED SCOTT'S TRESPASS SUIT

Circuit Court of St. Louis County, November Term, 1847.

State of Missouri   }
                         } ss.
County of St. Louis   }

Dred Scott, a man of color, by his attorneys, plaintiff in this suit, complains of Alexander Sandford, administrator of the estate of John Emerson, deceased, Irene Emerson and Samuel Russell defendants, of a plea of trespass that the said defendants, heretofore, to–wit, on the 1st day of July in the year 1846, at to-wit, the County of St. Louis aforesaid with force and arms assaulted said plaintiff, and then and there bruised and ill–treated him, and then and there put him in prison and kept and detained him in prison, and without any reason whatsoever for the space of one year, and then and there violating and contrary to law and against the will of said plaintiff; and said plaintiff avers that before and at the time of the committing of the grievance aforesaid, he, the said plaintiff, was then and there and still is a free person, and that the said defendants held and still hold him in slavery, and other wrongs to said plaintiff then and there did against the laws of the State of Missouri to the damage of the said plaintiff in the sum of £300, and therefore he sues.

C. VERDICT AGAINST SCOTT IN TRESPASS SUIT

April 30, 1847, April Term. A. Hamilton, Judge.

Dred Scott of color ⎫
vs.   ⎬ Trespass.
Irene Emmerson.   ⎭

This day come the parties by their attorney and comes also a jury . . . twelve good and lawful men, who being duly elected, tried and sworn the truth to speak upon the issue joined between the parties, upon their oaths, do find that the said defendant is not guilty in any manner and form as the plaintiff hath in his declaration complaint against her. Therefore it is considered that the said defendant go hence without day and recover of the said plaintiff her costs in this behalf expended. The plaintiff by his attorneys files a motion for a new trial herein. Set aside. . . .

Dred Scott   ⎫   Dred Scott   ⎫
   vs.   ⎬ Freedom.   vs.   ⎬ Freedom.
Irene Emmerson.   ⎭   Alex. Sandford,   ⎭
                                 Samuel Russell,
                                 Irene Emerson

It is ordered in this case that the plaintiff in these two suits make his election on or before the first day of the next term of this Court which of said suits he will continue to prosecute. . . .

D. NEW TRIAL ORDERED IN TRESPASS SUIT

Thursday December 2, 1847, November Term.

Dred Scott   ⎫
   vs.   ⎬
Irene Emmerson. ⎭

On consideration of the motion of the plaintiff for a new trial herein, it is ordered that the same be sustained, and that the verdict and judgment herein rendered be set aside and a new trial had.

E. FREEDOM SUIT ABANDONED

Thursday Feby 29, 1848, Nov. Term.

Dred Scott
 vs.
Alex. Sandford,
Samuel Russell,
Irene Emmerson
} Freedom.

This day comes said plaintiff by his attorneys and says that he will not further prosecute this suit. It is therefore considered that said defendants go hence without day and recover of said plaintiff their costs in this behalf, and have thereof execution.

F. DRED SCOTT HIRED OUT

Friday March 17th, 1848.

Dred Scott
 vs.
Irene Emmerson.
} Motion of Attorney for Defendant.

It is ordered that the Sheriff of St. Louis County take the said plaintiff into his possession and hire him out from time to time to the best advantage, during the pendency of this suit. And that he take bond from the hirer payable to the State of Missouri in the sum of $600 with good security conditioned that the said hirer shall not remove said plaintiff out of the jurisdiction of this Court; that he will pay the hire to said Sheriff and return said plaintiff at the expiration of the term for which he is hired, or as soon as this action is ended.

SOURCE: From the MS. Court Records of St. Louis County.

[AHC]

Supreme Court Chief Justice Roger B. Taney, Dred Scott Decision

March 6, 1857

Taney [1777–1864] succeeded Marshall as chief justice of the United States Supreme Court in 1835. Although inclined to a strict construction of the Constitution, he did little to weaken the theories of government set forth by Marshall. He was probably drawn into the delivery of the Dred Scott decision, a great obiter dictum, *by the sincere hope that the great prestige of a Supreme Court decision would settle forever the slavery question. This is the first case of an act of Congress, not relating to the judiciary itself, which was held void by the Supreme Court.*

— Note by Albert Bushnell Hart

THE QUESTION IS simply this: Can a negro, whose ancestors were imported into this country, and sold as slaves, become a member of the political community formed and brought into existence by the constitution of the United States, and as such become entitled to all the rights, and privileges, and immunities, guaranteed by that instrument to the citizen? One of which rights is the privilege of suing in a court of the United States in the cases specified in the constitution.

It will be observed, that the plea applies to that class of persons only whose ancestors were negroes of the African race, and imported into this country, and sold and held as slaves. The only matter in issue before the court, therefore, is, whether the descendants of such slaves, when they shall be emancipated, or who are born of parents who had become free before their birth, are citizens of a State, in the sense in which the word citizen is used in the constitution of the United States. And this being the only matter in dispute on the pleadings, the court must be understood as speaking in this opinion of that class only, that is, of those persons who are the descendants of Africans who were imported into this country, and sold as slaves. [...]

The words "people of the United States" and "citizens" . . . mean the same thing. [...] The question before us is, whether the class of persons described in the plea in abatement compose a portion of this people, and are constituent members of this sovereignty? [...]

In discussing this question, we must not confound the rights of citizenship which a State may confer within its own limits, and the rights of citizenship as a member of the Union. It does not by any means follow, because he has all the rights and privileges of a citizen of a State, that he must be a citizen of the United States. [...]

It is very clear [...] that no State can, by any act or law of its own, passed since the adoption of the constitution, introduce a new member into the political community created by the constitution of the United States. It cannot make him a member of this community by making him a member of its own. And for the same reason it cannot introduce any person, or description of persons, who were not intended to be embraced in this new political family, which the constitution brought into existence, but were intended to be excluded from it. [...]

It is true, every person, and every class and description of persons, who were at the time of the adoption of the constitution recognized as citizens in the several States, became also citizens of this new political body; but none other; it was formed by them, and for them and their posterity, but for no one else. [...]

It becomes necessary, therefore, to determine who were citizens of the several States when the constitution was adopted. . . .

In the opinion of the court, the legislation and histories of the times, and the language used in the declaration of independence, show, that neither the class of persons who had been imported as slaves, nor their descendants, whether they had become free or not, were then acknowledged as a part of the people, nor intended to be included in the general words used in that memorable instrument.

It is difficult at this day to realize the state of public opinion in relation to that unfortunate race, which prevailed in the civilized and enlightened portions of the world at the time of the declaration of independence, and when the constitution of the United States was framed and adopted. But the public history of every European nation displays it in a manner too plain to be mistaken.

They had for more than a century before been regarded as beings of an inferior order, and altogether unfit to associate with the white race, either in social or political relations; and so far inferior, that they had no rights which the white man was bound to respect; and that the negro might justly and lawfully be reduced to slavery for his benefit. He was bought and sold, and treated as an ordinary article of merchandise and traffic, whenever a profit could be made by it. This opinion was at that time fixed and universal in the civilized portion of the white race. It was regarded as an axiom in morals as well as in politics, which no one thought of disputing, or supposed to be open to dispute; and men in every grade and position in society daily and habitually acted upon it in their private pursuits, as well as in matters of public concern, without doubting for a moment the correctness of this opinion.

And in no nation was this opinion more firmly fixed or more uniformly acted upon than by the English government and English people. They not only seized them on the coast of Africa, and sold them or held them in slavery for their own use; but they took them as ordinary articles of merchandise to every country where they could make a profit on them, and were far more extensively engaged in this commerce than any other nation in the world.

The opinion thus entertained and acted upon in England was naturally impressed upon the colonies they founded on this side of the Atlantic. And, accordingly, a Negro of the African race was regarded by them as an article of property, and held, and bought and sold as such, in every one of the thirteen colonies which united in the declaration of independence, and afterwards formed the constitution of the United States. The slaves were more or less numerous in the different colonies, as slave labor was found more or less profitable. But no one seems to have doubted the correctness of the prevailing opinion of the time. . . .

The language of the declaration of independence is equally conclusive . . .

[. . .] "We hold these truths to be self-evident: that all men are created equal; that they are endowed by their Creator with certain unalienable rights; that among them is life, liberty, and the pursuit of happiness; that to secure these rights, governments are instituted, deriving their just powers from the consent of the governed."

The general words above quoted would seem to embrace the whole human family, and if they were used in a similar instrument at this day would be so understood. But it is too clear for dispute, that the enslaved African race were not intended to be included, and formed no part of the people who framed and adopted this declaration; for if the language, as understood in that day, would embrace them, the conduct of the distinguished men who framed the declaration of independence would have been utterly and flagrantly inconsistent with the principles they asserted; and instead of the sympathy of mankind, to which they so confidently appealed, they would have deserved and received universal rebuke and reprobation. [...]

But there are two clauses in the constitution which point directly and specifically to the Negro race as a separate class of persons, and show clearly that they were not regarded as a portion of the people or citizens of the government then formed.

One of these clauses reserves to each of the thirteen States the right to import slaves until the year 1808, if it thinks proper. . . . And by the other provision the States pledge themselves to each other to maintain the right of property of the master, by delivering up to him any slave who may have escaped from his service, and be found within their respective territories. [...] And these two provisions show, conclusively, that neither the description of persons therein referred to, nor their descendants, were embraced in any of the other provisions of the constitution; for certainly these two clauses were not intended to confer on them or their posterity the blessings of liberty, or of the personal rights so carefully provided for the citizen. [...]

The only two provisions which point to them and include them, treat them as property, and make it the duty of the government to protect it; no other power, in relation to this race, is to be found in the constitution; and as it is a government of special, delegated, powers, no authority beyond these two provisions can be constitutionally exercised. The government of the United States had no right to interfere for any other purpose but that of protecting the rights of the owner, leaving it altogether with the several States to deal with this race, whether emancipated or not, as each State may think justice, humanity, and the interests and safety of society, require. The States evidently intended to reserve this power exclusively to themselves.

[...] This court was not created by the constitution for such purposes. Higher and graver trusts have been confided to it, and it must not falter in the path of duty. [...]

And upon a full and careful consideration of the subject, the court is of opinion, that, upon the facts stated in the plea in abatement, Dred Scott was not a citizen of Missouri within the meaning of the constitution of the United States, and not entitled as such to sue in its courts; and, consequently, that the circuit court had no jurisdiction of the case, and that the judgment on the plea in abatement is erroneous.

[...] the plaintiff [...] admits that he and his wife were born slaves, but endeavors to make out his title to freedom and citizenship by showing that they were taken by their owner to certain places, hereinafter mentioned, where slavery could not by law exist, and that they thereby became free, and upon their return to Missouri became citizens of that State. [...]

The act of Congress, upon which the plaintiff relies, declares that slavery and involuntary servitude, except as a punishment for crime, shall be forever prohibited in all that part of the territory ceded by France, under the name of Louisiana, which lies north of thirty-six degrees thirty minutes north latitude, and not included within the limits of Missouri. And the difficulty which meets us at the threshold of this part of the inquiry is, whether Congress was authorized to pass this law under any of the powers granted to it by the constitution; for if the authority is not given by that instrument, it is the duty of this court to declare it void and inoperative, and incapable of conferring freedom upon any one who is held as a slave under the laws of any one of the States.

The counsel for the plaintiff has laid much stress upon that article in the constitution which confers on congress the power "to dispose of and make all needful rules and regulations respecting the territory or other property belonging to the United States;" but, in the judgment of the court, that provision has no bearing on the present controversy, and the power there given, whatever it may be, is confined, and was intended to be confined, to the territory which at that time belonged to, or was claimed by, the United States, and was within their boundaries as settled by the treaty with Great Britain, and can have no influence upon a territory afterwards acquired from a foreign government. It was a special provision for a known and particular territory, and to meet a present emergency, and nothing more. [...]

[…] The form of government to be established necessarily rested in the discretion of congress. […]

But the power of congress over the person or property of a citizen can never be a mere discretionary power under our constitution and form of government. The powers of the government and the rights and privileges of the citizen are regulated and plainly defined by the constitution itself. And when the territory becomes a part of the United States, the federal government enters into possession in the character impressed upon it by those who created it. It enters upon it with its powers over the citizen strictly defined, and limited by the constitution, from which it derives its own existence, and by virtue of which alone it continues to exist and act as a government and sovereignty. It has no power of any kind beyond it; and it cannot, when it enters a territory of the United States, put off its character, and assume discretionary or despotic powers which the constitution has denied to it. It cannot create for itself a new character separated from the citizens of the United States, and the duties it owes them under the provisions of the constitution. The territory being a part of the United States, the government and the citizen both enter it under the authority of the constiiution, with their respective rights defined and marked out; and the federal government can exercise no power over his person or property, beyond what that instrument confers, nor lawfully deny any right which it has reserved. […]

[…] in considering the question before us, it must be borne in mind that there is no law of nations standing between the people of the United States and their government, and interfering with their relation to each other […] if the constitution recognizes the right of property of the master in a slave, and makes no distinction between that description of property and other property owned by a citizen, no tribunal, acting under the authority of the United States, whether it be legislative, executive, or judicial, has a right to draw such a distinction, or deny to it the benefit of the provisions and guarantees which have been provided for the protection of private property against the encroachments of the government. Now, as we have already said in an earlier part of this opinion, upon a different point, the right of property in a slave is distinctly and expressly affirmed in the constitution. […] This is done in plain words — too plain to be misunderstood. And no word can be found in the constitution which gives congress a greater power over slave property, or which entitles property of that kind to less protection than property of any other description. The only power conferred is the power coupled with the duty of guarding and protecting the owner in his rights.

Upon these considerations, it is the opinion of the court that the act of congress which prohibited a citizen from holding and owning property of this kind in the territory of the United States north of the line therein mentioned, is not warranted by the constitution, and is therefore void; and that neither Dred Scott himself, nor any of his family, were made free by being carried into this territory; even if they had been carried there by the owner, with the intention of becoming a permanent resident. […]

[…] And it is contended, on the part of the plaintiff, that he is made free by being taken to Rock Island, in the State of Illinois.[…]

[…] As Scott was a slave when taken into the State of Illinois by his owner, and was there held as such, and brought back in that character, his *status,* as free or slave, depended on the laws of Missouri, and not of Illinois.

[AHC]

John Brown, Interrogation Concerning His Actions at Harpers Ferry

October 18, 1859

John Brown [1800–1859] "of Ossawatomie," was an abolitionist of that stern puritanical spirit [...] that feeds upon the Old Testament. In himself he saw a chosen instrument for visiting the iniquity of slavery upon its advocates. In Kansas he began retaliation upon pro-slavery settlers, and his desire for action in the anti-slavery cause culminated in his ill-planned raid on Harpers Ferry; but in defeat he showed himself such a man that he won the admiration of his enemies. This is from [a New York Herald] interview, after his capture, with Senator [James] Mason, Congressman [Clement] Vallandigham, and others.*

— *Note by Albert Bushnell Hart*

SENATOR MASON. CAN you tell us who furnished money for your expedition?

John Brown. I furnished most of it myself; I cannot implicate others. It is by my own folly that I have been taken. I could easily have saved myself from it, had I exercised my own better judgment rather than yielded to my feelings.

Mason. You mean if you had escaped immediately?

Brown. No. I had the means to make myself secure without any escape; but I allowed myself to be surrounded by a force by being too tardy. I should have gone away; but I had thirty odd prisoners, whose wives and daughters were in tears for their safety, and I felt for them. Besides, I wanted to allay the fears of those who believed we came here to burn and kill. For this reason I allowed the train to cross the bridge, and gave them full liberty to pass on. I did it only to spare the feelings of those passengers and their families, and to allay the apprehensions that you had got here in your vicinity a band of men who had no regard for life and property, nor any feelings of humanity.

Mason. But you killed some people passing along the streets quietly.

Brown. Well, sir, if there was anything of that kind done, it was without my knowledge. Your own citizens who were my prisoners will tell you that every possible means was taken to prevent it. I did not allow my men to fire when there was danger of killing those we regarded as innocent persons, if I could help it. They will tell you that we allowed ourselves to be fired at repeatedly, and did not return it.

A Bystander. That is not so. You killed an unarmed man at the corner of the house over there at the water-tank, and another besides.

Brown. See here, my friend; it is useless to dispute or contradict the report of your own neighbors who were my prisoners.

Mason. If you would tell us who sent you here, — who provided the means, — that would be information of some value.

Brown. I will answer freely and faithfully about what concerns myself, — I will answer anything I can with honor, — but not about others.

Mr. Vallandigham (who had just entered). Mr. Brown, who sent you here?

Brown. No man sent me here; it was my own prompting and that of my Maker, or that of the Devil, — whichever you please to ascribe it to. I acknowledge no master in human form.

Vallandigham. Did you get up the expedition yourself?

Brown. I did.

Vallandigham. Did you get up this document that is called a Constitution?

Brown. I did. They are constitution and ordinances of my own contriving and getting up.

Vallandigham. How long have you been engaged in this business?

Brown. From the breaking out of the difficulties in Kansas. Four of my sons had gone there to settle, and they induced me to go. I did not go there to settle, but because of the difficulties.

Mason. How many are there engaged with you in this movement?

Brown. Any questions that I can honorably answer I will, — not otherwise. So far as I am myself concerned, I have told everything truthfully. I value my word, sir.

Mason. What was your object in coming?

Brown. We came to free the slaves, and only that.

A Volunteer. How many men, in all, had you?

Brown. I came to Virginia with eighteen men only, besides myself.

Volunteer. What in the world did you suppose you could do here in Virginia with that amount of men?

Brown. Young man, I do not wish to discuss that question here.

Volunteer. You could not do anything.

Brown. Well, perhaps your ideas and mine on military subjects would differ materially.

Mason. How do you justify your acts!

Brown I think, my friend, you are guilty of a great wrong against God and humanity, — I say it without wishing to be offensive, — and it would be perfectly right for any one to interfere with you so far as to free those you wilfully and wickedly hold in bondage. I do not say this insultingly.

Mason. I understand that.

Brown. I think I did right, and that others will do right who interfere with you at any time and at all times. I hold that the Golden Rule, "Do unto others as ye would that others should do unto you," applies to all who would help others to gain their liberty.

Lieutenant Stuart. But don't you believe in the Bible?

Brown. Certainly I do.

Mason. Did you consider this a military organization in this Constitution? I have not yet read it.

Brown. I did, in some sense. I wish you would give that paper close attention.

Mason. You consider yourself the commander-in-chief of these "provisional" military forces.

Brown. I was chosen, agreeably to the ordinance of a certain document, commander-in-chief of that force.

Mason. What wages did you offer?

Brown. None.

Stuart. "The wages of sin is death."

Brown. I would not have made such a remark to you if you had been a prisoner, and wounded, in my hands.

A Bystander. Did you not promise a negro in Gettysburg twenty dollars a month?

Brown. I did not.

Mason. Does this talking annoy you?

Brown. Not in the least.

Vallandigham. Have you lived long in Ohio?

Brown. I went there in 1805. I lived in Summit County, which was then Portage County. My native place is Connecticut; my father lived there till 1805.

Vallandigham. Have you been in Portage County lately?

Brown. I was there in June last.

Vallandigham. When in Cleveland, did you attend the Fugitive Slave Law Convention there?

Brown. No. I was there about the time of the sitting of the court to try the Oberlin rescuers. 1 spoke there publicly on that subject; on the Fugitive Slave Law and my own rescue. Of course, so far as I had any influence at all, I was supposed to justify the Oberlin people for rescuing the slave, because I have myself forcibly taken slaves from bondage. I was concerned in taking eleven slaves from Missouri to Canada last winter. I think I spoke in Cleveland before the Convention. I do not know that I had conversation with any of the Oberlin rescuers. I was sick part of the time I was in Ohio with the ague, in Ashtabula County.

Vallandigham. Did you see anything of Joshua R. Giddings there?

Brown. I did meet him.

Vallandigham. Did you converse with him?

Brown. I did. I would not tell you, of course, anything that would implicate Mr. Giddings; but I certainly met with him and had conversations with him.

Vallandigham. About that rescue case?

Brown. Yes; I heard him express his opinions upon it very freely and frankly.

Vallandigham. Justifying it?

Brown. Yes, sir; I do not compromise him, certainly, in saying that.

Vallandigham. Will you answer this: Did you talk with Giddings about your expedition here?

Brown. No, I won't answer that; because a denial of it I would not make, and to make any affirmation of it I should be a great dunce.

Vallandigham. Have you had any correspondence with parties at the North on the subject of this movement?

Brown. I have had correspondence.

A Bystander. Do you consider this a religious movement?

Brown. It is, in my opinion, the greatest service man can render to God.

Bystander. Do you consider yourself an instrument in the hands of Providence?

Brown. I do.

Bystander. Upon what principle do you justify your acts?

Brown. Upon the Golden Rule. I pity the poor in bondage that have none to help them: that is why I am here; not to gratify any personal animosity, revenge, or vindictive spirit. It is my sympathy with the oppressed and the wronged, that are as good as you and as precious in the sight of God.

Bystander. Certainly. But why take the slaves against their will?

Brown. I never did.

Bystander. You did in one instance, at least

Stephens, the other wounded prisoner, here said, "You are right. In one case I know the negro wanted to go back."

Bystander. Where did you come from?

Stephens. I lived in Ashtabula County, Ohio.

Vallandigham. How recently did you leave Ashtabula Country?

Stephens. Some months ago. I never resided there any length of time; have been through there.

Vallandigham. How far did you live from Jefferson?

Brown. Be cautious, Stephens, about any answers that would commit any friend. I would not answer that.

[Stephens turned partially over with a groan of pain, and was silent.]

Vallandigham. Who are your advisers in this movement?

Brown. I cannot answer that. I have numerous sympathizers throughout the entire North.

Vallandigham. In northern Ohio?

Brown. No more there than anywhere else; in all the free States.

Vallandigham. But you are not personally acquainted in southern Ohio?

Brown. Not very much.

A Bystander. Did you ever live in Washington City?

Brown. I did not. I want you to understand, gentlemen, and [to the reporter of the "Herald"] you may report that, — I want you to understand that I respect the rights of the poorest and weakest of colored people, oppressed by the slave system, just as much as I do those of the most wealthy and powerful. That is the idea that has moved me, and that alone. We expected no reward except the satisfaction of endeavoring to do for those in distress and greatly oppressed as we would be done by. The cry of distress of the oppressed is my reason, and the only thing that prompted me to come here.

Bystander. Why did you do it secretly?

Brown. Because I thought that necessary to success; no other reason.

Bystander. Have you read Gerrit Smith's last letter?

Brown. What letter do you mean?

Bystander. The "New York Herald" of yesterday, in speaking of this affair, mentions a letter in this way: —

"Apropos of this exciting news, we recollect a very significant passage in one of Gerrit Smith's letters, published a month or two ago, in which he speaks of the folly of attempting to strike the shackles off the slaves by the force of moral suasion or legal agitation, and predicts that the next movement made in the direction of negro emancipation would be an insurrection in the South."

Brown. I have not seen the "New York Herald" for some days past; but I presume, from your remark about the gist of the letter, that I should concur with it. I agree with Mr. Smith that moral suasion is hopeless. I don't think the people of the slave States will ever consider the subject of slavery in its true light till some other argument is resorted to than moral suasion.

Vallandigham. Did you expect a general rising of the slaves in case of your success?

Brown. No, sir; nor did I wish it. I expected to gather them up from time to time, and set them free.

Vallandigham. Did you expect to hold possession here till then?

Brown. Well, probably I had quite a different idea. I do not know that I ought to reveal my plans. I am here a prisoner and wounded, because I foolishly allowed myself to be so. You overrate your strength in supposing I could have been taken if I had not allowed it. I was too tardy after commencing the open attack — in delaying my movements through Monday night, and up to the time I was attacked by the Government troops. It was all occasioned by my desire to spare the feelings of my prisoners and their families and the community at large. I had no knowledge of the shooting of the negro Heywood.

Vallandigham. What time did you commence your organization in Canada?

Brown. That occurred about two years ago; in 1858.

Vallandigham. Who was the secretary?

Brown. That I would not tell if I recollected; but I do not recollect. I think the officers were elected in May, 1858. I may answer incorrectly, but not intentionally. My head is a little confused by wounds, and my memory obscure on dates, etc.

Dr. Biggs. Were you in the party at Dr. Kennedy's house?

Brown. I was the head of that party. I occupied the house to mature my plans. I have not been in Baltimore to purchase caps.

Dr. Biggs. What was the number of men at Kennedy's?

Brown. I decline to answer that.

Dr. Biggs. Who lanced that woman's neck on the hill?

Brown. I did. I have sometimes practiced in surgery when I thought it a matter of humanity and necessity, and there was no one else to do it; but I have not studied surgery.

Dr. Biggs. It was done very well and scientifically. They have been very clever to the neighbors, I have been told, and we had no reason to suspect them, except that we could not understand their movements. They were represented as eight or nine persons; on Friday there were thirteen.

Brown. There were more than that.

Q. Where did you get arms? *A.* I bought them.

Q. In what State? *A:* That I will not state.

Q. How many guns? *A.* Two hundred Sharpe's rifles and two hundred revolvers, — what is called the Massachusetts Arms Company's revolvers, a little under navy size.

Q. Why did you not take that swivel you left in the house? *A.* I had no occasion for it. It was given to me a year or two ago.

Q. In Kansas?

A. No. I had nothing given to me in Kansas.

Q. By whom, and in what State? *A.* I decline to answer. It is not properly a swivel; it is a very large rifle with a pivot. The ball is larger than a musket ball; it is intended for a slug.

Reporter. I do not wish to annoy you; but if you have anything further you would like to say, I will report it.

Brown. I have nothing to say, only that I claim to be here in carrying out a measure I believe perfectly justifiable, and not to act the part of an incendiary or ruffian, but to aid those suffering great wrong. I wish to say, furthermore, that you had better — all you people at the South — prepare yourselves for a settlement of this question, that must come up for settlement sooner than you are prepared for it. The sooner you are prepared the better. You may dispose of me very easily, — I am nearly disposed of now; but this question is still to be settled, — this negro question I mean; the end of that is not yet. These wounds were inflicted upon me — both sabre cuts on my head and bayonet stabs in different parts of my body — some minutes after I had eased fighting and had consented to surrender, for the benefit of others, not for my own.[1] I believe the Major would not have been alive; I could have killed him just as easy as a mosquito when he came in, but I supposed he only came in to receive our surrender. There had been loud and long calls of "surrender" from us, — as loud as men could yell; but in the confusion and excitement I suppose we were not heard. I do not think the Major, or any one, meant to butcher us after we had surrendered.

An Officer. Why did you not surrender before the attack?

Brown. I did not think it was my duty or interest to do so. We assured the prisoners that we did not wish to harm them, and they should be set at liberty. I exercised my best judgment, not believing the people would wantonly sacrifice their own fellow-citizens, when we offered to let them go on condition of being allowed to change our position about a quarter of a mile. The prisoners agreed by a vote among themselves to pass across the bridge with us. We

---

[1] At the trial of Copeland the following evidence was given: —

Mr. Sennott. You say that when Brown was down you struck him in the face with your sabre?
Lieutenant Green. Yes.
Q. This was after he was down? *A.* Yes; he was down.
Q. How many times, Lieutanant Green, did you strike Brown in the face with your sabre after he was down? *A.* Why, sir, he was defending himself with his gun.
Mr. Hunter. I hope the counsel for the defense will not press such questions on them.

wanted them only as a sort of guarantee of our own safety, — that we should not be fired into. We took them, in the first place, as hostages and to keep them from doing any harm. We did kill some men in defending ourselves, but I saw no one fire except directly in self-defence. Our orders were strict not to harm any one not in arms against us.

Q. Brown, suppose you had every nigger in the United States, what would you do with them? A. Set them free.

Q. Your intention was to carry them off and free them? A. Not at all.

A Bystander. To set them free would sacrifice the life of every man in this community.

Brown. I do not think so.

Bystander. I know it. I think you are fanatical.

Brown. And I think you are fanatical. "Whom the gods would destroy they first make mad," and you are mad.

Q. Was it your only object to free the negroes? A. Absolutely our only object.

Q. But you demanded and took Colonel Washington's silver and watch? A. Yes; we intended freely to appropriate the property of slaveholders to carry out our object. It was for that, and only that, and with no design to enrich ourselves with any plunder whatever.

Bystander. Did you know Sherrod in Kansas? I understand you killed him.

Brown. I killed no man except in fair fight. I fought at Black Jack Point and at Osawatomie; and if I killed anybody, it was at one of these places.

[AHC]

The State of South Carolina, Ordinance of Secession and Declaration of Independence

December 20, 1860

On receiving the news of Abraham Lincoln's election [as president of the United States] the South Carolina legislature called a convention which passed the Ordinance of Secession December 20, 1860. This was done because, as the South Carolina declaration of independence stated: "A geographical line had been drawn across the Union, and all the states north of that line have united in the election of a man to the high office of President of the United States, whose opinions and purposes are hostile to slavery." Copies of this ordinance were forwarded to the other Southern states which passed similar ordinances, as follows: Mississippi, January 9, 1861; Florida, January 10; Alabama, January 11; Georgia, January 19; Louisiana, January 26; Texas, February 1. Delegates from the seceded states met at Montgomery, Alabama, February 4, 1861, and organized a provisional government. These states were afterwards joined by Virginia, April 17; Arkansas, May 6; and North Carolina, May 20.

— Note by Howard W. Preston

ORDINANCE OF SECESSION—1860.

AN ORDINANCE TO dissolve the Union between the State of South Carolina and other States united with her under the compact entitled "The Constitution of the United States of America."

We, the People of the State of South Carolina, in Convention assembled, do declare and ordain, and it is hereby declared and ordained, that the Ordinance adopted by us in Convention, on the

439

Twenty-third of May, in the year of our Lord one thousand seven hundred and eighty-eight, whereby the Constitution of the United States was ratified, and also all other Acts and parts of Acts of the General Assembly of the State ratifying amendments of the said Constitution, are hereby repealed, and the Union now subsisting between South Carolina and other States, under the name of the United States of America, is hereby dissolved.

In justification of the preceding ordinance was issued the following:

SOUTH CAROLINA DECLARATION OF INDEPENDENCE

The State of South Carolina, having determined to resume her separate and equal place among nations, deems it due to herself, to the remaining United States of America, and to the nations of the world, that she should declare the causes which have led to this act.

In the year 1765, that portion of the British Empire embracing Great Britain, undertook to make laws for the government of that portion composed of the thirteen American colonies. A struggle for the right of self-government ensued, which resulted, on the 4th of July, 1776, in a declaration by the colonies, "that they are, and of right ought to be, free and independent states, and that, as free and independent states, they have full power to levy war, to conclude peace, contract alliances, establish commerce, and do all other acts and things which independent states may of right do."

They further solemnly declared, that whenever any "form of government becomes destructive of the ends for which it was established; it is the right of that people to alter or abolish it, and to institute a new government." Deeming the government of Great Britain to have become destructive of these ends, they declared that the colonies "are absolved from all allegiance to the British crown, and that all political connection between them and the states of Great Britain is and ought to be totally dissolved."

In pursuance of this declaration of independence, each of the thirteen states proceeded to exercise its separate sovereignty; adopted for itself a constitution, and appointed officers for the administration of government in all its departments—legislative, executive, and judicial. For purpose of defense, they united their arms and their counsels; and, in 1778, they united in a league, known as the articles of confederation, whereby they agreed to intrust the administration of their external relations to a common agent, known as the Congress of the United States, expressly declaring in the first article, "that each state retains its sovereignty, freedom, and independence, and every power, jurisdiction, and right which is not, by this confederation, expressly delegated to the United States in Congress assembled."

Under this consideration the war of the Revolution was carried on, and on the 3d of September, 1783, the contest ended, and a definite treaty was signed by Great Britain, in which she acknowledged the independence of the colonies in the following terms:

Article I. His Britannic Majesty acknowledges the said United States, viz.: New Hampshire, Massachusetts Bay, Rhode Island and Providence Plantation, Connecticut, New York, New Jersey, Pennsylvania, Delaware, Maryland, Virginia, North Carolina, South Carolina, and Georgia, to be free, sovereign, and independent states; that he treats them as such; and for himself, his heirs, and successors, relinquishes all claim to the government, proprietary and territorial rights of the same, and every part thereof.

Thus was established the two great principles asserted by the colonies, namely, the right of a state to govern itself, and the right of a people to abolish a government when it becomes destructive of the ends for which it was instituted. And concurrent with the establishment of these principles was the fact that each colony became and was recognized by the mother country as a free, sovereign, and independent state.

In 1787, deputies were appointed by the states to revise the articles of confederation, and on September 17th, 1787, the deputies recommended for the adoption of the states the articles of union known as the constitution of the United States.

The parties to whom the constitution was submitted were the several sovereign states; they were to agree or disagree, and when nine of them agreed, the compact was to take effect among those concurring; and the general government, as the common agent, was then to be invested with their authority.

If only nine of the thirteen states had concurred, the other four would have remained as they then were—separate, sovereign states, independent of any of the provisions of the constitution. In fact, two of the states did not accede to the constitution until long after it had gone into operation among the other eleven; and during that interval, they exercised the functions of an independent nation.

By this constitution, certain duties were charged on the several states, and the exercise of certain of their powers not delegated to the United States by the constitution, nor prohibited by it to the states, are reserved to the states respectively, or to the people. On the 23d of May, 1788, South Carolina, by a convention of people, passed an ordinance assenting to this constitution, and afterwards altering her own constitution to conform herself to the obligation she had undertaken.

Thus was established, by compact between the states, a government with defined objects and powers, limited to the express words of the grant, and to so much more only as was necessary to execute the power granted. The limitations left the whole remaining mass of power subject to the clause reserving it to the state or to the people, and rendered unnecessary any specification of reserved powers.

We hold that the government thus established is subject to the two great principles asserted in the declaration of independence, and we hold further that the mode of its formation subjects it to a third fundamental principle, namely—the law of compact. We maintain that in every compact between two or more parties, the obligation is mutual—that the failure of one of the contracting parties to perform a material part of the agreement entirely released the obligation of the other, and that, where no arbiter is appointed, each party is remitted to his own judgment to determine the fact of failure with all its consequences.

In the present case that fact is established with certainty. We assert that fifteen of the states have deliberately refused for years past to fulfil their constitutional obligation, and we refer to their own statutes for the proof.

The constitution of the United States, in its fourth article, provides as follows:

"No person held to service or labor in one state, under the laws thereof, escaping into another, shall, in consequence of any law or regulation therein, be discharged from any service or labor, but shall be delivered up, on claim of party to whom such service or labor may be due."

This stipulation was so material to the compact that without it that compact would not have been made. The greater number of the contracting parties held slaves, and the state of Virginia had previously declared her estimate of its value by making it the condition of cession of the territory which now compose the states north of the Ohio river.

The same article of the constitution stipulates also for the rendition by the several states of fugitives from justice from the other states.

The general government, as the common agent, passed laws to carry into effect these stipulations of the states. For many years these laws were executed. But an increasing hostility on the part of the northern states to the institution of slavery has led to a disregard of their obligations, and the laws of the general government have ceased to affect the objects of the constitution. The states of Maine, New Hampshire, Vermont, Massachusetts, Connecticut, Rhode Island, New York, Pennsylvania, Illinois, Indiana, Ohio, Michigan, Wisconsin, and Iowa have enacted laws which either nullify the acts of Congress, or render useless any attempt to execute them. In many of these states the fugitive is discharged from the service of labor claimed, and in none of them has the state government complied with the stipulation made in the constitution. The state of New Jersey, at an early day, passed a law for the rendition of fugitive slaves in conformity with her constitutional undertaking; but the current of anti-slavery feeling has led her more recently to enact laws which render imperative the remedies provided by her own law, and by the laws of Congress. In the state of New York even the right of transit for a slave has been denied by her tribunals, and the states of Ohio and Iowa have refused to surrender to justice fugitives charged with murder and inciting servile insurrection in the state of Virginia. Thus the constitutional compact has been deliberately broken and disregarded by the non-slaveholding states, and the consequence follows that South Carolina is released from its obligation.

The ends for which this constitution was framed are declared by itself to be "to form a more perfect union, establish justice, insure domestic tranquility, provide for the common defence, protect the general welfare, and secure the blessings of liberty to ourselves and posterity."

These ends it endeavored to accomplish by a federal government, in which each state was recognized as an equal, and had separate control over its own institutions. The right of property in slaves was recognized by giving to free persons distinct political rights; by giving them the right to represent, and burdening them with direct taxes for three-fifths of their slaves; by authorizing the importation of slaves for twenty years, and by stipulating for the rendition of fugitives from labor.

We affirm that these ends for which this government was instituted have been defeated, and the government itself has been made destructive of them by the action of the non-slaveholding state. These states have assumed the right of deciding upon the propriety of our domestic institutions, and have denied the rights of property established in fifteen of the states and recognized by the constitution; they have denounced as sinful the institution of slavery; they have permitted the open establishment among them of societies whose avowed object is to disturb the peace and claim the property of the citizens of other states. They have encouraged and assisted thousands of our slaves to leave their homes, and those who remain have been incited by emissaries, books, and pictures to servile insurrection.

For twenty-five years this agitation has been steadily increasing, until it has now secured to its aid the power of the common government. Observing the forms of the constitution, a sectional party has found within that article establishing the executive department the means of subverting the constitution itself. A geographical line has been drawn across the Union, and all the states north of that line have united in the election of a man to the high office of President of the United States, whose opinions and purposes are hostile to slavery. He is to be entrusted with the administration of the common government, because he has declared that that "government cannot endure permanently half slave, half free," and that the public mind must rest in the belief that slavery is in the course of ultimate extinction.

This sectional combination for the subversion of the constitution has been aided in some of the states by elevating to citizenship persons who, by the supreme law of the land, are incapable of becoming citizens, and their votes have been used to inaugurate a new policy hostile to the south, and destructive of its peace and safety.

On the 4th of March next, this party will take possession of the government. It has announced that the south shall be excluded from the common territory; that the judicial tribunals shall be made sectional, and that a war must be waged against slavery until it shall cease throughout the United States.

The guarantees of the constitution will then no longer exist; the equal rights of the states will be lost. The slaveholding states will no longer have the power of self-government or self-protection, and the federal government will have become their enemies.

Sectional interest and animosity will deepen the irritation, and all hope of remedy is rendered vain by the fact that public opinion at the north has invested a great political error with the sanctions of a more erroneous religious belief.

We, therefore, the people of South Carolina, by our delegates in convention assembled, appealing to the Supreme Judge of the world for the rectitude of our intentions, have solemnly declared that the union heretofore existing between this state and the other states of North America is dissolved, and that the state of South Carolina has resumed her position among the nations of the world as a free, sovereign, and independent state, with full power to levy war, conclude peace, contract alliances, establish commerce, and to do all other acts and things which independent states may, of right, do.

And, for the support of this declaration, with a firm reliance on the protection of Divine Providence, we mutually pledge to each other, our lives, our fortunes, and our sacred honor.

[DIH]

Senator Jefferson Davis, Farewell Address to the U.S. Senate, "On Withdrawal from the Union"

January 21, 1861

The former Secretary of War and Vice President of the United States was a year older than Abraham Lincoln and also born in Kentucky. Davis here announces his resignation from the United States Senate on the principle of defending slavery for his home state of Mississippi, which had seceded from the Union on January 9. A few weeks later, in February 1861, Davis (1808–1889) became the President of the Confederate States of America.

The Civil War began in April. After the war's end in 1865, he was arrested and served two years in prison. He seems never to have repented for his support of slavery, his treason against the United States, or his leadership of a war that cost more than a half-million lives.

I RISE, Mr. President, for the purpose of announcing to the Senate that I have satisfactory evidence that the State of Mississippi, by a solemn ordinance of her people in convention assembled, has declared her separation from the United States. Under these circumstances, of course my functions are terminated here. It has seemed to me proper, however, that I should appear in the Senate to announce that fact to my associates, and I will say but very little more. The occasion does not invite me to go into argument; and my physical condition would not permit me to do so if it were otherwise; and yet it seems to become me to say something on the part of the State I here represent, on an occasion so solemn as this.

It is known to Senators who have served with me here that I have for many years advocated, as an essential attribute of State sovereignty, the right of a State to secede from the Union. Therefore, if I had not believed there was justifiable cause; if I had thought that Mississippi was acting without sufficient provocation, or without an existing necessity, I should still, under my theory of the Government, because of my allegiance to the State of which I am a citizen, have been bound by her action. I, however, may be permitted to say that I do think she has justifiable cause, and I approve of her act. I conferred with her people before that act was taken, counseled them then that if the state of things which they apprehended should exist when the convention met, they should take the action which they have now adopted.

I hope none who hear me will confound this expression of mine with the advocacy of the right of a State to remain in the Union, and to disregard its constitutional obligations by the nullification of the law. Such is not my theory. Nullification and secession, so often confounded, are indeed antagonistic principles. Nullification is a remedy which it is sought to apply within the Union, and against the agent of the States. It is only to be justified when the agent has violated his constitutional obligation, and a State, assuming to judge for itself, denies the right of the agent thus to act, and appeals to the other States of the Union for a decision; but when the States themselves, and when the people of the States, have so acted as to convince us that they will not regard our constitutional rights, then, and then for the first time, arises the doctrine of secession in its practical application.

A great man who now reposes with his fathers, and who has been often arraigned for a want of fealty to the Union, advocated the doctrine of nullification, because it preserved the Union. It was because of his deep-seated attachment to the Union, his determination to find some remedy for existing ills short of a severance of the ties which bound South Carolina to the other States, that Mr. John C. Calhoun advocated the doctrine of nullification, which he proclaimed to be peaceful, to be within the limits of State power, not to disturb the Union, but only to be a means of bringing the agent before the tribunal of the States for their judgment.

Secession belongs to a different class of remedies. It is to be justified upon the basis that the States are sovereign. There was a time when none denied it. I hope the time may come again, when a better comprehension of the theory of our Government, and the inalienable rights of the people of the States, will prevent any one from denying that each State is a sovereign, and thus may reclaim the grants which it has made to any agent whomsoever.

I therefore say I concur in the action of the people of Mississippi, believing it to be necessary and proper, and should have been bound by their action if my belief had been otherwise; and this brings me to the important point which I wish on this last occasion to present to the Senate. It is by this confounding of nullification and secession that the name of a great man, whose ashes now mingle with his mother earth, has been invoked to justify coercion against a seceded State. The phrase "to execute the laws," was an expression which General Jackson applied to the case of a State refusing to obey the laws while yet a member of the Union. That is not the case which is now presented. The laws are to be executed over the United States, and upon the people of the United States. They have no relation to any foreign country. It is a perversion of terms; at least it is a great misapprehension of the case, which cites that expression for application to a State which has withdrawn from the Union. You may make war on a foreign State. If it be the purpose of gentlemen, they may make war against a State which has withdrawn from the Union; but there are no laws of the United States to be executed within the limits of a seceded State. A State finding herself in the condition in which Mississippi has judged she is, in which her safety requires that she should provide for the maintenance of her rights out of the Union, surrenders all the benefits, (and they are known to be many,) deprives herself of the advantages, (they are known to be great,) severs all the ties of affection, (and they are close and enduring,) which have bound her to the Union; and thus divesting herself of every benefit, taking upon herself every burden, she claims to be exempt from any power to execute the laws of the United States within her limits.

I well remember an occasion when Massachusetts was arraigned before the bar of the Senate, and when then the doctrine of coercion was rife and to be applied against her because of the rescue of a fugitive slave in Boston. My opinion then was the same that it is now. Not in a spirit of egotism, but to show that I am not influenced in my opinion because the case is my own, I refer to that time and that occasion as containing the opinion which I then entertained, and on which my present conduct is based. I then said, if Massachusetts, following her through a stated line of conduct, chooses to take the last step which separates her from the Union, it is her right to go, and I will neither vote one dollar nor one man to coerce her back; but will say to her, God speed, in memory of the kind associations which once existed between her and the other States.

It has been a conviction of pressing necessity; it has been a belief that we are to be deprived in the Union of the rights which our fathers bequeathed to us, which has brought Mississippi into her present decision. She has heard proclaimed the theory that all men are created free and equal, and this made the basis of an attack upon her social institutions; and the sacred Declaration of Independence has been invoked to maintain the position of the equality of the races. That Declaration of Independence is to be construed by the circumstances and purposes for which it was made. The communities were declaring their independence; the people of those communities were asserting that no man was born—to use the language of Mr. Jefferson—booted and spurred to ride over the rest of mankind; that men were created equal—meaning the men of the political community; that there was no divine right to rule; that no man inherited the right to govern; that there were no classes by which power and place descended to families, but that all stations were equally within the grasp of each member of the body-politic. These were the great principles they announced; these were the purposes for which they made their declaration; these were the ends to which their enunciation was directed. They have no reference to the slave; else, how happened it that among the items of arraignment made against George III was that he endeavored to do just what the North has been endeavoring of late to do—to stir up insurrection among our slaves? Had the Declaration announced that the Negroes were free and equal, how was the Prince to be arraigned for stirring up insurrection among them? And how was this to be enumerated among the high crimes which caused the colonies to sever their connection with the mother country? When our Constitution was formed, the same idea was rendered more palpable, for there we find provision made for that very class of persons as property; they were not put upon the footing of equality with white men—not even upon that of paupers and convicts; but, so far as representation was concerned, were discriminated against as a lower caste, only to be represented in the numerical proportion of three fifths.

Then, Senators, we recur to the compact which binds us together; we recur to the principles upon which our Government was founded; and when you deny them, and when you deny to us the right to withdraw from a Government which thus perverted threatens to be destructive of our rights, we but tread in the path of our fathers when we proclaim our independence, and take the hazard. This is done not in hostility to others, not to injure any section of the country, not even for our own pecuniary benefit; but from the high and solemn motive of defending and protecting the rights we inherited, and which it is our sacred duty to transmit unshorn to our children.

I find in myself, perhaps, a type of the general feeling of my constituents towards yours. I am sure I feel no hostility to you, Senators from the North. I am sure there is not one of you, whatever sharp discussion there may have been between us, to whom I cannot now say, in the presence of my God, I wish you well; and such, I am sure, is the feeling of the people whom I represent towards those whom you represent. I therefore feel that I but express their desire when I say I hope, and they hope, for peaceful relations with you, though we must part. They may be mutually beneficial to us in the future; as they have been in the past, if you so will it. The reverse may bring disaster on every portion of the country; and if you will have it thus, we will invoke the God of our fathers, who delivered them from the power of the lion, to protect us from the ravages of the bear; and thus, putting our trust in God and in our own firm hearts and strong arms, we will vindicate the right as best we may.

In the course of my service here, associated at different times with a great variety of Senators, I see now around me some with whom I have served long; there have been points of collision; but whatever of offense there has been to me, I leave here; I carry with me no hostile remembrance. Whatever offense I have given which has not been redressed, or for which satisfaction has not been demanded, I have, Senators, in this hour of our parting, to offer you my apology for any pain which, in heat of discussion, I have inflicted. I go hence unencumbered of the remembrance of any injury received, and having discharged the duty of making the only reparation in my power for any injury offered.

Mr. President, and Senators, having made the announcement which the occasion seemed to me to require, it only remains to me to bid you a final adieu.

[IS]

President Abraham Lincoln, First Inaugural Address

March 4, 1861

Running against three other candidates in the highly charged political atmosphere of 1860—with the southern states on the verge of secession and the fate of the Union clearly in the balance—Abraham Lincoln won the presidency for the Republicans with a minority of the total popular vote: 1.8 million against a total of 2.6 million for the other three candidates, the southern Democrat John C. Breckenridge, the "northern" Democrat Stephen A. Douglas, and John Bell of the conservative Constitutional Union Party. Lincoln's victory in the Electoral College was convincing, however, with 180 electoral votes against seventy-two for Breckenridge, twelve for Douglas, and thirty-nine for Bell. There were some very closely contested states in 1860. Lincoln carried California, for example, with a majority of only 657 votes out of well over 100,000.

On March 4, 1861, with unprecedented security provided by Washington police and the U.S. Cavalry, Lincoln rode without incident in a carriage from Willard's Hotel to the Capitol accompanied by outgoing President Buchanan. He then stood on a platform off the Capitol's east wing, with the structure's unfinished dome and scaffolding looming in the background, to take the oath of office as the sixteenth president from Chief Justice Roger Taney. In the half-hour speech that followed, Lincoln attempted at once to assure the South that it had nothing to fear from his Republican administration, reiterating his long-held position that he had no plans and no authority to interfere with the institution of slavery where it then existed; but also promising that he would defend the Union and the property of the federal government. He didn't shrink from mentioning the prospect of a civil war, but asked for calm and thoughtful deliberation, declaring plainly that if it came, it wouldn't be the federal government that started it. The magnificent final paragraph derived at least partially from the suggestions of William Seward, who was about to take office as Lincoln's secretary of state. Five weeks later, on April 12, 1861, Confederate forces opened fire on Fort Sumter in Charleston harbor.

— Note by John Grafton

Fellow-citizens of the United States:

IN COMPLIANCE WITH a custom as old as the Government itself, I appear before you to address you briefly, and to take, in your presence, the oath prescribed by the Constitution of the United States to be taken by the President, before he enters on the execution of his office.

I do not consider it necessary, at present, for me to discuss those matters of administration about which there is no special anxiety or excitement. Apprehension seems to exist among the people of the southern States that, by the accession of a Republican Administration, their property and their peace and personal security are to be endangered. There has never been any reasonable cause for such apprehension. Indeed, the most ample evidence to the contrary has all the while existed, and been open to their inspection. It is found in nearly all the published speeches of him who now addresses you. I do but quote from one of those speeches, when I declare that "I have no purpose, directly or indirectly, to interfere with the institution of slavery in the States where it exists." I believe I have no lawful right to do so; and I have no inclination to do so. Those who nominated and elected me, did so with the full knowledge I had made this, and made many similar declarations, and had never recanted them. And, more than this, they placed in the platform, for my acceptance, and as a law to themselves and to me, the clear and emphatic resolution which I now read:

"*Resolved,* That the maintenance inviolate of the rights of the States, and especially the right of each State to order and control its own domestic institutions according to its own judgment exclusively, is essential to that balance of power on which the perfection and endurance of our political fabric depend; and we denounce the lawless invasion by armed force of the soil of any State or Territory, no matter under what pretext, as among the gravest of crimes."

I now reiterate these sentiments; and in doing so, I only press upon the public attention the most conclusive evidence of which the case is susceptible, that the property, peace, and security of no section are to be in anywise endangered by the now incoming Administration.

I add, too, that all the protection which, consistently with the Constitution and the laws, can be given will be cheerfully given to all the States when lawfully demanded, for whatever cause, as cheerfully to one section, as to another.

There is much controversy about the delivering up of fugitives from service or labor. The clause I now read is as plainly written in the constitution as any other of its provisions:

"No person held to service or labor in one State under the laws thereof, escaping into another, shall, in consequence of any law or regulation therein, be discharged from such service or labor, but shall be delivered up on claim of the party to whom such service or labor may be due."

It is scarcely questioned that this provision was intended by those who made it for the reclaiming of what we call fugitive slaves; and the intention of the lawgiver is the law.

All members of Congress swear their support to the whole Constitution—to this provision as well as any other. To the proposition, then that slaves whose cases come within the terms of this clause "shall be delivered up," their oaths are unanimous. Now, if they would make the effort in good temper, could they not, with nearly equal unanimity, frame and pass a law by means of which to keep good that unanimous oath?

There is some difference of opinion whether this clause should be enforced by national or by state authority; but surely that difference is not a very material one. If the slave is to be surrendered, it can be of but little consequence to him or to others, by which authority it is done. And should any one, in any case, be content that this oath shall go unkept, on a merely unsubstantial controversy as to how it shall be kept?

Again, in any law upon this subject, ought not all the safeguards of liberty known in the civilized and humane jurisprudence to be introduced, so that a free man is not, in any case, surrendered as a slave? And might it not be well at the same time to provide by law for the enforcement of that clause in the Constitution which guarantees that "the citizens of each State shall be entitled to all privileges and immunities of citizens in the several States?"

I take the official oath to-day with no mental reservations, and with no purpose to construe the Constitution or laws by any hypercritical rules. And while I do not choose now to specify particular acts of Congress as proper to be enforced, I do suggest that it will be much safer for all, both in official and private stations, to conform to and abide by all those acts which stand unrepealed, than to violate any of them, trusting to find impunity in having them held to be unconstitutional.

It is seventy-two years since the first inauguration of a President under our national Constitution. During that period fifteen different and very distinguished citizens have in succession administered the executive branch of the government. They have conducted it through many perils, and, generally with great success. Yet, with all this scope for precedent, I now enter upon the same task for the brief constitutional term of four years, under great and peculiar difficulties.

A disruption of the Federal Union, heretofore only menaced, is now formidably attempted. I hold that in the contemplation of universal law and of the Constitution, the Union of these States is perpetual. Perpetuity is implied, if not expressed, in the fundamental law of all national governments. It is safe to assert that no government proper ever had a provision in its organic law for its own termination. Continue to execute all the express provisions of our national Constitution, and the Union will endure forever, it being impossible to destroy it except by some action not provided for in the instrument itself.

Again, if the United States be not a government proper, but an association of States in the nature of contract merely, can it, as a contract, be peaceably unmade by less than all the parties who made it? One party to a contract may violate it—break it, so to speak; but does it not require all too lawfully rescind it? Descending from these general principles we find the proposition that in legal contemplation the Union is perpetual, confirmed by the history of the Union itself.

The Union is much older than the Constitution. It was formed, in fact, by the Articles of Association in 1774. It was matured and continued in the Declaration of Independence in 1776. It was further matured, and the faith of all the then thirteen States expressly plighted and engaged that it should be perpetual, by the Articles of Confederation, in 1778. And, finally, in 1787, one of the declared objects for ordaining and establishing the Constitution, was to form a more perfect Union. But if the destruction of the Union by one or by a part only of the States be lawfully possible, the Union is less than before, the Constitution having lost the vital element of perpetuity.

It follows from these views that no State, upon its own mere motion, can lawfully get out of the Union; that resolves and ordinances to that effect are legally void; and that acts of violence within any State or States against the authority of the United States, are insurrectionary or revolutionary, according to circumstances.

I therefore consider that, in view of the Constitution and the laws, the Union is unbroken, and, to the extent of my ability, I shall take care, as the Constitution itself expressly enjoins upon me, that the laws of the Union shall be faithfully executed in all the States. Doing this, which I deem to be only a simple duty on my part I shall perfectly perform it, so far as is practicable, unless my rightful masters, the American people, shall withhold the requisition, or, in some authoritative manner, direct the contrary.

I trust this will not be regarded as a menace, but only as the declared purpose of the Union that it will constitutionally defend and maintain itself.

In doing this there need be no bloodshed or violence, and there shall be none unless it is forced upon the national authority.

The power confided to me, *will be used to hold, occupy, and possess the property and places belonging to the Government,* and collect the duties and imposts; but beyond what may be necessary for these objects there will be no invasion, no using of force against or among the people anywhere.

Where hostility to the United States shall be so great and so universal as to prevent competent resident citizens from holding the Federal offices, there will be no attempt to force obnoxious strangers among the people that object. While the strict legal right may exist of the Government to enforce the exercise of these offices, the attempt to do so would be so irritating, and so nearly impracticable withal, that I deem it better to forego for the time the uses of such offices.

The mails, unless repelled, will continue to be furnished in all parts of the Union.

So far as possible, the people everywhere shall have that sense of perfect security which is most favorable to calm thought and reflection.

The course here indicated will be followed, unless current events and experience shall show a modification or change to be proper;

and in every case and exigency my best discretion will be exercised according to the circumstances actually existing, and with a view and hope of a peaceful solution of the national troubles, and the restoration of fraternal sympathies and affections.

That there are persons, in one section or another, who seek to destroy the Union at all events, and are glad of any pretext to do it, I will neither affirm nor deny. But if there be such, I need address no word to them.

To those, however, who really love the Union, may I not speak, before entering upon so grave a matter as the destruction of our national fabric, with all its benefits, its memories, and its hopes? Would it not be well to ascertain why we do it? Will you hazard so desperate a step, while any portion of the ills you fly from, have no real existence? Will you, while the certain ills you fly to, are greater than all the real ones you fly from? Will you risk the commission of so fearful a mistake? All profess to be content in the Union, if all constitutional rights can be maintained. Is it true, then, that any right, plainly written in the Constitution has been denied? I think not. Happily the human mind is so constituted, that no party can reach to the audacity of doing this.

Think, if you can, of a single instance in which a plainly-written provision of the Constitution has ever been denied. If, by the mere force of numbers, a majority should deprive a minority of any clearly-written constitutional right, it might, in a moral point of view, justify revolution; it certainly would, if such right were a vital one. But such is not our case.

All the vital rights of minorities and of individuals are so plainly assured to them, by affirmations and negations, guaranties and prohibitions in the Constitution, that controversies never arise concerning them. But no organic law can ever be framed with a provision specifically applicable to every question which may occur in practical administration. No foresight can anticipate, nor any document of reasonable length contain, express provisions for all possible questions. Shall fugitives from labor be surrendered by national or by State authorities? The Constitution does not expressly say. Must Congress protect slavery in the Territories? The Constitution does not expressly say. From questions of this class, spring all our constitutional controversies and we divide upon them into majorities and minorities.

If the minority will not acquiesce, the majority must, or the government must cease. There is no other alternative for continuing the government but acquiescence on the one side or the other. If a minority in such case, will secede rather than acquiesce, they make a precedent which in turn will ruin and divide them, for a minority of their own will secede from them, whenever a majority refuses to be controlled by such a minority. For instance, why may not any portion of a new confederacy, a year or two hence, arbitrarily secede again, precisely as portions of the present Union now claim to secede from it? All who cherish disunion sentiments, are now being educated to the exact temper of doing this. Is there such perfect identity of interests among the States to compose a new Union as to produce harmony only, and prevent renewed secession? Plainly, the central idea of secession is the essence of anarchy.

A majority held in restraint by constitutional checks and limitations and always changing easily with deliberate changes of popular opinions and sentiments is the only true sovereign of a free people. Whoever rejects it, does, of necessity, fly to anarchy or to despotism. Unanimity is impossible; the rule of a majority, as a permanent arrangement, is wholly inadmissible. So that, rejecting the majority principle, anarchy or despotism in some form is all that is left.

I do not forget the position assumed by some that constitutional questions are to be decided by the Supreme Court, nor do I deny that such decisions must be binding in any case upon the parties to a suit, as to the object of that suit, while they are also entitled to very high respect and consideration in all parallel cases by all other departments of the government. And while it is obviously possible that such decision may be erroneous in any given case, still the evil effect following it, being limited to that particular case, with the chance that it may be overruled and never become a precedent for other cases, can better be borne than could the evils of a different practice.

At the same time the candid citizen must confess that if the policy of the government upon the vital questions affecting the whole people is to be irrevocably fixed by decisions of the Supreme Court, the instant they are made, as in ordinary litigation between parties in personal actions, the people will have ceased to be their own masters, unless having to that extent practically resigned their government into the hands of that eminent tribunal.

Nor is there in this view any assault upon the court or the judges. It is a duty from which they may not shrink, to decide cases properly brought before them; and it is no fault of theirs if others seek to turn their decisions to political purposes. One section of our country believes slavery is right, and ought to be extended, while the other believes it is wrong and ought not to be extended. This is the only substantial dispute. The fugitive slave clause of the constitution, and the law for the suppression of the foreign slave trade, are each as well enforced, perhaps, as any law can ever be in a community where the moral sense of the people imperfectly supports the law itself. The great body of the people abides by the dry legal obligation in both cases, and a few break over in each. This, I think, cannot be perfectly cured, and it would be worse in both cases after the separation of the sections, than before. The foreign slave trade, now imperfectly suppressed, would be ultimately revived, without restriction, in one section; while fugitive slaves, now only partially surrendered, would not be surrendered at all by the other.

Physically speaking we cannot separate. We cannot remove our respective sections from each other, nor build an impassable wall between them. A husband and wife may be divorced, and go out of the presence and beyond the reach of each other, but the different parts of our country cannot do this. They cannot but remain face to face; and intercourse, either amicable or hostile, must continue between them. Is it possible, then, to make that intercourse more advantageous or more satisfactory after separation than before? Can aliens make treaties easier than friends can make laws? Can treaties be more faithfully enforced between aliens than laws can among friends? Suppose you go to war, you cannot fight always; and when, after much loss on both sides, and no gain on either, you cease fighting, the identical questions as to terms of intercourse are again upon you.

This country, with its institutions, belongs to the people who inhabit it. Whenever they shall grow weary of the existing government, they can exercise their constitutional right of amending, or their revolutionary right to dismember or overthrow it. I cannot be ignorant of the fact that many worthy and patriotic citizens are desirous of having the national constitution amended. While I make no recommendation of amendment, I fully recognize the full authority of the people over the whole subject, to be exercised in either of the modes prescribed in the instrument itself, and I should, under existing circumstances, favor, rather than oppose, a fair opportunity being afforded the people to act upon it.

I will venture to add, that to me the convention mode seems preferable, in that it allows amendments to originate with the people themselves, instead of only permitting them to take or reject propositions originated by others not especially chosen for the purpose and which might not be precisely such as they would wish either to accept or refuse. I understand that a proposed amendment to the Constitution which amendment, however, I have not seen, that has passed Congress, to the effect that the Federal Government shall never interfere with the domestic institutions of the States, including that of persons held to service. To avoid misconstruction of what I have said, I depart from my purpose not to speak of particular amendments, so far as to say that, holding such a provision to now be implied constitutional law, I have no objection to its being made express, and irrevocable.

The chief magistrate derives all his authority from the people, and they have conferred none upon him to fix the terms for the separation of the States. The people themselves also can do this, if they choose, but the Executive, as such, has nothing to do with it. His duty is to administer the present government as it came to his hands, and to transmit it unimpaired by him to his successor. Why should there not be a patient confidence in the ultimate justice of the people? Is there any better or equal hope in the world? In our present differences is either party without faith of being in the right? If the Almighty Ruler of nations, with his eternal truth and justice, be on your side of the North, or on yours of the South, that truth and that justice will surely prevail by the judgment of this great tribunal, the American people. By the frame of the Government under which we live, this same people have wisely given their public servants but little power for mischief, and have with equal wisdom provided tor the return of that little to their own hands at very short intervals. While the people retain their virtue and vigilance, no administration, by any extreme wickedness or folly, can very seriously injure the Government in the short space of four years.

My countrymen, one and all, think calmly and well upon this whole subject. Nothing valuable can be lost by taking time.

If there be an object to hurry any of you, in hot haste, to a step which you would never take deliberately, that object will be frustrated by taking time; but no good object can be frustrated by it.

Such of you as are now dissatisfied still have the old Constitution unimpaired, and on the sensitive point, the laws of your own framing under it; while the new administration will have no immediate power, if it would, to change either.

If it were admitted that you who are dissatisfied hold the right side in the dispute, there still is no single reason for precipitate action. Intelligence, patriotism, Christianity, and a firm reliance on Him who has never yet forsaken this favored land, are still competent to adjust, in the best way, all our present difficulties.

In your hands, my dissatisfied fellow-countrymen, and not in mine, is the momentous issue of civil war. The government will not assail you. You can have no conflict, without being yourselves the aggressors. You have no oath registered in Heaven to destroy the government, while I shall have the most solemn one to "preserve, protect, and defend" it.

I am loath to close. We are not enemies, but friends. We must not be enemies. Though passion may have strained, it must not break our bonds of affection.

The mystic chords of memory, stretching from every battle-field and patriot grave, to every living heart and hearthstone all over this broad land, will yet swell the chorus of the Union, when again touched, as surely they will be, by the better angels of our nature.

[FDS]

Major-General Benjamin Butler, Query Regarding "Contraband" to the Secretary of War Simon Cameron

July 30, 1861

For the first year of the war, President Lincoln and Congress did not bend to what seemed inevitable to many who were more aggressive about abolishing slavery. Generals Fremont and Butler saw early opportunities, in their campaigns in slave states, to free slaves by declaring them "contraband." To do so legally was a matter of dispute and not well settled until President Lincoln decided the next year that indeed the purpose of the war, beyond union, was emancipation, the destruction, once and for all, of America's detestable "institution."

Secretary of War Cameron replied on August 8 that Butler had overstepped himself: "You will . . . neither authorize nor permit any interference by the troops under your command with the servants of peaceable citizens in a house or field, nor will you in any manner encourage such citizens to leave the lawful service of their masters, nor will you, except in cases where the public good may seem to require it, prevent the voluntary return of any fugitive to the service from which he may have escaped."

HEADQUARTERS DEPARTMENT OF VIRGINIA,
FORTRESS MONROE, JULY 30, 1861

HON. SIMON CAMERON, Secretary of War:—
SIR: By an order received on the morning of the 26th July from Major-General Dix, by a telegraphic order from Lieut.-General

461

Scott, I was commanded to forward, of the troops of this department, four regiments and a half, including Col. Baker's California
regiment, to Washington, via Baltimore. This order reached me at
2 o'clock A.M., by special boat from Baltimore. Believing that it
emanated because of some pressing exigency for the defence of
Washington, I issued my orders before daybreak for the embarka-
tion of the troops, sending those who were among the very best
regiments I had. In the course of the following day they were all
embarked for Baltimore, with the exception of some 400, for
whom I had not transportation, although I had all the transport
force in the hands of the quartermaster here, to aid the Bay line of
steamers, which, by the same order from the Lieut.-General, was
directed to furnish transportation.

Up to and at the time of the order I had been preparing for an
advance movement, by which I hoped to cripple the resources of
the enemy at Yorktown, and especially by seizing a large quantity
of negroes who were being pressed into their service in building the
entrenchments there. I had five days previously been enabled to
mount for the first time, the first company of light artillery, which
I had been empowered to raise, and they had but a single rifled
cannon, an iron six-pounder. Of course, every thing must and did
yield to the supposed exigency and the orders. This ordering away
the troops from this department, while it weakened the posts at
Newport News, necessitated the withdrawal of the troops from
Hampton, where I was then throwing up entrenched works to enable me to hold the town with a small force, while I advanced up
the York or James River. In the village of Hampton there were a
large number of negroes, composed in a great measure of women
and children of the men who had fled thither within my lines for
protection, who had escaped from marauding parties of rebels who
had been gathering up able-bodied blacks to aid them in constructing their batteries on the James and York Rivers. I had employed
the men in Hampton in throwing up entrenchments, and they
were working zealously and efficiently at that duty, saving our soldiers from that labor under the gleam of the midday sun. The
women were earning substantially their own subsistence in wash-
ing, marketing, and taking care of the clothes of the soldiers, and
rations were being served out to the men who worked for the support of the children. But by the evacuation of Hampton, rendered
necessary by the withdrawal of troops, leaving me scarcely

5,000 men outside the Fort, including the force at Newport News, all these black people were obliged to break up their homes at Hampton, fleeing across the creek within my lines for protection and support. Indeed, it was a most distressing sight to see these poor creatures, who had trusted to the protection of the arms of the United States, and who aided the troops of the United States in their enterprise, to be thus obliged to flee from their homes, and the homes of their masters who had deserted them, and become fugitives from fear of the return of the rebel soldiery, who had threatened to shoot the men who had wrought for us, and to carry off the women who had served us, to a worse than Egyptian bondage. I have, therefore, now within the Peninsula, this side of Hampton Creek, 900 negroes, 300 of whom are able-bodied men, 30 of whom are men substantially past hard labor, 175 women, 225 children under the age of 10 years, and 170 between 10 and 18 years, and many more coming in. The questions which this state of facts presents are very embarrassing.

First, what shall be done with them? and, *Second,* What is their state and condition?

Upon these questions I desire the instructions of the Department.

The first question, however, may perhaps be answered by considering the last. Are these men, women, and children, slaves? Are they free? Is their condition that of men, women, and children, or of property, or is it a mixed relation? What their *status* was under the Constitution and laws, we all know. What has been the effect of rebellion and a state of war upon that *status?* When I adopted the theory of treating the able-bodied negro fit to work in the trenches as property liable to be used in aid of rebellion, and so contraband of war, that condition of things was in so far met, as I then and still believe, on a legal and constitutional basis. But now a new series of questions arises. Passing by women, the children, certainly, cannot be treated on that basis; if property, they must be considered the encumbrance rather than the auxiliary of an army, and, of course, in no possible legal relation could be treated as contraband. Are they property? If they were so, they have been left by their masters and owners, deserted, thrown away, abandoned, like the wrecked vessel upon the ocean. Their former possessors and owners have causelessly, traitorously, rebelliously, and, to carry out the figure, practically abandoned them to be swallowed up by the winter storm of starvation. If property, do they not become the property of the salvors? but we, their salvors, do not need and will not hold such property, and will assume no such ownership: has not, therefore, all proprietary relation ceased? Have they not become, thereupon, men, women, and children? No longer under ownership of any kind, the fearful relics of fugitive masters, have they not by their masters' acts, and the state of war, assumed the condition, which we hold to be the normal one, of those made in God's image. Is not every constitutional, legal, and moral requirement, as well to the runaway master as their relinquished slaves, thus answered? I confess that my own mind is compelled by this reasoning to look upon them as men and women. If not free born, yet free, manumitted, sent forth from the hand that held them never to be reclaimed.

Of course, if this reasoning, thus imperfectly set forth, is correct, my duty, as a humane man, is very plain. I should take the same care of these men, women, and children, houseless, homeless, and unprovoked for, as I would of the same number of men, women, and children, who, for their attachment to the Union, had been driven or allowed to flee from the Confederate States. I should have no doubt on this question, had I not seen it stated that an order had been issued by General McDowell in his department, substantially forbidding all fugitive slaves from coming within his lines, or being harbored there. Is that order to be enforced in all military departments? If so, who are to be considered fugitive slaves? Is a slave to be considered fugitive whose master runs away and leaves him? Is it forbidden to the troops to aid or harbor within their lines the Negro children who are found therein, or is the soldier, when his march has destroyed their means of subsistence, to allow them to starve because he has driven off the rebel masters? Now, shall the commander of a regiment or battalion sit in judgment upon the question, whether any given black man has fled from his master, or his master fled from him? Indeed, how are the free born to be distinguished? Is one any more or less a fugitive slave because he has labored upon the rebel entrenchments? If he has so labored, if I understand it, he is to be harbored. By the reception of which, are the rebels most to be distressed, by taking those who have wrought all their rebel masters desired, masked their battery or those who have refused to labor and left the battery unmasked?

I have very decided opinions upon the subject of this order. It does not become me to criticize it, and I write in no spirit of criticism, but simply to explain the full difficulties that surround the enforcing it. If the enforcement of that order becomes the policy of the Government, I, as a soldier, shall be bound to enforce it steadfastly, if not cheerfully. But if left to my own discretion, as you may have gathered from my reasoning, I should take a widely different course from that which it indicates.

In a loyal State I would put down a servile insurrection. In a state of rebellion I would confiscate that which was used to oppose my arms, and take all that property, which constituted the wealth of that State, and furnished the means by which the war is prosecuted, beside being the cause of the war; and if, in so doing, it should be objected that human beings were brought to the free enjoyment of life, liberty, and the pursuit of happiness, such objection might not require much consideration.

Pardon me for addressing the Secretary of War directly upon this question, as it involves some political considerations as well as propriety of military action. I am, sir, your obedient servant,

BENJAMIN F. BUTLER

[FDS]

President Abraham Lincoln, Preliminary Emancipation Proclamation

September 22, 1862

In the midst of the Civil War, the Preliminary Emancipation Proclamation helped change the moral focus of the northern states toward ending slavery rather than primarily for maintaining the union. To the surprise of the nation and to some of the members of his own cabinet, President Lincoln put it forward soon after a Union Army victory (or stalemate) at Antietam. He believed the document was "giving fair warning of what was to come on January 1, 1863."[1] In the one hundred days that separated the preliminary and final proclamations, the vital details—that the slaves in any of the states that were still "in rebellion" would gain their freedom—were slowly but surely accepted and embraced by the majority of the citizens of the North.

BY THE PRESIDENT of the United States of America.

A Proclamation.

I, Abraham Lincoln, President of the United States of America, and Commander-in-Chief of the Army and Navy thereof, do hereby proclaim and declare that hereafter, as heretofore, the war will be prosecuted for the object of practically restoring the constitutional relation between the United States, and each of the States, and the people thereof, in which States that relation is, or may be, suspended or disturbed.

---

[1] Douglas L. Wilson. *Lincoln's Sword: The Presidency and the Power of Words.* New York. Alfred A. Knopf. 2006. 133.

That it is my purpose, upon the next meeting of Congress to again recommend the adoption of a practical measure tendering pecuniary aid to the free acceptance or rejection of all slave States, so called, the people whereof may not then be in rebellion against the United States and which States may then have voluntarily adopted, or thereafter may voluntarily adopt, immediate or gradual abolishment of slavery within their respective limits; and that the effort to colonize persons of African descent, with their consent, upon this continent, or elsewhere, with the previously obtained consent of the Governments existing there, will be continued.

That on the first day of January in the year of our Lord, one thousand eight hundred and sixty-three, all persons held as slaves within any State, or designated part of a State, the people whereof shall then be in rebellion against the United States shall be then, thenceforward, and forever free; and the executive government of the United States, including the military and naval authority thereof, will recognize and maintain the freedom of such persons, and will do no act or acts to repress such persons, or any of them, in any efforts they may make for their actual freedom.

That the executive will, on the first day of January aforesaid, by proclamation, designate the States, and part of States, if any, in which the people thereof respectively, shall then be in rebellion against the United States; and the fact that any State, or the people thereof shall, on that day be, in good faith represented in the Congress of the United States, by members chosen thereto, at elections wherein a majority of the qualified voters of such State shall have participated, shall, in the absence of strong countervailing testimony, be deemed conclusive evidence that such State and the people thereof, are not then in rebellion against the United States.

That attention is hereby called to an Act of Congress entitled "An Act to make an additional Article of War" approved March 13, 1862, and which act is in the words and figure following:

"Be it enacted by the Senate and House of Representatives of the United States of America in Congress assembled, That hereafter the following shall be promulgated as an additional article of war for the government of the army of the United States, and shall be obeyed and observed as such:

"Article-All officers or persons in the military or naval service of the United States are prohibited from employing any of the forces under their respective commands for the purpose of returning fugitives from service or labor, who may have escaped from any persons to whom such service or labor is claimed to be due, and any officer who shall be found guilty by a court martial of violating this article shall be dismissed from the service.

"Sec.2. And be it further enacted, That this act shall take effect from and after its passage."

Also to the ninth and tenth sections of an act entitled "An Act to suppress Insurrection, to punish Treason and Rebellion, to seize and confiscate property of rebels, and for other purposes," approved July 17, 1862, and which sections are in the words and figures following:

"Sec.9. And be it further enacted, That all slaves of persons who shall hereafter be engaged in rebellion against the government of the United States, or who shall in any way give aid or comfort thereto, escaping from such persons and taking refuge within the lines of the army; and all slaves captured from such persons or deserted by them and coming under the control of the government of the United States; and all slaves of such persons found on (or) being within any place occupied by rebel forces and afterwards occupied by the forces of the United States, shall be deemed captives of war, and shall be forever free of their servitude and not again held as slaves.

"Sec.10. And be it further enacted, That no slave escaping into any State, Territory, or the District of Columbia, from any other State, shall be delivered up, or in any way impeded or hindered of his liberty, except for crime, or some offence against the laws, unless the person claiming said fugitive shall first make oath that the person to whom the labor or service of such fugitive is alleged to be due is his lawful owner, and has not borne arms against the United States in the present rebellion, nor in any way given aid and comfort thereto; and no person engaged in the military or naval service of the United States shall, under any pretense whatever, assume to decide on the validity of the claim of any person to the service or labor of any other person, or surrender up any such person to the claimant, on pain of being dismissed from the service."

And I do hereby enjoin upon and order all persons engaged in the military and naval service of the United States to observe, obey, and enforce, within their respective spheres of service, the act, and sections above recited.

And the executive will in due time recommend that all citizens of the United States who shall have remained loyal thereto throughout the rebellion, shall (upon the restoration of the constitutional relation between the United States, and their respective States, and people, if that relation shall have been suspended or disturbed) be compensated for all losses by acts of the United States, including the loss of slaves.

In witness whereof, I have here unto set my hand, and caused the seal of the United States to be affixed.

Done at the City of Washington this twenty-second day of September, in the year of our Lord, one thousand, eight hundred and sixty-two, and of the Independence of the United States the eighty seventh.

[Signed:] Abraham Lincoln
By the President

[Signed:] William H. Seward
Secretary of State

[ARCH]

President Abraham Lincoln, Final Emancipation Proclamation

January 1, 1863

On January 12, Confederate President Jefferson Davis responded to his rival president's proclamation in a message to his congress: "The people of this Confederacy . . . cannot fail to receive this proclamation as the fullest vindication of their own sagacity in foreseeing the uses to which the dominant party in the United States intended from the beginning to apply their power; nor can they cease to remember with devout thankfulness that it is to their own vigilance in resisting the first stealthy progress of approaching despotism that they owe their escape from consequences now apparent to the most skeptical."

William W. Brown, an author and former slave, wrote at the time, "'What shall be done with the slaves if they are freed?' You had better ask, 'What shall we do with the slaveholders if the slaves are freed?' The slave has shown himself better fitted to take care of himself than the slaveholder."

While the Emancipation Proclamation freed the slaves in Confederate states and areas, it did not free them elsewhere. That comprehensiveness would have to wait until the Thirteenth Amendment to the Constitution, not ratified until the end of 1865.

WHEREAS, ON THE twenty-second day of September, in the year of our Lord one thousand eight hundred and sixty-two, a proclamation was issued by the President of the United States containing among other things the following, to wit:

"That on the first day of January, in the year of our Lord one thousand eight hundred and sixty-three, all persons held as slaves within any State or designated part of a State, the people whereof shall then be in rebellion against the United States, shall be then, thenceforth and forever free; and the Executive Government of the United States, including the military and naval authorities thereof, will recognize and maintain the freedom of such persons, and will do no act or acts to repress such persons, or any of them, in any efforts they may make for their actual freedom.

"That the Executive will, on the first day of January aforesaid, by proclamation, designate the States and parts of States, if any, in which the people therein respectively shall then be in rebellion against the United States, and the fact that any State, or the people thereof, shall on that day be in good faith represented in the Congress of the United States by members chosen thereto, at elections wherein a majority of the qualified voters of such State, shall have participated, shall, in the absence of strong countervailing testimony, be deemed conclusive evidence that such State and the people thereof are not then in rebellion against the United States."

Now, therefore, I, Abraham Lincoln, President of the United States, by virtue of the power in me vested as Commander-in-chief of the Army and Navy of the United States in time of actual armed rebellion against the authority and Government of the United States, and as a fit and necessary war measure for suppressing said rebellion, do, on this first day of January, in the year of our Lord one thousand eight hundred and sixty-three, and in accordance with my purpose so to do, publicly proclaimed for the full period of one hundred days from the day of the first above-mentioned order and designate, as the States and parts of States wherein the people thereof respectively are this day in rebellion against the United States, the following, to wit: Arkansas, Texas, Louisiana, except the parishes of St. Bernard, Plaquemines, Jefferson, St. John, St. Charles, St. James, Ascension, Assumption, Terre Bonne, Lafourche, St. Mary, St. Martin, and Orleans, including the City of New Orleans. Mississippi, Alabama, Florida, Georgia, South-Carolina, North-Carolina, and Virginia, except the forty-eight counties designated as West Virginia, and also the counties of Berkeley, Accomac, Northampton, Elizabeth City, York, Princess Ann, and Norfolk, including the cities of Norfolk and Portsmouth, and which excepted parts are, for the present, left precisely as if this proclamation were not issued.

And by virtue of the power and for the purpose aforesaid, I do order and declare that all persons held as slaves within said designated States and parts of States are, and henceforward shall be free; and that the Executive Government of the United States, including the Military and Naval authorities thereof, will recognize and maintain the freedom of said persons.

And I hereby enjoin upon the people so declared to be free, to abstain from all violence, unless in necessary self-defense, and I recommend to them that in all cases, when allowed, they labor faithfully for reasonable wages.

And I further declare and make known that such persons of suitable condition will be received into the armed service of the United States to garrison forts, positions, stations, and other places, and to man vessels of all sorts in said service.

And upon this act, sincerely believed to be an act of justice, warranted by the Constitution, upon military necessity, I invoke the considerate judgment of mankind and the gracious favor of Almighty God.

In witness whereof, I have here unto set my hand and caused the seal of the United States to be affixed.

[L.S.]

Done at the City of Washington, this first day of January, in the year of our Lord one thousand eight hundred and sixty-three, and of the Independence of the United States of America the eighty-seventh.

ABRAHAM LINCOLN

BY THE PRESIDENt—WILLIAM H. SEWARD,
Secretary of State

[FDS]

President Abraham Lincoln, "Gettysburg Address," Delivered at the Dedication to the Cemetery at Gettysburg

November 19, 1863

Massachusetts orator Edward Everett, wrote Lincoln on November 20 to say, "I should be glad if I could flatter myself that I came as near the central idea of the occasion in two hours as you did in two minutes." Lincoln replied: "In our respective parts yesterday, you could not have been excused to make a short address, nor I a long one. I am pleased to know that, in your judgment, the little I did say was not entirely a failure."[1] The Gettysburg Address has become, second only to the Declaration of Independence, the most famous speech in American history.

FOUR SCORE AND seven years ago our fathers brought forth on this continent, a new nation, conceived in Liberty, and dedicated to the proposition that all men are created equal.

Now we are engaged in a great civil war, testing whether that nation, or any nation so conceived and so dedicated, can long endure. We are met on a great battle-field of that war. We have come to dedicate a portion of that field, as a final resting place for those

---

[1] "Lincoln spoke only 105 or 110 words a minute, in part because he paused often for emphasis," writes Ronald C. White. Jr., in *Lincoln's Greatest Speech* (New York: Simon and Schuster. 2002. 165).

who here gave their lives that that nation might live. It is altogether fitting and proper that we should do this.

But, in a larger sense, we can not dedicate—we can not consecrate—we can not hallow—this ground. The brave men, living and dead, who struggled here, have consecrated it, far above our poor power to add or detract. The world will little note, nor long remember what we say here, but it can never forget what they did here. It is for us the living, rather, to be dedicated here to the unfinished work which they who fought here have thus far so nobly advanced. It is rather for us to be here dedicated to the great task remaining before us—that from these honored dead we take increased devotion to that cause for which they gave the last full measure of devotion—that we here highly resolve that these dead shall not have died in vain—that this nation, under God, shall have a new birth of freedom—and that government of the people, by the people, for the people, shall not perish from the earth.

ABRAHAM LINCOLN
November 19, 1863

[FDS]

Major-General W. T. Sherman, Letter to the Mayor and City Council of Atlanta

September 12, 1864

Like him or not, Major-General William Tecumseh Sherman's moral bearing on the war was always deeply considered and clearly explained: "You cannot qualify war in harsher terms than I will. War is cruelty, and you cannot refine it; and those who brought war into our country deserve all the curses and maledictions a people can pour out." The Union had no general more effective than he at carrying out bold missions, and Sherman's "March to the Sea" was indeed devastating to property in the South and the Confederacy's war capabilities.

HEADQUARTERS MILITARY DIVISION OF THE MISSISSIPPI,
in the field, Atlanta, Georgia, September 12, 1864

James M. Calhoun, *Mayor* E. E. Rawson *and* S. C. Wells,
representing City Council of Atlanta

GENTLEMEN: I have your letter of the 11th, in the nature of a petition to revoke my orders removing all the inhabitants from Atlanta. I have read it carefully, and give full credit to your statements of the distress that will be occasioned, and yet shall not revoke my orders, because they were not designed to meet the humanities of the case, but to prepare for the future struggles in which millions of good people outside of Atlanta have a deep interest. We must have peace, not only at Atlanta, but in all America.

To secure this, we must stop the war that now desolates our once happy and favored country. To stop war, we must defeat the rebel armies which are arrayed against the laws and Constitution that all must respect and obey. To defeat those armies, we must prepare the way to reach them in their recesses, provided with the arms and instruments which enable us to accomplish our purpose. Now, I know the vindictive nature of our enemy, that we may have many years of military operations from this quarter; and, therefore, deem it wise and prudent to prepare in time. The use of Atlanta for warlike purposes is inconsistent with its character as a home for families. There will be no manufactures, commerce, or agriculture here, for the maintenance of families, and sooner or later want will compel the inhabitants to go. Why not go now, when all the arrangements are completed for the transfer, instead of waiting till the plunging shot of contending armies will renew the scenes of the past month? Of course, I do not apprehend any such thing at this moment, but you do not suppose this army will be here until the war is over. I cannot discuss this subject with you fairly, because I cannot impart to you what we propose to do, but I assert that our military plans make it necessary for the inhabitants to go away, and I can only renew my offer of services to make their exodus in any direction as easy and comfortable as possible.

You cannot qualify war in harsher terms than I will. War is cruelty, and you cannot refine it; and those who brought war into our country deserve all the curses and maledictions a people can pour out. I know I had no hand in making this war, and I know I will make more sacrifices to-day than any of you to secure peace. But you cannot have peace and a division of our country. If the United States submits to a division now, it will not stop, but will go on until we reap the fate of Mexico, which is eternal war. The United States does and must assert its authority, wherever it once had power; for, if it relaxes one bit to pressure, it is gone, and I believe that such is the national feeling. This feeling assumes various shapes, but always comes back to that of Union. Once admit the Union, once more acknowledge the authority of the national Government, and, instead of devoting your houses and streets and roads to the dread uses of war, I and this army become at once your protectors and supporters, shielding you from danger, let it come from what quarter it may. I know that a few individuals cannot resist a torrent of error and passion, such as swept the South into rebellion, but you can point out, so that we may know those who desire a government, and those who insist on war and its desolation.

You might as well appeal against the thunder-storm as against these terrible hardships of war. They are inevitable, and the only way the people of Atlanta can hope once more to live in peace and quiet at home, is to stop the war, which can only be done by admitting that it began in error and is perpetuated in pride.

We don't want your Negroes, or your horses, or your houses, or your lands, or anything you have, but we do want and will have a just obedience to the laws of the United States. That we will have, and, if it involves the destruction of your improvements, we cannot help it.

You have heretofore read public sentiment in your newspapers that live by falsehood and excitement; and the quicker you seek for truth in other quarters, the better. I repeat then that, by the original compact of Government, the United States had certain rights in Georgia, which have never been relinquished and never will be; that the South began war by seizing forts, arsenals, mints, custom-houses, etc., etc., long before Mr. Lincoln was installed, and before the South had one jot or title of provocation. I myself have seen in Missouri, Kentucky, Tennessee, and Mississippi, hundreds and thousands of women and children fleeing from your armies and desperadoes, hungry and with bleeding feet. In Memphis, Vicksburg, and Mississippi, we fed thousands upon thousands of the families of rebel soldiers left on our hands, and whom we could not see starve. Now that war comes home to you, you feel very different. You deprecate its horrors, but did not feel them when you sent carloads of soldiers and ammunition, and molded shells and shot, to carry war into Kentucky and Tennessee, to desolate the homes of hundreds and thousands of good people who only asked to live in peace at their old homes, and under the Government of their inheritance. But these comparisons are idle. I want peace, and believe it can only be reached through union and war, and I will ever conduct war with a view to perfect and early success.

But, my dear sirs, when peace does come, you may call on me for anything. Then will I share with you the last cracker, and watch with you to shield your homes and families against danger from every quarter.

Now you must go, and take with you the old and feeble, feed and nurse them, and build for them, in more quiet places, proper habitations to shield them against the weather until the mad passions of men cool down, and allow the Union and peace once more to settle over your old homes at Atlanta. Yours in haste,

W. T. SHERMAN,
Major-General commanding

[FDS]

President Abraham Lincoln, Second Inaugural Address

March 4, 1865

With characteristic economy and generosity, Abraham Lincoln surveyed the past four years of war and directed the divided country to look ahead and "Bind up the nation's wounds." The abolitionist and author Frederick Douglass, who was present at the President's second inaugural, admiringly observed that "the address sounded more like a sermon than a state paper."

At this second appearing to take the oath of the presidential office, there is less occasion for an extended address than there was at the first. Then a statement, somewhat in detail, of a course to be pursued, seemed fitting and proper. Now, at the expiration of four years, during which public declarations have been constantly called forth on every point and phase of the great contest which still absorbs the attention, and engrosses the energies of the nation, little that is new could be presented. The progress of our arms, upon which all else chiefly depends, is as well known to the public as to myself; and it is, I trust, reasonably satisfactory and encouraging to all. With high hope for the future, no prediction in regard to it is ventured.

On the occasion corresponding to these four years ago, all thoughts were anxiously directed to an impending civil war. All dreaded it, all sought to avert it. While the inaugural address was being delivered from this place, devoted altogether to *saving* the Union without war, insurgent agents were in the city seeking to *destroy* it without war—seeking to dissolve the Union, and divide effects, by negotiation. Both parties deprecated war; but one of them would *make* war rather than let the nation survive; and the other would *accept* war rather than let it perish. And the war came.

One eighth of the whole population were colored slaves, not distributed generally over the Union, but localized in the Southern part of it. These slaves constituted a peculiar and powerful interest. All knew that this interest was, somehow, the cause of the war. To strengthen, perpetuate, and extend this interest was the object for which the insurgents would rend the Union, even by war; while the government claimed no right to do more than to restrict the territorial enlargement of it. Neither party expected for the war, the magnitude, or the duration, which it has already attained. Neither anticipated that the *cause* of the conflict might cease with, or even before, the conflict itself should cease. Each looked for an easier triumph and a result less fundamental and astounding. Both read the same Bible, and pray to the same God; and each invokes His aid against the other. It may seem strange that any men should dare to ask a just God's assistance in wringing their bread from the sweat of other men's faces; but let us judge not that we be not judged. The prayers of both could not be answered; that of neither has been answered fully. The Almighty has His own purposes. "Woe unto the world because of offences! for it must needs be that offences come; but woe to that man by whom the offence cometh!" If we shall suppose that American Slavery is one of those offences which, in the providence of God, must needs come, but which, having continued through His appointed time, He now wills to remove, and that He gives to both North and South, this terrible war, as the woe due to those by whom the offence came, shall we discern therein any departure from those divine attributes which the believers in a Living God always ascribe to Him? Fondly do we hope—fervently do we pray—that this mighty scourge of war may speedily pass away. Yet, if God wills that it continue, until all the wealth piled by the bond-man's two hundred and fifty years of unrequited toil shall be sunk, and until every drop of blood drawn with the lash, shall be paid by another drawn with the sword, as was said three thousand years ago, so still it must be said "the judgments of the Lord, are true and righteous altogether."

With malice toward none; with charity for all; with firmness in the right, as God gives us to see the right, let us strive on to finish the work we are in; to bind up the nation's wounds; to care for him who shall have borne the battle, and for his widow, and his orphan—to do all which may achieve and cherish a just and lasting peace, among ourselves, and with all nations.

[FDS]

Lieutenant-General Ulysses S. Grant of the Army of the Potomac and Commander of the Confederate States General Robert E. Lee, Correspondence Regarding Surrender

April 9, 1865

President Lincoln had authorized his Lieutenant-General Ulysses S. Grant (1822–1885) to negotiate with Confederate Commander Robert E. Lee (1807–1870) in the surrender of the Confederacy's most important army, and Lee, foreseeing the destruction of his men, finally conceded defeat. Though Grant and Lee had met while serving in the Mexican War, Appomattox Courthouse (Clover Hill), Virginia, was their first meeting as equals. Grant then drafted the concluding terms of surrender on the spot.

HEADQUARTERS ARMIES OF THE UNITED STATES,
April 9, 1865

GENERAL R. E. LEE:
Commanding C. S. Army:
GENERAL: Your note of yesterday is received. As I have no authority to treat on the subject of peace the meeting proposed for 10 A.M. to-day could lead to no good. I will state, however, general, that I am equally anxious for peace with yourself, and the whole North entertain the same feeling. The terms upon which peace can be had are well understood. By the South laying down their arms they will hasten that most desirable event, save thousands of human

lives, and hundreds of millions of property not yet destroyed. Sincerely hoping that all our difficulties may be settled without the loss of another life, I subscribe myself,

Very respectfully, your obedient servant,

U. S. GRANT,
Lieutenant-General, U. S. Army

April 9, 1865

LIEUT. GEN. U. S. GRANT,
Commanding C. S. Armies:

GENERAL: I received your note of this morning on the picket-line, whither I had come to meet you and ascertain definitely what terms were embraced in your proposal of yesterday with reference to the surrender of this army. I now request an interview in accordance with the offer contained in your letter of yesterday for that purpose.

Very respectfully, your obedient servant,

R. E. LEE,
General

HEADQUARTERS ARMIES OF THE UNITED STATES,
Appomattox Court-House, Va., April 9, 1865

GENERAL R. E. LEE,
Commanding C. S. Army:

GENERAL: In accordance with the substance of my letter to you of the 8th instant, I propose to receive the surrender of the Army of Northern Virginia on the following terms, to wit: Rolls of all the officers and men to be made in duplicate—one copy to be given to an officer to be designated by me, the other to be retained by such officer or officers as you may designate; the officers to give their individual paroles not to take up arms against the Government of the United States until properly exchanged, and each company or regimental commander sign a like parole for the men of their commands. The arms, artillery, and public property to be parked and stacked, and turned over to the officers appointed by me to receive them. This will not embrace the side-arms of the officers, nor their private horses or baggage. This done, each officer and man will be allowed to return to their homes, not to be disturbed by United States authority so long as they observe their paroles and the laws in force where they may reside.

Very respectfully,

U. S. GRANT,
Lieutenant-General

[FDS]

General Robert E. Lee, Farewell Address to the Confederate Army of Northern Virginia

April 10, 1865

Having surrendered on April 9, Lee, according to his son, remarked to his waiting soldiers of the Army of Northern Virginia, " 'Men, we have fought through the war together; I have done my best for you; my heart is too full to say more,' " and then "he bade them good-bye and told them to return home and become good citizens." Lee became the president of Washington University in Virginia (renamed Washington and Lee after his death).

HEADQUARTERS, ARMY OF NORTHERN VIRGINIA,
April 10, 1865

AFTER FOUR YEARS' of arduous service, marked by unsurpassed courage and fortitude, the Army of Northern Virginia has been compelled to yield to overwhelming numbers and resources. I need not tell the survivors of so many hard-fought battles, who have remained steadfast to the last, that I have consented to this result from no distrust of them; but, feeling that valour and devotion could accomplish nothing that could compensate for the loss that would have attended the continuation of the contest, I have determined to avoid the useless sacrifice of those whose past services have endeared them to their countrymen. By the terms of the agreement, officers and men can return to their homes and remain there until exchanged. You will take with you the satisfaction that proceeds from the consciousness of duty faithfully performed; and

I earnestly pray that a merciful God will extend to you His blessing and protection. With an increasing admiration of your constancy and devotion to your country, and a grateful remembrance of your kind and generous considerations of myself, I bid you an affectionate farewell.

R. E. Lee,
General

[FDS]

President Abraham Lincoln, Last Public Address

April 11, 1865

With the Confederacy's capital, Richmond, taken, Confederate R. E. Lee's forces surrendered, President Abraham Lincoln spoke from the White House on the inevitable "reconstruction" of the South. Four days later he was dead, assassinated by a Confederate fanatic.

WE MEET THIS evening, not in sorrow, but in gladness of heart. The evacuation of Petersburg and Richmond, and the surrender of the principal insurgent army, give hope of a righteous and speedy peace whose joyous expression cannot be restrained. In the midst of this, however, He from whom all blessings flow must not be forgotten. A call for a national thanksgiving is being prepared, and will be duly promulgated. Nor must those whose harder part gives us the cause of rejoicing, be overlooked. Their honors must not be parceled out with others. I myself was near the front, and had the high pleasure of transmitting much of the good news to you; but no part of the honor, for plan or execution, is mine. To Gen. Grant, his skilful officers, and brave men, all belongs. The gallant Navy stood ready, but was not in reach to take active part.

By these recent successes the re-inauguration of the national authority—reconstruction—which has had a large share of thought from the first, is pressed much more closely upon our attention. It is fraught with great difficulty. Unlike a case of a war between independent nations, there is no authorized organ for us to treat with. No one man has authority to give up the rebellion for any other man. We simply must begin with, and mould from, disorganized and discordant elements. Nor is it a small additional embarrassment that we, the loyal people, differ among ourselves as to the mode, manner, and means of reconstruction.

As a general rule, I abstain from reading the reports of attacks upon myself, wishing not to be provoked by that to which I cannot properly offer an answer. In spite of this precaution, however, it comes to my knowledge that I am much censured for some supposed agency in setting up, and seeking to sustain, the new State government of Louisiana. In this I have done just so much as, and no more than, the public knows. In the Annual Message of Dec. 1863 and accompanying Proclamation, I presented a plan of reconstruction (as the phrase goes) which, I promised, if adopted by any State, should be acceptable to, and sustained by, the Executive government of the nation. I distinctly stated that this was not the only plan which might possibly be acceptable; and I also distinctly protested that the Executive claimed no right to say when, or whether members should be admitted to seats in Congress from such States. This plan was, in advance, submitted to the then Cabinet, and distinctly approved by every member of it. One of them suggested that I should then, and in that connection, apply the Emancipation Proclamation to the theretofore excepted parts of Virginia and Louisiana; that I should drop the suggestion about apprenticeship for freed-people, and that I should omit the protest against my own power, in regard to the admission of members to Congress; but even he approved every part and parcel of the plan which has since been employed or touched by the action of Louisiana. The new constitution of Louisiana, declaring emancipation for the whole State, practically applies the Proclamation to the part previously excepted, It does not adopt apprenticeship for freed-people; and it is silent, as it could not well be otherwise, about the admission of members to Congress. So that, as it applies to Louisiana, every member of the Cabinet fully approved the plan. The message went to Congress, and I received many commendations of the plan, written and verbal; and not a single objection to it, from any professed emancipationist, came to my knowledge, until after the news reached Washington that the people of Louisiana had begun to move in accordance with it. From about July 1862, I had corresponded with different persons, supposed to be interested, seeking a reconstruction of a State government for Louisiana. When the message of 1863, with the plan before mentioned, reached New-Orleans, Gen. Banks wrote me that he was confident the people, with his military co-operation, would reconstruct, substantially on that plan. I wrote him, and some of them to try it; they tried it, and the result is known. Such only has been my agency in getting up the Louisiana government. As to sustaining it, my promise is out, as before stated. But, as bad promises are better broken than kept, I shall treat this as a bad promise, and break it, whenever I shall be convinced that keeping it is adverse to the public interest. But I have not yet been so convinced.

I have been shown a letter on this subject, supposed to be an able one, in which the writer expresses regret that my mind has not seemed to be definitely fixed on the question whether the seceded States, so called, are in the Union or out of it. It would perhaps, add astonishment to his regret, were he to learn that since I have found professed Union men endeavoring to make that question, I have *purposely* forborne any public expression upon it. As appears to me that question has not been, nor yet is, a practically material one, and that any discussion of it, while it thus remains practically immaterial, could have no effect other than the mischievous one of dividing our friends. As yet, whatever it may hereafter become, that question is bad, as the basis of a controversy, and good for nothing at all—a merely pernicious abstraction.

We all agree that the seceded States, so called, are out of their proper practical relation with the Union; and that the sole object of the government, civil and military, in regard to those States is to again get them into that proper practical relation. I believe it is not only possible, but in fact, easier to do this, without deciding, or even considering, whether these States have ever been out of the Union, than with it. Finding them safely at home, it would be utterly immaterial whether they had ever been abroad. Let us all join in doing the acts necessary to restoring the proper practical relations between these States and the Union; and each forever after, innocently indulge his own opinion whether, in doing the acts, he brought the States from without, into the Union, or only gave them proper assistance, they never having been out of it.

The amount of constituency, so to speak, on which the new Louisiana government rests, would be more satisfactory to all, if it contained fifty, thirty, or even twenty thousand, instead of only about twelve thousand, as it does. It is also unsatisfactory to some that the elective franchise is not given to the colored man. I would myself prefer that it were now conferred on the very intelligent, and on those who serve our cause as soldiers. Still the question is not whether the Louisiana government, as it stands, is quite all that is desirable. The question is, "Will it be wiser to take it as it is, and help to improve it; or to reject, and disperse it?" "Can Louisiana be brought into proper practical relation with the Union *sooner* by *sustaining*, or by *discarding* her new State government?"

Some twelve thousand voters in the heretofore slave-state of Louisiana have sworn allegiance to the Union, assumed to be the rightful political power of the State, held elections, organized a State government, adopted a free-state constitution, giving the benefit of public schools equally to black and white, and empowering the Legislature to confer the elective franchise upon the colored man. Their Legislature has already voted to ratify the constitutional amendment recently passed by Congress, abolishing slavery throughout the nation. These twelve thousand persons are thus fully committed to the Union, and to perpetual freedom in the state—committed to the very things, and nearly all the things the nation wants—and they ask the nation's recognition and its assistance to make good their committal. Now, if we reject, and spurn them, we do our utmost to disorganize and disperse them. We in effect say to the white men, "You are worthless or worse—we will neither help you, nor be helped by you." To the blacks we say "This cup of liberty which these, your old masters, hold to your lips, we will dash from you, and leave you to the chances of gathering the spilled and scattered contents in some vague and undefined when, where, and how." If this course, discouraging and paralyzing both white and black, has any tendency to bring Louisiana into proper practical relations with the Union, I have, so far, been unable to perceive it. If, on the contrary, we recognize, and sustain the new government of Louisiana the converse of all this is made true. We encourage the hearts, and nerve the arms of the twelve thousand to adhere to their work, and argue for it, and proselyte for it, and fight for it, and feed it, and grow it, and ripen it to a complete success. The colored man too, in seeing all united for him, is inspired with vigilance, and energy, and daring, to the same end. Grant that he desires the elective franchise; will he not attain it sooner by saving the already advanced steps toward it, than by running backward over them? Concede that the new government of Louisiana is only to what it should be as the egg is to the fowl; we shall sooner have the fowl by hatching the egg than by smashing it. Again, if we reject Louisiana, we also reject one vote in favor of the proposed amendment to the national Constitution. To meet this proposition, it has been argued that no more than three-fourths of those States which have not attempted secession are necessary to validly ratify the amendment. I do not commit myself against this, further than to say that such ratification would be questionable, and sure to be persistently questioned; while ratification by three-fourths of all the States would be unquestioned and unquestionable.

I repeat the question. "Can Louisiana be brought into proper practical relation with the Union *sooner* by *sustaining* or by *discarding* her new State Government?"

What has been said of Louisiana will apply generally to other States. And yet so great peculiarities pertain to each state, and such important and sudden changes occur in the same state; and withal, so new and unprecedented is the whole case that no exclusive and inflexible plan can safely be prescribed as to details and collaterals. Such an exclusive, and inflexible plan, would surely become a new entanglement. Important principles may, and must, be inflexible.

In the present *"situation,"* as the phrase goes, it may be my duty to make some new announcement to the people of the South. I am considering, and shall not fail to act, when satisfied that action will be proper.

[FDS]

The Thirteenth Amendment to the Constitution

December 6, 1865

In January 1864, Senator John Henderson of Missouri proposed the Thirteenth Amendment to the Constitution, whereby slavery would be outlawed throughout the Union. In April 1864 the Senate approved it; the House of Representatives approved it on January 31, 1865; it became law on December 6, 1865, when twenty-seven of the thirty-six states ratified it. Kentucky did not ratify the amendment until 1976; Mississippi ratified it in 1995.

SECTION 1. NEITHER slavery nor involuntary servitude, except as a punishment for crime whereof the party shall have been duly convicted, shall exist within the United States, or any place subject to their jurisdiction.

SECTION 2. Congress shall have power to enforce this article by appropriate legislation.

[FDS]

Source and Author Guide

[ACH]   *Source Book and Bibliographical Guide for American Church History*. Edited by Peter G. Mode. Menasha, Wisconsin: George Banta Publishing Company. 1921.

[AHC]   *American History Told by Contemporaries*. Four Volumes. Edited by Albert Bushnell Hart. New York: Macmillan. 1917.

[AHD]   *American Historical Documents 1000–1904*. The Harvard Classics. Edited by Charles W. Eliot (CWE). Volume 43. New York: P. F. Collier and Son Company. 1910.

[AIH]   *Great Documents in American Indian History*. Wayne Moquin and Charles Van Doren. New York: Da Capo. 1995.

[APP]   *The American Presidency Project* by Gerhard Peters and John T. Woolley. http://www.presidency.ucsb.edu/index.php

[AST]   Abolition of the Slave Trade. The Schaumburg Center for Research in Black Culture. The New York Public Library. Accessed February 26, 2015. http://abolition.nypl.org/texts/us_constitution/5/?_utma=10456805.190678389.1421713661.1424982082.1424982082.1&_utmb=10456805.6.10.1424982082&_utmc=10456805&_utmx=-&_utmz=10456805.1424982082.1.1.utmcsr=google|utmccn=%28organic%29|utmcmd=organic|utmctr=%28not%20provided%29&_utmv=-&_utmk=119047049

[COV]   *The Code of Virginia with the Declaration of Independence, Constitution of the United States, etc.* John M. Patton. Richmond, Virginia: W. F. Ritchie. 1849.

[CS]   Thomas Paine. *Common Sense*. Mineola, New York: Dover. TKTK.

[DAAL]   *The Dover Anthology of American Literature,* Volume 1. Bob Blaisdell. Mineola, New York: Dover. 2014.

[DAH]   *Documents of American History*. Volume I: to 1898; 10th ed. Henry Steele Commager and Milton Cantor. Englewood Cliffs, New Jersey: Prentice Hall. 1988. Volume 2: Since 1898; 7th ed. Henry Steele Commager. New York: Appleton-Century-Crofts. 1963.

[DI]   *The Declaration of Independence and Other Great Documents of American History, 1775–1865*. John Grafton. Mineola, New York: Dover. 2000.

[DIH]   *Documents Illustrative of American History, 1606–1863*. Howard W. Preston. New York: G. P. Putnam's Sons. 1886.

[EI]   *Essays on Immigration*. Bob Blaisdell. Mineola, New York: Dover. 2011.

[ETP]   *The Essential Thomas Paine*. Edited by John Dos Passos. Mineola, New York: Dover. 2008. (Originally 1940.)

[FDS]   *Famous Documents and Speeches of the Civil War*. Bob Blaisdell. Mineola, New York: Dover. 2006.

[GIA]   *Great Inaugural Addresses*. James Daley. Mineola, New York: Dover. 2010.

[GSAA]   *Great Speeches by African Americans*. James Daley. Mineola, New York: Dover. 2006.

[GSAW]   *Great Speeches by American Women*. James Daley. Mineola, New York: Dover. 2008.

[GSFD]   *Great Speeches by Frederick Douglass*. James Daley. Mineola, New York: Dover. 2013.

[GSNA]   *Great Speeches by Native Americans*. Bob Blaisdell. Mineola, New York: Dover. 2000.

[IS]   *Infamous Speeches: From Robespierre to Osama bin Laden*. Bob Blaisdell. Mineola, New York: Dover. 2011.

[LD]   *Landmark Decisions of the U. S. Supreme Court*. James Daley. Mineola, New York: Dover. 2006.

[LLA]   *Littel's Living Age*. Volume 18 (July, August, September, 1848). Boston: E. Littell and Company.

[LOE]   Horace Mann. *Lectures on Education*. Boston: Wm. B. Fowle and N. Capen. 1845.

[NARA] National Archives & Records Adminstration. archives. gov (also ourdocuments.gov)

[OJLC] *Original Journals of the Lewis and Clark Expedition, 1804–1806*. Volume 7. Reuben Gold Thwaites. New York: Dodd, Mead and Co. 1905.

[RHE] *Readings in the History of Education: A Collection of Sources and Readings to Illustrate the Development of Educational Practice, Theory, and Organization*. Ellwood P. Cubberley. Boston: Houghton Mifflin Company. 1920.

[SDIA] *Select Documents Illustrative of American History, 1606–1775*. William McDonald. New York: Macmillan. 1904.

[SDIUS] *Select Documents Illustrative of the History of the United States, 1776–1861*. William McDonald. New York: Macmillan. 1909.

[SN] *Slave Narratives of the Underground Railroad*. Christine Rudisel and Bob Blaisdell. Mineola, New York: Dover. 2014.

[USC] *The United States Constitution: The Full Text with Supplementary Materials*. Bob Blaisdell. Mineola, New York: Dover. 2009.

[WGS] *The World's Great Speeches*. Fourth edition. Lewis Copeland **(LC)**, Lawrence W. Lamm and Stephen J. McKenna. Mineola, New York: Dover. 1999.

Bibliography

Albert Bushnell Hart and Edward Charming. American History Leaflets. *Colonial and Constitutional*, New York: A. Lovell and Co., 1894.

Richard D. Heffner. *A Documentary History of the United States.* Expanded edition. New American Library, Mentor: New York. 1965.

Robert V. Hine and Edwin R. Bingham. *The American Frontier: Readings and Documents.* Boston: Little, Brown. 1972.

Ben Perley Poore.*The Federal and State Constitutions, Colonial Charters and Other Organic Laws of the United States.* Washington. 1877.

Christine Rudisel and Bob Blaisdell. *Slave Narratives of the Underground Railroad*, Mineola, New York: Dover, 2014.

Edwin Clarence Stedman and Ellen Mackay Hutchinson. *A Library of American Literature from the Earliest Settlement to the Present Time.* New York. 1888–1890.

David R. Wrone and Russell S. Nelson, Jr. *Who's the Savage?: A Documentary History of the Mistreatment of the Native North Americans.* Greenwich, Connecticut. New York: Fawcett. 1973.

A CATALOG OF SELECTED
DOVER BOOKS
IN ALL FIELDS OF INTEREST

A CATALOG OF SELECTED DOVER
BOOKS IN ALL FIELDS OF INTEREST

100 BEST-LOVED POEMS, Edited by Philip Smith. "The Passionate Shepherd to His Love," "Shall I compare thee to a summer's day?" "Death, be not proud," "The Raven," "The Road Not Taken," plus works by Blake, Wordsworth, Byron, Shelley, Keats, many others. 96pp. 5³⁄₁₆ x 8¼. 0-486-28553-7

100 SMALL HOUSES OF THE THIRTIES, Brown-Blodgett Company. Exterior photographs and floor plans for 100 charming structures. Illustrations of models accompanied by descriptions of interiors, color schemes, closet space, and other amenities. 200 illustrations. 112pp. 8⅜ x 11. 0-486-44131-8

1000 TURN-OF-THE-CENTURY HOUSES: With Illustrations and Floor Plans, Herbert C. Chivers. Reproduced from a rare edition, this showcase of homes ranges from cottages and bungalows to sprawling mansions. Each house is meticulously illustrated and accompanied by complete floor plans. 256pp. 9⅜ x 12¼.
0-486-45596-3

101 GREAT AMERICAN POEMS, Edited by The American Poetry & Literacy Project. Rich treasury of verse from the 19th and 20th centuries includes works by Edgar Allan Poe, Robert Frost, Walt Whitman, Langston Hughes, Emily Dickinson, T. S. Eliot, other notables. 96pp. 5³⁄₁₆ x 8¼. 0-486-40158-8

101 GREAT SAMURAI PRINTS, Utagawa Kuniyoshi. Kuniyoshi was a master of the warrior woodblock print — and these 18th-century illustrations represent the pinnacle of his craft. Full-color portraits of renowned Japanese samurais pulse with movement, passion, and remarkably fine detail. 112pp. 8⅜ x 11. 0-486-46523-3

ABC OF BALLET, Janet Grosser. Clearly worded, abundantly illustrated little guide defines basic ballet-related terms: arabesque, battement, pas de chat, relevé, sissonne, many others. Pronunciation guide included. Excellent primer. 48pp. 4³⁄₁₆ x 5¾.
0-486-40871-X

ACCESSORIES OF DRESS: An Illustrated Encyclopedia, Katherine Lester and Bess Viola Oerke. Illustrations of hats, veils, wigs, cravats, shawls, shoes, gloves, and other accessories enhance an engaging commentary that reveals the humor and charm of the many-sided story of accessorized apparel. 644 figures and 59 plates. 608pp. 6⅛ x 9¼.
0-486-43378-1

ADVENTURES OF HUCKLEBERRY FINN, Mark Twain. Join Huck and Jim as their boyhood adventures along the Mississippi River lead them into a world of excitement, danger, and self-discovery. Humorous narrative, lyrical descriptions of the Mississippi valley, and memorable characters. 224pp. 5³⁄₁₆ x 8¼. 0-486-28061-6

ALICE STARMORE'S BOOK OF FAIR ISLE KNITTING, Alice Starmore. A noted designer from the region of Scotland's Fair Isle explores the history and techniques of this distinctive, stranded-color knitting style and provides copious illustrated instructions for 14 original knitwear designs. 208pp. 8⅜ x 10⅞. 0-486-47218-3

Browse over 9,000 books at www.doverpublications.com

CATALOG OF DOVER BOOKS

ALICE'S ADVENTURES IN WONDERLAND, Lewis Carroll. Beloved classic about a little girl lost in a topsy-turvy land and her encounters with the White Rabbit, March Hare, Mad Hatter, Cheshire Cat, and other delightfully improbable characters. 42 illustrations by Sir John Tenniel. 96pp. 5³⁄₁₆ x 8¼.   0-486-27543-4

AMERICA'S LIGHTHOUSES: An Illustrated History, Francis Ross Holland. Profusely illustrated fact-filled survey of American lighthouses since 1716. Over 200 stations — East, Gulf, and West coasts, Great Lakes, Hawaii, Alaska, Puerto Rico, the Virgin Islands, and the Mississippi and St. Lawrence Rivers. 240pp. 8 x 10¾.
0-486-25576-X

AN ENCYCLOPEDIA OF THE VIOLIN, Alberto Bachmann. Translated by Frederick H. Martens. Introduction by Eugene Ysaye. First published in 1925, this renowned reference remains unsurpassed as a source of essential information, from construction and evolution to repertoire and technique. Includes a glossary and 73 illustrations. 496pp. 6⅛ x 9¼.   0-486-46618-3

ANIMALS: 1,419 Copyright-Free Illustrations of Mammals, Birds, Fish, Insects, etc., Selected by Jim Harter. Selected for its visual impact and ease of use, this outstanding collection of wood engravings presents over 1,000 species of animals in extremely lifelike poses. Includes mammals, birds, reptiles, amphibians, fish, insects, and other invertebrates. 284pp. 9 x 12.   0-486-23766-4

THE ANNALS, Tacitus. Translated by Alfred John Church and William Jackson Brodribb. This vital chronicle of Imperial Rome, written by the era's great historian, spans A.D. 14-68 and paints incisive psychological portraits of major figures, from Tiberius to Nero. 416pp. 5³⁄₁₆ x 8¼.   0-486-45236-0

ANTIGONE, Sophocles. Filled with passionate speeches and sensitive probing of moral and philosophical issues, this powerful and often-performed Greek drama reveals the grim fate that befalls the children of Oedipus. Footnotes. 64pp. 5³⁄₁₆ x 8 ¼.   0-486-27804-2

ART DECO DECORATIVE PATTERNS IN FULL COLOR, Christian Stoll. Reprinted from a rare 1910 portfolio, 160 sensuous and exotic images depict a breathtaking array of florals, geometrics, and abstracts — all elegant in their stark simplicity. 64pp. 8⅜ x 11.   0-486-44862-2

THE ARTHUR RACKHAM TREASURY: 86 Full-Color Illustrations, Arthur Rackham. Selected and Edited by Jeff A. Menges. A stunning treasury of 86 full-page plates span the famed English artist's career, from *Rip Van Winkle* (1905) to masterworks such as *Undine, A Midsummer Night's Dream,* and *Wind in the Willows* (1939). 96pp. 8⅜ x 11.
0-486-44685-9

THE AUTHENTIC GILBERT & SULLIVAN SONGBOOK, W. S. Gilbert and A. S. Sullivan. The most comprehensive collection available, this songbook includes selections from every one of Gilbert and Sullivan's light operas. Ninety-two numbers are presented uncut and unedited, and in their original keys. 410pp. 9 x 12.
0-486-23482-7

THE AWAKENING, Kate Chopin. First published in 1899, this controversial novel of a New Orleans wife's search for love outside a stifling marriage shocked readers. Today, it remains a first-rate narrative with superb characterization. New introductory Note. 128pp. 5³⁄₁₆ x 8¼.   0-486-27786-0

BASIC DRAWING, Louis Priscilla. Beginning with perspective, this commonsense manual progresses to the figure in movement, light and shade, anatomy, drapery, composition, trees and landscape, and outdoor sketching. Black-and-white illustrations throughout. 128pp. 8⅜ x 11.   0-486-45815-6

Browse over 9,000 books at www.doverpublications.com

THE BATTLES THAT CHANGED HISTORY, Fletcher Pratt. Historian profiles 16 crucial conflicts, ancient to modern, that changed the course of Western civilization. Gripping accounts of battles led by Alexander the Great, Joan of Arc, Ulysses S. Grant, other commanders. 27 maps. 352pp. 5⅜ x 8½. 0-486-41129-X

BEETHOVEN'S LETTERS, Ludwig van Beethoven. Edited by Dr. A. C. Kalischer. Features 457 letters to fellow musicians, friends, greats, patrons, and literary men. Reveals musical thoughts, quirks of personality, insights, and daily events. Includes 15 plates. 410pp. 5⅜ x 8½. 0-486-22769-3

BERNICE BOBS HER HAIR AND OTHER STORIES, F. Scott Fitzgerald. This brilliant anthology includes 6 of Fitzgerald's most popular stories: "The Diamond as Big as the Ritz," the title tale, "The Offshore Pirate," "The Ice Palace," "The Jelly Bean," and "May Day." 176pp. 5⅜ x 8½. 0-486-47049-0

BESLER'S BOOK OF FLOWERS AND PLANTS: 73 Full-Color Plates from Hortus Eystettensis, 1613, Basilius Besler. Here is a selection of magnificent plates from the *Hortus Eystettensis,* which vividly illustrated and identified the plants, flowers, and trees that thrived in the legendary German garden at Eichstätt. 80pp. 8⅜ x 11. 0-486-46005-3

THE BOOK OF KELLS, Edited by Blanche Cirker. Painstakingly reproduced from a rare facsimile edition, this volume contains full-page decorations, portraits, illustrations, plus a sampling of textual leaves with exquisite calligraphy and ornamentation. 32 full-color illustrations. 32pp. 9⅜ x 12¼. 0-486-24345-1

THE BOOK OF THE CROSSBOW: With an Additional Section on Catapults and Other Siege Engines, Ralph Payne-Gallwey. Fascinating study traces history and use of crossbow as military and sporting weapon, from Middle Ages to modern times. Also covers related weapons: balistas, catapults, Turkish bows, more. Over 240 illustrations. 400pp. 7¼ x 10⅛. 0-486-28720-3

THE BUNGALOW BOOK: Floor Plans and Photos of 112 Houses, 1910, Henry L. Wilson. Here are 112 of the most popular and economic blueprints of the early 20th century — plus an illustration or photograph of each completed house. A wonderful time capsule that still offers a wealth of valuable insights. 160pp. 8⅜ x 11. 0-486-45104-6

THE CALL OF THE WILD, Jack London. A classic novel of adventure, drawn from London's own experiences as a Klondike adventurer, relating the story of a heroic dog caught in the brutal life of the Alaska Gold Rush. Note. 64pp. 5³⁄₁₆ x 8¼. 0-486-26472-6

CANDIDE, Voltaire. Edited by Francois-Marie Arouet. One of the world's great satires since its first publication in 1759. Witty, caustic skewering of romance, science, philosophy, religion, government — nearly all human ideals and institutions. 112pp. 5³⁄₁₆ x 8¼. 0-486-26689-3

CELEBRATED IN THEIR TIME: Photographic Portraits from the George Grantham Bain Collection, Edited by Amy Pastan. With an Introduction by Michael Carlebach. Remarkable portrait gallery features 112 rare images of Albert Einstein, Charlie Chaplin, the Wright Brothers, Henry Ford, and other luminaries from the worlds of politics, art, entertainment, and industry. 128pp. 8⅜ x 11. 0-486-46754-6

CHARIOTS FOR APOLLO: The NASA History of Manned Lunar Spacecraft to 1969, Courtney G. Brooks, James M. Grimwood, and Loyd S. Swenson, Jr. This illustrated history by a trio of experts is the definitive reference on the Apollo spacecraft and lunar modules. It traces the vehicles' design, development, and operation in space. More than 100 photographs and illustrations. 576pp. 6¾ x 9¼. 0-486-46756-2

Browse over 9,000 books at www.doverpublications.com

A CHRISTMAS CAROL, Charles Dickens. This engrossing tale relates Ebenezer Scrooge's ghostly journeys through Christmases past, present, and future and his ultimate transformation from a harsh and grasping old miser to a charitable and compassionate human being. 80pp. 5³⁄₁₆ x 8¼. 0-486-26865-9

COMMON SENSE, Thomas Paine. First published in January of 1776, this highly influential landmark document clearly and persuasively argued for American separation from Great Britain and paved the way for the Declaration of Independence. 64pp. 5³⁄₁₆ x 8¼. 0-486-29602-4

THE COMPLETE SHORT STORIES OF OSCAR WILDE, Oscar Wilde. Complete texts of "The Happy Prince and Other Tales," "A House of Pomegranates," "Lord Arthur Savile's Crime and Other Stories," "Poems in Prose," and "The Portrait of Mr. W. H." 208pp. 5³⁄₁₆ x 8¼. 0-486-45216-6

COMPLETE SONNETS, William Shakespeare. Over 150 exquisite poems deal with love, friendship, the tyranny of time, beauty's evanescence, death, and other themes in language of remarkable power, precision, and beauty. Glossary of archaic terms. 80pp. 5³⁄₁₆ x 8¼. 0-486-26686-9

THE COUNT OF MONTE CRISTO: Abridged Edition, Alexandre Dumas. Falsely accused of treason, Edmond Dantès is imprisoned in the bleak Chateau d'If. After a hair-raising escape, he launches an elaborate plot to extract a bitter revenge against those who betrayed him. 448pp. 5³⁄₁₆ x 8¼. 0-486-45643-9

CRAFTSMAN BUNGALOWS: Designs from the Pacific Northwest, Yoho & Merritt. This reprint of a rare catalog, showcasing the charming simplicity and cozy style of Craftsman bungalows, is filled with photos of completed homes, plus floor plans and estimated costs. An indispensable resource for architects, historians, and illustrators. 112pp. 10 x 7. 0-486-46875-5

CRAFTSMAN BUNGALOWS: 59 Homes from "The Craftsman," Edited by Gustav Stickley. Best and most attractive designs from Arts and Crafts Movement publication — 1903–1916 — includes sketches, photographs of homes, floor plans, descriptive text. 128pp. 8¼ x 11. 0-486-25829-7

CRIME AND PUNISHMENT, Fyodor Dostoyevsky. Translated by Constance Garnett. Supreme masterpiece tells the story of Raskolnikov, a student tormented by his own thoughts after he murders an old woman. Overwhelmed by guilt and terror, he confesses and goes to prison. 480pp. 5³⁄₁₆ x 8¼. 0-486-41587-2

THE DECLARATION OF INDEPENDENCE AND OTHER GREAT DOCUMENTS OF AMERICAN HISTORY: 1775-1865, Edited by John Grafton. Thirteen compelling and influential documents: Henry's "Give Me Liberty or Give Me Death," Declaration of Independence, The Constitution, Washington's First Inaugural Address, The Monroe Doctrine, The Emancipation Proclamation, Gettysburg Address, more. 64pp. 5³⁄₁₆ x 8¼. 0-486-41124-9

THE DESERT AND THE SOWN: Travels in Palestine and Syria, Gertrude Bell. "The female Lawrence of Arabia," Gertrude Bell wrote captivating, perceptive accounts of her travels in the Middle East. This intriguing narrative, accompanied by 160 photos, traces her 1905 sojourn in Lebanon, Syria, and Palestine. 368pp. 5⅜ x 8½. 0-486-46876-3

A DOLL'S HOUSE, Henrik Ibsen. Ibsen's best-known play displays his genius for realistic prose drama. An expression of women's rights, the play climaxes when the central character, Nora, rejects a smothering marriage and life in "a doll's house." 80pp. 5³⁄₁₆ x 8¼. 0-486-27062-9

Browse over 9,000 books at www.doverpublications.com

DOOMED SHIPS: Great Ocean Liner Disasters, William H. Miller, Jr. Nearly 200 photographs, many from private collections, highlight tales of some of the vessels whose pleasure cruises ended in catastrophe: the *Morro Castle, Normandie, Andrea Doria, Europa,* and many others. 128pp. 8⅞ x 11¾. 0-486-45366-9

THE DORÉ BIBLE ILLUSTRATIONS, Gustave Doré. Detailed plates from the Bible: the Creation scenes, Adam and Eve, horrifying visions of the Flood, the battle sequences with their monumental crowds, depictions of the life of Jesus, 241 plates in all. 241pp. 9 x 12. 0-486-23004-X

DRAWING DRAPERY FROM HEAD TO TOE, Cliff Young. Expert guidance on how to draw shirts, pants, skirts, gloves, hats, and coats on the human figure, including folds in relation to the body, pull and crush, action folds, creases, more. Over 200 drawings. 48pp. 8¼ x 11. 0-486-45591-2

DUBLINERS, James Joyce. A fine and accessible introduction to the work of one of the 20th century's most influential writers, this collection features 15 tales, including a masterpiece of the short-story genre, "The Dead." 160pp. 5³⁄₁₆ x 8¼.
0-486-26870-5

EASY-TO-MAKE POP-UPS, Joan Irvine. Illustrated by Barbara Reid. Dozens of wonderful ideas for three-dimensional paper fun — from holiday greeting cards with moving parts to a pop-up menagerie. Easy-to-follow, illustrated instructions for more than 30 projects. 299 black-and-white illustrations. 96pp. 8⅜ x 11.
0-486-44622-0

EASY-TO-MAKE STORYBOOK DOLLS: A "Novel" Approach to Cloth Dollmaking, Sherralyn St. Clair. Favorite fictional characters come alive in this unique beginner's dollmaking guide. Includes patterns for Pollyanna, Dorothy from *The Wonderful Wizard of Oz,* Mary of *The Secret Garden,* plus easy-to-follow instructions, 263 black-and-white illustrations, and an 8-page color insert. 112pp. 8¼ x 11. 0-486-47360-0

EINSTEIN'S ESSAYS IN SCIENCE, Albert Einstein. Speeches and essays in accessible, everyday language profile influential physicists such as Niels Bohr and Isaac Newton. They also explore areas of physics to which the author made major contributions. 128pp. 5 x 8. 0-486-47011-3

EL DORADO: Further Adventures of the Scarlet Pimpernel, Baroness Orczy. A popular sequel to *The Scarlet Pimpernel,* this suspenseful story recounts the Pimpernel's attempts to rescue the Dauphin from imprisonment during the French Revolution. An irresistible blend of intrigue, period detail, and vibrant characterizations. 352pp. 5³⁄₁₆ x 8¼. 0-486-44026-5

ELEGANT SMALL HOMES OF THE TWENTIES: 99 Designs from a Competition, Chicago Tribune. Nearly 100 designs for five- and six-room houses feature New England and Southern colonials, Normandy cottages, stately Italianate dwellings, and other fascinating snapshots of American domestic architecture of the 1920s. 112pp. 9 x 12. 0-486-46910-7

THE ELEMENTS OF STYLE: The Original Edition, William Strunk, Jr. This is the book that generations of writers have relied upon for timeless advice on grammar, diction, syntax, and other essentials. In concise terms, it identifies the principal requirements of proper style and common errors. 64pp. 5⅜ x 8½. 0-486-44798-7

THE ELUSIVE PIMPERNEL, Baroness Orczy. Robespierre's revolutionaries find their wicked schemes thwarted by the heroic Pimpernel — Sir Percival Blakeney. In this thrilling sequel, Chauvelin devises a plot to eliminate the Pimpernel and his wife. 272pp. 5³⁄₁₆ x 8¼. 0-486-45464-9

AN ENCYCLOPEDIA OF BATTLES: Accounts of Over 1,560 Battles from 1479 B.C. to the Present, David Eggenberger. Essential details of every major battle in recorded history from the first battle of Megiddo in 1479 B.C. to Grenada in 1984. List of battle maps. 99 illustrations. 544pp. 6½ x 9¼. 0-486-24913-1

ENCYCLOPEDIA OF EMBROIDERY STITCHES, INCLUDING CREWEL, Marion Nichols. Precise explanations and instructions, clearly illustrated, on how to work chain, back, cross, knotted, woven stitches, and many more — 178 in all, including Cable Outline, Whipped Satin, and Eyelet Buttonhole. Over 1400 illustrations. 219pp. 8⅜ x 11¼. 0-486-22929-7

ENTER JEEVES: 15 Early Stories, P. G. Wodehouse. Splendid collection contains first 8 stories featuring Bertie Wooster, the deliciously dim aristocrat and Jeeves, his brainy, imperturbable manservant. Also, the complete Reggie Pepper (Bertie's prototype) series. 288pp. 5⅜ x 8½. 0-486-29717-9

ERIC SLOANE'S AMERICA: Paintings in Oil, Michael Wigley. With a Foreword by Mimi Sloane. Eric Sloane's evocative oils of America's landscape and material culture shimmer with immense historical and nostalgic appeal. This original hardcover collection gathers nearly a hundred of his finest paintings, with subjects ranging from New England to the American Southwest. 128pp. 10⅝ x 9.
0-486-46525-X

ETHAN FROME, Edith Wharton. Classic story of wasted lives, set against a bleak New England background. Superbly delineated characters in a hauntingly grim tale of thwarted love. Considered by many to be Wharton's masterpiece. 96pp. 5³⁄₁₆ x 8¼.
0-486-26690-7

THE EVERLASTING MAN, G. K. Chesterton. Chesterton's view of Christianity — as a blend of philosophy and mythology, satisfying intellect and spirit — applies to his brilliant book, which appeals to readers' heads as well as their hearts. 288pp. 5⅜ x 8½.
0-486-46036-3

THE FIELD AND FOREST HANDY BOOK, Daniel Beard. Written by a co-founder of the Boy Scouts, this appealing guide offers illustrated instructions for building kites, birdhouses, boats, igloos, and other fun projects, plus numerous helpful tips for campers. 448pp. 5³⁄₁₆ x 8¼. 0-486-46191-2

FINDING YOUR WAY WITHOUT MAP OR COMPASS, Harold Gatty. Useful, instructive manual shows would-be explorers, hikers, bikers, scouts, sailors, and survivalists how to find their way outdoors by observing animals, weather patterns, shifting sands, and other elements of nature. 288pp. 5⅜ x 8½. 0-486-40613-X

FIRST FRENCH READER: A Beginner's Dual-Language Book, Edited and Translated by Stanley Appelbaum. This anthology introduces 50 legendary writers — Voltaire, Balzac, Baudelaire, Proust, more — through passages from *The Red and the Black, Les Misérables, Madame Bovary,* and other classics. Original French text plus English translation on facing pages. 240pp. 5⅜ x 8½. 0-486-46178-5

FIRST GERMAN READER: A Beginner's Dual-Language Book, Edited by Harry Steinhauer. Specially chosen for their power to evoke German life and culture, these short, simple readings include poems, stories, essays, and anecdotes by Goethe, Hesse, Heine, Schiller, and others. 224pp. 5⅜ x 8½. 0-486-46179-3

FIRST SPANISH READER: A Beginner's Dual-Language Book, Angel Flores. Delightful stories, other material based on works of Don Juan Manuel, Luis Taboada, Ricardo Palma, other noted writers. Complete faithful English translations on facing pages. Exercises. 176pp. 5⅜ x 8½. 0-486-25810-6

Browse over 9,000 books at www.doverpublications.com

FIVE ACRES AND INDEPENDENCE, Maurice G. Kains. Great back-to-the-land classic explains basics of self-sufficient farming. The one book to get. 95 illustrations. 397pp. 5⅜ x 8½. 0-486-20974-1

FLAGG'S SMALL HOUSES: Their Economic Design and Construction, 1922, Ernest Flagg. Although most famous for his skyscrapers, Flagg was also a proponent of the well-designed single-family dwelling. His classic treatise features innovations that save space, materials, and cost. 526 illustrations. 160pp. 9⅜ x 12¼.
0-486-45197-6

FLATLAND: A Romance of Many Dimensions, Edwin A. Abbott. Classic of science (and mathematical) fiction — charmingly illustrated by the author — describes the adventures of A. Square, a resident of Flatland, in Spaceland (three dimensions), Lineland (one dimension), and Pointland (no dimensions). 96pp. 5³⁄₁₆ x 8¼.
0-486-27263-X

FRANKENSTEIN, Mary Shelley. The story of Victor Frankenstein's monstrous creation and the havoc it caused has enthralled generations of readers and inspired countless writers of horror and suspense. With the author's own 1831 introduction. 176pp. 5³⁄₁₆ x 8¼. 0-486-28211-2

THE GARGOYLE BOOK: 572 Examples from Gothic Architecture, Lester Burbank Bridaham. Dispelling the conventional wisdom that French Gothic architectural flourishes were born of despair or gloom, Bridaham reveals the whimsical nature of these creations and the ingenious artisans who made them. 572 illustrations. 224pp. 8⅜ x 11. 0-486-44754-5

THE GIFT OF THE MAGI AND OTHER SHORT STORIES, O. Henry. Sixteen captivating stories by one of America's most popular storytellers. Included are such classics as "The Gift of the Magi," "The Last Leaf," and "The Ransom of Red Chief." Publisher's Note. 96pp. 5³⁄₁₆ x 8¼. 0-486-27061-0

THE GOETHE TREASURY: Selected Prose and Poetry, Johann Wolfgang von Goethe. Edited, Selected, and with an Introduction by Thomas Mann. In addition to his lyric poetry, Goethe wrote travel sketches, autobiographical studies, essays, letters, and proverbs in rhyme and prose. This collection presents outstanding examples from each genre. 368pp. 5⅜ x 8½. 0-486-44780-4

GREAT EXPECTATIONS, Charles Dickens. Orphaned Pip is apprenticed to the dirty work of the forge but dreams of becoming a gentleman — and one day finds himself in possession of "great expectations." Dickens' finest novel. 400pp. 5³⁄₁₆ x 8¼.
0-486-41586-4

GREAT WRITERS ON THE ART OF FICTION: From Mark Twain to Joyce Carol Oates, Edited by James Daley. An indispensable source of advice and inspiration, this anthology features essays by Henry James, Kate Chopin, Willa Cather, Sinclair Lewis, Jack London, Raymond Chandler, Raymond Carver, Eudora Welty, and Kurt Vonnegut, Jr. 192pp. 5⅜ x 8½. 0-486-45128-3

HAMLET, William Shakespeare. The quintessential Shakespearean tragedy, whose highly charged confrontations and anguished soliloquies probe depths of human feeling rarely sounded in any art. Reprinted from an authoritative British edition complete with illuminating footnotes. 128pp. 5³⁄₁₆ x 8¼. 0-486-27278-8

THE HAUNTED HOUSE, Charles Dickens. A Yuletide gathering in an eerie country retreat provides the backdrop for Dickens and his friends — including Elizabeth Gaskell and Wilkie Collins — who take turns spinning supernatural yarns. 144pp. 5⅜ x 8½. 0-486-46309-5

HEART OF DARKNESS, Joseph Conrad. Dark allegory of a journey up the Congo River and the narrator's encounter with the mysterious Mr. Kurtz. Masterly blend of adventure, character study, psychological penetration. For many, Conrad's finest, most enigmatic story. 80pp. 5³⁄₁₆ x 8¼. 0-486-26464-5

HENSON AT THE NORTH POLE, Matthew A. Henson. This thrilling memoir by the heroic African-American who was Peary's companion through two decades of Arctic exploration recounts a tale of danger, courage, and determination. "Fascinating and exciting." — *Commonweal.* 128pp. 5⅜ x 8½. 0-486-45472-X

HISTORIC COSTUMES AND HOW TO MAKE THEM, Mary Fernald and E. Shenton. Practical, informative guidebook shows how to create everything from short tunics worn by Saxon men in the fifth century to a lady's bustle dress of the late 1800s. 81 illustrations. 176pp. 5⅜ x 8½. 0-486-44906-8

THE HOUND OF THE BASKERVILLES, Arthur Conan Doyle. A deadly curse in the form of a legendary ferocious beast continues to claim its victims from the Baskerville family until Holmes and Watson intervene. Often called the best detective story ever written. 128pp. 5³⁄₁₆ x 8¼. 0-486-28214-7

THE HOUSE BEHIND THE CEDARS, Charles W. Chesnutt. Originally published in 1900, this groundbreaking novel by a distinguished African-American author recounts the drama of a brother and sister who "pass for white" during the dangerous days of Reconstruction. 208pp. 5⅜ x 8½. 0-486-46144-0

THE HUMAN FIGURE IN MOTION, Eadweard Muybridge. The 4,789 photographs in this definitive selection show the human figure — models almost all undraped — engaged in over 160 different types of action: running, climbing stairs, etc. 390pp. 7⅞ x 10⅝. 0-486-20204-6

THE IMPORTANCE OF BEING EARNEST, Oscar Wilde. Wilde's witty and buoyant comedy of manners, filled with some of literature's most famous epigrams, reprinted from an authoritative British edition. Considered Wilde's most perfect work. 64pp. 5³⁄₁₆ x 8¼. 0-486-26478-5

THE INFERNO, Dante Alighieri. Translated and with notes by Henry Wadsworth Longfellow. The first stop on Dante's famous journey from Hell to Purgatory to Paradise, this 14th-century allegorical poem blends vivid and shocking imagery with graceful lyricism. Translated by the beloved 19th-century poet, Henry Wadsworth Longfellow. 256pp. 5³⁄₁₆ x 8¼. 0-486-44288-8

JANE EYRE, Charlotte Brontë. Written in 1847, *Jane Eyre* tells the tale of an orphan girl's progress from the custody of cruel relatives to an oppressive boarding school and its culmination in a troubled career as a governess. 448pp. 5³⁄₁₆ x 8¼.
0-486-42449-9

JAPANESE WOODBLOCK FLOWER PRINTS, Tanigami Kônan. Extraordinary collection of Japanese woodblock prints by a well-known artist features 120 plates in brilliant color. Realistic images from a rare edition include daffodils, tulips, and other familiar and unusual flowers. 128pp. 11 x 8¼. 0-486-46442-3

JEWELRY MAKING AND DESIGN, Augustus F. Rose and Antonio Cirino. Professional secrets of jewelry making are revealed in a thorough, practical guide. Over 200 illustrations. 306pp. 5⅜ x 8½. 0-486-21750-7

JULIUS CAESAR, William Shakespeare. Great tragedy based on Plutarch's account of the lives of Brutus, Julius Caesar and Mark Antony. Evil plotting, ringing oratory, high tragedy with Shakespeare's incomparable insight, dramatic power. Explanatory footnotes. 96pp. 5³⁄₁₆ x 8¼. 0-486-26876-4

Browse over 9,000 books at www.doverpublications.com